Gerhard Vinken
Zones of Tradition - Places of Identity

Urban Studies

für Martina

Gerhard Vinken, born in 1961, holds the chair of heritage studies (Denkmalpflege) at the University of Bamberg. His research focuses on urban studies and built heritage, heritage politics, and international heritage cultures. He is a founding member of the Center for Heritage Studies and Technologies (KDWT) in Bamberg.

Gerhard Vinken
Zones of Tradition - Places of Identity
Cities and Their Heritage

We acknowledge support by the Open Access Publication Fund of the Otto-Friedrich-Universität Bamberg.

Bibliographic information published by the Deutsche Nationalbibliothek
The Deutsche Nationalbibliothek lists this publication in the Deutsche Nationalbibliografie; detailed bibliographic data are available in the Internet at http://dnb.d-nb.de

This work is licensed under the Creative Commons Attribution 4.0 (BY) license, which means that the text may be remixed, transformed and built upon and be copied and redistributed in any medium or format even commercially, provided credit is given to the author. For details go to http://creativecommons.org/licenses/by/4.0/.
Creative Commons license terms for re-use do not apply to any content (such as graphs, figures, photos, excerpts, etc.) not original to the Open Access publication and further permission may be required from the rights holder. The obligation to research and clear permission lies solely with the party re-using the material.

First published in 2021 by transcript Verlag, Bielefeld
© Gerhard Vinken

Cover layout: Kordula Röckenhaus, Bielefeld
Cover illustration: Palermo, Porta Felice, © Gerhard Vinken 2019
Translated by Graeme Curry unless otherwise indicated
Printed by Majuskel Medienproduktion GmbH, Wetzlar
Print-ISBN 978-3-8376-5446-2
PDF-ISBN 978-3-8394-5446-6
https://doi.org/10.14361/9783839454466
ISSN of series: 2747-3619
eISSN of series: 2747-3635

Printed on permanent acid-free text paper.

Contents

Setting the Framework

1 The Heritage of Cities
An Introduction 9

2 The Crises of the Modern City
Place and Trajectorial Space 19

3 The Distinctiveness of Cities
Heritage as a Mode of Reproduction 37

4 The Spaces of the Monument
Exposing – Framing – Zoning 47

Zoning the City. Heritage and Modernity

5 Tashkent / Uzbekistan
Conflicting Relations. Mahalla, Soviet Modernism, Global City 65

6 Basel / Switzerland
The *Heimat* Zone. Planning the 'Historic' Town 83

7 New York / USA
Zoning in America. Beauty, History and Real Estate 97

8 Düsseldorf / Germany
Size Matters. Modern Megastructures as Heritage.. 121

Doing Tradition. Heritage Politics and Identity-Building

9 **Cologne / Germany**
Islands of Tradition. Heritage Politics from the Nazi Era to Postwar Reconstruction....... 135

10 **Berlin / Germany**
Monumental Revision. A Capital between Ruin and Restoration 149

11 **Palermo / Italy**
A Dark Legacy. Surviving through Remembering 159

12 **Frankfurt / Germany**
Clone City. An Insatiable Thirst for Authenticity.. 171

Reclaiming Heritage. Conflict, Contestation, Canonization

13 **Palermo / Italy**
Appropriations. The Canonization of the City in Early Travel Literature 191

14 **New York / USA**
Sharing Heritage? Heinrich Heine in the Bronx... 227

15 **Salvador da Bahia / Brazil**
Whose Heritage? Globalization and Local Practices in the Pelourinho District 233

16 **New Orleans / USA**
Contested Heritage. African-American Culture in a Southern City 243

References 265

Illustration Credits 315

Acknowledgments 321

Setting the Framework

1 The Heritage of Cities
An Introduction

Cities are: dynamic, chaotic, dense, big, heterogeneous, anonymous, meaningful, inscrutable, dazzling, contradictory, eternal. And so on. Studying cities in terms of their heritage means focusing on issues different to those addressed by conventional debates on monuments and conservation. The city slices through the images of homogeneity that the concept of heritage often invokes, whether in terms of homeland/*Heimat*, region or even nation, and that also contaminate recent debates such as those on heritage communities, for instance around indigenous heritage.[1] Cities are distinguished by density and heterogeneity, and by comparatively high levels of dynamism, both social and spatial. As a result, debates over heritage, over the ways heritage is articulated and the ways claims to heritage are staked, merge with other structures of the imagination. Even if these, too, are at times not entirely free of traces of essentialism, the heritage of cities nonetheless reveals unmistakably that heritage production is a process.

It is thus no accident that new topics in the theory of heritage conservation have often emerged on the territory of urban heritage conservation. For instance, the concept of the monument, which, since the 19th century, had been focused on the individual monument, on exceptional architecture, was successfully enlarged around 1900 via the concept of the urban ensemble. This concept embraced not only everyday architectures but also the spatial relations between buildings and their broader environment.[2] The trend towards conceiving of heritage as a societal process or discourse[3] and the inclusion of non-material aspects also occurred internationally with an emphasis on urban heritage conservation. In the USA, calls for heritage conservation to become more "than a cult of antiquarians", for its conceptualization as a matter for society as a whole, emerged as early as the 1960s. This resulted in the establishment of the Historic District as a preferential preservation tool.[4] With its focus on the city, the European

---

1   Cf. Adell, Between Imagined Communities, 2015.
2   Breuer, Ensemble, 1989.
3   Smith, Uses of Heritage, 2006; Harrison, Critical Approaches, 2013.
4   Quoted in: Murtagh, Keeping Time, 2006, 50–51. Cf. the essay on New York in this volume (Chapter 7).

Architectural Heritage Year 1975 also gave the topic a major boost. In the run-up to the event, demands by 'reformists' from countries including Germany for a new, more social conception of conservation[5] were thwarted by the heritage conservation establishment, which criticized the "almost medically therapeutic zeal" with which "urban-social matters" were being approached and the "tendency to think of and to accept conservation primarily in connection with urban planning considerations".[6] The primacy of this defence of conservation as a matter of protecting the original material substance was fateful and meant that in Germany, to this day, the "conserve as found" conception is prescribed in law and rarely questioned.[7] Only recently have calls for greater participation begun to have an impact on official procedures, not coincidentally in the sphere of urban heritage conservation once again.[8] The heritage of cities is without doubt a key issue for the future, and not only because ever greater numbers of people live in cities. It also poses a challenge because, in their dynamism and heterogeneity, urban heritage figurations often resist established conceptions of heritage typified by concepts such as endurance and persistence, homogeneity and integrity.[9] When we consider cities, it is particularly clear how hard it is to speak about heritage without also speaking about social and political issues, about interest groups, and ultimately about questions of power.[10]

The city, as should not be forgotten when considering questions of urban heritage, was long considered the locus of modern life and in many societies still represents the "open" locus of aspiration that enables liberation from traditional ties. For long phases in the modern period, city planning was dominated by a powerful hostility to tradition. In the shaping and reframing of urban spaces in line with functionalist technological ideals, the vital tasks of meaning-making and identity-formation were neglected.[11] With the renaissance of antitechnicist urban research, Jane Jacobs, among others, drew attention to social cohesion and community-making processes,[12] while Kevin Lynch focused on the production of the image of the city and its orientation function in a very broad sense.[13] This new conception of the city as a meaningful living environment – an environment that 'means' in the literal sense – also revived the topic of its "heritage" in debates about city planning, architecture and conservation. A foundational text in the section **Setting the Framework** explores this conflict between habitat and technology-driven planning, between "place" und "trajectorial space", as the one in which the

---

5   Scheurmann, Konturen und Konjunkturen, 2018, 254–261.
6   According to Georg Mörsch in: Mörsch/Vereinigung der Landesdenkmalpfleger, Denkmalpflege 1975, 1976, 87–89.
7   See Vinken, Escaping Modernity, 2017.
8   See Sandmeier/Selitz, Das Kommunale Denkmalkonzept, 2020. Lisa Marie Selitz is currently completing a dissertation on the topic of *Erhalten – Erneuern – Beteiligen. Partizipation als Verhandlungsgegenstand der städtebaulichen Denkmalpflege* (working title, forthcoming 2021).
9   See Sophie Stackmann's dissertation on *Integrität als Konzept für das Erbe der Vergangenheit – eine kritische Lektüre* (working title, forthcoming 2021).
10 Harvey, Heritage Pasts, 2001.
11 Cf. for example, the essay on Cologne in this volume (Chapter 9).
12 Jacobs, Death and Life, 1961.
13 Lynch, The Image of the City, 1960.

formatting of heritage in modern urban space must also be decided. The latent tension between the designation of the city as both "modern" and "significant" or "meaningful" is a leitmotif in many of the essays collected in this volume.

In reducing the heritage question to a social one, however, we do not do justice to the complexity of the issue. After all, cities are not only characterized by heterogeneity and contradictions, dynamism and fluidity; as "ancient" nodes and meaningful habitats, they are often also privileged sites of heritage, characterized by a high degree of architectural and structural tradition and stability – of "monumentality" in other words. Of course, their perdurability should not be understood in static terms; urban spaces are subject to penetration and layering, connections, disruptions and breaks. The fundamental observation that many cities are distinct not only in terms of their ambience, but also with regard to their structures, spaces and architectural manifestations, is one that Aldo Rossi was able to demonstrate vividly with reference to the European city.[14] Rossi did not focus his thought on a concept of heritage – or did so only to the extent that the "urban artefacts" and structural features and peculiarities of a city can be used to derive a specific local (in Rossi's terms a "rational") architecture. And yet his *Architecture of the City* details key elements (alongside urban artefacts primary elements, locus, aura, etc.) that should be analysed in order to understand the built heritage of cities. For Rossi, the city, with its layers of deposits and overlays, reutilizations and reinterpretations, continuities and breaks, is more than a passive stone stage-set: it becomes an effective "actor" by prestructuring significations, "setting" standards, suggesting ways of reading (or not) that may become active in processes of constituting and claiming heritage. Drawing on these considerations, heritage may be considered a specific mode of reproduction rather than a mode of production.[15] This approach, outlined by an interdisciplinary research cluster on "The Intrinsic Logic of Cities"[16] attempts to open ways to seeing heritage as a social practice without disregarding specific "given features" of the urban environment that contribute to the particularity or distinctiveness of urban heritage.[17]

This position in no way contradicts the view formally articulated by Critical Heritage Studies, according to which heritage heritage has no intrinsic value but only value that is socially negotiated, communicated and made.[18] As early as 1903, in his influential work *The Modern Cult of Monuments*, the Austrian art historian and conservationist Alois Riegl described built heritage as a phenomenon of reception.[19] If today we correctly understand heritage to be a social practice, the question of what is specific to this practice and which concept of practice we wish to apply nonetheless often remains underarticulated.[20] My working hypothesis is that heritage positions itself as a practice of reproduction or making permanent, a practice whose key principle is the projection of

---

14 Rossi, The Architecture of the City, 1984 (1966).
15 Kirshenblatt-Gimblett, From Ethnology to Heritage, 2004.
16 Berking/Löw, Die Eigenlogik der Städte, 2008.
17 Cf. the essay on *The Distinctiveness of Cities* in this volume (Chapter 3).
18 Smith, Uses of Heritage, 2006.
19 Riegl, The modern cult of monuments, 1982 (1903).
20 Harrison, Understanding the Politics, 2009.

endurance forwards into the future. And many "political" treatments of the concept of heritage very much underestimate that these processes appear to be determined more by phenomena belonging to the repressed and the unconscious than by intentions and political goals – a circumstance that the French philosopher Jacques Derrida summarized in his concept of hauntology.[21]

These preliminary remarks cannot do much more than roughly outline the field in which my approaches to cities and their heritage have been undertaken. The aim of this collection of texts is less to make a contribution to theory than to establish a research practice that seeks explorative and occasionally playful access as a means of revealing the scintillating complexity of urban heritage via constantly proliferating cross-sections and shifting perspectives. At the same time, these studies, which were written over a period of more than ten years, also seek to go beyond established approaches to urban heritage, most of which are tied to specific disciplines. To put it another way, I attempt to take approaches from the archaeological sciences, which take heritage in its materiality seriously and which also concern themselves with historical monuments and city quarters, topography, city layouts and plot structures, and fuse them with methods of inquiry drawn from the social sciences, which focus on the processes by which heritage is formed and reproduced. In this, particular attention is paid to urban places and spaces and to the relevant orderings and relationships within them that often have a lasting effect on heritage. The contribution made to heritage-making by different spatial practices is expanded upon in detail in one of the introductory chapters.[22]

* * *

The section entitled **Zoning the City: Heritage and Modernity** focuses on the intersection of spatial segregation and heritage-making processes, and on the question of how the often-contradictory demands made of the city (identification, orientation vs. function, market, etc.) are each organized in a spatial sense. By bringing to bear insights from critical spatial theory, patterns can be recognized here that are often reproduced over long periods and through political ruptures, and that are reinterpreted and re-evaluated in accordance with the changing conditions. The first example to be considered is the Uzbek capital of Tashkent, a city that, since the colonial period, has been shaped by the dual structure of modernity – tradition and a variety of planning logics (Asian-Islamic, "Western" – Tsarist and Soviet, etc.). It is only against the background of these spatial-social constellations that conflicts over cities' heritage develop their full depth. In societal debates around tradition and identity, which are permeated by social, ethical and ideological tensions, a question central to all heritages discourses is clearly articulated: that of the "right" way to live.

---

21   In *Specters of Marx* (originally published in French in 1993) Jacques Derrida develops the concept of "hauntology", a philosophy of haunting, in which the repressed returns as a ghost and deploys its potency for society in a spectral, in-between status (Derrida, Specters of Marx, 1994). Sophie Stackmann theorizes heritage as spectral in her dissertation *Integrität als Konzept für das Erbe der Vergangenheit – eine kritische Lektüre* (working title, forthcoming 2021).

22   Cf. the essay on *The Spaces of the Monument* in this volume (Chapter 4).

Overall, the texts collected in this section show that the making of heritage enclaves, historic districts and similar urban heritage formations can be understood less in terms of intentional heritage-planning than as a complex interplay of established structures within the urban environment and societal processes of value attribution. It is the specific features of the urban environment and the attributions of meaning embedded latently within them that first offer the specific possibility of claiming, reactivating and formulating heritage. The fact that this social process of ascribing value is itself also pre-structured (and subject to historical shifts) by means of categories such as race, class and gender is self-evident. Since the publication of my book *Zone Heimat* in 2010, I have frequently discussed how practices of spatial separation and segregation can take the form of heritage-making (or more precisely heritage-formation).[23] The European *Altstadt* (old town, historic city centre) – or rather its production – involves the articulation of anti-modern images of nostalgia and ideological residues that were formed within European Romanticism and remain effective in the evaluative standards, goals and aesthetic norms of urban heritage to this day. This is discussed in detail in the book with respect to the Swiss city of Basel. However, "historic" quarters and districts are not the result of a desire to protect or preserve; their existence can rather be ascribed to the specific goals of modernization that were formulated since the 19th century and the planning practices that went along with them. By means of zoning, the establishment of specific building zones, the *Altstadt* is afforded a place in the modernized urban body; it is this spatial segregation that first makes possible the integration of contradictory development goals in the modern city.

Zoning and the establishment of Historic Districts have been inextricably intertwined from the start. This can be seen clearly with respect to the development of preservation legislation, for instance in the USA. As one of the key achievements of modern city planning, zoning pursues a strategy of outward demarcation and inward homogenization. For America's Historic Districts, established as "special zones", this leads to the aesthetic homogenization of urban heritage, which can be read as a yearning for the "lost" integrity of the "good old days". The processes of homogenization that go hand-in-hand with the declaration of a Historic District are associated with the flattening of heterogeneity and difference and the elimination of everything that is foreign or alien. The example of New York makes clear that these fantasies of homogenization and demarcation via heritage-zoning are fuelled in equal part by social and by economic interests. In the case of the Historic Districts, the modernization of the zone aims not only at formal and aesthetic standardization "in the image of the old" but also at the creation of socially homogeneous neighbourhoods (in terms of ethnicity and class), and ultimately at the safeguarding of property values.

From a German perspective, what is remarkable about heritage preservation law in the United States is the fact that urban heritage conservation, in particular, is considered a societal undertaking, and that the use of participatory mechanisms, up to and including the involvement of residents in listing processes, has become the norm. The 'innocent' wish of preservationists and many residents for "historic" and beautiful

---

23   For a comprehensive overview, see: Vinken, Zone Heimat, 2010; Vinken, Im Namen der Altstadt, 2016.

urban spaces has nonetheless been corrupted by the prevailing patterns of ownership and power: the spatial and legal demarcation of historic quarters and the social desire for segregation are directly linked. It is a tension that is increasingly also articulated in German debates, for instance in the conflict around the role of heritage conservation in processes of gentrification,[24] or in calls emanating from the left for the protection of established populations and their social and cultural networks. In the image of a homogeneous and socially vulnerable established (East German) population defending itself against mobile and privileged (Western and global) newcomers of all kinds we certainly see repeated patterns of defensiveness and fear of otherness latent in concepts associated with identity formation, such as *Heimat* and neighbourhood.

Heritage – armed with claims about background, origin, permanence and identity – has established itself as a (necessary) counterpoint to a 'modern' present, which is progressing, forgetful of tradition, towards a wide-open future. At a time when many countries are including the remnants of modernism on lists of protected monuments, this dialectical process, in which the origins of the heritage concept lie, reaches its conclusion. Taking as an example the debate over the heritage of modernism in Düsseldorf, I discuss how perspectives are shifting now that the megastructures from which the preservationist movement once sought to protect the city from are themselves being recognized as worthy of preservation, and how new fronts and arguments are emerging in this debate about urban heritage.

The section on ***Doing Tradition: Heritage Politics and Identity-Building*** pays closer attention to the political aspects of urban heritage That heritage structures in urban spaces are being harnessed not only to desires for prestige and distinctiveness, but also to revisionist and reactionary conceptions of history, can be demonstrated with reference to three German case studies, each of them subtly different and all located somewhere between restoration, reconstruction and revitalization. However, these are not examples of the national instrumentalization of heritage politics; rather, the cases of Cologne, Berlin and Frankfurt make it possible to reveal the ideological implications of such projects, which understand themselves to be unpolitical and the innocuous continuation of local traditions. Characteristic of such projects, which can be located in time between post-war reconstruction and the recent present, are lines of argument that invoke aesthetics in support of the "historic" framing of urban areas, and by the same token reject modernism and the modern formal language. Moreover, the efforts expended on urban heritage that are examined here are underpinned by promises of continuity, in that they are presented as "recovering" or "regaining" something by means of repair, restoration or reconstruction. In this way, the act of *making* and its political and societal goals are effectively disguised. It is therefore all the more important to recall these acts, in order to promote critical engagement with cultural heritage and to allow for multiperspectivity and contradiction.

The image of a static and homogeneous identity that characterizes many urban restoration projects is opposed to this goal. In Cologne, it is not well known that the current *Altstadt* is the result of a reconstruction campaign that was driven by heritage conservation and that sought to preserve the identity of a city almost entirely destroyed

---

24   Takahashi, Berlin Heritage Conservation, 2018.

in the war. It is even less well known that the area which was rebuilt did not exist in this form before the comprehensive rehabilitation efforts of the 1930s and 40s. The fantasies of homogenization that were radicalized and reinterpreted in racist terms during the era of Nazi rule were revitalized in the post-war era in the vestments of (supposedly unpolitical) compromise formulae. The consequences of these acts of repression are deeply inscribed in the appearances of German cities: to this day they can be read in the ongoing debates within institutional heritage conservation, a field which, shielded by claims of scientific objectivity, considers itself to be unpolitical and seeks to cast its abstention on questions of heritage and heritage politics as a virtue.[25]

It is hardly surprising that other actors move in to fill this gap. The particularly vehement wave of reconstructionism that has been rolling over Germany since the 1980s has largely suppressed other debates on city planning in the public consciousness, establishing standards to which heritage conservation can no longer refuse to conform: restoration and reconstruction "in renewed splendour" are once more in vogue.[26] In Berlin, one can see where this unholy alliance might lead. Around the newly reconstructed palace of the Hohenzollern Kaisers, a combination of restoration, reconstruction and rehabilitation is creating a historic centre that is full of nostalgia for Prussia and its megalomaniacal imperial fantasies. The aim is to erase memories of the historically and ideologically divided heritage landscape of central Berlin. A city shaped by destruction and ruptures, whose heterogeneity is again approaching pre-war levels, is marginalizing and suppressing undesirable narratives, particularly East German perspectives and cultures of remembrance. Yet even this level of revisionism is surpassed by the beloved fake historic districts of cities such as Dresden and Hildesheim, or, as analysed here, Frankfurt am Main. In Frankfurt, urban heritage takes the form of a homogeneous *Altstadt* clone, brand new and constructed above an underground car park. Marketed as "reconstructions", these projects are revisionist erasures that thin out and contaminate urban heritage. Such practices can thus be located within the grand narrative of the European city: the tale of the good old days. It is this one narrative of original, meaningful order that is opposed to the presumed senselessness and formlessness of the present – a narrative that was already used to encourage a moral and aesthetic renewal of society by the conservative reformers of the 19th century,[27] and one with which, more recently, UKIP and the now defunct Brexit Party campaigned for Britain to leave the European Union, illustrating their arguments with images of Poundbury, Prince Charles's fake Olde England suburb near Dorchester.[28]

Today, the boundary between heritage figuration and historically themed architecture has in many regards become fluid – materially, aesthetically, ideologically. The repoliticization of debates about heritage, which has finally reached Germany not least

---

25   Vinken, Erbe und Emotionen, forthcoming 2021.
26   Buttlar, Denkmalpflege statt Attrappenkult, 2011. Cf. the essay on Berlin in this volume (Chapter 10).
27   Pugin, Contrasts, 1836; Pugin, Gothic Architecture, 1920 (1821–1838).
28   Website YouTube, Building for the Future, marketing trailer UKIP. Cf.: Vinken, Erbe und Emotionen, forthcoming, 2021.

in the form of the "decolonize" movement, can therefore only be welcomed. And I understand my book to be, among other things, a plea for the stakeholders in this debate to become more aware of their social responsibility, in order to reformulate heritage as a contribution to productive coexistence in a pluralistic and heterogeneous society. My text on the Sicilian capital, Palermo, reveals what an urban community can achieve when various actors understand the heritage of the city to be a political platform that can be used to bring about positive social change. By means of a coordinated heritage politics that attempts to draw together a disparate range of voices, a real turn-around has been accomplished in recent decades in a city that appeared irredeemably lost to organized crime. The reappropriation of the city by its residents was in fact achieved in the name of an urban heritage that aimed to counter the established narrative of a "city of crime", attracting significant support. Alongside determined political coordination, the key to success was the involvement of a variety of political and social groups as well as a broad palette of activities. These embedded conventional heritage conservation measures, such as inventorization and restoration of monuments, in a broad spectrum of support measures as well as social and educational projects in order to achieve a revitalization and rehabilitation of the historic centre, to stop processes of decline and desertion, and to disseminate new hope.

Finally, the section **Reclaiming Heritage. Conflicts, Contestation, Canonization** examines the potential of heritage to generate conflict. The focus here turns to social processes of contesting and reclaiming heritage, and to the highly varied constellations of actors involved. These are often manifestations of conflicts between global and local perspectives. Interwoven with them, however, though not paralleling them entirely, are other dynamics, which can be gathered together under the heading of the canonization of heritage. Canonization reflects fundamental power relations; it strengthens, marginalizes and contests heritage.[29] Yet cultural heritage is fundamentally a phenomenon grounded in collective perception and requires consensus to be effective. The various texts presented here provide arguments and observations that may help to evaluate these processes of negotiation and meaning-making, but ultimately it is always a matter of perspective and the standards applied, i.e. of positionality.

The chapter on how Sicily's cultural heritage came to be included in the (northern) European canon of taste and culture through the writings of the pioneer travellers of the late 18th century shows, with reference to Palermo, that the conflict between the global and the local is anything but new. It is possible to read this story as one in which Sicily grows closer to Europe, as an Enlightenment project that is associated with a major increase in positive knowledge (archaeological, historical art-historical, etc.). Yet it is clear that a significant body of knowledge was also lost in this process of canonization: not only the legacy of Arab-Norman culture, but also mediaeval sites were excluded from the local canon after failing to satisfy the aesthetic judgment of the representatives of the northern Enlightenment. The irony, not further elaborated in the chapter, is that these same Enlightenment thinkers, in their later garb as Romantics, were to rediscover the Middle Ages, raising it up as a model for their respective national cultures. These acts by which Sicily was 'discovered' certainly fit the pattern of colonialism:

---

29   Silverman, Contested Cultural Heritage, 2011.

questions of evaluation and, above all, of evaluative hegemony are matters of power and are accompanied by marginalization and loss.

In this context, the "foreign" and the "familiar" are certainly ambivalent and shifting categories. In the name of heritage, the foreign can be appropriated as exotic or as a primal origin, or else can be excluded and eliminated as hostile, inappropriate, ugly.[30] In addition, travelling heritage also provides a good opportunity to study processes of contextualization, framing, rejection and appropriation.[31] In this context, an essay on a "German" monument in the Bronx explores the emotional residues of heritage making. A monument forced to "travel" by anti-Semitism was adopted by the German community in New York and then banished to the Bronx; processes of appropriation and marginalization, destruction and redemption are are revealed as through a magnifying glass.

The tension between global and local evaluations is analysed once again with regard to Salvador da Bahia (Brazil). The starting point here is the rehabilitation, with international support, of the city's Pelourinho district, one of the largest contiguous Baroque city centres in the Americas, which was recently granted UNESCO World Heritage status. The rehabilitation of an important urban monument has taken its toll in terms of displacement, population transfer, and the weakening of social and cultural ties. The complexity of this example emerges from the fact that the former centre of the global slave trade is today a vital tourist destination, above all for Brazilians who come here to seek reconnect with their African roots. The *africanità* which is ascribed to the city is located less in its colourful building traditions, however, than in its cultural practices – precisely those aspects of its heritage that have experienced significant weakening as a result of the forces of homogenization and gentrification to which the historic centre has been subject as part of the heritage-making process. The lines of conflict and ambivalences are not always easy to resolve in a former city of slavery that is energetically reclaiming its African heritage, and that is assigned a specific role in the national consciousness: For in Bahia's urban heritage are also articulated the highly fragmented conflicts that surround the definition of a Brasilian identity.

Similar questions can be asked from a different perspective about New Orleans's Black heritage. In contrast to Brazil, the official historiography of the United States is unambiguously white; Blackness is not a component of American identity as a matter of course, as it is in Brazil. To this day, Black culture is generally considered to represent an exteriority. The starting point for my examination of this are the many irreversible instances of destruction that the city experienced in the disastrous floods caused by Hurricane Katrina in 2005. I analyse changes that have taken place in the city since reconstruction and the suppression of Black heritage artefacts, a phenomenon that takes its place in a long history of marginalization, domestication and commercial exploitation. In this context, once again, the urgent question arises of what we want to speak about when we speak about the heritage of a city; who can this "we" be? On which side do we wish to place ourselves? Here we can observe how racist discrimination proliferates monstrously, even in discourses around cultural heritage and indeed precisely in

---

30 Vinken, Das Erbe der Anderen, 2015.
31 Juneja, Mobile Heritage, 2015.

these discourses. The re-politicization of this debate, which is being pursued by Post-Colonial and Critical Heritage Studies, has already reached "the streets" of our cities in the form of the conflicts over Confederate monuments, the decolonization movement and Black Lives Matter activists. To research urban heritage is to write against the homogenization latent in established conceptions of cultural heritage; it means analysing heritage process in their contradictory modes of reproduction in the knowledge that the question of heritage is always a political one.

2 The Crises of the Modern City[1]
Place and Trajectorial Space

> As we know, the great obsession of the nineteenth century was history [...]. The present age may be the age of space instead. We are in an era of the simultaneous, of juxtaposition, of the near and the far, of the side-by-side, of the scattered.
> (Michel Foucault)[2]

Two categories of space, the place and the trajectorial space, are paradigmatic figures of space in the modern city.[3] The two concepts articulate the contrary and irreconcilable demands and functions the city has faced since the age of industrialization. To this day, an especially conspicuous feature of our cities are areas where a conflict plays out that remains unresolved: the conflict between the spaces of habitation, of human encounter and exchange, and the 'trajectories', open spaces of traffic, which are supposed to guarantee unlimited access and unhindered passage, an undisturbed "flow" – the spaces, in a word, that I will in the following call trajectorial spaces.

Urban planning as an independent discipline came into being first and foremost as a set of procedures of the organization of space aiming to arrange various "functions", including abidance/encounter and connection/rapid transit, in one and the same space. Yet the different attempts to provide a rational subdivision, order, and "zoning" of the urban surface according to different functions, and the call for "traffic-friendly" cities in particular, in fact led to a crisis Alexander Mitscherlich aptly described as the "inhospitability" of the city.[4] The hypothesis that this effect can be attributed directly to the intrusion of the trajectorial space into the dense core spaces of the cities is supported by Marc Augé's theoretical reflections on space.[5] Even in simple geometric terms, the

---

1   Translation from the German by Gerrit Jackson with assistance from Johanna Blokker.
2   Foucault, Different Spaces, 1998 (1967), 175.
3   On the term "trajectorial space" cf. Vinken, Ort und Bahn, 2008, and Knoblauch/Löw, The Re-Figuration, 2020; Löw, Re/figure(e)/ation, 2020.
4   Mitscherlich, Unwirtlichkeit unserer Städte, 1965.
5   Augé, Non-Places, 1995 (1992).

"centers" or "crossroads" that are places block the axes and paths that lead from one place to another.[6] Yet what I have described as a conflict between the different "demands" on the city reaches deeper. For the city center is one of those "anthropological places" Augé has described as identical, relational, and historical to the extent that they embody the "particularity" of a city: their various elements and practices can be seen as interrelated, and they convey continuity and stability not in the form of dissociated recollection but as participation.[7] It is into the city centers, as spaces "where individual itineraries can intersect and mingle,"[8] that the trajectorial space enters and with it a new spatial category of the "non-place." For the trajectorial space can be grouped with those spaces of transit and travelling Augé has called "the archetype of *non-place*."[9] To conceive place and trajectorial space as forming a dichotomic constellation means, moreover, to acknowledge that they tend to exclude each other, rather than constituting partial spaces that integrate into a larger shared space. The conflicts of the modern city cannot indeed be resolved by shifting the distribution of "space" in favor of one or the other pole. The history of modern urban development can be read in this perspective as a series of attempts to overcome a fundamental conflict over space with inadequate means. In a study of the example of Le Corbusier, the following analysis will examine how the trajectorial space becomes the paradigm of the modern city in the functionalist utopias, and will ask which qualities and potentials for conflict break the traditional urban spaces apart. Organic urban planning sought to reconcile place and trajectory; the example of Rudolf Schwarz, one of its champions, illustrates the factors that made the failure of this reconciliation inevitable.

The trajectory is the product and the icon of traffic. Long before mechanized individual traffic becomes a mass phenomenon that defines the cityscape, "traffic" begins to change the way people think about the city. Urban planning becomes traffic planning. Modernization now means a "correction" of the city,[10] a removal of its constrictions, a process of breaking open – and that includes opening the city toward its environment. As the fortification walls of old European cities are razed, the contrast that has long defined them – that between city and country – is dissolved.[11] Industrialization and, later, a new degree of mobility give this development additional dynamism, as well as creating a double problem: the congestion of the urban core, with the attendant negative consequences for the health of its residents; and the cancerous growth of developments in the surrounding countryside. From the Garden City movement onward, all influential urban utopias seek to remedy this doubly negative balance by conceiving city and country as a unified space for planning purposes.[12] The implementation by means of urban planning of a new reality that transcends the traditional dualism culminates in the concept of the urban landscape. In 1949, the architect and urban planner Rudolf

---

6 Augé, Non-Places, 1995 (1992), 57
7 Augé, Non-Places, 1995 (1992), 52–55.
8 Augé, Non-Places, 1995 (1992), 66.
9 Augé, Non-Places, 1995 (1992), 86. Italics in the original. In the same context, Augé also introduces the highway as a prominent non-place (ibid., 79).
10 Gurlitt, Handbuch des Städtebaues, 1920, 240–288.
11 Warnke, Natur nach dem Fall, 1994; Vinken, Die neuen Ränder, 2005.
12 Fehl/Rodríguez-Lores, Die Stadt wird in der Landschaft sein, 1997, 19–54.

Schwarz, seeking to establish the urban landscape as the general model of postwar reconstruction, writes: "The large city has become fluid, it flows out into its landscape, filling it to the brim. [...] City and country have come into flux, and out of their murky intermixture the urban landscape crystallizes."[13] The urban cores, too, are accordingly subjected to a process of space planning guided by criteria of order and functionality, which instate the guiding vision of a clearly structured city rich in greenery and open spaces, a hygienic and "traffic-friendly" urban landscape traversed by – ideally: intersection-free – roads and railroads embedded in wide green areas.

That the city is categorized as a space that can be planned, controlled, and subdivided is the trajectorial space's first triumph. The trajectory turns out in this regard to be the agent of a homogeneous "Euclidean" space conceived as preexisting what is in it; seen from the trajectory, everything becomes a destination – or an obstacle. The tabula rasa, the empty and zonable space in which the modern city comes into being and at whose mercy it has been ever since, is the trajectorial space. The sway of this space has changed the heterogeneous spatial structure of the traditional city, which Marc Augé has described as a fabric of interrelations between interpenetrating and overlapping places as well as an "active place."[14] Le Corbusier's urban projects and utopias present an illustrative example that can help us gain a better understanding of this process and the specific qualities of the trajectorial space. For as we will see, the great variety of such projects designed by the man who was probably the single most influential protagonist of functionalist urban planning[15] at once marks a radical end point of the trajectorial space's dominance over the city.

The motif of the trajectory already occupies a central position in Le Corbusier's early urban utopias. He first comes to public notice as an urban planner at the Paris Autumn Salon of 1922, where he presents his project of a "Contemporary City for Three Million Inhabitants" (figs 1, 2).[16]

The *Ville Contemporaine* is considered the first ever functionalist urban development project.[17] For the first time, the urban area is strictly divided into spatially separate zones that also differ in their formal designs – a downtown of skyscrapers is surrounded by a residential city consisting of linear residential structures meandering across wide open spaces and, further out, by factory areas with the associated working-class housing estates. The project's main feature is the generous use of open space in conjunction with a high population density; the architect described his design as a "vertical garden city." Buildings occupy only five percent of the total area; the slender high-rises are set several hundred meters apart.

---

13   Schwarz, Von der Bebauung, 1949, 205–206.
14   Augé, Non-Places, 1995 (1992), 66.
15   Huse, Le Corbusier in Selbstzeugnissen, 1976, 56–79. See the recent summary discussion in Petrilli, L'urbanistica, 2006.
16   Le Corbusier, The City of To-morrow, 1987 (1925), 176–177.
17   Huse, Le Corbusier in Selbstzeugnissen, 1976, 56, 59–63.

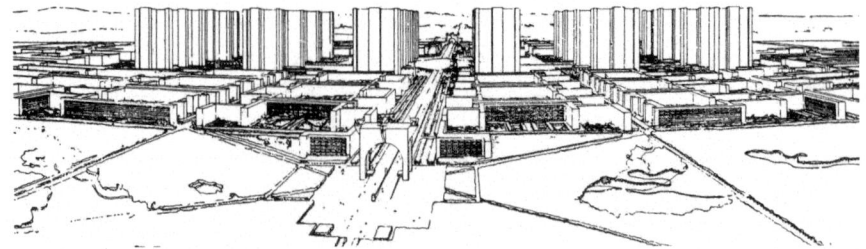

Figure 1: "Contemporary City for Three Million Inhabitants", overview, Le Corbusier 1922

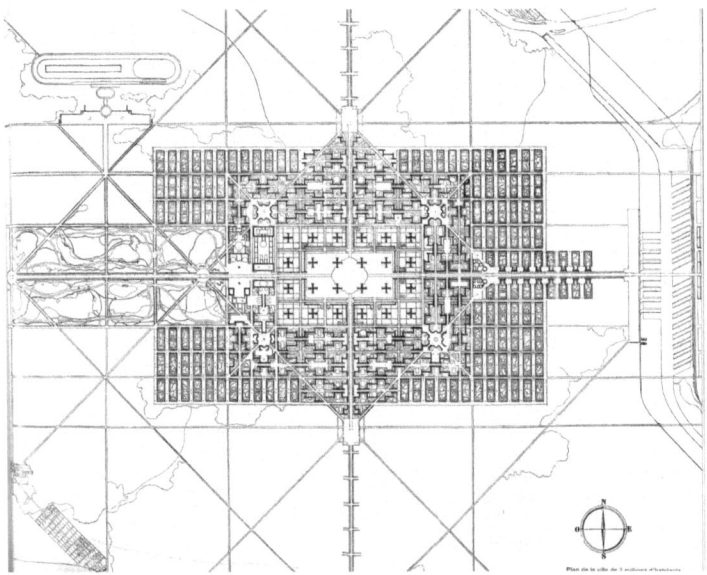

Figure 2: "Contemporary City for Three Million Inhabitants", layout, Le Corbusier 1922

The center of the entire project is given to traffic, with a landing field for air taxis atop a multi-level train station. Numerous highways and roads provide access to the entire metropolitan area, forming a complex fabric of thoroughfares of gradated capacity. The ornamental aspect of this fabric, which patently owes more to a concern for formal aesthetics than to functional considerations, renders it glaringly obvious that the trajectory is the project's guiding principle. The building designs, too, derive from this primacy of the trajectory. From roads and parking levels, elevators, as "vertical mass transit," catapult people to their workplaces and apartments off the hallways of the meandering blocks. Despite the inclusion of dedicated pedestrian levels, the enormous dimensions and spaces of the "Contemporary City" are designed for rapid movement, for the car and the driver. A multi-lane highway reserved for individual traffic forms the rigorously geometrical layout's spine. The fact that this highway, moving away from the city center, abruptly narrows down to a much smaller road highlights the representative and symbolic function of the so-called *grande traversée*, whose beginning and end are designated by triumphal arches: the center of the modern city marks the triumph of the automobile. In this regard, the project renders a very literal interpretation of the concept of "Fordism": Le Corbusier reiterates the fundamental disposition of Ford's groundbreaking car factory in Detroit, a gigantic industrial compound whose layout obeys rational considerations, with a central production line linking the various elements.

Despite the highway axis dominating the project, the *Ville Contemporaine* remains committed to the tradition of centralistic urban layouts. Still, the consequences of the city's integration into, and subordination to, the trajectorial space are unmistakable. Ample spaces designed to enable a neat separation of functions as well as a high degree of mobility isolate and distance the individual elements from one another, privileging gazing over doing, driving past over lingering. The density and superimposition of structures of interrelation and spaces of action of the traditional city disintegrates into a space conceived from the perspective of the trajectory and furnished with architectonic sculptures. The rich choreography of visual axes between these elements Le Corbusier presented in various drawings[18] is best seen in the sequences that emerge as one drives past them (fig. 3). The city becomes an aggregation of marginal objects in a trajectorial space to be traversed in rapid movement.

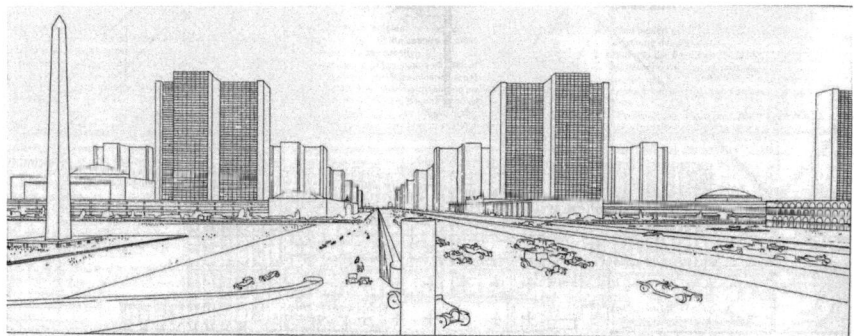

Figure 3: "Contemporary City for Three Million Inhabitants", view from the central highway, Le Corbusier 1922

In the 1930s, Le Corbusier elaborated his Contemporary City into the *Ville Radieuse*, the "Radiant City".[19] The spatially separate zones (administrative, residential, industrial, recreational) are now placed in alternation along the central highway. The conveyor belt of traffic has become the sole defining principle giving the urban design its

---

18   Le Corbusier, Œuvre complète, 1960, 34–39.
19   Le Corbusier, La ville radieuse, 1935.

structure and shape, creating the arbitrarily extensible linear city.[20] This renders the integration of the city into a space conceived as total (and homogeneous) even more obvious. The radiant city itself is trajectory-shaped, perfectly aligned, dynamic, endless. The trajectory is the principle of this space in two ways: as a principle of distancing and remote views; and as the principle of a homogeneous functional space of movement that presupposes additional homogeneous spaces dedicated to specific functions such as habitation, work, etc.

The trajectory remains the leitmotif of Le Corbusier's urban planning well into the postwar era. As early as 1929, he had designed ribbon-shaped megastructures that would snake through the bays of Rio de Janeiro (fig. 4) like the sandworms of Frank Herbert's desert planet. Not much later, he wanted to connect two outlying suburbs of Algiers with similar linear cities (fig. 5).[21]

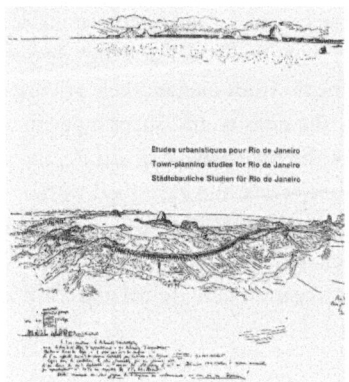

Figures 4, 5: Urban planning for Rio de Janeiro, "Project Obus" for Algiers, Le Corbusier 1929 and 1931

The central aim of these visions is to achieve a complete synthesis of trajectory and residential unit. The new urban form consists of wide highways atop a gigantic support structure made of reinforced concrete into which apartment units are inserted; in the case of Algiers, Le Corbusier's plans included housing for no less than 180,000 inhabitants. The arterial road is the "roof" of a ribbon-shaped apartment block on stilts; habitation is formally and literally subordinate to the trajectory. In a gesture almost of modesty, the revolutionary structure of this urban utopia is motivated as a technical alteration to the urban structure: "The project provides the city with what it urgently needs: rapid transit and apartments."[22] In fact, it entails massive interventions into the spatial structure that are illuminating for our inquiry into the qualities of the trajectorial space, as they concern its relation to the old city and to the surrounding countryside. Indicatively enough, the first point, the relation between the trajectorial space and the

---

20 Le Corbusier, La ville radieuse, 1935, 170.
21 Le Corbusier, Precisions on the present State, 2015 (1930), 233–245; and see Boesiger/Girsberger, Le Corbusier, 1999, 324–328.
22 Boesiger/Girsberger, Le Corbusier, 1999, 327.

old city, was only of marginal interest to Le Corbusier. In many sketches, built-up areas are indicated by nothing more than summary hatching. His linear city is, first and foremost, a grand system for automotive traffic that "frees" the old city "of confusion and clutter [...] without interfering with the existing state of affairs in any way."[23] For, the conciliatory argument goes, "nothing is easier than to build, with little disturbance, supports of reinforced concrete rising well above the roofs of existing neighborhoods."[24] Rather than "scraping off [and] removing" "that swarming mass that until now has clung to the ground like a rigid crust" – these words are meant to describe a reorganization of the historic center of Paris[25] – the design calls for traffic to traverse the old Rio with its heterogeneous spaces and layered components on stilts. Transcended by the technological constructions of the new machine age, the old city languishes in the shadow of the trajectory.

The distancing and marginalization of the old city we can observe in this instance is positively a precondition for the new kind of urban landscape to which Le Corbusier plans to give shape. This urban landscape, rather than consisting of city and countryside, abruptly confronts both with the trajectorial space and its architectonic implementation. Seen through the eyes of the creator-architect, nature and architecture allow each other to appear in the most flattering light: "The whole site began to speak [...] of architecture [...]. The city announced itself by the only line that can harmonize with the vehement caprice of the mountains: the horizontal."[26] The freedom of the open road corresponds to the freedom of the distanced gaze: "The steamers that passed, magnificent and moving constructions of modern times, suspended in the space above the city, found a response, an echo, a rejoinder there."[27] At night, in particular, ships entering the harbor would come upon a magnificent spectacle whose effect would surpass that of New York's skyline. This urban utopia of a grand form composed, in sculptural fashion, into the landscape aims both at total functionality and at the aesthetic appeal of distanced spectatorship, uniting two central qualities of non-places: constituted to meet specific purposes, they do not engender spaces of encounter and assembly, instead establishing unambiguous and functionalized relationships between the isolated individual and the space.[28] The highway on stilts moreover permits no more than a passing glance at the existing places with their centers and crossroads. In the privilege it accords to the distant view, too, this "trajectorial-city" belongs to the spaces of transit occupied by travelers.

The *Cité linéaire industrielle* (fig. 6), a project Le Corbusier begins drafting in 1942–43, represents the synthesis and quintessence of his ideas about urban development.[29] In

---

23   Boesiger/Girsberger, Le Corbusier, 1999, 324.
24   Le Corbusier, Precisions on the present State, 2015 (1930), 242.
25   Le Corbusier, The City of To-morrow, 1987 (1925), 280–281. At the time, Le Corbusier planned to build a "Contemporary City," the *Ville Voisin* (named after a automobile brand), in the center of Paris (ibid., 277–289).
26   Le Corbusier, Precisions on the present State, 2015 (1930), 245.
27   Le Corbusier, Precisions on the present State, 2015 (1930), 245.
28   Augé, Non-Places, 1995 (1992), 96–97.
29   Le Corbusier, L'Urbanisme des Trois Établissements humains, 1959, 97–125. On the genesis of the "industrial linear city" cf. Fehl/Rodríguez-Lores, Die Stadt wird in der Landschaft sein, 1997, 153–158.

this "industrial linear city," which is conceived as the centerpiece of a comprehensive reorganization of space, the trajectory becomes the principle of the global order of space and indeed of civilization as a whole.

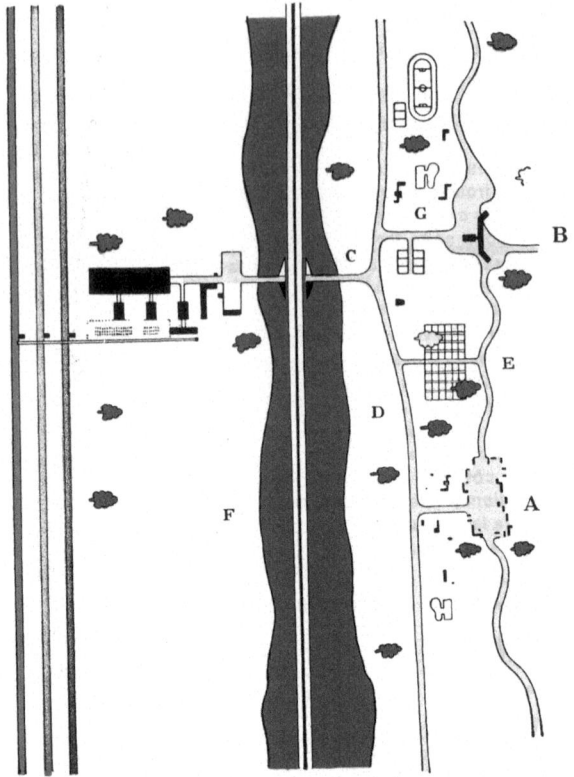

Figure 6: "Industrial Linear City", Le Corbusier/ASCORAL 1942–43

In several sketches, Le Corbusier lays out the vision of a global order of space based on gigantic urban belts that extend across the continents from harbor to harbor. The slightly cryptic annotation reads in translation: "The world has spread across the entire surface of the earth, from one pole to the other and even across the poles themselves, a world made up of storage facilities, gigantic productive forces, and transit and transportation infrastructure."[30] The industrial linear city is a loose aggregation of factory compounds, residential units, and infrastructure along transportation and traffic routes laid out in parallel lines. At its center runs a highway – wide green spaces shield the rest of the city from its noise – reserved for individual traffic (!). At some distance from it, the various routes of freight traffic run in parallel to it: road, railroad, and canal. The factory zones are inserted between these lines. On the other side of the highway are apartments, communal buildings such as athletic and recreation centers, and cultural

---

30   Quoted in: Boesiger/Girsberger, Le Corbusier, 1999, 336.

and administrative facilities. This urban landscape lacks all traditional urban attributes, or rather: it is conceived as the antithesis to the historic city: loose, permeated by greenery, and dynamic rather than dense, built of stone, and centered. The trajectory as the principle of spatial order creates functionally unambiguous and homogeneous zoned spaces in order to realize the explicit aim of the functionalist urban models. The industrial linear city, too, clearly evinces the qualities of the trajectorial space. The city is reduced to spatially isolated zones, each composed of homogeneous functional units devoted to habitation, work, and play; modern man, ideally, is always efficient: now as a sleeper, now as an eater, now as a worker. The city's resident becomes its user – especially so on the central trajectory, which remains Le Corbusier's privileged perspective of its representation. Here, as in all non-places, man is free from his "usual determinants" and "no more than what he does or experiences in the role of [...] driver."[31]

Le Corbusier's urbanistic proposals are remarkably consistent in the way they take the concept of the functionalist city to its logical extreme – also as regards its spatial dispositions. In the linear city, the modern city is entirely conceived around the central trajectory – and with the trajectory a non-place has intruded into the center of the urban fabric and broken it apart into isolated zones, modes of access, and views. Linear cities have played a supporting role at best in the history of urban development.[32] Yet beyond such instances in which the trajectory formally shapes the modern city, most evidently so in the linear urban forms, we can note structural changes – or rather, spatial dislocations – that result from the rise of the trajectorial space as the new paradigm of urban development. A direct path leads from the trajectory and the trajectorial space to the crisis of the modern city and its "inhospitability" mentioned above. In the historical perspective, however, responsibility for this development is borne not by utopian visions of the linear city but rather by the organic urban models that prevailed in the postwar era, promising to correct the construction flaws of the functionalist city[33] by replacing a mechanical and "empty" order with one that would be "animated," meaningful, and lively. In his influential textbook *Organische Stadtbaukunst* (The Art of Organic Urban Development, published 1948),[34] Hans Bernhard Reichow dedicates himself to a renewal of the city as a harmonious entity "in accord with the laws of life", and to the "development of a cohesive, organically structured, ordered, and integrated metropolitan body possessing natural and meaningful unity".[35] The new urban landscape is to be based on a cellular and hierarchically gradated structure, from the single-family residential unit to the apartment block, from the neighborhood to the urban district. Green spaces or woodlands and agricultural areas separate the individual urban cells or neighborhoods from one another. Metaphors taken from the (human) organism undergird this structure of order. Cells and organs, arteries and nerve cords are to be placed in organic – which is also to say, meaningful and purposive – arrangement. This image,

---

31　Augé, Non-Places, 1995 (1992), 103.
32　Fehl/Rodríguez-Lores, Die Stadt wird in der Landschaft sein, 1997, and Kainrath, Die Bandstadt, 1997.
33　Cf. the summary discussion in Düwel/Gutschow, Städtebau in Deutschland, 2001, 165–174.
34　Reichow, Organische Stadtbaukunst, 2005 (1948).
35　Reichow, Organische Stadtbaukunst, 2005 (1948), 59.

it would seem, assigns places as well as trajectories their respective locations within a shared whole, the "urban body." And yet, as I will show in the following, the city under the aegis of the organic has been no less subject to the dominance of the trajectorial space and its non-places.

The champions of organic urban planning took far from negative views of technology, traffic, and mobility. Just like Le Corbusier, they claimed to have the right answers to the new demands the city faced; they, too, were heralds of modern progress. As early as 1928, Rudolf Schwarz, a theorist of the modern city whose importance has not yet been fully recognized, had devoted a book to the "path-breaking power of technology";[36] in his subsequent writings, he had repeatedly placed the demands of the age of mechanization, the "intrusion of technology into the cities,"[37] at the center of his reflections on urban development.[38] When Schwarz was appointed head of general planning for the rebuilding of Cologne in 1946, he drafted an urban landscape that would subject the entire Cologne Bight to a new spatial structure. *Das neue Köln* (The New Cologne),[39] a programmatic book published in connection with these plans, illustrates the project in striking graphic representations that show the Cologne Bight as a network of more or less autonomous urban units (fig. 7).

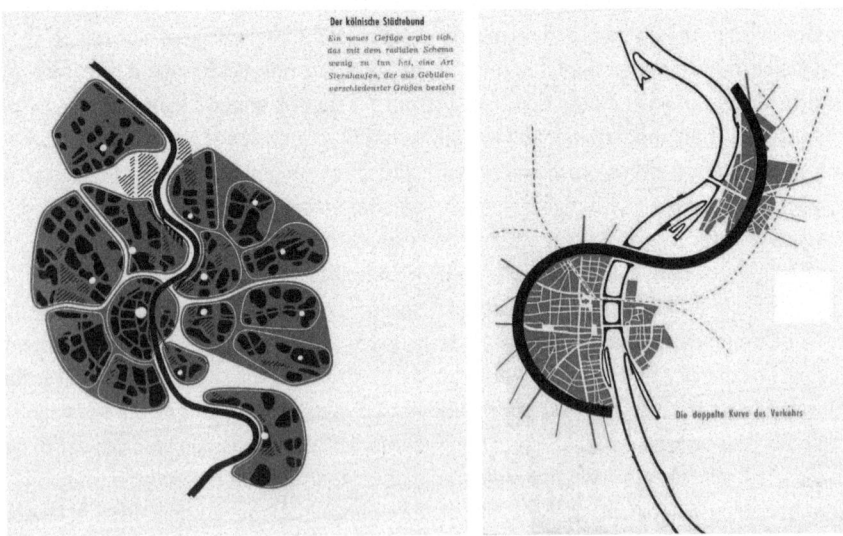

Figures 7, 8: "The Cologne Federation of Cities" – "Double City Cologne and Mülheim", Rudolf Schwarz 1950

This "federation of cities" is shown in sketches deliberately designed to recall the images of cells and nuclei in biology textbooks. Upon closer examination, however, the heritage of the functional city is tangible in the plans for Cologne not only in the rational

---

36   Schwarz, Wegweisung der Technik, 1979 (1928).
37   Schwarz, Das neue Köln, 1950, 11.
38   See the recent detailed discussion in Pehnt/Strohl, Rudolf Schwarz, 1997.
39   Schwarz, Das neue Köln, 1950.

organization of the region as a whole but also, quite concretely, in the figure of the "double city" (fig. 8): the urban nucleus of Cologne, as the "acropolis" (*Hochstadt*) and "city of education and community," is complemented by Mülheim as the "city of labor," a structure that unmistakably recalls the linear-city conceptions. The two centers are organized along two conveyor belts, the "double curve" of traffic, formed by the river Rhine and a planned new highway. Mülheim itself functions as a linear city along a central trajectory, quite as proposed by Le Corbusier for industrial cities; the "acropolis" (*Hochstadt*) of Cologne, by contrast, is "embraced and delimited" by the highway – a configuration we will need to discuss in greater detail.

In fact, Rudolf Schwarz had closely studied the industrial linear city as early as 1941, when he worked on the plans for Thionville (Diedenhofen), on which his proposals for Cologne would later draw.[40] The drafts for the organically structured "urban landscape of Diedenhofen"[41] were commissioned by the National Socialists, who sought to redevelop war-ravaged Lorraine, which had come under German occupation, radically Germanizing and modernizing it in the process. In this context, Schwarz transformed the guiding model of an organic structure into a concrete structural schema that profoundly influenced the German debates of the postwar era, not least importantly through his widely read 1949 programmatic essay *Von der Bebauung der Erde* (On the development of the earth),[42] which explicitly describes the organic urban landscape as an elaboration of the linear city (fig. 9).

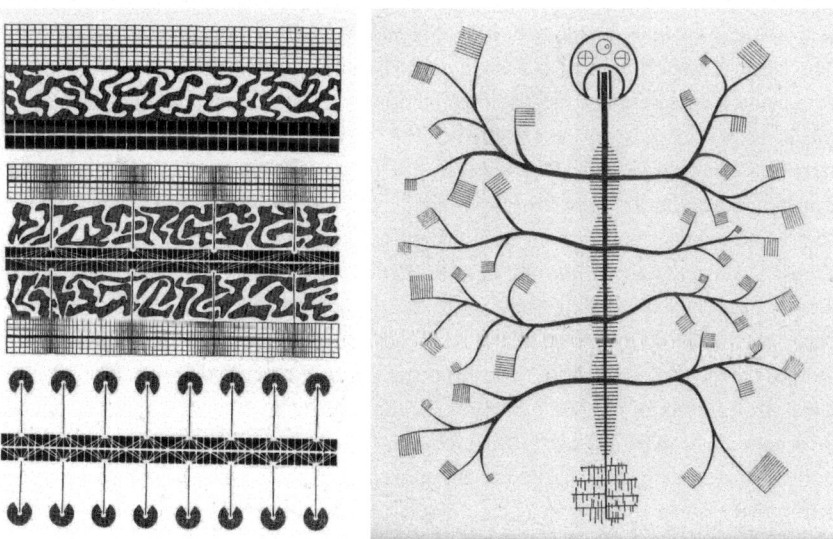

Figures 9, 10: "Development Scheme from the Linear City to the Urban Landscape" –"Industrial Ribbon with Residential Developments and 'Hochstadt'", *Rudolf Schwarz 1949*

---

40   Pehnt/Strohl, Rudolf Schwarz, 1997, 100–112.
41   Schwarz, Stadtlandschaft Diedenhofen, 1943.
42   Schwarz, Von der Bebauung der Erde, 1949.

A "three-ribbon city" (with an industrial, a green, and a residential ribbon), mirrored across one axis, becomes a five-ribbon city with a central industrial ribbon, and finally an industrial ribbon with residential developments forming lateral appendages. Another illustration (fig. 10), which depicts a schematic view of the entire urban landscape as it was to be realized in Cologne as well, confirms the extent to which the linear element of the central trajectory has penetrated the organic plans: here, too, the city's spine and its structurally dominant element is the "maelstrom of the industrial zone." This model city, however, is enriched by the addition of a new element. Whereas Le Corbusier puts issues of transportation front and center, which leads to a design that seeks to insert the zoned city as smoothly as possible into the trajectorial space, the organic model has two poles. The residential cells are arranged in relation to the transportation belt without adopting its spatial structure, forming their own centers of gravity. Schwarz compares this pattern to the spatial organization of a cathedral: the length of the central nave is flanked by chapels that are accessible and yet intimate and self-enclosed spaces, just as the autonomous spatial units of a "pearl necklace" of residential cells are arrayed along the "maelstrom of the industrial zone."[43]

The trajectorial space of the industrial linear city has thus been reinterpreted into a polar order of the sort that is characteristic for the entire concept of the urban landscape. City and countryside, too, are presented as interrelated categories: the city, Schwarz writes, is "another countryside. The landscape exists doubly, once spread out outside as countryside, and then comprised in a narrow space, transformed into head and countenance, as city."[44] The city itself is accordingly a "double entity." It is a home, homelike, associated with domesticity and the female; but at once also "disclosed toward the open and wedded to the man."[45] This polar order is also, and primarily, a spatial order. On the one hand, the city as a home is "pervaded by the power of places" that can be assigned to the "forever unvarying processes of human lives" and are charged with "the unceasing repetitions of the quotidian." "That means much for planning. In order for residential developments to be able to become a home, their dimensions must remain within the compass life can pervade." Every narrow domain "must contain everything that belongs to the generation of community life."[46] The anthropological place, it would seem, has been rehabilitated in this theory as one "pole" of considerations in urban development. Complementing his theory of the place, Schwarz elaborates a theory of the trajectorial space. The figure that to his mind marks the polar opposite of the home is traffic, as the expression of openness par excellence. This pole, he argues, did not fully develop until traffic was mechanized. The man of old, the pedestrian, now shared the city with man as the "commander of technology, with great speeds and spaces at his disposal."[47] The human being of the modern era is accordingly described as a double creature, at once "pre-technological" and "meta-

---

43 The image continues with an equation between the altar, the inner sanctum, and the "acropolis" (*Hochstadt*) or "central sun", Schwarz, Von der Bebauung, 1949, 106.
44 Schwarz, Gegenstand des Städtebaus, 1997 (1948), 218.
45 Schwarz, Von der Bebauung, 1949, 196.
46 Schwarz, Von der Bebauung, 1949, chapter "Die Stadt", 193–212.
47 Schwarz, Das neue Köln, 1950, 11–12.

technological"; as a pedestrian and "conductor and director of technology."[48] This double being, Schwarz argues in his essay on "Das neue Köln," necessarily requires a double structure of his habitat: "the ample and spacious city and the other one for the quiet and precious things and the homes of human sentiment."[49] The new city of Schwarz, we might translate, merges place and trajectory.

How is this simultaneity conceived in spatial terms? How can place and trajectory be integrated in such a fashion that neither pole takes on the spatial qualities of the other, with the attendant adverse effects? For the "double entity" of the new city to be realized in full, Schwarz is convinced, both components need to "mature into their fully developed figure."[50] This process of the clarification of home and technology, of place and trajectory described here as one of maturation also implies a radical reconstruction and reorganization of the city. And once again, the guiding figure of modernization is the trajectorial space and the structure it imposes: "The technical [component], in particular, must be developed to its full clarity and size, as unconstrained as possible by petty considerations. The large conveyor belts of traffic must flow through the lands in free movement and be equipped with everything required for a smooth discharge of traffic," Schwarz writes – Le Corbusier would have concurred without qualification. These wide-open spaces of knowledge must then "be complemented by a meta-technological component that, undisturbed by technology and its traffic, is the province of unencumbered man."[51] This privilege accorded to one pole, that of the trajectorial space, provides, in the practice of urban planning, the argument that it is necessary to reorganize the city in order to make it traffic-friendly. Still, from now on – and no earlier theorist has put it quite so clearly – the urban planner's task is double: not only must he create wide and fluid spaces; he must also "restitute" to the pedestrian city its proper dimensions, since traffic, Schwarz writes, had brought about "the general dissolution of the historic town center."[52] In Le Corbusier's model, the city was an uncompromising trajectorial space; in the organic model, it becomes a space traversed by polar opposites, "the dynamic [space] of the belts of traffic and the static one of the pedestrian". "Belt and domain," Schwarz writes in looking back on his work on the plans for Cologne, "needed to be woven into each other."[53]

The Cologne plans offer insight into the details of how the modern dichotomy of place and trajectorial space was to be translated into a new spatial order – and analyzing them can help us detect the flaws in the procedures applied to attain this goal. As we saw, the "maelstrom of technology" remained the principle on which the urban landscape's order was based; in the Cologne Bight, the highway from Cologne to Mülheim would be one such trajectory. The trajectory has the double function of providing

---

48 Schwarz, Das neue Köln, 1950, 11–12.
49 Schwarz, Das neue Köln, 1950, 11–12.
50 Schwarz, Das neue Köln, 1950, 12.
51 Schwarz, Das neue Köln, 1950, 12.
52 Schwarz, Das neue Köln, 1950, 11.
53 Schwarz, Der Aufbau zerstörter Städte, 1997 (1955), 220.

access to, and imposing order upon, space: "Rapid traffic fringes the place, branching off from its fringe toward its center" (fig. 11).⁵⁴

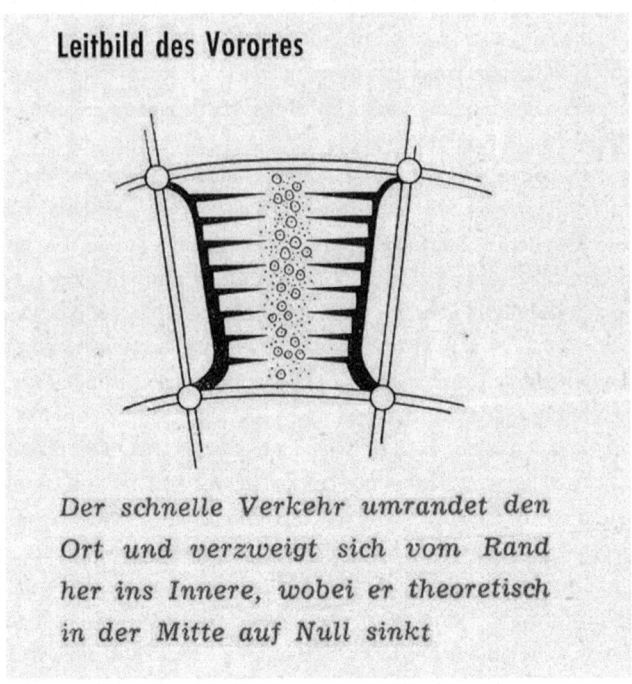

Figure 11: *"General Concept of the Suburb"*, *Rudolf Schwarz 1950*

This second task of the trajectory, here designated by the term "fringing," which was already recognizable in the sketch "The double curve of traffic" (fig. 8), merits closer examination. Unlike Mülheim, an industrial town fed, and bisected, by the trajectory as though by a conveyor belt, the urban nucleus of Cologne is fringed by the trajectory, which turns it into an island of sorts. This constellation returns in the structure imposed on the urban cores. The "reorganization of the inner city" looks peaceful and hardly spectacular in the plans: it shows the newly organized, largely independent residential neighborhoods, each comprehended by higher-order roads. These multi-lane arterial roads are laid out wide enough to accommodate not only car traffic, but also the tramway on its own track bed separate from the street. The "general concept" summarizes this method as follows: "Calm and internally complete neighborhoods need to be formed and separated from one another, and the suitable means to this end is the thoroughfare."⁵⁵ "Internally complete" – that refers to the desired autonomy of these units, which usually comprise several parishes and generally coincide with a school district. Traffic infrastructure, as Schwarz puts it concisely in the same context, has "today almost taken on the function formerly fulfilled by city walls; it delimits and circumscribes

---

54   Schwarz, Das neue Köln, 1950, 29.
55   Schwarz, Das neue Köln, 1950, 43.

the quarter. The planner will fringe the latter with such roads and distance it from adjacent quarters."[56] The trajectory is here not just the central element of spatial planning; it is also meant to supply the definition and protection classically afforded by the city wall: the trajectorial space and its non-places are suddenly charged with circumscribing and assembling.

The mismatched comparison between the highway and the city wall reveals where the blind spot of the project of organic reconciliation lies. For there is no spatial overlap between the wall and the trajectory: whereas the wall separates an (open) outside from a (protected, enclosed) inside, expansiveness from narrowness, city from countryside, the trajectorial space cannot serve as a boundary in this sense. As an agent of the infinite, open, and expanding vector space, it occupies adjacent spaces in order to subject them to its order. Schwarz was in fact perfectly aware that the two spaces to be "woven into each other" were incommensurable opposites: "The fact remains that modern traffic requires urban planning on a different spatial and temporal scale than the traffic of the old cities, largely defined by pedestrians. Modern traffic requires wide, fluid belts to be rapidly traversed. The driver condenses the space he traverses, whereas the pedestrian gradually gains access to it."[57] Yet Schwarz's use of the term "condensed" to describe the trajectorial space quite plainly shows the inadequacy of the instruments he proposes. The two spaces and their different scales cannot indeed be interwoven into peaceful coexistence in a greater space of the urban totality. The condensed space of the trajectory evinces a characteristic urge to unrestrained expansion. It is unsuitable as the boundary of a small-scale "interior" because as a consequence, the emptiness and distancing of the trajectorial space invade the protective urban spaces of guarding and assembling. The plans for Cologne are clear evidence in this regard: in Schwarz's conception, the expressways that enclose the neighborhoods are to be as "frontage-free" as possible. Rather than being lined by businesses, roads should preferably widen into square-like exterior spaces used as parking lots interspersed with tall and large administrative buildings that, erected at large distances, "are more commensurate with the scale of the belt."[58] The trajectory exports its scale into the spaces adjacent to it, transforming them into space congruous to itself. Distancing and emptiness, the qualities of the trajectorial space, distinctly come to the fore. The new city Schwarz imagines already faintly suggests the specific qualities of the car city Venturi and Scott Brown taught us to recognize in their exemplary study of Las Vegas (fig. 12).[59] Seen from the highway, the city in this model shrivels into an agglomeration of isolated buildings on the edges of wide parking areas, while omnipresent advertising billboards and information signage provide the required rapid orientation.

---

56 Schwarz, Das neue Köln, 1950, 29.
57 Schwarz, Das neue Köln, 1950, 11–12.
58 Schwarz, Der Aufbau zerstörter Städte, 1997 (1955), 221.
59 Venturi/Brown/Izenour, Learning from Las Vegas, 1972.

Figure 12: Traditional city and car city. Rome and Las Vegas, Robert Venturi/Denise Scott Brown 1972.

The urban landscape of Cologne, with its desired "interweaving of belt and domain," was not realized except in isolated locations; but it served as a guiding model in the rebuilding of many war-ravaged cities. The reorganization of Essen into a "shopping city with direct Autobahn access," for instance, begun under mayor Gustav Heinemann, who would later be Federal President of West Germany, clearly evinces comparable structures. The historic urban core is "fringed" by a wide ring road directly connected to the Ruhrschnellweg highway. Constricted and isolated rather than "delimited and circumscribed," Essen's center has been rebuilt as a commercial and business district.[60] As envisioned by Le Corbusier and Rudolf Schwarz, parking garages function as hinges between the trajectorial space and the "pedestrian area" where the driver switches "roles," becoming a consumer. The trajectorial space thus abuts a functional zone that is no less spatially homogeneous; the city under the sway of the trajectory is pervaded by nonplaces: it is not a place of encounter and assembly.[61]

Le Corbusier probably saw the extent of the conflict between the traditional city and the new trajectorial spaces more clearly than did the champions of the organic urban landscape. In his vision, the old cities have in the machine age sunken into a sort of enchanted oblivion: "The beauty and splendor of the concentric city derived from the royal roads; but where the railroad, appearing on the scene, ignored it and passed it

---

60 Loth, Essens Wiederaufbau, 2005, 131–133.
61 Löw/Vinken, Die Dichte der Entleerung, 2007.

by in a wide arc, the city fell asleep."[62] Yet even if the future the architect confidently envisions belongs to the "villes vertes," the "vertical garden cities" and "unités d'habitation" embedded in green areas, he does not foresee a complete disappearance of the traditional "radiocentric cities." In accordance with their origins, he sees them located, as "cities of exchange," at the intersections of the major traffic arteries.[63] And although sweeping "surgical" interventions ought to prepare these sleeping beauties for the future,[64] Le Corbusier fears a collision between the linear city and the traditional city: "Attentive measures will be able to prevent the industrial city from penetrating and altogether dissolving in the concentric city: a wide protective greenbelt will need to be laid out around the old city, a belt of fields, meadows, and forests. This peaceful space enables people from both spheres to meet, allows for a rapprochement and harmonious exchange between them: one city brings to this meeting the enormous tension of machine technology; the other, the pertinacity of things that are, as it were, forever unchanging, having been contemplated, experienced, and tested for a long time."[65] The city, as a place of assembly, now appears as nothing more than a monument to forever unchanging things. And protecting the trajectorial space, with its functional efficiency and beauty, from the relics of the old world requires a wide *cordon sanitaire*. Indicatively enough, the city of the past is to be embedded in peaceful greenery, a schema we can trace back all the way to the romantic ruin in the park; Le Corbusier's plans for the new Paris had envisioned a similar setting in which the national monuments would be "salvaged."[66] Modern life, however, has moved into the dynamic spaces of transit. In Le Corbusier's city, as Hugo Häring wrote, man is "a mere visitor, merely passing through."[67]

---

62   Le Corbusier, L'Urbanisme des Trois Établissements humains, 1959, 102.
63   Le Corbusier, Concerning Town Planning, 1948 (1946). The new spatial order, composed of industrial linear cities, radiocentric cities, and agricultural production units, is laid out in detail in Le Corbusier, Les trois établissements humains, 1946.
64   Surgery rather than the paltry remedies of traditional medicine: that was already the architect's motto in his first comprehensive work on urban planning, see Le Corbusier, The City of To-morrow, 1987 (1925), 258–273. For a more detailed discussion of the proposed modernization measurements to be implemented during rebuilding, see also Le Corbusier, Concerning Town Planning, 1948 (1946).
65   Le Corbusier, L'Urbanisme des Trois Établissements humains, 1959, 102.
66   On the plan to 'salvage' the national heritage in the *Ville Voisin*, see Le Corbusier, The City of Tomorrow, 1987 (1925), 287–289. Cf the essay on *The Spaces of the Monument* in this volume (Chapter 4).
67   Hugo Häring, Zwei Städte, in: Die Form, 2/1926, 172–175, quoted in: Düwel/Gutschow, Städtebau in Deutschland, 2001, 71.

3 The Distinctiveness of Cities[1]
Heritage as a Mode of Reproduction

> In the dispositions of towns and cities are manifesed the memory of societies and landscapes.
> (Karl Schlögel)[2]

The concept of *Eigenlogik* – of a city's particular or intrinsic logic – has contributed to the debate which is now attempting to comprehend the ways in which every city is particular and different from all other cities, and to understand how this particularity takes definite form and is stabilized.[3] At first glance, built heritage would seem to play an obvious leading role in this function. Indeed, a city's built heritage is considered to be almost definitive of with its particularity and identity. However, seeing the "identity" or "DNA" of a city in its built heritage is an essentializing shortcut that runs counter to the concept of *Eigenlogik*. *Eigenlogik* might be understood as a 'mode of reproduction' that is operative in locally specific and long-lasting ways and is unconsciously implicit in all practices and routines.[4] That is to say, *Eigenlogik* as a locally operative praxis should be traceable also in those processes and practices through which heritage is reclaimed and shaped, interpreted and handed down. It is accordingly first and foremost the making and managing of a city's heritage that constitutes a rewarding field of study.[5]

The local as a research problem

What is 'local' about a built monument? At first glance, this would seem to be a simple matter, given the monument's fixed location. Upon closer inspection, however, locality turns out to be a parameter fraught with questions. All discourses of heritage, from the official designation to the attribution of 'meaning', evidently refer to contexts that

---

1   Translation from the German by Gerrit Jackson with assistance from Johanna Blokker.
2   Karl Schlögel in the preface to Anziferow, Die Seele Petersburgs, 2003 (1922), 38.
3   Berking/Löw, Die Eigenlogik der Städte, 2008; Löw, The City as Experiential Space, 2013.
4   Bockrath, Städtischer Habitus, 2008, 76.
5   Frank, Wall memorials and heritage, 2016 (2009).

are barely, or not at all, tied to local circumstances, a fact that has come to be recognized as a major problem; note, for instance, how the World Heritage label spreads Western notions of value in parts of the world where people have very different understandings of collective memory and abide by different concepts of heritage.[6] And this is not, as many claim, just another effect of globalization; it is a problem that is as old as heritage preservation itself. When local construction businesses in post-revolutionary France dismantled the walls of the abbey at Cluny – Europe's most significant medieval monastery complex – to burn the stones for quicklime, it was scholars from Paris such as Prosper Mérimée who travelled to Burgundy to save the abbey. It was a civil servant with Berlin's building inspectorate, Karl Friedrich Schinkel, who 'discovered' the ruins of the abbey at Chorin as a national monument; in the countryside of Brandenburg it had fallen into oblivion, and locals were using it as a stable, among other things. The discovery of the Venus de Milo, too, initially elicited only a tepid local response. Even today, the ways in which global elites and local residents judge the value of cultural heritage often differ considerably.[7] The history of preservation is also the history of an attribution of meaning performed by outsiders. And even when the significance of a monument is undisputed on the local level, the local is not the framework within which this significance is attributed to it. Instead, local processes of recognizing and ascribing value to a monument generally take place in relation to global, national and regional frameworks. On the one hand, recent experience in the field of World Heritage in particular has produced striking evidence that local acceptance is indispensable to sustainable monument preservation. Yet on the other, in the logic of international heritage policies, value is defined precisely with regard to a monument's general significance: 'universal' heritage enjoys the highest status. By comparison, 'merely' national or regional significance would seem to carry a penalty; the local stands at the very bottom of this hierarchy.

This may be one reason why differences in local ascriptions of value have rarely been the focus of significant research. To be sure, differences between urban and rural populations, between higher and lower levels of education, between laypeople and heritage professionals – all have meanwhile become topics of scholarly interest. The extent to which cities belonging to a similar cultural sphere nevertheless reach decidedly different conclusions regarding the value of their heritage is a question that has not, however, been closely examined. Do these processes reflect city-specific features regarding, for instance, the selection and treatment of architectural monuments? Are there differences among the meanings attributed to comparable monuments in different cities? An initial study undertaken by the urban studies group at the Technical University in Darmstadt seems to confirm our sense that the issue presents a fertile field of research awaiting exploration: a comparative look at the ways in which reference groups of monuments – in this case medieval buildings – are treated in the three Hessian cities of Mainz, Frankfurt and Darmstadt, and an analysis of the significance they hold for each city's self-

---

6   Ashworth/Graham/Tunbridge, Pluralising Pasts, 2007.
7   Vinken, Pranger von Bahia, 2015.

image, turns up revealing differences, including initial evidence for widely diverging local constructions of identity.[8]

Local history and *Eigenlogik*

In Frankfurt, the Middle Ages are a firmly established parameter in the self-image of a trading city steeped in tradition. The *Dom* (the city's main church) and the *Römer* (the medieval town hall), both of which were rebuilt after World War II, seem to occupy such an unquestionably central position in Frankfurt's urban self-image that preservationists feel no need to pay them particular attention. Instead, they focus their energies primarily on the 'unloved' monuments: post-war and industrial buildings such as the central market hall, now slated for conversion. In the perspective of city marketers, the *Römerberg* or main square in Frankfurt's old town, like the skyline dominated by the towers of German and international banks represents one of the main go-to vehicles of the city's brand, which can be adapted to appeal to individual target audiences. An island of tradition focused on the *Römer* and set before a backdrop of skyscrapers – this is the contrast in which the city probably recognizes itself most fully. A shriveled medieval remnant, an appendix, one might think; and yet a decisive point of reference and a conceptual lynchpin at the centre of vigorous debates over building policies, such as those currently revolving around plans for new construction and planned reconstruction at the site of the *Technisches Rathaus*, a large post-war administrative complex slated for demolition.[9]

The situation in Wiesbaden is different. A spa town that is not particularly rich in relics of medieval culture, the city, to quote its leading architectural preservationist, Martin Horsten, "shows astonishingly little passion" for the monuments of its early history. Experts cherish the Romanesque Sonnenberg castle, an impressive complex whose history reaches back into the 12th century, as well as the medieval town fortifications, as incomparable monuments of the era's military architecture. In the 19th century, during the rise of *Rheinromantik*, the castle was developed as a tourist destination for paying visitors and was staged as the terminus of a picturesque promenade through the spa gardens; it quickly became a popular postcard motif. Even today, however, it is proving difficult to elicit public interest in this neglected object; questions regarding the uses of the city's extensive parks, by contrast, routinely draw a great deal of public attention.

The situation in Darmstadt is more difficult to describe. The former artists' colony *Mathildenhöhe*, a famous Art-Nouveau ensemble, is unrivalled as the city's premier piece of architectural heritage and is currently being considered for nomination to the World Heritage list; the great public interest in plans to erect new buildings in the area demonstrates that it is not only outsiders who recognize the ensemble's significance. In the highly heterogeneous cityscape, where post-war rebuilding has had a profound impact, architectures of different eras appear in impassive contiguity. In the early 20th century,

---

8   Vinken, Lokale Sinnstiftung, 2011.
9   The *Dom-Römer Areal* planned at that time has now been realized (cf. the essay on Frankfurt in this volume (Chapter 12).

the city added an additional story to the *Weißer Turm*, a remnant of the town's old fortifications now located next to a major department store, with the explicit aim of improving the structure's visibility and prominence amid a city that had grown larger and taller around it. Additional vestiges of fortifications stand, slightly perplexed, outside the *Darmstadtium* convention centre, as well as in a nearby green space (these remains can be a little difficult to find). According to Nikolaus Heiss, the city's appointed preservationist, Darmstadt values all eras of its past. The goal is to exhibit the city's history in its variety, operating on the broadest basis possible. As to the Middle Ages, they occupy their allotted place without much ado, as well-restored and clearly labelled architecture.

This initial and cursory diagnosis is neither coincidental nor arbitrary. There are tangible reasons why the Middle Ages are of different relative significance to the three cities I have discussed. Frankfurt, the modern banking metropolis, is identified as a medieval establishment by its very name: legend has it that the town arose near a ford (*Furt*) held by the Franks and once used by Charlemagne to escape his Saxon pursuers. The *Römer* represents two central features of the city's self-image: the German kings were crowned here, and, perhaps even more salient, the building housed the most important market of this free imperial city and mercantile centre – a tradition that Frankfurt likes to regard as living on, uninterrupted, into the present. By reconstructing and simulating 'medieval' showpieces, Frankfurt keeps its mythical roots in sight. A city that has dedicated itself to global trade finds stability in an assertion of its origins set in stone: we are reminded that monument preservation is always also a medium of self-assurance.

By contrast, Wiesbaden, the erstwhile ducal residence and present-day state capital, sees itself primarily as a spa town. Although it was already known for its baths in antiquity and during the later reign of Charlemagne, the city did not rise to supraregional significance until the 19th century, when it became known as the "Nice of the North"; its baths, casinos and expansive parks attracted the courts of the German emperors, and in their train, it became a meeting point for the wealthy and fashionable from all over the world. To this day, the facilities that define Wiesbaden – sometimes called "Pensionopolis" (Retiree-opolis) – as a spa town and ducal residence, namely its gardens, representative bathhouses and villas, dominate the city's self-image. The Middle Ages simply do not fit into this picture: they bring connotations of the dark, the primitive and the provincial to mind that are incompatible with the desired image of a fashionable, elegant and modern resort town. If the Middle Ages have a place here, it is in the form of a *point de vue*, a picturesque ruin set in a park that frames and tames its otherness as a showpiece. That was indeed what happened in the 19th century, although as more recent history shows, this adaptation was not enough to build an emotional attachment to Wiesbaden's medieval monument among the city's residents.

Darmstadt presents a less clear-cut diagnosis. The town was granted its charter as a city in the 14th century. Its history is inextricably tied to that of the palace, which was expanded in a representative fashion in the Renaissance and Baroque periods. The old town, whose history reached back into the Middle Ages, burned down almost entirely in 1944 and was rebuilt after the war on a new street plan; outside the city centre, by contrast, many historic buildings were reconstructed. The result is a paradoxical picture that is difficult to read at first glance: a modern city is surrounded by architectural monuments from various eras. A former ducal seat whose economy is dominated by service industries and public administration, the city has always been oriented towards the palace and never developed a strong civic image of its own. When the university moved into the palace, Darmstadt became an academic centre. Yet, other competing images continue to exist, including Darmstadt as "City of the Arts", as "City Amid Forests" and, the favourite of preservationists, as "Art-Nouveau City". Who can dispute that the *Mathildenhöhe* is more important to Darmstadt's image than are its medieval town walls? Still, these stand as a generally accepted part of the city's architectural heritage, living in placid coexistence with their more renowned neighbour; the different parts of this city's history do not interfere with each other. These findings merit further study, which may contribute to a more defined hypothesis about the way in which *Eigenlogik* operates.

With all this in mind, a fertile field in which to begin the scholarly examination of urban *Eigenlogik* would be a comparative exploration of the ways locals engage with cultural heritage, a look at the local specificity of how heritage is 'made and managed'. A second and, to my mind, even more interesting line of inquiry would address the special character of built heritage as a phenomenon of permanence having a physical basis, and thus as a medium of collective memory.[10] In her work on *The Sociology of Space*, Martina Löw has shown how any production of space must be described as taking place in an interplay between given physical circumstances and social practices.[11] How exactly can we conceptualize this interplay in relation to urban *Eigenlogik*? Helmuth Berking speaks of an "elective affinity among spatial organization, the physical environment, and cultural dispositions".[12] He continues: "Urbanity is associated with patterns of perception and emotion, of action and interpretation that, taken together, constitute what we can call the urban *doxa*".[13] How does this "association", this elective affinity between a built environment and cultural dispositions, come into being, how does it take definite form, stabilize and reproduce? With a view to built heritage as a privileged subset of the physical world, can we say that it operates in this interplay as a stabilizer of such interrelations – that it operates, to use Ulf Matthiesen's term, as an amplifier of *Eigenlogik*?[14]

Memory

We are used to thinking of the distinctiveness of a city in terms of the particularity and permanence of its urban spaces and architectures. A city's built heritage, in particular, is seen as making a significant contribution to the formation of its urban identity. Theoretically ambitious conceptualizations of the interplay between the specific and historically-developed urban environments and social valuation processes first emerged in

---

10   Halbwachs, Das kollektive Gedächtnis, 1950.
11   Löw, The Sociology of Space, 2016 (2001).
12   Helmuth Berking and Martina Löw in their introduction to: Die Eigenlogik der Städte, 2008, 8.
13   Berking, Skizzen zur Erforschung der Stadt und der Städte, 2008, 23. Italics in the original.
14   Lecture held by Ulf Matthiesen at the colloquium "Space, Place, Power" in Darmstadt in January 2011.

the 1960s. The timing was not coincidental: resistance to the dictates of modernist instrumental functionalism arose in the name not only of the city's image and its individuality,[15] but also of the regional and the local. Against the doctrine of the International Style and its claim to universal validity, critics took recourse to the specific site and its history. The famous book *Architecture of the City* published by the architect and theorist Aldo Rossi in 1966 strikes me as containing several particularly interesting points that might be taken up by the hypothesis of *Eigenlogik*.[16] The city, Rossi writes, has a biography that is manifest in its buildings and spatial structures. This biography is a matter not so much of sedimented history but rather of collective memory, an unconscious that participates actively in present-day processes of urban design and interpretation. This point is of decisive importance for a city's future viability, Rossi argues in a radical turn away from technocratic planning traditions, since the productive creation of new architecture is impossible without recourse to this 'memory'. Rossi indeed reads the city's architecture as a 'mode of reproduction', or as "conditioned and conditioning", to use his own words.[17]

This mode of reproduction, Rossi goes on to argue, is anchored in permanent structures such as the urban layout and local architectural typologies of a city, but most importantly in its so-called "primary elements": its key buildings, which are the privileged sites where meaning aggregates. And it is these key buildings, which are profoundly imprinted on the collective memory, that can be described as built heritage in the full sense of the term.[18] The meaning and great significance these monuments have for the city, Rossi argues – and this argument is particularly interesting in our context – are tied to their permanence, to their survival as vehicles of meaning that is not bound to functions more strictly conceived. To the contrary, Rossi writes, these buildings retain their ability to define the image and identity of a city even as their functions change and even after they have lost all 'useful' function.[19]

Rossi's *Architecture of the City* seeks to conceptualize the elective affinity between the attribution of meaning and the physical circumstances as the result of an interplay between permanent meaningful structures and buildings on the one hand, social practices of value ascription on the other; it is in this sense that architecture is 'conditioned and conditioning'. Urban spaces are, according to this view, not merely the products of design and planning processes, of changing social actions and attributions. Rather, they themselves 'inform' the social actions performed on them and with them. The material givens of a city do not merely reflect general and local power relations and interests, they actually shape and stabilize social actions and lend them their specific local character. To my mind, Rossi's theses read like a theory of *Eigenlogik* avant la lettre: each city is individual and each is particular because it reproduces its features in a constant interplay of proposed meanings and attributions, a dynamic process in which the permanent architectural elements act as stabilizing factors. In the following sections, I will

---

15 Lynch, The Image of the City, 1960.
16 Rossi, The Architecture of the City, 1984 (1966).
17 Rossi, The Architecture of the City, 1984 (1966), 32.
18 Rossi, The Architecture of the City, 1984 (1966), 22.
19 Rossi, The Architecture of the City, 1984 (1966), 88–94.

examine the question of how these architectural elements, and built heritage in particular, act as amplifiers of *Eigenlogik*. Since I am exploring largely uncharted territory, I can only offer a sketch of some major aspects of the issue.

Permanence

Built heritage is involved in processes of collective meaning (re)production in a very special way. Its privileged role in the stabilization of urban distinctiveness is a virtue of its social construction as a permanent and stable marker of identity. The monument is permanent – not so much in its physical existence (which of course is limited) but rather in its construction as heritage – at least for as long as it is recognized as such.[20] All production of meaning that envisions heritage produces permanence. Practices in the field of heritage preservation aim at perpetuation and reproduction, at making their object everlasting and present – not unlike the liturgy: eternity achieved by means of ceaseless reenactments. On a side note, this construction of permanence explains all measures directed at heritage preservation, down to the creation of replicas and reconstructions.[21]

My first hypothesis, then, is that heritage is predestined to serve the formation and amplification of city-specific modes of reproduction because the attribution of permanence is intrinsic to it. Heritage preservation, as a 'liturgy of commemoration', is by design a mode of reproduction. Dominant among the practices and routines that are directed at, and constitute, the monument are those that are framed as reproduction or re-enactment. The authority of heritage is rooted in an assertion of its permanence, and this permanence is delegated to its materiality. But it is again important to note that this property of permanence is not to be confused with the actual material presence of the heritage object, which may be attenuated to the point of complete disappearance; rather, it is an integral structural component of the concept of the monument. The power of the monument lies in this very ability to attract new ascriptions of meaning and to legitimize them by virtue of its apparent permanence. These processes of meaning attribution are not unrestrained, however, but are structurally stable and directional to a large degree. This is because every ascription of meaning to a built object, if it is to be successful, must adhere to the perpetuating formula of the liturgical: that is, it must be a "reproduction".

That is my second hypothesis on heritage as an amplifier of *Eigenlogik*: to be successful, an attribution of meaning to a monument must be a reproduction or re-enactment, one which in extreme cases can also accommodate breaks and contradictions. The monument's material construction is necessary to its complex figure of permanence. On the one hand, the physical reality of the monument produces and enables the notion of simple duration in time, and hence its credibility or authority as heritage. On the other

---

20 Pred, Place as Historically Contingent Process, 1984.
21 Nerdinger, Geschichte der Rekonstruktion, 2010.

hand, the physical substance of the monument literally serves as the material on which successive attributions of meaning can be inscribed.[22]

Alienness

The monument is the product of an attribution of stability: it is a permanent sign and a sign of permanence. The attribution of collective meaning to such objects and the aggregation of (originally religious) practices around them that promised physical permanence were among the earliest cultural activities of human society, as was the production of them. Particularly illustrative examples include prehistoric megaliths and sites such as Stonehenge. Yet the decisive point about these objects is not their permanence as such, but rather their ability to store meaning. By 'store' I do not mean that they serve as passive reservoirs, but that they can act as vehicles of meaning, vehicles driving an ongoing process in which meaning is rendered relevant to the present in a relational fashion. The authority of the 'always already' is coupled to current relevance by the monument's physical reality. The latter lends the monument its presence: it is visibly and palpably part of the spaces in which we live. But at the same time and just as evidently, as the very definition of the monument implies, its origins do not lie in our own time. In its physical reality it precedes us, it is "old". Alois Riegl, the great theorist of the monument of the turn of the 20th century, wrote a treatise on the "modern cult of monuments" in which he ascribed central significance to what he called "age value" (*Alterswert*).[23] The most salient quality the monument possessed, he believed, was not its historic value, not its ability to attest to a past era, but rather its quality of being visibly and palpably old. It is this quality that enables us to experience the fundamental truth that becoming and passing never cease; it is this quality that allows us to participate on an emotional level in something that exceeds our own limitations, that reaches far into the past and the future.[24]

The monument's age, authenticated by its physical reality, engenders a highly powerful double experience: that of familiarity – the object has always been there – as well as that of alienness – the object is not of our time, and thus not (entirely) ours. It projects from a different time, from another world into ours. Our interpretations and attributions of meaning do not entirely exhaust it; hence, the monument is alien in the sense that it is not (entirely) comprehensible. Built heritage cannot be understood in a concrete way because many aspects of it may be incomplete, fragmentary or just 'missing': aspects such as the circumstances of its production, the stages of its transmission, or its original use or meaning. At the same time it is inaccessible in a very fundamental way simply because it is old, and thus produces a figure of difference relative to current and past interpretations and attributions.

---

22 Wohlleben, Theoretische Grundlagen, 1999. The intangible heritage would require a separate study at this point with regard to its *Eigenlogik* effects.
23 Riegl, Der moderne Denkmalkultus, 1903.
24 Riegl, Der moderne Denkmalkultus, 1903, 150.

Now the figure of difference so produced, which eludes complete comprehension or resolution into a precisely defined meaning, by no means makes the monument any weaker. On the contrary, its aura and authority are directly linked to this (attribution of) alienness, alterity or excess. In his book on *Bau und Überbau* (Structure and Superstructure), the art historian Martin Warnke has described the Gothic cathedral as a figure of excess or '*Überschuss*'.[25] The question he was trying to answer was this: What motivated people in the Middle Ages to erect these gigantic buildings, which by virtue of their sheer size and the effort and expense required to build them are conceivable only as the joint accomplishments of many different social groups? How was it possible to keep these social groups with their divergent interests committed to a shared goal for many decades? Warnke's novel idea is that the cathedral is a "figure of excess" that eludes any attempt to offer a final or complete interpretation or to subordinate it in its entirety to any specific intention or plan. It is precisely because the cathedral literally "surmounts" everything that it can become, beyond all divergent interests, becoming a screen on which community can be projected, that it can serve as a vehicle of collective meaning.

The monument is more than the "witness who can be interrogated again and again" which heritage preservation institutions like to invoke. It is more than a product of competing 'makings' and processes of negotiation. Its meaning resides in the very fact that it is inexhaustible: a figure of excess whose authority and ability to sustain the emergence of consensus are ultimately rooted in a double experience – that of its evident permanence and its evident alienness.

Mode of reproduction

Built heritage is constructed as a figure of excess that proves resistant to complete interpretive comprehension and time and again requires reinterpretation. With regard to the interrelation between built heritage and *Eigenlogik*, another point is crucial. The attribution of meaning to a monument is indeed fundamentally open in the sense that it is always incomplete; but it is by no means open in the sense of being unrestricted or free of presuppositions. Readings or attributions of meaning in the context of built heritage are oriented towards an origin – not unlike the exegeses of a sacred book, the meaning of which is obscure and yet presumed across all interpretive approaches to be present and powerfully operative. The relevance of the monument is rooted not in its current topicality but in its authenticity. The logic of the attribution of meanings is the current exegesis of something that is said again and again; it is the act of rendering present an older, original and hence true meaning.

This ability to render the past present also proves to be a structural bridge across profound ruptures. When the power of interpretation shifts radically, for example, in the transition from a colonial to a postcolonial society, heritage is transformed. Exactly what is important is now different. The Jesuit church may be joined by the pillory. Yet even these new interpretations, as scholars in the field of postcolonial studies have emphasized again and again, are not trapped between the alternatives of affirmation or

---

25 Warnke, Bau und Überbau, 1984.

rejection, but instead create palimpsestic appropriations, fusions whose heterogeneity allows them to melt down older and contradictory layers of meaning as well, suspending the various origins.[26] The monument is accordingly not (or certainly not first and foremost) a mirror of conflicting powers of interpretation or successive processes of negotiation. Operative in it are echoes of older attributions: repressed and almost illegible information regarding its meaning, which is now present only in the form of displacements, disfigurations and palimpsestic inscriptions – and which, not unlike the unconscious, nonetheless has an effect, helping to shape present-day attributions of meaning. [27] A structural form of self-reference is characteristic of the monument, a mode of reproduction that persists through all 'makings'.

---

26 Lagae, From Patrimoine partagé, 2008.
27 For Derrida heritage is a ghostly phenomenon, "haunting" us with older, latent or unconscious layers of meaning; cf. Derrida, Specters of Marx, 1994 (1993).

4 The Spaces of the Monument
Exposing – Framing – Zoning

> We are able to perceive objects only as parts of a spatial arrangement. Being social is therefore explained in a fundamental way by the spatial orderings in which we are embedded.
>
> (Martina Löw)[1]

The construction and production of the spaces of monuments has received little attention and has never been systematically researched. Despite the spatial turn, heritage conservation has a certain ongoing spatial blindness that is built into its origins. It is "a true daughter of historicism"[2] and was given its form as a discipline in the late 19th century. The highest task of the historic monument was originally to commemorate and immortalize the great moments of history. Worth protecting as a "piece of national existence",[3] the historic building presents itself as a historical document of a previous age that is worth preserving, and, on account of its age, as a fragile, endangered "remnant". From the temporal perspective of "survival", the task of heritage conservation is one of constant care and maintenance, of "preservation" – a procedure that should ideally be neutral. As Georg Dehio, one of the early theorists of heritage conservation from the turn of the 19th century – a moment so productive of new disciplinary programmes – put it: "conserve, do not restore".[4] More recent additions to the stipulations of the heritage-conservation catechism, such as preservation of substance and reversibility also argue for minimizing the impact of conservation measures.[5] And conversely, every intervention is considered a falsification. Every embellishment and "renovation", copy and reconstruction goes against a practice that exists as an unbroken chain going back to

---

1   Löw, Space Oddity, 2015, 7.
2   Dehio, Denkmalschutz und Denkmalpflege, 1988 (1905), 97.
3   Dehio, Denkmalschutz und Denkmalpflege, 1988 (1905), 92. For a critical perspective cf. Riegl, Neue Strömungen, 1995 (1905), 220–223.
4   Dehio, Denkmalschutz und Denkmalpflege, 1988 (1905), 102. Cf. Scheurmann, Vom Konservieren und Restaurieren, 2005.
5   For a critical view: Petzet, Reversibility, 1992.

the 19th century and is considered an exception that can only be justified by exceptional circumstance such as destruction in war.⁶ The history of heritage conservation is correspondingly presented as a story of progress, in the course of which the norms for the sensitive and appropriate treatment of monuments have become ever more stringent, leading to the ultimate triumph of the obligation towards neutrality – that is until the outbreak of postmodernism, which caused much valuable ground to be lost to visual and pictorial effects, reconstruction, and simulation.⁷

The uncompromising notion that every conceivable interference with a monument is equivalent to an act of destruction has also been repeatedly expressed since the earliest theories of the monument. Its target is the *vandalisme restaurateur*: those embellishments, purifications and reconstructions undertaken in the name of historical accuracy.⁸ The call to let monuments "die in peace" is a consequence of the view that every intervention necessarily means appropriation and alienation: "We have no right whatever to touch them",⁹ was how the English writer, art historian and social philosopher John Ruskin justified this ideal, which later became known as the principle of *"non toccare"*.¹⁰ It should be noted, however, that the supposed neutrality of this principle is only prima facie. Even those ruins entering the twilight of their years in "untouched" beauty only become monuments through systematic measures, such as the allocation of a special status (as monuments that are legally withdrawn from all forms of use). And, above all: it is tied to the ascription of a peculiar spatial status that differs from the functional spaces of modernity. It is precisely in consideration of the substance of the radically neutral ideal of *"non toccare"* that it becomes clear that every historic building is the outcome of planning decisions and spatial operations, which are therefore to be considered as literally constitutive of monuments. An analysis of these procedures not only shows significant differences regarding spatial practices of monumentalization, it also generates new criteria for categorizing and evaluating practices of heritage conservation and urbanism and is, moreover, certainly relevant to the theory of space.

The precondition for the shift in perspective described here was established by the art historian Alois Riegl, who applied his reception-theory approach to the theory of heritage conservation.¹¹ In the context of his effort to fundamentally reconceptualize the "modern cult of monuments" Riegl considered that the central category of the mon-

---

6   On the debates on reconstruction in Germany: Sauerländer, Erweiterung des Denkmalbegriffs, 1975 and Lipp/Petzet, Vom modernen zum postmodernen Denkmalkultus, 1994.
7   On the state of this debate cf. Meier/Will, Paradigmenwechsel, 2005.
8   Eugène-Emmanuel Viollet-le-Duc, the leading theorist of the 19th century, also a strong critic of the *vandalisme restaurateur*, was, however, in favour of critical completion: "To restore a building is not to preserve it, to repair, or rebuild it; it is to reinstate it in a condition of completeness which could never have existed at any given time." Viollet-le-Duc, On Restoration, 1875, 9 (originally Dictionnaire raisonné, 1875, VIII:14–34, 14).
9   Ruskin, The Seven Lamps, 1849, 187.
10 Used in this sense by Cesare Brandi, cf. Brandi, Teoria del Restauro, 1963.
11 Kemp, Kunstwerk und Betrachter, 1988, 241–242.

ument in the 19th century, that of "historical value", had given way to "age-value".[12] Typical of the new age, he wrote, was "the effort to grasp all physical and psychological experiences not in their objective essence, but in their subjective appearance, i.e. in the effects that they have on the subject".[13]

For Riegl, the replacement of historical value by age-value corresponds to a shift in the effect of the monument (*Denkmalwirkung*) from an experience of culture (*Bildungserlebnis*) to one of feeling (*Gefühlserlebnis*), as well as to a related "mass efficacy" (*Massenwirksamkeit*; which Riegl also described as a "socialist tendency"). In contrast to the exclusive historical value that rests on conventions and knowledge, age-value as "visible antiquity" is accessible to all. In this way, it conveys a quasi-religious "irresistible feeling of participation in the eternal cycle of becoming and passing away" that promises sentimental modern humans "complete redemption".[14] Age-value is thus also a temporal category,[15] one, however, that is not grounded in the substance of the monument but its effect. By means of this turn towards effect, the spatial preconditions of the monument – largely ignored by the theory of the monument – come into view: the perspective and the standpoint of the observer, just as the location of the monument in space, and finally the production of space itself. All measures that constitute and preserve monuments create spaces.[16] Today, it is above all the field of Memory Studies that has started to follow this path again.

For the historian Pierre Nora, the past is given to us as something radically "other" ("radicalement autre"), an "hallucination artificielle", as a world from which we are forever separated and which may only be experienced under conditions of a "régime de discontinuité". The "truth of memory" lies in the fact that this discontinuity may be removed at one stroke ("qui d'un coup la supprime"). Sites of memory are, from this perspective, places where a subtle interplay of insurmountable distance from and unguarded nearness to the past is staged.[17] This ambiguity of the monument, which is the focus of a paradoxical interplay of distancing and appropriation, has shaped the various forms of spatial production that have accompanied the monument since its institutionalization. They can be described as a sequence of processes of inclusion and exclusion, which can switch from exposing and framing to isolation and exclusion. The

---

12   Riegl, Der moderne Denkmalkultus, 1995 (1903). A translation of this text does exist (Riegl, The modern Cult of Monuments, 1982). However, to remain as true as possible to the wording of the passages cited here, we have opted to translate them ourselves.
13   Riegl, Der moderne Denkmalkultus, 1995 (1903), 156–157.
14   Riegl, Der moderne Denkmalkultus, 1995 (1903), 150.
15   With regard to Riegl, Wolfgang Kemp spoke of a "dehistoricization through temporalization", Kemp, Gesammelte Aufsätze, 1995, 220.
16   There are several relevant passages in Riegl's book on the modern cult of the monument, including, in the chapter on the relationship of present-day values to the cult of the monument: "For age-value, even more energetically than historical value, must oppose the ripping-out of a monument from its previous, quasi-organic contexts and its confinement in museums [...]." Riegl, Der moderne Denkmalkultus, 1995 (1903), 177.
17   Nora, Between memory and history, 1996, 12. Our translation remains as close as possible to the wording of the original; cf. Nora, Les Lieux de Mémoires, 1997 (1984–1992), xxxi–xxxii.

background to this shift is an intensifying fundamental conflict at the heart of modernity: the tension between heritage and contemporaneity, between origin and progress, a conflict that – originally grasped dialectically – ultimately finds its culmination in the functional spaces of the modern city.

Exposing/Monumentalization

In her book *The Sociology of Space*, the sociologist Martina Löw illustrated her theses on the social production of space with reference to Jerusalem's Wailing Wall.[18] The composer and pianist Josef Tal describes two very different impressions of space that he received on successive visits to the wall. The first time he approached it through "a dense network of narrow, winding alleyways," of the Arab Old City and ended "all of a sudden [...] in front of a sheer wall of huge stone blocks. High above there was a slender strip of blue sky between the confined walls of the alleyway" (fig. 1). On his second visit, after the Six Day War, "the tangle of alleyways in front of the Wailing Wall was cleared. Today, the approach to the wall is via a large, expansive tract that provides space for thousands of visitors" (fig. 2).

Figure 1: Jerusalem, Wailing Wall, around 1910

Tal observed that, although these were "the same stone blocks" that he was visiting, their "language" had been changed by the new surroundings. While the closeness of the space had originally made the wall of the destroyed temple appear more powerful, awakening the impression that the divine presence was hovering "inaccessibly above the immeasurable stone", the constellation had changed as a result of the creation of the wide-open plaza in front of the wall, giving prayer there "a different sense": "The broad space [...] sends their wailing echo in the breadth instead of in the height."[19]

---

18   Löw, The Sociology of Space, 2016 (2001), 129–130, 136–139, 144–145.
19   All quotes from Löw, The Sociology of Space, 2016 (2001), 129–130.

Figure 2: Jerusalem, Wailing Wall today (Photo: EvgeniT 2013)

Löw uses this example to illustrate the physical aspect of the constitution of space before subsequently examining how institutionalized arrangements, such as power relationships, are reproduced in space.[20] With regard to the example of the Wailing Wall, this concerns the transformation of a religious space into a "security-oriented" space shaped by the "secular demonstration of power".[21] The interventions at Jerusalem's Wailing Wall that Josef Tal describes were politically motivated. Following the capture of East Jerusalem by the Israeli army, Israel planned to develop the city as the symbolic capital of the Israeli state – a development in which the framing of the Wailing Wall as a national monument and the principal locus of political and religious identity played a key role.[22] But there is indeed a long tradition of such spatial practices in the service of heritage politics. In the 19th century, it was established practice to expose monuments by means of demolition – a technique known as *dégagement* or *isolement* – so as to give them a new *mise en scène* in the form of an open square in front of them or around them. Conventionally considered as a means of establishing symbols of the grandeur of power, this was monumentalization in the most literal sense, namely the establishment of a spatial disposition for the newly established category of the historic monument. Exposing is, as the example of the mediaeval cathedrals shows, the definitive procedure for the constitution of monuments.

Today, nearly every cathedral presents itself as an isolated or disengaged monumental building whose western façade, topped with towers, is visible across a large and usually symmetrical square or plaza (fig. 3). This image, which we take for granted today and which is closely associated with the building type of the cathedral, is in fact the result of modern urban-planning measures, an early example of which was documented by the architect Le Corbusier for Notre-Dame de Paris (fig. 4).[23]

---

20   Löw, The Sociology of Space, 2016 (2001), 144.
21   Löw, The Sociology of Space, 2016 (2001), 145.
22   Ricca, Shifting Symbolism, 2005.
23   Le Corbusier, The City of To-Morrow, 1987 (1925), 269.

 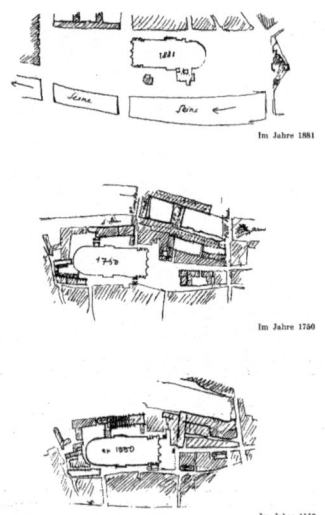

Figure 3: Paris, Notre-Dame (Photo: J. Blum 2006)
Figure 4: Paris, Exposing Notre-Dame, Le Corbusier 1919

Prior to this, Notre-Dame had, like nearly all sacred buildings in similar urban settings, been situated in a densely built neighbourhood. In mediaeval city centres, large open spaces were usually only reserved for the market. Nor were the lines of sight of main thoroughfares oriented towards religious buildings – whether their towers or main façades. Furthermore, the unimpeded view of these grand structures was also obscured by smaller buildings, such as market stalls or masons' lodges, as well as residential houses, which were often built right up against the walls of the great churches. In the Baroque period, as can be seen in Le Corbusier's drawings, the first efforts were made to create a grander setting for the churches by establishing small squares in front of them. Yet the major work of clearing the cathedral squares generally only took place after they had been classified as *monuments historiques*. The aim of the measures that first made it possible to experience the west façades as the "principal view" and an iconic image was not only to expose this façade to panoramic view, thereby transforming it, but also to enhance the effect of the churches on urban space at a distance. In Paris, this was achieved by creating connections with the Seine quays, undertaken as part of a large-scale urban rehabilitation of the *Île de la Cité*. This creation of a new *mise en scène* for historic buildings can be linked to the great modernization projects of European cities, which were largely defined in terms of axial streets and grand squares. In Paris, for instance, the key modernization initiatives of the 19th century went hand in hand with the creation of "broad, purposeful thoroughfares connecting monuments, radiating from *places*, endowed with uniform architecture, and their perspectives closed at each end by some public structure."[24] Laid bare within the body of the city, those mon-

---

24   Jordan, Transforming Paris, 1995, 195. Italics in the original.

uments, churches or public buildings serve as *points-de-vue* for the new boulevards hat Baron Haussmann had blasted through the densely built quartiers of central Paris.

The presentation of 'important' religious buildings as panoramically visible monuments in open squares soon established itself as a convention in European urban planning. The contrast of these monuments' effect on space and on the observer before and after they were laid bare may still be experienced today by comparing Notre-Dame de Paris and Strasbourg Minster. In the case of the latter, no drastic measures were undertaken. The exquisite west façade of Strasbourg's cathedral with its exuberant stone ornamentation looms up suddenly out of narrow lanes, marking a sudden break in the cityscape; in concrete terms, a sudden shift of scale, materiality and status. It is an experience of contrast comparable to Tal's observation of the Wailing Wall as cited above. The "confined walls of the alleyway", to use Tal's own words again, cause the stones to "appear more powerful", significantly enhancing the sense that the ornate Gothic façades are reaching towards the heavens. A comparison of the two cathedrals also reveals the main effect of exposure: the enhancement of grandeur (distancing, overview, order, clarity) and monumentality. Instead of sequences, intersections, intermixing and overlapping, the Paris constellation invokes completeness and wholeness and produces an emphatic sense of standing-for-itself.

Yet in Tal's statements about the Wailing Wall, a note of ambiguity can also clearly be heard, one that is inherent to the exposing of monuments. On the one hand, this practice aims at the power of the image and monumentalization in the literal sense. On the other hand, it comes at the price of a weakening that can be grasped as a kind of secularization. While it appeared to Tal, in his account of his first visit, that the Almighty hovered "inaccessibly above the immeasurable stone", now the open space before the exposed wall "sends their wailing echo in the breadth instead of in the height"[25] and hence, in plain terms, no longer to God. Tal adds to his description of this transformation that he "will be aware of comparing the Wailing Wall with a museum object".[26] Although the comparison made here between monument and museum was immediately withdrawn, it is highly suggestive. When religious objects are placed in a museum, they are reassessed and revalued as cultural objects, and they enter the canon of bourgeois culture. This goes hand in hand with a weakening of their original significance. In concrete terms, it is a secularization. An anecdote from Cologne sheds some light on the tension that Tal notes between the temple of the muses and religious practice. According to the story, once a week a peasant woman from the Eifel region used to appear in Cologne's Wallraf Richartz Museum of art, where she would pray at a particular altarpiece, until the museum finally stopped her: the museum was a place of exhibition, not of prayer.[27]

In terms of the disposition of space, the comparison made by Tal between the monument and the museum is revealing. By being exposed, the monument, like the museum piece, is prepared, removed from its context so as to be placed on display as an autonomous 'masterpiece' and exemplum.[28] The transformation of buildings into

---

25   Quoted in: Löw, The Sociology of Space, 2016 (2001), 144, 129.
26   Quoted in: Löw, The Sociology of Space, 2016 (2001), 130.
27   Brock, Inszenierung und Vergegenwärtigung, 1997.
28   The consequences of this are discussed in detail in: O'Doherty, Inside the White Cube, 1986.

monuments and their canonization as objects of national secular worship is institutionalized by means of spatial operations that originate in the context of the museum: isolating and framing, and stressing display value over use value. As a central institution of civic learning and culture, the museum can make use of a formally codified framing to undertake this isolation and reinterpretation in the service of aesthetic and moral education. By contrast, the exposure and decontextualization of monuments in the heterogeneous spaces of the city carries the risk of producing an ambiguous figure. In spatial terms, exposure threatens to turn into a lack of mediation, a shift from the *permanent, exemplary, eloquent* monument to the *artificial, isolated, dumb* foreign body. Baron Hausmann's urban planning intervention already evoked this effect in the people of his time. The journalist Louis Veuillot wrote in 1867 about the changes to the French capital: "The new Paris will never have a history and will kill off the scent of the history of the old Paris. [...] Even the old monuments that have been left standing say nothing, because everything around them is changed. Notre Dame and the Tower of St Jacques are no more in their places than the Obelisk [which was first brought from Egypt in 1836 and set up on the Place de la Concorde, author's note], and seem to have been imported from remote places as vain curiosities."[29] The historic monuments that were exposed and positioned as *points-de-vue* for the new axial streets evoked the impression of having been implanted in their modernized environment. This 'foreignness' of the historic buildings led Veuillot to conclude that the new Paris was without history. The severing of the connection between the monument and its traditional environment makes the link to the past appear precarious. The monument requires mediation to be legible. For historic buildings, the question of the appropriate mediation of a monument appears above all as a problem of framing.

Framing/Mediation

The history of the theory and practice of framing and staging historic monuments has still to be written. The thoughts of Karl Friedrich Schinkel shed a great deal of light on notions of the appropriate framing of the historic building in the early years of its institutionalization. Schinkel was not only the leading architect of his generation, but also the first Prussian state conservator and the 'father' of German heritage conservation.[30] His first restoration project in the province of Brandenburg concerned the ruins of Chorin Abbey, north of Berlin. It was to become a highly successful monument, and, as a unique early example of North German brick Gothic has graced the cover of many surveys of monuments in the region.[31]

Schinkel, who 'rediscovered' the ruins of the former Cistercian abbey during his 1816 tours of inspection, found the complex of buildings in a state of deep dereliction and neglect, in parts turned over to agricultural use. He made a dedicated effort to rescue this forgotten monument. This included the completion of numerous drawings in

---

29   Quoted in: Benevolo, History of Modern Architecture, 1971 (1960), 134.
30   Huse, Deutsche Texte, 1984, 62–83.
31   Vinken, Die künstlerische Entdeckung, 2001, 339–341.

Figure 5: Chorin, "Lateral view of the Abbey, as viewed from the field", Karl Friedrich Schinkel 1816/17

1816/17, which were probably intended for publication.[32] It is likely that Schinkel was inspired by the portfolio that Friedrich Gilly had produced of Marienburg castle in East Prussia in the late 18th century, whose restoration was now imminent – not least because of Gilly's powerful drawings, which had also enjoyed considerable commercial success (1799–1803). Schinkel's drawings aim to present the ruins as, above all, something memorable that can be experienced. Traces of contemporary agricultural activity are hidden. Troublesome extensions and refittings are ignored. For the largest work, entitled "Main view seen from field" (*Hauptansicht vom Felde gesehen*), the chosen perspective emphasizes the largely undamaged portions, giving an impression of intactness. Other representations, attractively composed from an artistic perspective, anticipate Schinkel's presentation of Chorin as a monument (fig. 5). The abbey ruins are here exposed on a broad green and framed by groups of trees, a suggestion that was later taken up by the landscape architect Peter Joseph Lenné: whose plan shows the monument embedded in a landscaped park, enabling a constantly shifting variety of surprising views of the spectacular brick building.[33] Schenkel's drawings of Chorin evoke the Romantic motif of ruins in a park, as emblematically established in through Caspar David Friedrich's engagement with the ruins of Eldena Abbey near Greifswald.[34]

The transformation of a derelict and forgotten old building into a 'valuable historical document' goes together with the establishment of certain aesthetic and spatial concepts. In Chorin, the landscaped gardens around the ruins were composed to enable the varying and surprising views of the spectacular brick building, as mentioned above. The ideal presentation of a monument here includes exposing and framing: measures Schinkel believed emphasized the monumental character of the building, allowing its intended pedagogical effect to unfold completely. Framing thus initiates a double movement: isolation and close focus in the service of exact objectifying perception, and

---

32   Berndt, Chorin, 1997.
33   Karg, Die Landschaftsgestaltung, 1987.
34   Vinken, Die künstlerische Entdeckung, 2001, 340–342.

simultaneously, even more so than in the case of the exposed or 'disengaged' cathedrals, the foundation of a new 'pictorial' unity that requires a certain distance to capture.[35]

The embedding and framing of historic monuments in green landscapes subsequently also became a popular procedure for historic buildings located within cities. It was particularly valued wherever urban redevelopment generated a need for the creation of new spatial relationships – as with the Tour Saint-Jacques, as mentioned above. A good example is the treatment of city gates, which lost their function during the modernization and expansion of urban areas. In the debates on their preservation – as I have shown for the case of Basel – the possibility of effectively integrating them in the grand public spaces of the modern city played an important role.[36] When Basel's walls were torn down, the initial plan, in order to create a promenade on the model of Vienna, was to replace St Alban's gate with a square containing fountains and greenery. The decision to preserve St Alban's and two further city gates went hand in hand with some revealing changes. First, the gate was extensively restored, in a way one could classify as iconization. The aesthetically problematic isolation of that gate due to the removal of the wall was to be ameliorated by the construction of a neo-Gothic 'picturesque guardhouse'. At the same time, the plans for the area around the gate were significantly altered and a landscaped park was created around the mediaeval building (fig. 6). The image of the 'ancient, greying' city gate, framed by trees, was soon a beloved postcard motif.

Figure 6: Basel, St Alban's gate with newly laid-out park, around 1875

---

35 Gamper, Die Natur ist republikanisch, 1998, particularly the chapter "Der Rahmenblick", 135–156; cf. also Langen, Anschauungsformen, 1965, particularly the chapter "Einleitung. Das Prinzip der Rahmenschau. Begriffsbestimmung", 5–44.
36 See Vinken, Die neuen Ränder, 2005. Cf. the essay on Basel in this volume (Chapter 6).

Isolation/Exclusion

The embedding of historic buildings in parks is still practised today. Good examples include the ruins of many bombed-out churches that have been repurposed as war memorials and survive in the last meagre green spaces of Germany's modernized cities. In many respects, Hanover's Aegidienkirche is typical. Originally situated in the densely built city centre, after the rubble of war had been cleared, the church's ruins were initially left standing in isolation, surrounded by a carpark. The plans for the rebuilding of Hanover paid no heed to the historic grid of streets or the traditional form of closed-perimeter block construction from the pre-war period. The creation of suburban-style terraced housing along less dense, greener, more 'modern' lines left the ruins of the church, which had once served as the major symbol of identity and the dominant landmark of the district, literally on their own. As in many similar cases, a small park with trees can provide only meagre coverage for this sudden loss of relationships. This case provides a first impression of how the 'Romantic' correlation of the monument with its surroundings has significantly shifted in the modern period. The high period of avant-garde modernism formulated the new ideal of *Être-du-temps* in a break with tradition and the past. In architecture, a rigorous functionalism undermined the meaning of historical forms of building. In this way, the historic building is stripped of its relevance for contemporary creations and reduced to its role as a historical 'document'. This neutralization is also manifest, as we can see, in the spatial dispositions of the monuments: exposing and framing turn into isolation and exclusion.

The principal witness for the conflict between heritage and contemporaneity that is being fought in the modern city is Le Corbusier, one of the protagonists of a functionalist modernity.[37] The Swiss architect, whose 1922 *Ville Contemporaine*, a "contemporary city for two million inhabitants" was the first Fordist urban utopia,[38] was also responsible for the Athens Charter (1933), the founding manifesto of modern urban planning.[39] This was the first time that an attempt had been made to produce binding standards for heritage conservation. During the urgently necessary modernization of cities, according to the Charter's fifth chapter ("The Historic Heritage of Cities") "Architectural assets must be protected" if they "are the expression of a former culture and if they respond to a universal interest".[40] Yet the Charter places tight restrictions on the protection of historic monuments, which should only be preserved "if their preservation does not entail the sacrifice of keeping people in unhealthy condition" and "if it is possible to remedy their detrimental presence by means of radical measures".[41] What this shows is that heritage now needed to fit in with spaces defined in terms of the new standards of rationality, functionality, hygiene. The now precarious position of built heritage is

---

37   On Le Corbusier's urbanist projects and their spatial implications cf. the essay on the Crises of the Modern City in this volume (Chapter 2).
38   See Le Corbusier, Œuvre complète, 1960, 34–39; cf. Le Corbusier, The City of To-morrow, 1987 (1925), particularly 163–177.
39   Le Corbusier, The Athens Charter, 1973 (1933), 41–105.
40   Le Corbusier, The Athens Charter, 1973 (1933), 86.
41   Le Corbusier, The Athens Charter, 1973 (1933), 87.

reflected in its relationship to the functional spaces of the modern city. The Charter's provisions for planning measures as they relate to historic buildings are limited to a few, dry comments. According to the Charter, "The destruction of the slums around historic monuments will provide an opportunity to create verdant areas."[42] The historic buildings embedded in the green corridors of the functional city again evoke the romantic image of the ruins in their park landscape. Yet this is less a mechanism of mediation than a case of isolation and contrast. As for the surrounding architecture, the Charter warns that "using styles of the past [...] for new structures erected in historic areas has harmful consequences" [and] "will [not] be tolerated in any form".[43]

The now spatially irremediable antagonism that arises here between heritage and the contemporary city – which can be viewed in terms of the incommensurable concepts of meaning and function – runs through many of Le Corbusier's urban planning projects, including his plan to rebuild central Paris, which, as *Ville Voisin* (fig. 7), was to be ambiguously given the name of a luxury automobile brand.[44]

Figure 7: The new centre of Paris. "Ville Voisin", Le Corbusier 1925

To apply the principles developed for the "contemporary city", the radical proposal was to demolish the area north of the Rue Rivoli up to the Gare du Nord, and thus to destroy the historic Marais and Les Halles districts, which had remained largely intact through Haussmann's alterations. They were to be replaced by a group of high-rises, which were to rear up out of green spaces transected by multi-lane highways. Le Corbusier countered the inevitable fierce criticism that this proposed 'destruction' of the French capital would have brought with two lines of argument. On the one hand, he placed his car-centred city in the tradition of the great urban regeneration projects undertaken since the Renaissance, and particularly the remodelling under Baron Haussmann.[45] This is the context in which the sketches for the exposing of Notre-Dame were made. Grand contemporary urban planning, as Corbusier understood it, has always

---

42 Le Corbusier, The Athens Charter, 1973 (1933), 88.
43 Le Corbusier, The Athens Charter, 1973 (1933), 88.
44 Le Corbusier, The City of To-morrow, 1987 (1925), 277–289.
45 Le Corbusier, The City of To-morrow, 1987 (1925), 258–273.

been major "surgery" rather than "medicine": "a genuine sense of liberty drives one to cut, to open up".⁴⁶

The second argument looks towards the question of the historical identity of a city and sees this as upheld by the great *chef d'œuvres* of each era: Notre-Dame and the Louvre, Sacré Cœur and the Eiffel Tower. As long as these key monuments are preserved, Paris will still be Paris – and, as the drawing makes clear, the tower blocks of the *Ville Voisin* are themselves self-consciously positioned in the tradition of these monuments of identity formation and city branding.⁴⁷ Polemically, Le Corbusier underlines the relationship between the *Ville Voisin* and Paris's built heritage more strongly: "In this scheme the historical past, our common heritage, is respected. More than that, it is *rescued*."⁴⁸ In the new city, in which no more than five percent of the land area is to be built upon, major sites of interest can be exposed and embedded harmonically in green spaces with trees and hedgerows: "The 'Voisin' scheme would isolate the whole of the ancient city and bring back peace and calm from Saint-Gervais to the Étoile. The districts of the *Marais*, the *Archives*, the *Temple*, etc., would be demolished. But the ancient churches would be preserved. They would stand surrounded by verdure [...]. In this way the past becomes no more dangerous to life, but finds instead its true place within it."⁴⁹ Displayed in the green spaces with no context, however, the old monuments have the appearance of foreign bodies within the rational beauty of the urban machine. In contrast to the open squares or Romantic parks of the 19ᵗʰ century, in the shadow of the tower blocks, the monuments have no possibility of imposing themselves on the surrounding space. The garden, once a mediating frame, here functions as a neutral *cordon sanitaire*, an insulating band from the functional spaces of the contemporary city. The dialectical play of exposing and framing has been transformed into isolation and lack of mediation.

Island/Zone

The procedures of isolation and exclusion that we can observe here are not limited to individual monuments.⁵⁰ The 'island of tradition' (*Traditionsinsel*) has been an established concept in urban planning since the 1930s.⁵¹ The precursor to this was the growth of an interest in vernacular architecture and the 'historic ensemble', which went hand in hand with an expansion of the concept of the historic monument beyond its formerly exclusive focus on grand individual buildings (castles, churches, town halls).⁵² The early German *Heimatschutz* movement made effective use of the new medium of the fine art book to promote the idea of the harmonic constellation of buildings and their setting in

---

46 Author's translation; the original passage is as follows : "Un véritable besoin de libération pousse à couper, à ouvrir [...]." Le Corbusier, Urbanisme, 1925, 254.
47 Le Corbusier, Precisions on the present State, 2015 (1930), 174–177.
48 Le Corbusier, The City of To-morrow, 1987 (1925), 287. Italics in the original.
49 Le Corbusier, The City of To-morrow, 1987 (1925), 287–288. Italics in the original.
50 For details of the consequences: Vinken, Zone Heimat, 2010.
51 On the concept of the *Traditionsinsel* cf. the essay on Cologne in this volume (Chapter 9).
52 For a recent overview: Jakobi, Die Heimatschutzbewegung, 2005.

nature.⁵³ The focus of institutionalized heritage conservation shifted from individual buildings to heritage areas. The 'island of tradition' is a figure of consensus and compromise between a model of heritage conservation that is strongly focused on visual impact and a functionalist urban planning that wishes to reshape the city as part of a radical and traffic-oriented modernization. It took the destruction of wartime aerial bombardment to make such plans for complete urban redesign a real possibility. For all their shock at the huge scale of the devastation, nearly everyone involved in post-war rebuilding also saw the destruction as a major opportunity. In Cologne, for instance, the wartime Mayor, Robert Brandes, had already begun to ponder: "If the destruction of our cities has any purpose, [then it is that of] clarifying the spiritual and intellectual foundations for planning *the city of the future* and showing the way to this great goal [...]. Entirely new cities will come into existence. At root, surviving districts are a burden."⁵⁴ Many conservationists shared the euphoria of a new beginning and welcomed the destruction as an "opportunity that was unlikely to come again" to remove the "dirty slums" and "tastelessness" of the Wilhelmine period.⁵⁵ In view of the widespread destruction, the establishment of "historic centres" (*historischer Kerne*) on a modest scale emerged as the preferred means of reinforcing urban identities that had been weakened.

These old town islands, as has not only become evident in recent years,⁵⁶ do not depend on either authenticity or continuity. The plans made by Hamburg's city planner, Fritz Schumacher, have come down to us, I which he proposed "joining together [surviving buildings] somewhere to create a 'historic centre' however modest."⁵⁷ Hanover's 'old town' was indeed created after the war using this procedure: the few half-timbered houses that had not been destroyed were removed from the city centre, which was rebuilt on 'car-friendly' lines, and assembled near the reconstructed *Marktkirche*, creating an artificial 'island of tradition'.⁵⁸

The plans of the architect and city planner Wilhelm Riphan for the rebuilding of Cologne are instructive regarding the new spatial order.⁵⁹ The "backbone of the plan" is the reorganization of the transport infrastructure, which would have entirely reshaped the structure of the city.⁶⁰ The rebuilt Mediaeval churches were to be isolated and "set as jewels in the [newly established] green corridors of the city centre.⁶¹ On the Rhine front, Riphan also deviated from a modern layout by establishing an 'island of tradition', justifying this in a way that might sound familiar: "The rebuilding of the area around

---

53 For instance, the *Blaue Bücher* series, which sold in large numbers (published by Karl Robert Langewiesche since 1902) or the nine volumes of Schultze-Naumburg, Kulturarbeiten, 1901–1917.
54 Brandes, Wiederaufbau und Gemeindeverwaltung, 1944, 1. Italics in the original.
55 Huppertz, Schönere Zukunft, 1945/1947, 2–3.
56 Cf. the essay on Frankfurt in this volume (Chapter 12), and Vinken, Im Namen der Altstadt, 2016.
57 Fritz Schumacher, Zum Wiederaufbau Hamburgs, 1948, quoted in: Beseler/Gutschow, Kriegsschicksale Deutscher Architektur, 1988, XLVIII.
58 Beseler/Gutschow, Kriegsschicksale Deutscher Architektur, 1988, 250–251.
59 For a detailed discussion: Vinken, Zone Heimat, 2010, 157–178 and the essay on Cologne in this volume (Chapter 9).
60 Huppertz, Schönere Zukunft, 1945/1947, 4.
61 Huppertz, Schönere Zukunft, 1945/1947, 7–8.

Great St. Martin's (rehabilitation of the old town) with the old market will make it possible to preserve what is original and unique about Cologne".[62] The drawing included to illustrate the newly laid out Rhine front reveals clearly the contrast sought between the functionalist post-war modernism and the 'reservation' of tradition that was only tolerated at the edge (see figure 8 in chapter 9 on Cologne in this volume). The fact that this part of the city centre, which had only been restored as a model old town during the Nazi dictatorship, was then in large part rebuilt on 'historical' terms and remains established as Cologne's old town today is one of the great ironies of Cologne's history.[63]

In the 'island of tradition', two central modernist procedures for the constitution of monuments – isolation and exclusion – are transferred from the individual monument to the ensemble. Old town quarters are to be experienced as clearly set apart. To this end, they are subject to ongoing processes of homogenization, via urban beautification and heritage conservation efforts, via the removal of every 'foreign' trace – and now once more via the large-scale construction of historicizing or replica buildings, as in Frankfurt, Hildesheim, Dresden or Potsdam (fig. 8).[64]

Figure 8: *Actually brand new. Potsdam Old Market Square (Photo: M. Moldovan 2019)*

As discrete old town quarters, they may only be experienced within their defined boundaries by means of special treatment, specifically through the definition and enforcement of a stylistic code, design regulations that also apply to new builds, and replicas. Only through procedures of distancing and isolation can old town zones be distinguished from their modern surroundings, which is what grants them their visual power.

---

62   Riphahn, Grundgedanken zur Neugestaltung, 1945, 7–8.
63   Cf. Vinken, Zone Heimat, 2010, 157–178, and the essay on Cologne in this volume (Chapter 9).
64   Cf. Vinken, Im Namen der Altstadt, 2016, and the essay on Frankfurt in this volume (chapter 12).

Zoning the City. Heritage and Modernity

5 Tashkent / Uzbekistan
Conflicting Relations. Mahalla, Soviet Modernism, Global City

> These golden valleys – dear Uzbekistan,
> The courageous spirit of your ancestors is with you!
> *(national anthem of the Republic of Uzbekistan, 1992)*

The complexity of the various formations that make up Tashkent's urban heritage is immediately apparent, and the cityscape of Uzbekistan's capital is dominated by signs of unredeemed promises and structural contradictions. The fragmentary nature of its spaces, which resist being organized into a meaningful whole, has been discussed many times before.[1] Contrasting forms of urbanism and life blend in complex ways. This is more than apparent in the city's spatial structures. The stark contrasts between the modernist Soviet city with its wide and imposing spaces of power and the large-scale architecture constructed since independence are immediately apparent. Yet, in structural terms, both the newly erected shopping and administrative district, built in the late-modern steel and glass of a global city, and the grand neo-Timurdic buildings of postcolonial Uzbekistan stand in the tradition of spaces of control and the representation of state power of the Soviet metropolis.[2] In terms of urban space, it can be shown that the deeper break is with the traditional 'mahallas', which invoke an entirely different conception of the city and the urban, and whose formless sprawl penetrates and undermines the zoned 'trajectory space' of the districts of central authority.[3]

Tashkent is like a magnifying glass articulating all the complex contradictions and negotiations around the 'correct' way to modernize and to join the globalized world – including the ubiquitous question of what role (which and whose) traditions can and

---

1 Hartung, Hauptstadtinszenierung, 2012, 79–81.
2 Hartung, Hauptstadtinszenierung, 2012, 79.
3 On the concept of trajectory space, cf. Vinken, Ort und Bahn, 2008; Löw, In welchen Räumen, 2020; and the essay on *The Crises of the Modern City* in this volume (Chapter 2).

should play. This chapter turns its attention to the contradictory dynamics of branding and appropriation strategies within Tashkent's heterogeneous urban spaces. Representative examples of urban heritage are analysed from different perspectives and at different scales: in addition to historic monuments and built heritage, the focus is on spatial structures and social spaces, cultural traditions and heritage politics.

Regressive Identity Politics and Urban Heritage

In Uzbekistan, questions of heritage are always also questions of national self-presentation. By means of a concerted cultural and heritage policy, the young state is seeking to generate a national identity that it has never possessed.[4] Uzbekistan is not an organic unity that corresponds to some linguistic or cultural area, but rather has its origins in colonialism. It came into existence in the 19th century as the Tsarist Russian Governate General of Turkestan. Tashkent has been the capital ever since. The country received its current geographical borders under Soviet rule as the Uzbek Socialist Republic. Uzbekistan, "the most populous and arguably the most culturally diverse of all Central Asian States",[5] is full of tensions and contradictions, including those between the majority Uzbeks and the Tajik and Kazakh minorities, as well as the 'Russians' (themselves a heterogeneous group), who are strongly represented in Tashkent, and the descendants of the Koreans forcibly resettled by Stalin in 1937. Although Cyrillic was replaced by the Latin alphabet in 1990, both scripts are still common in the Tashkent cityscape. Alongside the Uzbek language, Russian remains the lingua franca of the educated classes.

The government is systematically pursuing an orchestrated heritage policy that utilizes Uzbekistan's cultural legacy to establish a national 'brand'. One example of this is the revival of the myth of the Silk Road, which had a precursor in the *Project Silk Road*, launched in 1988 with support from UNESCO.[6] And UNESCO continues to pursue identity-political goals in the field of immaterial heritage, for instance, by supporting traditional handicrafts, particularly weaving.[7] Whether it wants to or not, it thereby also supports the regressive identity politics of Uzbekistan's authoritarian and patriarchal elites – both new and old.[8] A central element in these identity politics is the synthetic-

---

4   Laura L. Adams has published a monograph extensively analysing nation building in post-Soviet Uzbekistan, with a focus on the culture of national festivals, cf. Adams, The Spectacular State, 2010.
5   Kosmarski, Grandeur and Decay, 2011, 33.
6   Mentges, The Role of UNESCO, 2012, 216.
7   Mentges, The Role of UNESCO, 2012, 114–115.
8   Adams, The Spectacular State, 2010, 47–58 and passim; Mentges, The Role of UNESCO, 2012.

seeming cult of Timur and the establishment of Timur as the "Father of the Nation" and legendary "Founder of the Uzbek State".[9]

Figure 1: *Timur rides again. Equestrian statue in front of Hotel Uzbekistan (Photo: J. Blokker 2014)*

In 1993, in a highly symbolic act, a statue of Timur riding a horse was placed overlooking the city's central square, which also now bears his name, in a spot that was formerly occupied by sculptures of Stalin (1940) and Marx and Engels (1967) (fig. 1).[10] The so-called Timurdic style, which draws from sources including Iranian architecture, influenced most of Tashkent's grandest buildings,[11] including City Hall, the parliament, the senate building and Amir Timur Museum. The latter functions as both a museum of Timur and the Timurids and symbolically of the Uzbek nation; it is also depicted on the 1000 sum banknote (fig. 2): architecture as bricks-and-mortar heritage politics.[12]

---

9   Timur (Temür ibn Taraghai Barlas, also known as Timur Lenk ‚Timur the Lame, Tamerlane) completed the Islamization of Central Asia in the 14th century, following the conquests of the Mongol conquests and made Samarkand to the capital of his short-lived empire, which stretched from the Caspian Sea to India and incorporated large swathes of Western and Central Asia. On the Timurdic rebranding, see Paskaleva, Ideology in Brick and Tile, 2015, 419; Kosmarski, Grandeur and Decay, 2011, 42; Adams, The Spectacular State, 2010, 38–43; and Bell, Redefining National Identity, 1999, 188.
10 Hartung, Hauptstadtinszenierung, 2012, 76–77. Cf. also Adams, The Spectacular State, 2010, 25–32, which contains a list of streets and squares renamed since 1990.
11 Meuser, Architektur in Zentralasien, 2012, 62–63.
12 Hartung, Hauptstadtinszenierung, 2012, 75.

Figure 2: Brick-and-mortar heritage politics. The Amir Timur Museum in the "Timurid" style (Photo: Rjruiziii 2009)

Uzbekistan's authoritarian government has been emphasizing the country's membership of the Islamic cultural sphere ever since independence, making a clean break with the Soviet doctrine of state secularism. This has been used to recentre 'traditional' ways of life and social roles. Alongside secularism and 'Western' lifestyles, values such as gender equality have been suppressed in favour of patriarchal structures.[13] Particularly the mahallas – the traditional semi-autonomous neighbourhoods – have been invested with the hope that they could provide anchors of cultural and social identity – hopes that, in the context of reactionary and repressive social and cultural politics, can, as we will see, be subject to critical examination.

A Dual Urban Structure

The caesuras and contradictions that immediately strike every traveller to Tashkent bear witness to a colonial period characterized by upheavals and catastrophes. Uzbekistan's capital, today the home of two million people, stood for a long time in the shadow of Samarkand and Bukhara, and underwent a period of dynamic development only after the Russian conquest.[14] As the capital of the Governate General of Turkestan, Tashkent was expanded in splendid fashion under Tsarist rule. The ancient Asian and Islamic settlement with its characteristic structures was joined by a colonial new town, which was intended to act as the engine of rapid growth, and which, following connection to the railway network in 1898, transformed Tashkent into a city of 200,000 in 1910;

---

13 At the same time, however, the government pursues a model of loyal Islam and severely represses hardline Islamist tendencies, often as a pretext for threating opposition movements with detention, torture and jail.
14 On the general history of the city, cf. Lorenz, Stadtgeschichte Taschkents, 2012.

it ultimately became one of the largest cities in the Tsarist empire.[15] As the capital of the Uzbek Socialist Soviet Republic from 1924, Tashkent became the largest industrial city in Central Asia, particularly when the Soviet Union transferred heavy industry that was vital to the war effort to its southern territories, the harder for the invading Germans to reach.[16] The population exceeded one million as early as 1965.[17] Plans to rebuild Tashkent as a Soviet metropolis had already been forged in 1964, but it was the 1966 earthquake that provided the opportunity to subject the devastated city to a structural overhaul. The rebuilding of Tashkent as a large-scale planned city based on industrially fabricated large blocks was conceived of as a national flagship project that would demonstrate the capabilities of the Soviet community of nations.[18] Following the demise of the Soviet Union, the rebuilding of Tashkent as a national capital and global city – of which the Soviet-era rebuilding may be considered a precursor – was an opportunity to position some large-scale government architecture and palaces of glass and steel in the open spaces of the Soviet city.

It has often been said that Tashkent has exhibited a dual urban structure since Tsarist times.[19] This is characteristic of colonial cities and can be traced back to the powerful need for segregation on the part of the colonisers. The Tsarist new town, whose centre can still be traced in the street plan around the central Amir Timur Square, was positioned some five kilometres east of the old town; the two parts only merged later on, with the Ankhor Canal acting as the visible border between them.[20] The stark contrast between the organic Islamic-Asian city and the planned Tsarist colonial city has been noted by many travellers:[21] on the one hand, a "labyrinthine network of streets around the grand bazaar with its traditional mud-brick architecture, on the other, the imperial echo of Saint Petersburg in the tradition of 18th century European urban planning [...]".[22] This European city was largely built over by later Soviet planners; only occasionally does one come across corridor streets between closed-perimeter blocks on the European scale within the rational Soviet urban machine.

This duality has in essence persisted, despite some claims to the contrary, down to the present day.[23] While Soviet modernization efforts might have sought to overcome the division by building over both the Tsarist city and the Islamic town, the modernization plans forged in Moscow were largely left unimplemented. Even the ambitious *Mosohlproekt* (1937–38), a massive reconstruction campaign that envisaged to erect large four-storey blocks around a dense central district was only executed in a rudimentary way (along the central axis).[24] The old and the new – partially constructed – cities remained largely separate. When Tashkent was rebuilt following the 1966 earthquake,

---

15 Lorenz, Stadtgeschichte Taschkents, 2012, 107–108; Kosmarski, Grandeur and Decay, 2011, 39–41.
16 Hartung, Hauptstadtinszenierung, 2012, 82.
17 Lorenz, Stadtgeschichte Taschkents, 2012, 107–108.
18 Hartung, Hauptstadtinszenierung, 2012, 83.
19 Lorenz, Stadtgeschichte Taschkents, 2012; Stronski, Tashkent, 2010, 254.
20 Lorenz, Stadtgeschichte Taschkents, 2012, 107.
21 Lorenz, Stadtgeschichte Taschkents, 2012, 95.
22 Hartung, Hauptstadtinszenierung, 2012, 82.
23 Stronski, Tashkent, 2010, 254
24 Stronski, Tashkent, 2010, 48, 54, 56–71.

many buildings were demolished in both the Tsarist and the traditional residential areas to make room for an extensive planned city on the models of Le Corbusier or Niemeyer.[25] What emerged was an exemplary administrative and commercial center, the very definition of a functionally-zoned and interconnected city with demonstratively emphasized avenues and traffic corridors (fig. 3).[26] Owing to the lack of private transport, the promise of modernity associated with these plans has still not been fulfilled. Irregular clusters of huge apartment blocks stand around erratically within the loose grid of the planned city, whose spaces barely strike the observer as urban.[27]

Figure 3: Urban planning on a grand scale. View from the Hotel Uzbekistan over Amir Timur Square (Photo: J. Blokker 2014)

Yet the city's historical dualism has not been overcome – merely transformed. What may strike the Western visitor is that this apparently functional and Fordist city of trajectories is not content to conform to a rational pattern of cleanly delineated zones but continues to be subverted and infiltrated by urban forms from earlier cultural eras. At the edges of the modern functional spaces can be found "microspaces of improvised living: market stalls, rows of booths [...]."[28] Along the main roads, which may have as many as twelve lanes and are frequently screened off behind concrete walls or fences designed to hide them from sight, the informally proliferating single-storey dwellings of the mahalla[29] residential areas may be seen from time to time, their irregular and

---

25   Chukhovich, Building the Living East, 2012, 220, 225.
26   Cf. the essay on *The Crises of the Modern City* in this volume (Chapter 2).
27   Hartung speaks of "landmarks of urban dissolution", Hartung, Hauptstadtinszenierung, 2012, 84.
28   Hartung, Hauptstadtinszenierung, 2012, 85.
29   For an overview of the history, transformation and organization of the mahalla: Sievers, Uzbekistan's Mahalla, 2002.

often unpaved streets appearing suburban or even rural (fig. 4).³⁰ There could be no greater contrast between these two forms of the city. Here, the large-scale, grand city of trajectories, there the small-scale system of compounds, its winding system of cul-de-sacs screened off from passing traffic.³¹ The mahallas, residential districts organized on neighbourhood lines, are vital for the cultural and social order of traditional groups in Uzbek society (more on this below). Spatially, these districts are structured by the needs of their inhabitants to live and communicate, and not by those of crossing and transit: the modern zones and the trajectory city are subverted and undermined by the network city of the mahalla; the dualism of Tashkent's space has been transformed into a contradictory meshwork.³²

Figure 4: An informally proliferating residential district. Mahalla in Tashkent (Photo: J. Blokker 2014)

Meanwhile, within this complex pattern, the spatial and ethnic divide between Asians and Europeans remains. The cause of this was, in the first instance, that the newly built apartments were originally intended for skilled workers and other privileged individuals, of whom Russians made up the majority; above all, however, there has always been and continues to be a strong resistance to life in large apartment blocks among Uzbeks and other Asian population groups as a result of their cultural and social customs.³³ Sources from the 1970s make sharply clear how extreme the

---

30   Hartung, Hauptstadtinszenierung, 2012, 86.
31   On the structure of the compound, cf. Hartung, Hauptstadtinszenierung, 2012, 90–92.
32   Tashkent is thus Le Corbusier's very nightmare: the creator of the Fordist city was constantly concerned with preventing the organic city he considered as deficient in terms of both spatial and sanitary terms, from infecting the beauty and health of his functionalist city machine, cf. Vinken, Ort und Bahn, 2008, and the essay on *The Crises of the Modern City* in this volume (Chapter 2).
33   Stronski, Tashkent, 2010, 270.

ongoing segregation was then, describing the "Uzbek" districts (mahallas) as no-go areas for "Russians".[34]

'Civilizing the Orient'

This simultaneity of the zoned trajectory city and the small-scale and largely informal neighbourhoods is the result of an unresolved conflict of modernity. Up until Uzbekistan's independence, urban planning meant modernization on the Western model and was, as can be seen, closely associated with the goal of 'civilizing the Orient', i.e. the region's Islamic-Asian heritage. Over a huge area, civilizing was a euphemism for eliminating. The Russian colonial city was built a secure distance from the old Tashkent as usual; from a Western perspective, the Asian city was defective, dirty, narrow. The broad, lantern-lit boulevards and stone buildings of the new town were the antithesis of the unmappable alleyways with their 'primitive' mud-brick huts.[35] Not only the colonized population was excluded from the European city but also the workers and poor that had been drawn to Tashkent; they were settled outside the colonial city. Such segregation is an expression of a sense of superiority that fears those who are subject to discrimination as a source of infection and violence – and the origin of the desire to recast the 'oriental' in the mould of the European.[36] Under the Soviets, this civilizing mission was seen in historical-materialistic terms, namely as the political task of overcoming class contradictions and redeeming a 'backward' society. Yet this mission had no less of a destructive effect on the traditional residential quarters. Moreover, the Soviets' efforts at modernization were far more directly aggressive towards the old town; in 1929, plans were even laid to tear it down completely and create a park in its place.[37] While it proved impossible to implement this and similar projects, zoning regulations, improvements to sanitation and construction projects were performed under the paradigm of modernization, aiming at "progress" and "civilization".[38]

From the Western perspective, the goal of creating consistent living standards throughout Soviet society required planned cities, large blocks and the elimination of the "'urban village' of chaotically arranged mud-brick homes".[39] Urban planning was an aspect of social and cultural policy that aimed at eliminating a 'backward' culture and implementing ideologically founded re-education. Even the scale of the apartments was designed to encourage the spread of European nuclear-family norms. The replacement of compounds that were home to extended families by apartment blocks manufactured on an industrial scale also fulfilled the desire for social control. In the new city, children would no longer be cared for in private compounds, but in centralized state-run nurseries, while kitchens were kept deliberately small in order

---

34   Kosmarski, Grandeur and Decay, 2011, 48.
35   Lorenz, Stadtgeschichte Taschkents, 2012, 95–96.
36   Lorenz, Stadtgeschichte Taschkents, 2012, 96.
37   Stronski, Tashkent, 2010, 54.
38   Stronski, Tashkent, 2010, 57–58.
39   Stronski, Tashkent, 2010, 60.

to encourage family members to eat separately from each other in canteens provided for this purpose in schools and factories.[40] Nor did the often-remarked-upon (and rightly so!) formal 'orientalization' of the prefabricated high-rises contradict the goals of development and progress. The often elaborate decorations – mass produced concrete components based on 'oriental' designs often derived from traditional Uzbek textile patterns – were intended to evoke an Uzbek "national style", in accordance with Stalin's dictum that national culture under the dictatorship of the proletariat should be "national in form, socialist in content" (figs 5, 6).[41]

Figures 5, 6: "National in form, socialist in content". Soviet housing blocks with 'oriental' decoration (Photos: J. Blokker 2014)

The imposition of egalitarian apartments for nuclear families went hand-in-hand here with the cultivation of an "oriental-arabesque" regional style.[42] After 1966, very few Soviet planners and architects seriously considered adapting rational spatial planning procedures and industrial housing construction to the lifestyles of the Turkic population of the city and analysing in concrete terms the extent to which the mahalla system could be integrated into socialist planning.[43] The architect Mitkhat Bulatov, for instance, argued that the "mahalla spirit" had to be destroyed, but could still be transformed into a

---

40   Lorenz, Stadtgeschichte Taschkents, 2012, 113–115.
41   Stalin, Deviations on the National Question, 1942 (1930), 207.
42   On the concepts of the national and the regional in this context, cf. Chukhovich, Building the Living East, 2012, 217–218. Even Stalinist architecture in Tashkent had made an attempt at mimicking the language of regional forms (albeit filtered through neo-historicism), as paradigmatically realised in the Alisher Navoi Theatre completed in 1947; Navoi Prospekt, which was laid out in 1937, destroyed much of the old city, replacing it with modern buildings of culture and governance featuring "typically Uzbek" forms of construction. Oswald/Demydovets, Bauten und Projekte, 2012, 193–195.
43   Stronski, Tashkent, 2010, 146–153; Chukhovich, Building the Living East, 2012, 225–230.

kind of Soviet "micro-district".⁴⁴ The few significant experiments in this direction after 1966 included the experimental avantgarde building in Micro-District C-27 (1975), where Korobtsev and Khalilova created piles of residential cubes that ensured each family had a private outdoor space.⁴⁵ Also spectacular is the Zhemchug high-rise, which has been called a "vertical mahalla". Designed by Odetta Aidinova, this sixteen-floor residential tower includes an interior courtyard for each set of three storeys as a semi-public common area.⁴⁶ However, these are all exceptions, prototypes that never entered mass production; and the two contradictory city forms – planned city and mahalla – continue to exist as parallel worlds.

Processes of Self-Discovery. Heritage und Heritage Communities

On independence, the modern/oriental binary pair was deprived of its colonial logic. The state no longer represented 'European' modernity, with its sense of a calling to oppose 'backwardness' and 'underdevelopment' – alongside the exotic, the dark and the alien – in the name of enlightenment, secularization and rationalism. Yet in Tashkent there is still little evidence of coherent urban planning that is focused on the needs of the inhabitants or takes account of the elements that make up their culture. The expansion of the centre, as mentioned above, which aims to centre to create a global city and a modern economic hub, unabashedly built on the grandeur and power of the Soviet city, even if individual buildings were "de-Russified" in the course of their modernization.⁴⁷ The trajectory spaces that are now often branded as "Timurdic" are antiurban and do little to promote the development of public life; now as before, they ignore the patterns of life of the majority of the city's inhabitants and the spaces of their everyday lives. Götz Burggraf considers the development of public space in Tashkent since 1991 as the "reflection of a two-way process of self-discovery": while state agencies have attempted to create expressions of national identity and to represent this effectively in the public space, representatives of civil society are pursuing a different set of interests; the "double nature" of the city is being consolidated by the fixation on major projects and an ineffective system for balancing different interests.⁴⁸ As Hartung points out, "Eternal Tashkent", the glossy official publication commemorating Tashkent's development that was published in 1998, presents the old city as something that should hurry up and vanish.⁴⁹ When the presidency changed hands in 2017, it came with hopes of politi-

---

44   Stronski, Tashkent, 2010, 151.
45   Meuser, Architektur in Zentralasien, 2012, 56.
46   Meuser, Architektur in Zentralasien, 2012, 57 and Oswald/Demydovets, Bauten und Projekte, 2012, 214–215. Cf. also Kalinovsky, Laboratory of Socialist Development, 2018, 125.
47   These include the Senate Building and the House of the Ministries, Oswald/Demydovets, Bauten und Projekte, 2012, 190–191 and Hartung, Hauptstadtinszenierung, 2012, 84–85. On the post-socialist cityscape cf. Adams, The Spectacular State, 2010, 25–33.
48   Burggraf, Der öffentliche Raum, 2012, 152, 155. Hartung observes that characterizing the endless uninhabited spaces of the government quarter as "public space" is problematic. Hartung, Hauptstadtinszenierung, 2012, 79.
49   Hartung, Hauptstadtinszenierung, 2012, 86–87.

cal reform and greater economic openness. Yet the status of the 'oriental' city remains precarious under the new ruler. The *Tashkent City* project (2017) followed the established pattern of a late modern glass-and-steel city of business and bureaucracy.[50] Its realization necessitated the prior clearance of two mahallas, whose residents were rehoused elsewhere.[51] At least the *Modern Mahalla* project is now giving some thought to the future development and modernization of the traditional residential areas. This project proposes to "redesign" 505 neighbourhoods, and plans that are circulating show major structural changes, which is likely to mean rebuilding from scratch.[52] At the same time, the backlog of massive apartment buildings requiring rehabilitation in the wide-open spaces of the Soviet-era residential areas has reached an alarming level.

It is clear that the various layers of the city's architectural history enjoy very different degrees of attention and appreciation among the different heritage communities. For international professionals and lovers of architecture, Tashkent is no longer an "undiscovered gem", especially given the large expanses of occasionally spectacular Soviet modernism that have survived and produced so many iconic structures. These include Tashkent's underground stations,[53] the state circus[54], the Hotel Uzbekistan[55], the Chorsu Bazaar (fig. 7)[56] and the State Museum of History of Uzbekistan (fig. 8) to name but a few.

Such icons of the city enjoy enormous popularity, at least among those educated Tashkent residents who are interested in architecture; they are shown to visitors with great pride. Crucially, however, my Uzbek Master's students explicitly did not evaluate them as "monuments" in the sense of built heritage, although many are important sites of identification, including the circus, which was one of the largest in the Soviet Union, and the Chorsu Bazaar at the heart of the decimated old city (fig. 8).[57] Growing identification with the city's Soviet-era cultural buildings was most recently seen in protests at the demolition of the Dom cinema, a concrete structure from the early 1980s.[58] By contrast, the mass-manufactured housing blocks, for all the complexity of their façade decoration, enjoy considerably less popularity. It seems that, in them, the memory of the destruction of the Islamic city and its lifeworlds – by earthquake *and* bulldozer – is still alive.

---

50 Matyakubova, Tashkent City, 2018, 3
51 Matyakubova, Tashkent City, 2018, 5–7.
52 Matyakubova, Tashkent City, 2018, 7–8, with reference to an article from 2017, cf. Sovremennoi mahalle radi ne vse, GazetaUz, 20 August 2017.
53 Website Matador Network, To see the best art and architecture.
54 Oswald/Demydovets, Bauten und Projekte, 2012, 228–229.
55 Oswald/Demydovets, Bauten und Projekte, 2012, 234–235.
56 Oswald/Demydovets, Bauten und Projekte, 2012, 220–221.
57 In March 2014, I held a day-long teaching seminar in Tashkent at the Usbekisch-Deutschen Zentrum für Architektur und Bauwesen (UDZ), an academic institution operated jointly by the Potsdam University of Applied Sciences and the Tashkent Institute of Architecture and Civil Engineering as part of the Uzbek-German master's degree course in building conservation and heritage conservation. Topics covered included historic preservation and the preservation of international cultural heritage. There was a lively discussion of the status of individual architectures and structures. This was continued during excursions in the city, most of which were led by students.
58 Matyakubova, Tashkent City, 2018, 8–10.

Figure 7: Iconic Soviet Modernism: Chorsu Bazaar

Figure 8: State Museum of History (Photos: J. Blokker 2014)

The only structures referred to literally as historic monuments or built heritage by the Master's students (as well as presumably by most of Tashkent's cultural tourists) are showpieces of Islamic architectures, of the kind that have been granted UNESCO World

Heritage status in Samarkand and other sites,[59] but are relatively poorly represented in Tashkent. The most frequently mentioned example in Tashkent is the – much renovated – Kukeldash Madrasa (fig. 9). It has again been used as a Koran school in recent years, and appears to stand as a placeholder for old Tashkent, which from this position, near the dome of the grand bazaar, can be hard to detect amidst the modern cityscape.

Figure 9: UNESCO World Heritage. Kukeldash Madrasa (Photo: J. Blokker 2014)

Another point of reference that serves as a source of identity formation, according to my observations, is the new religious centre that has developed around Hazrat Imam Mosque since it opened in 2007. Created by means of extensive restoration and reconstruction, the Timurdic ensemble includes mosques, madrassas and mausoleums dating from the 16th to the 19th centuries, and contains the oldest surviving copy of the Koran.[60] These complexes and monuments, however, have little influence on the city; Soviet planning has left them isolated and insular. From the perspective of classical architectural conservation, by contrast, the traditional residential districts, the often faceless mahallas, are entirely invisible. Yet for historically informed urban planning, this is an absolutely vital layer of the city. It is no exaggeration to say that the possibility of reconciling tradition and future will above all be decided by how Tashkent deals with the traditional urban spaces of these neighbourhoods.[61]

Uzbekistan's mahallas are not treated as historic monuments, but are perceived as culturally significant spaces, as heritage of the kind that helps to form identities in the broad sense that surpasses the mere concept of cultural heritage. There is no possibility

---

59 Website Wikipedia, List of World Heritage Sites in Uzbekistan.
60 Dieckmann, Tausend und eine Macht, 2014.
61 For details of the challenges and the new legal regulations since 1991: Sievers, Uzbekistan's Mahalla, 2002, 118–152.

of productively steering tradition here by means of legal stipulations aimed at conserving material substance or preventing alterations. As sites of constant transgression and transformation, the houses and compounds of Tashkent's mahallas are rarely more than a century old. In their wealthier areas (given the inward orientation of their structure, it is often hard to identify the personal wealth of those who live there), gentrification has set in. This gentrification has seen many unauthorized cases of privatization of common lands and public space.[62] The withering away of the mixed-use mahalla structures into purely residential districts appears unstoppable, with the loss of the once indispensable mahalla house and the infrastructure of small neighbourhood centres with their tradespeople's compounds, kiosks, shops and teahouses.[63] New residential areas, for all that they pass on traditional ways of living together, are often hard to tell apart from European-style suburbs.

Since the mahalla is such a highly loaded symbol for "Uzbek" culture and way of life, its future is the crucial question for the 'right' path to modernization. This is where the conflicts between traditional ways of life and the constantly shifting demands of a globalized society play out; and this is where the question arises of how and in which spaces the inhabitants of Tashkent wish to live and will be able to live in the future. The city's official concepts and framework plans are reluctant to engage with this question. There is no master plan for socially responsible, sustainable and culturally sensitive urban planning. In view of the significance that the mahallas have not only for the identity of the Uzbek people but also in concrete terms for the everyday life of the city,[64] scholars and activists have rightly called for more transparency, communication and participation in the city's planning measures.[65] Though the demolition of traditional residential areas, and the compulsory resettlement that this entails, regularly provokes opposition, the residents' room to manoeuvre is often narrow as a consequence of their limited ownership rights. They also suffer from crumbling infrastructure caused by a lack of investment in mahallas that are facing long-term rehabilitation measures. In the short-term, a system to manage complaints and fair compensation for those facing rehousing would bring relief; but in the long term, what is needed is a system for balancing the interests of the city and its citizens that has a firm institutional and legal basis, e.g. the establishment of binding property rights and procedures for civic participation in planning processes.[66]

Traditional Urban Spaces – Contaminated Heritage?

Clearly this goes beyond problems of compensation and civic participation; it ultimately concerns the fundamental issue of the 'right' way of living – a question that emphatically

---

62 Kosmarski, Grandeur and Decay, 2011, 52–53.
63 Hartung, Hauptstadtinszenierung, 2012, 92.
64 In 1989 around one third of Tashkent's residents still lived in mahallas, Sievers, Uzbekistan's Mahalla, 2002, 117.
65 Matyakubova, Tashkent City, 2018, 9.
66 Matyakubova, Tashkent City, 2018, 7.

invokes that of the 'right' way of life. At its heart, this concerns the issue of what kind of space will be given over to tradition in a society that is conceiving of its own path to modernity. Most authors, however, see the mahalla as having already provided an answer to the question of the right way to live in Tashkent.⁶⁷ Western authors praise the mahalla as a paradise of compounds, perfectly adapted to the climate, earthquake-proof, in tune with the local way of life, organic, ancient and "still successful after all this time": all that remains, in their view, is thus to capture the essence of the Asian city and its mahalla structure and adapt this to current needs.⁶⁸ In local descriptions of the city and in guides for travellers, Tashkent's traditional districts are often glorified as an earthly paradise.⁶⁹ Academic authors, who seek to cast a critical gaze over Uzbek urban policy, also see these as places "of community and connectedness".⁷⁰

Figure 10: Mahalla – a paradise of compounds? (Photo: Varandej 2015)

To my mind, these statements need to be challenged from two directions. The first concerns the plausibility of such a planning approach. Is it desirable for a city with a population in the millions to favour such a low-density form of architecture even in central areas? How can a city with an endless expanse of single-storey residential compounds meet all of the new challenges ahead, such as those of urban sprawl: excessive land use and expensive infrastructure, not only for local public transport but also for energy and water – problems that will likely only intensify with accelerating climate change? Is it even possible to reconcile the mahalla with a property sector run on free-market lines, or would these areas have to be collectivized to facilitate a less-intensive

---

67 For a critical perspective, see Sievers, Uzbekistan's Mahalla, 2002, 123.
68 Hartung, Hauptstadtinszenierung, 2012, 93.
69 Website Uzbek Travel, About Uzbekistan.
70 Matyakubova, Tashkent City, 2018, 5.

form of residential building in highly desirable city-centre areas? Living centrally in one- to two-storey, small-scale structures is a pattern we tend to find elsewhere in informal settlements that are largely free of market forces. In addition, it is possible to identify fault lines between the supposed "paradise of compounds" and a pluralistic and democratic (and gender-equitable) community life. Mahallas do not have public spaces in the full sense of the word, but rather form closed enclaves that are decoupled from passing traffic. Similar to gated communities, they systematically exclude social change and intermixing.[71] Such infrastructure as exists serves only the neighbourhood; the mahallas are socially homogeneous and exclusive. One cannot simply pick a mahalla, but strict rules are enforced about who may move in; leaving voluntarily may also lead to ostracization.[72]

The mahalla, one must constantly remind oneself, is far more than merely a spatial unit in the sense of a neighbourhood. In the Arab and Asian world, it is a widespread and legally acknowledged instrument of institutional self-government for city districts, with an elected leader and a council of elders.[73] The mediating function that it plays between families and the state is traditionally also connected with powerful functions for social regulation and control – something that the Soviet authorities encouraged and exploited.[74] The mahalla is "one of only a few effective traditional structures that can unite representatives of various ethnic and religious groups through the creation of a common identity based on shared residence. However, throughout the history of these communities, political authorities have often attempted to manipulate these institutions to enhance the state's legitimacy".[75] The post-independence project to strengthen the mahalla follows in this tradition.[76] The process of "mahallization"[77] is an inherent aspect of an authoritarian heritage and identity policy.[78] The process is ambivalent at least: "Thus, the old neighborhood institution *malhalla* – which existed even throughout the Soviet era and represents an interface between state and local communities – is more or less instrumental as a new organizational unit of political control, using old patterns of social practices: Family, kinship and patriarchal structure organize the life of citizens on a local level."[79]

Even if some authors stress the mediating role of the mahallas and compare them with the NGOs that operate in the cities of the Global South, it is hard to deny that they stand less for the self-organization of an egalitarian society of citizens than for the stabilization of a patriarchal structure that is defined by "blood ties" and kinship.

---

71 Goziev, Mahalla, 2015.
72 Sievers, Uzbekistan's Mahalla, 2002, 98, 136.
73 Sievers, Uzbekistan's Mahalla, 2002, 95–102.
74 Sievers, Uzbekistan's Mahalla, 2002, 113–114.
75 Dadabaev, Community life, 2013, 181.
76 For details, see Sievers, Uzbekistan's Mahalla, 2002, 118–120, 131–150.
77 Also "malhallization". On the concept, see Mentges, The Role of UNESCO, 2012, 220. The spelling "malhalla" is unusual in Uzbekistan.
78 It has been accompanied by a process of juridification and formalization that may actually serve to weaken the institution in the long term. Sievers refers to this as "grassroots absolutism", Sievers, Uzbekistan's Mahalla, 2002, 152–154, 152.
79 Mentges, The Role of UNESCO, 2012, 220. Italics in the original.

Human rights groups point out that the Uzbek government uses mahallas to suppress dissidents, religious minorities and women and to curtail their rights.[80] When I was teaching in Tashkent, I became aware that the topic of the mahalla was not an easy one for the ethnically and culturally heterogeneous groups of students to discuss, and that it was easier to speak openly in private contexts. The level of social pressure exerted on individuals by their surroundings in everyday situations (such as when choosing whom to marry) was perceptibly high (even if it was accepted as unavoidable). My impression was that the dominant speakers, who tended to be Uzbek men, saw the mahalla as a largely unambivalent frame of reference and source of identity, while the Russians, Korean women, and Uzbek women were more likely to remain silent on the topic. The complaint was voiced, for instance, that women were expected to move to their husband's mahalla (and to the house of their parents-in-law) after marriage and were often forced to break off all contacts to their mahalla of origin – and hence to their parents and other relatives.[81]

The question of the mahalla makes particularly clear just how complex issues of "urban heritage" become as soon as we look beyond the narrow concept of "built heritage" and take into account the space of the city as a whole and the structural, social and emotional aspects of urban life. Only when we take all of these together can we see the various formations of urban heritage. Sustainable urban development, to sum up this chapter's findings, depends directly on how the various heritage formations can be articulated and weighted to be included in future plans and transformation processes. In general terms, urban heritage, as the case of Tashkent demonstrates clearly, is easy to instrumentalize, whether for heritage politics, nation building or branding, as well as for reactionary or repressive social politics. The example of the mahallas makes clear that patriarchal social structures with their mechanisms of control and repression are being defended and consolidated in Tashkent's debates over planning policy and urban development – and this in the name of tradition and cultural heritage.

---

80 The Equal Rights Trust, After the Padishah, 2016, in particular 168–169.
81 On this, cf. also Sievers, Uzbekistan's Mahalla, 2002, 99.

6 Basel / Switzerland
The *Heimat* Zone. Planning the 'Historic' Town

> ... la forme d'une ville change plus vite, hélas,
> que le cœur d'un mortel !
> ...the form a city takes more quickly shifts,
> alas, than does the mortal heart!
> *(Charles Baudelaire)* [1]

Roadside signs have started appearing in Germany that draw attention to a nearby *Historische Altstadt* (which reads approximately as "Historic Old Town"). That raises the question of whether there can also be non-historical old towns. Lamenting 'manufactured antiquity' has a long history. In his notorious 1933 speech "Zur Rettung der deutschen Altstadt" (On Saving the German Old Town), the art historian Wilhelm Pinder condemned both "Old Heidelberg" and "Old Nuremberg" as fakes – the result in each case of historicist renovations and assimilating infill construction.[2] In particular, to the critical visitor, those famous German Old Towns that have been marketed to tourists for decades can seem like little more than theatrical trickery. The market for this manufactured antiquity has been booming since German unification. However, my question about the 'making' of *Altstadt* is not primarily concerned with the fake or simulated antiquity of many 'historic' town quarters but rather the claims of historicity and authenticity inherent in the concept of *Altstadt* itself. Talk of a badly planned and disfigured, faked and simulated Old Town implicitly assumes that there could be a real and authentic one: the 'real' *Altstadt* as something that has passively come down to us, as historical remains or a document that emerges out of another time and into ours and requires protection from impudent modernity. Yet *Altstadt* is also a phenomenon against which the question of true or false, real or manufactured comes up short. For the making of *Altstadt* is deeply rooted in the history of the city, and, more specifically, in the practices and methods of modern urban planning.[3]

---

1 Baudelaire, The Flowers of Evil, 1998 (1857), 175.
2 Pinder, Rede am Tag für Denkmalpflege und Heimatschutz, 1934, 127.
3 For a full exploration of this thesis: Vinken, Zone Heimat, 2010.

Altstadt is a construct in several regards:

- *Altstadt* emerges as the dialectical counter-image of the modern city. In contrast to the acceleration, destruction and alienation of modernity, *Altstadt* offers endurance, order and a sense of home. In brief, the modern city and the modern urban experience are antecedent to the notion of the Old Town.
- *Altstadt* is not a remnant of urban modernization, but a product of it. The construction of the 'historic' town centre is founded in a differentiation of urban space, which, in the form of zoning, is at the heart of modern urban planning.
- And finally: *Altstadt* is not the result of preservation or conservation, but of willful intervention. Rehabilitation is a specific form of modernization that undertakes sanitary, social and aesthetic homogenization. By this means, synthetic islands of tradition are accorded to the modern city, with its lack of boundaries and its dynamism, as special zones.

Counter-Image

Simplifying somewhat, one could say that the Old Town came about during the first modern cultural movement: Romanticism. In 1801, Ludwig Tieck left Berlin, whose "labyrinthine regularity" had become unbearable to him. For his famous book, *Outpourings of an Art-Loving Friar*, he reinvented Albrecht Dürer's Nuremberg. Old Nuremberg, with its winding alleyways, old-fashioned (*"altväterischen"*) houses and churches, tiny round-paned windows was for him a symbol of a German golden age, a "vigorous centre of German art".[4] Against modernity, with its experiences of dissolution and loss, Romanticism sets the feeling, the character, the soul that it finds in the image of the German *Altstadt*: "German art was once a pious youth, reared at home among relatives and within the walls of a little town. Now that it has grown older it has become a polished man of the world who in ridding himself of his provincialism has sacrificed his feeling, his individuality, his very soul".[5] The city as the vessel of the soul plays an important role in the iconography of Romanticism. In his drawing "Dürer and Raphael before the Throne of Art",[6] Franz Pforr turns "old German" Nuremberg into a kind of attribute of the German artist, while Rome plays the same role for his opposite number, the equally revered Raphael. In Friedrich Overbeck's 1810 portrait of Franz Pforr,[7] the Nazarene, who died young, is portrayed in the position "in which he would perhaps have felt happiest":[8] From an arbour, the observer's gaze is drawn through the alleyways of an old German town towards an Italian coast: pious, orderly domesticity is embodied

---

4   Wackenroder/Tieck, Outpourings, 1975 (1797), 49.
5   Wackenroder/Tieck, Outpourings, 1975 (1797), 55.
6   Etching based on a lost drawing.
7   Berlin, Nationalgalerie.
8   Wesenberg, Nationalgalerie Berlin, 2001, 317.

in the intricate and varied beauty of the *Altstadt* with its obedience to a higher order, which in turn opens onto the landscape.

In the dynamic flux of industrialization, the evocation of the good old town took on a new aspect. As a symbol of natural order and integrity, *Altstadt* became the counter-image of the modern city, which was experienced as lacking boundaries, structure and stability. A telling example is the presentation of a city in Pugin's *Contrasts*[9] (fig. 1).

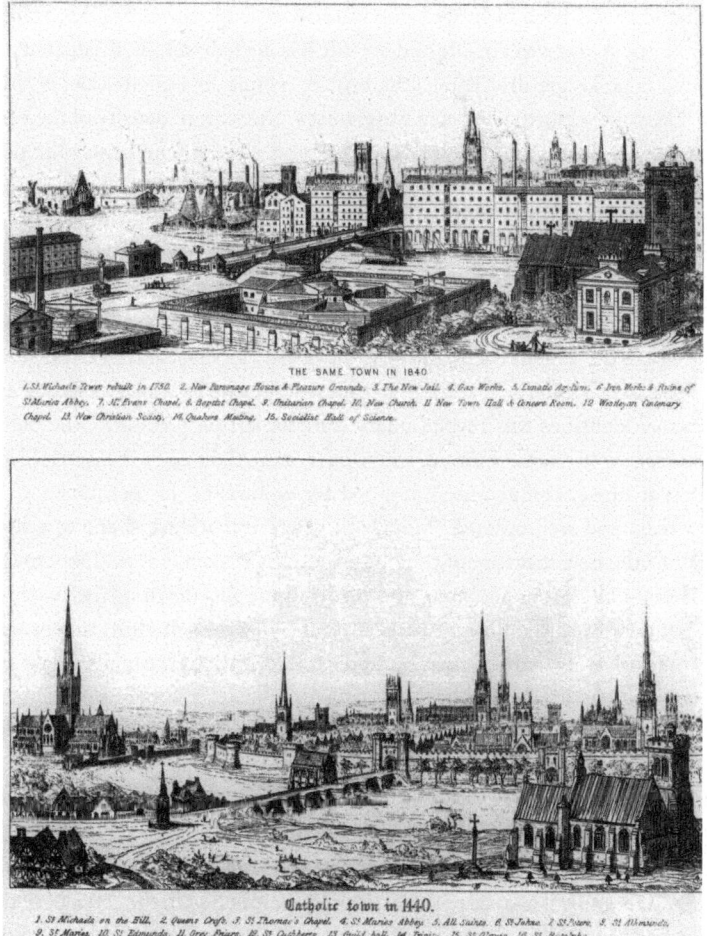

Figure 1: "Contrasts". *View of a City 1840 and 1440, A. W. N. Pugin 1841*

In this architectural pamphlet, the initiator of the Gothic Revival seeks to prove the superiority of Gothic architecture over Classicism, which he considers degenerate and pagan. The accompanying engravings show the titular "contrasts" – good and bad: a fictitious contemporary city is contrasted with an idealized view of the same town from around 1440. Modern history is presented as an age of decadence and decline. Front

---

9   Pugin, Contrasts, 1841.

and centre stands the prison, the new poorhouse, as an emblem of modernity; behind it, fenced off, the madhouse – modernity as discipline and punishment. Modernity becomes distance from God: in the foreground to the right, the grand new parsonage, set down in isolation, casts a shadow over the church, while the old churchyard has been replaced by a pleasure ground; in the background on the left, the large abbey, placed outside the walls in the Roman manner stands in a state of ruin next to the ironworks. Modernity is presented as destruction, including the destruction of manifest architectural order: shortened church towers compete with belching smokestacks; the harmonious silhouette has been destroyed; the waterfront is obscured by giant warehouses. The clear boundary between inside and outside has been dissolved, dissipated; the edge of the town is no longer discernible; the bridge, rebuilt on a giant scale, is reduced to a chasm-like void, a cutting between warehouses. The vibrant density of the centre has given way to the depressing crush of industry and gloomy tenements. The new town here reflects a society whose social and moral order is out of kilter. The historic town is drafted as its counter-image – the embodiment of divine, organic order.

If *Altstadt* here represents order in a disorderly time, it is even more a symbol of permanence in a time of increasing acceleration. The order that the Old Town embodies is that of the permanent, the eternal, the self-evident. In this way, *Altstadt* is constituted precisely where the experience of the city underwent its most extreme transformation in the course of modernity: in relation to time. An oft-cited passage in Baudelaire's Les fleurs du mal identifies this revolutionary transformation precisely: "The old Paris is gone (the form a city takes more quickly shifts, alas, than does the mortal heart!)."[10] Since ancient times, architecture has stood for endurance, for permanence. The city offered a fixed and well-ordered framework, a space that gave shape to a life full of variety. With the new measure of time given – from Dickens's *Hard Times* to Chaplin's *Modern Times* – by the monotonous and untiring up-and-down of the machines, the pistons of the railway, the flow of workers on the way to their shift, this order-giving stone framework is also carried away by modern acceleration. The tempos have switched place, man has been left behind by the transformations of his environment. Modernity is accompanied from the start by an experience of alienation and uprootedness that is perceived as nostalgia, longing for home, or cultural pessimism.

From this perspective, the city/Old Town binary is revealed to be a special case of one of modernity's central configurations: the dialectical construction of history as a present that is moving towards the future, on the one hand, and as tradition, on the other. The new demand for radical contemporaneity, which culminated in the concept of the avant garde, discredited tradition as old in the sense of outdated, incongruous, of the past. On the other hand, the dialectical concept of history emerged from a figure of origins; the progressive present creates tradition as a concept of permanence, familiarity, the eternally valid. He who measures everything against the present will, following Hegel, make the past into heritage.[11] In the accelerated transformation of industrialization, experience of the city splits. Next to modern Paris, Capital of the 19th Century, *vieux Paris* appears as a powerful image of all that is familiar and threatened, and as the (lost)

---

10   Baudelaire, The Flowers of Evil, 1998 (1857), 175.
11   Choay, The Invention, 2001, 131–152.

Heimat. The concept of *Altstadt* splits the flow of time, excluding from the present a 'previously'; it distinguishes the contemporary from the conventional, the historical, or better, the permanent: the 'always already' of tradition. The invention of *Altstadt* out of the experience of modernity is clearly inscribed in Pugin's illustration: tellingly, his contrast of the Gothic city and the modern one is not arranged chronologically as before and after. The image of the mediaeval city is constructed by means of its modern view. Here, the *Altstadt* is the image of an ideal type, the counter-image of the new – false – city.

Altstadt is a figure of origin and tradition wrested from the diktat of modern *être-du-temps* as a place of quasi-timelessness. Yet the concrete Old Town, those 'historic' areas in the hearts of our cities, are also constructions in several regards. Old Towns do not come about as a result of neutral processes such as preservation or conservation. They are generated during the modernization of cities, more precisely in processes of spatial differentiation and homogenization that are at the heart of every instance of urban modernization.[12] The case of Basel, a city whose history, in contrast to that of so many German cities, is not fractured by wartime destruction and post-war reconstruction, outlines these processes of heritage-making clearly and concisely.

According a Place

The construction of *Altstadt* has its origin in the transformations that a city undergoes in the early stages of modernization: when the Old Town is accorded to a rapidly expanding urban area as its "core".[13] This initial phase is defined by the boundary, which once again reveals itself to be the constitutive figure *par excellence*.[14] The city of Basel retained a full set of fortifications well into the 19th century. Until 1856, the gates were locked at night. A broad strip of open land in front of the walls was left unbuilt to maintain a clear field of fire.[15] The city's fortifications thus remained a definite boundary – physically, legally and economically – until the threshold of industrialization. And yet the Trojan Horse of progress had already found its way into the city: the railway. The first station (serving the Strasbourg–Basel Railway) had been kept within the city proper by means of an elaborate and expensive expansion of the city walls. The newly constructed railway gate was locked at night like all the others: a remarkable and pointless attempt to use conventional means to retain mastery over the incoming tide of revolutionary change. The dynamic potential of this new mode of transport created new facts and necessities on the ground. With the decision in 1857 to build the new Central Station outside the walls, the old defences were implicitly abandoned. The law to expand the city of 1859 paved the way for the moats to be filled in, new entrances to be created and the walls and earthworks to be removed. The fortifications were dismantled in stages between

---

12 Fehl, Stadt-Umbau, 1995, 13.
13 Vinken, Die neuen Ränder, 2005.
14 Simmel, Sociology, 2009, in particular "Excursus on Social Boundary", 551–570.
15 Siegfried, Basels Entfestigung, 1923, 91–92.

1861 and 1878 (fig. 2).[16] In their place, in imitation of Vienna, a circular promenade was created.

Figure 2: Modern Times. View of Basel with the new Station in front of the defortified city, lithograph by Jean Baptiste Arnout 1865

Naturally, these measures were undertaken in the name of modernization. Basel needed to open itself up to its rapidly expanding suburbs, and the circular promenade was to serve as the pivot point by regulating the flow of traffic. The ring also promised social and sanitary benefits: recreation for all, health, fresh air for a densely built city.[17] Last but not least, it was thought of as a beautification measure, as a grand new setting for the city and a stage for modern life. This complete ring of parks and alleys is beautiful, healthful and practical – in short, it is modern, the new face of the city. The *Promenadenring* was the antithesis of the city walls: open instead of closed, dynamic rather than set in stone, connecting instead of protecting. Although it is an emblem of modernity, the ring also contains a powerful moment of continuity. It recalls the city's old boundaries within the modern cityscape. It is not a mere dividing line, but a space with its own order, whose configuration decisively changed how the Old Town is perceived. It is significant, in this regard, that elements of the old fortifications have been utilized in the promenade. Three of Basel's five city gates have been kept as physical documents of the old boundary;[18] more precisely, they were repurposed as monuments.[19] Their restoration was not undertaken in order to re-establish a specific historical state. Rather, it aimed to be characteristic, to recreate a typical 'mediaeval city gate' or even 'Basel city gate', one whose character – that of venerable antiquity, military and economic power, pride – was to be established via aesthetic means (figs 3, 4). The gates'

---

16   Kreis, Abbruch und Aufbruch, 1995.
17   Falter, Grünflächen der Stadt Basel, 1984, 43.
18   Siegfried, Basels Entfestigung, 1923, 140–146; Kreis, Abbruch und Aufbruch, 1995, 223–228.
19   Helmig/Matt, Inventar Basler Stadtbefestigung, 1989.

character as historical monuments was completed by placing them in small, landscaped parks.

Figures 3, 4: Basel, St. Alban's Gate in 1863 and following its restoration in 1872.

The old city gates, whose atmospheric staging as historic monuments owes a debt to bourgeois notions of culture and education, are the most prominent architectural sites around the promenade ring. The monumental gates certify its authenticity as the fortifications' representative and heir. Beyond this, they also cut across the ring's self-referential space. By evoking the opening and closing functions of the city walls, they inscribe the interior-exterior antagonism of the old boundary into the new one. In this, however, there is a decisive drift of meaning: the boundary function of the wall, its establishment of 'interior' and 'exterior' is translated by the ring into 'old' and 'new'. The binary pair ancient town/extensions here superimposed upon the subtexts original/model and organic/planned. It was Heidegger who stated that "a boundary is not that at which something stops but [...] that from which something *begins its presencing*."[20] And so the promenade ring accords the modern city an interior: an interior that frames itself as particular, as *Heimat*. The urban planning measures undertaken in the name of modernization thus simultaneously transformed the status of the old quarter of town into an *Altstadt* that is the heart and soul of the new city.

Special Zone

These transformations of an older part of town into an *Altstadt* in the sense of a core, centre and origin are preconditions for the concrete generation of 'historic' quarters,

---

20 Heidegger, Building Dwelling Thinking, 1971 (1951), 152. Italics in the original.

which occurs in parallel to or, more precisely, as an inherent component of modernization. Of course, not every part of the old city is today part of Basel's *Altstadt*. Since the removal of the city walls, large areas of the city's centre have been modernized to form a central business district and often renovated several times in quick succession.[21] Nevertheless, Basel's impressive urban substance provides an image of a Swiss German *Altstadt* that is very 'well preserved' over a large area. Paradoxically, this image is in large part generated by the mediaeval 'faubourgs' (*Spalenvorstadt*; *St. Alban-Vorstadt*) that were incorporated into the expanded city in the late Middle Ages through enlargement of its ring of walls. While some 70 percent of houses inside the ring have been rebuilt since 1875,[22] the resulting impression is quite heterogeneous. In substantive terms, coherent groups of buildings from the pre-industrial age remain in the area around the Minster and near the Rhine as well as on the slopes above (e.g. Heuberg, Nadelberg, Spalenberg, Leonhardsberg), while other parts have been transformed into a modern business district (fig. 5).

Figure 5: "Altstadt" and 19th-century business district. Basel, Marktplatz and Sattelgasse (Photo: Koch 1898)

---

21 Brönnimann, Basler Bauten, 1973; Stolz/Bühler, Basel im 19. Jahrhundert, 1979.
22 Meier, Basel einst und jetzt, 1993, 10.

The area inside the ring is differentiated by topographic means: the so-called *Talstadt* or "valley town" around the market has traditionally contained the most important thoroughfares and shopping streets, which run down towards the old bridge over the Rhine. The old 'faubourgs' and the less convenient hillsides were residential areas or craftsmen's quarters; the *Münstersporn*, which shields the lower town from the Rhine, was long marked by the presence of the Church. Modernization intensified these differences: traffic and trade on the one hand, peace and quiet on the other; even partially neglected areas such as those along the banks of the Birsig river, which crossed the city openly until 1897.

Are today's 'historic' quarters, therefore, remnants of the old city that were not subject to modernization and have since been granted official protection? On more careful examination, a different picture is revealed. The precondition for the emergence of homogeneous old-town districts as 'zones of tradition' is a bundle of urban-planning measures. First, and most significantly, it is a result of spatial differentiation, which has been accompanied by legal provisions and specific building regulations. Basel's *Altstadt* quarters are the result of zoning, i.e. planning legislation that defines business district and 'historic' areas as different zones, and of a modernization practice that aesthetically homogenizes each of these zones. Strictly speaking, Basel's famed *Altstadt* came into existence as a planning zone.

Urban planning emerged as a separate discipline in the late 19th century as a means of regulating the modernization of cities. It initially concentrated on formulating general rules and guidelines and applying them as blanket measures: this is modernization as homogenization. Basel was no exception, and early attempts were made to create uniform rules for the entire city – by defining the minimum width of streets, for instance.[23] For the town centre, this regulation of the streets in accordance with the needs of modern transport infrastructure was known as "correction": this was a major undertaking that required all the houses on at least one side of a street to be torn down one by one to gain a relatively modest increase in width. Because of the size of the compensation payments to owners, this process was only economically and politically viable for a few main shopping streets. Above all, however, the compromises that were necessary to maintain a uniform appearance throughout the city left both parts of Basel unsatisfied. The minimum street width that it was possible to achieve in the centre at great expense around the turn of the century was considered inadequate for the extensions and the modern suburbs.[24] The first generally binding planning laws for Basel were passed in 1919. Significantly, they did not apply to the city centre, but only to the extensions.[25]

Paradoxically, the solution to this problem was the result of radically functionalist urban planning. Its key concept is spatial differentiation, encapsulated in the concept of the zone.[26] The blueprint was given by Le Corbusier, who placed the idea of functional zones at the heart of his thought. In his first functionalist model of a city, "a contemporary city for three million inhabitants" (1922), commercial and administrative, res-

---

23 Ratschläge, 315, 1864.
24 Ratschläge, 315, 1864, 7–8.
25 Ratschläge, 2257, 1919.
26 Vinken, Sonderzone Heimat, 2006.

idential and industrial areas are spatially segregated.[27] The functional zones, such as the high-rise business district and the residential districts of large housing blocks that surround it, are also subject to different formal design criteria. Although these radical ideas were initially rejected, the principle of zoning would be adopted universally as the basis of urban modernization. When the first generally binding rules for the whole of Basel were developed in the 1930s, it was divided into planning zones (*Bauzonen*).[28] This also marked the establishment of the

Altstadt in legal terms. For the first time, parts of the city centre that had previously been designated "Planning Zone 5" (*Bauzone 5*) and "Correction Area" (*Korrektionsgebiet*) were defined as *Schutzzonen Altstadt* (Protection Zones), and subject to a special set of building regulations.[29] The *Schutzzonen Altstadt*, however, were, although they were designated as protection zones, were likewise planning zones, and conservation legislation in the proper sense was not established until 1977.[30] The *Schutzzone Altstadt* is what we call a special zone with special rules for building in existing fabric. Whether a new building is constructed, or an old building is renovated remains a question of profitability. All that is asked is that new buildings fit in with the existing structures so that modernization occurs in the image of the Old Town. In place of a general requirement to build to a height of five storeys, as applies to the rest of the city centre, here, individual requirements are based on existing structures. But the regulations applied to new builds within the rehabilitation zone change the parameters of the cost-benefit analysis. Height limits, in particular, reduce the expected return and tend to discourage this kind of investment, instead benefitting the rehabilitation or restoration of historic structures. Thus without considerable support from the city via a local tax, known as the *Arbeitsrappen* (work cent), large-scale renovation would not have been possible.[31] The "clean division between the town centre correction areas and the Old Town rehabilitation zones (*Altstadtzonen*)"[32] created the spatial conditions for the ongoing special treatment of the *Altstadt*, which soon became known as the rehabilitation area (*Sanierungsgebiet*).

"Rehabilitation" added a new urban remodelling process to the established procedure of "correction". The business district was "corrected" (which means rebuilt on a larger scale) to meet investors' expectations of a return, while "rehabilitation" of the "protection zones" created an *Altstadt*. It is important to emphasize that in this context, rehabilitation must also be understood as modernization; at heart it is a kind of radical homogenization of the special zones, one that calls for the "aesthetic and sanitary recovery of the [...] Old Town."[33] Homogenization thus occurs on two levels: on the one hand, as modernization in line with the latest sanitary, social and planning standards; on the other, as beautification according to the conservative doctrine of *Heimatschutz*.

---

27 Le Corbusier, Œuvre complète, 1960, 34–39.
28 Wyss, Denkmalpflege in Basel, 1988; Boerlin, Denkmalschutzrecht Basel Stadt, 1974, 27–28.
29 Ratschläge, 3769, 1939, to which was appended the "Decision of the Great Council regarding the establishment of two zone plans for the area of Basel City" (*Grossratsbeschluss betreffend die Festsetzung von zwei Zonenplänen für das Gebiet von Basel-Stadt*).
30 Nertz, Umgang des Baslers, 1991, 106.
31 Meier, Basler Arbeitsrappen, 1984.
32 Comment, Basler Arbeiter-Zeitung, 24 September 1945.
33 Burckhardt, Altstadtsanierung, 1945/1946, 1.

In the name of sanitation and ventilation, built-over yards were cleared out ("*entkernt*") and cleaned up (figs 6, 7).

Figures 6, 7: "Clearing out". Sanitization project for the block Schneidergasse – Nadelberg – Spalenberg – Rosshofgasse, 1945

The old unit of the narrow townhouse was replaced by the more practical division into apartments: "a shower-bath in every home" was the slogan of renovation in line with modern sanitary standards.[34] Social homogenization was a desirable side effect. The so-called reintegration of the slums into the economic cycle often led to major population transfers and the exclusion of marginal groups.

"For sanitary, economic and aesthetic improvement, we particularly welcome the clearing of structures from courtyards and gardens, the creation of space between buildings, the removal of additions and particularly rooftop extensions, height reduction, the improvement of shop fittings, and the removal of intrusive elements" (1945).[35] Modernization thus did not take place behind unchanging façades: rehabilitation meant above all – and the degree to which this was the case is often underestimated – aesthetic homogenization, whose impact direction has remained unbroken to this day. We will give a few examples of this. The first is as unspectacular as it is telling. The house at Petersplatz 3[36] appears to have been remodelled several times, most recently in the 19th century, when it received a new façade (fig. 8). The aim of restoration was to remove all these diverse traces, particularly those of 'copyist' historicism, which had been branded as misguided. The 'French' shutters were replaced by the more 'solid' variety common in Basel, shop windows were removed, as were the cornices: all "urban" ambitions that looked to Paris or Vienna were replaced by Old Basel cosiness (fig. 9). Here now stood a house with a brand-new pitched roof as though it had never been any different, the epitome of 'authentic' Old Basel rectitude, timeless and tasteful: *Heimat*.

---

34   Arbeitsbeschaffungsbehörden, Altstadt heute und morgen, 1945.
35   Materialien zum Sanierungsgesetz, 1945/1956.
36   Meier, Basler Arbeitsrappen, 1984, 214–215.

Figures 8, 9: Basel, Petersplatz 3, 1962 and following restoration in 1963 (Photos Eidenbenz; Hoffmann)

In 1953, the Art Nouveau-influenced façade of a kindergarten built in 1905 apparently became a foreign body in the *Altstadt* quarter and an annoyance (fig. 10).[37] During the restoration the gable decorating the façade was removed. The foreign-looking mansard roof was replaced by an upper storey in keeping with the area, with mullioned windows, wooden external shutters and a pitched roof (fig. 11). In a more affluent time, the ground floor would probably also have been completely 'dehistoricized', as the the heavy rustication of the socle and the round window and door openings now stand in peculiar contrast to the *Heimatschutz* style of the upper storey.

Overall, a major effort was made to create an *Altstadt* that was profitable and tasteful in equal measure. In many cases, several narrow houses were merged and had storeys added so that it is almost impossible to see how they used to look.[38] New buildings also had to comply with regulations for materials, volumes, and roof and window forms. The model for this was a synthetic and largely ahistorical type of house. On many streets, everything 'alien' has been removed. Only one voice is still permitted to speak, a radical *Heimatschutz* style which, using the same details in every case, is supposed to give Basel's Old Town its unmistakable character: mullioned windows with plain frames and wooden shutters are the leitmotif alongside the inevitable dormer windows (fig. 12, 13).

---

37 Meier, Basler Arbeitsrappen, 1984, 435–436.
38 E.g. in the Marktgasse. Cf. Meier, Basler Arbeitsrappen, 1984, 279–280.

Figures 10, 11: Basel, Mittlere Strasse 79, built in 1905, before and after restoration in 1953

Figures, 12, 13: Basel, Spalenvorstadt 28–20, in 1957 and in 1984 (Photos Peter Heman; Eidenbenz)

The rehabilitation of Basel's historic quarters has become increasingly demanding in conservation terms over the years; for instance, when it comes to dealing with the original material substance of the structures. The guiding aesthetic principles, however, remain unchanged to this day.[39] The results of this decades-long urban beautification strategy are homogenized 'historic' quarters that differ considerably from the surrounding business districts and that are perceived, despite their separation in space, as "Basel's Old Town". This is an achievement of urban planning whose benefits are obvious and yet whose ambiguous aspects should not be overlooked. The longing for a present that is progressing toward the future is a very modern experience; so too is the need for a history rooted in the local and particular. It is this particular constellation that feeds the desire for an *"Altstadt"*, which is accorded to the modern city as a *"Heimat* zone".

---

39 Wyss, Basler Spuren, 1987.

7 New York / USA
Zoning in America. Beauty, History and Real Estate

> The Right of Cities to be Beautiful
> (Walter Muir Whitehill, 1966)[1]

New York revels in its image as a city of constant reinvention, of permanent change. Yet this dynamism takes a high toll on even the city's most iconic architecture, as books such as *Lost New York* (1968) have vividly demonstrated.[2] Relatively early in the city's history, before the midpoint of the 19th century, awareness of the disadvantages of the relentless rebuilding was already expressed in terms of complaints at the dominant "pull-down-and-build-over spirit".[3] In fact, New York has been the site of several decisive historic preservation battles: the conflict over Pennsylvania Station (fig.1), which was torn down in 1963, is considered the catalyst for the historic preservation movement in the USA.[4]

Above all, however, it was the struggles around Greenwich Village that took the discussion over heritage conservation in a whole new direction.[5] This was a debate that also had a lasting effect in Germany, decisively influencing prominent authors such as Mitscherlich.[6]

---

1   Muir Whitehill, The Right of Cities, 1966, as a consequence of the famous US-Supreme Court's ruling in Berman v. Parker 1954 (348 U.S. 26); see below.
2   Silver, Lost New York, 1968.
3   Goldstone/Dalrymple, A Guide to New York City, 1976, 17–18.
4   Plosky, Fall and Rise of Pennsylvania Station, 1999.
5   Flint, Wrestling with Moses, 2011.
6   It is no coincidence that Alexander Mitscherlich draws on Jacobs' 1961 *Death and Life* in his 1965 polemic *Die Unwirtlichkeit unserer Städte. Anstiftung zum Unfrieden*.

Figure 1: A catalyst. Demolition of New York's Pennsylvania Station 1965

The Battle of Greenwich Village

The uniqueness of "The Village" is owed to its origins. Established in 1790 as overflow for the city that had outgrown its boundaries, when the surveys to plan New York's legendary grid were undertaken in 1811, Greenwich Village was already too built-up to be assimilated to the meshwork plan of large-scale streets and blocks designed to ensure that the city would conform to a regular plan in the future. This district around and to the north of Washington Square, formerly occupied by people of modest means, soon developed into wealthy middle-class area. Then, as the rich moved further north, it became first a home for immigrants, and then, by the 1920s at the latest, a legendary home for bohemians and artists, keeping its outsider status in the post-war years thanks to an association with political radicalism and the lesbian and and gay rights movement.[7] "The Village remained a bucolic neighbourhood within a bustling metropolis, a quaint sanctuary just a few blocks from the skyscrapers of the world's first vertical city. But Greenwich Village's map had a metaphoric resonance as well: rejecting orderliness, refusing conformity, repelling the grid."[8] In the 1950s, this dense neighbourhood with such a significant place in the city's fabric was supposed to be torn down in a slum clearance and rebuilt on New York's standard gridiron pattern. This was part of the urban renewal programme in whose name the all-powerful New York city planner Robert Moses flattened entire districts to make room for urban expressways and standardised blocks. Some 130 buildings would have been demolished in the redevelopment, and 150 families would have needed to be rehoused.[9] The plan also included extending 5th Avenue to the south, right through Washington Square, whose iconic triumphal arch is one of the Village's most distinctive landmarks – a plan that, in 1958, *The New Yorker's*

---

7   Wetzsteon, Republic of Dreams, 2002; Strausbaugh, The Village, 2013.
8   Wetzsteon, Republic of Dreams, 2002, 4.
9   Flint, Wrestling with Moses, 2011, 62.

influential architecture critic described as "a piece of unqualified vandalism".[10] A deeply committed citizens' initiative arose to save the small-scale, mixed-use artists' district, so steeped in tradition, and it was ultimately successful in preventing the destruction of "The Village" (fig. 2).[11]

Figure 2: Civic resistance. Protest poster ca. 1952/59

In her best-selling opus magnum, *The Death and Life of Great American Cities*,[12] the campaign's most prominent spokesperson, Jane Jacobs (fig. 3), denounced the loss of organically developed urban structures with their heterogeneous mix of uses, stressing the importance of neighbourhoods as part of the living fabric of a city.

Figure 3: Jane Jacobs (Photo 1961)

---

10   Quoted in: Flint, Wrestling with Moses, 2011, 80.
11   Gratz, Authentic Urbanism, 2003.
12   Jacobs, Death and Life, 1961.

The possibility of safeguarding the Village from destruction in the long term was based on new legislative instruments that had been introduced in the USA in the 1950s. It is telling that this did not come about as a result of preservation orders in the narrow sense but rather through zoning regulations. The passing of the NYC Zoning Resolution in 1961 in fact marked a major departure in the history of planning in New York. It divided the city into three different kinds of zoning district: residential, commercial and manufacturing.[13] The NYC Zoning Resolution replaced New York's original zoning laws, which dated from 1916, and with a considerable number of amendments, it remains in force to this day. These regulations granted The Village a certain degree of protection. Yet they said nothing about historic preservation. Conservation activists saw the possibility of adding provisions on "aesthetic zoning" for "historic neighbourhoods", about which there had been much discussion at the time, to the new zoning regulations, using this as a means of establishing protection for building historic urban ensembles. In the end, stipulations concerning what was also known as "historic and aesthetic zoning" (discussed below in greater detail) were not incorporated into the NYC Zoning Resolution; still, a degree of protection had been obtained.[14] The new law was to come into effect after a year's grace period: in the embattled Village, this led to 150,000 planning applications for major projects being received, which would have irreversibly transformed the character of the area.[15] This was prevented by means of an emergency statute, which remained in place until the new zoning laws came into force.

For a truly effective historical preservation law, New York City had to wait until 1965 and the New York City Landmarks Law. It established a body, the New York City Landmarks Preservation Commission, charged with ordering the preservation of landmarks, landmark sites and historic districts.[16] In 1969, Greenwich Village joined Brooklyn heights and SoHo in being designated one of the first historic districts in the city; it was also the largest, covering 60 blocks (figs 4, 5).

New York was far from leading the way in this regard, with 50 municipalities throughout the United States being quicker to establish historic districts. Yet in the decade following the adoption of the NYC Landmark Law, not only were 400 buildings classified as landmarks, 23 additional historic districts were also created.[17] By 2014, their number had expanded to 114 and more than a quarter of properties in Manhattan had become subject to some kind of heritage conservation requirement[18] – on its face, a huge testament to the success of the new preservation instrument.

---

13 For a detailed overview, see Wood, Preserving New York, 2008, 230–233.
14 Website The New York Preservation Archive Project, 1961 New York Zoning Resolution.
15 Whalen, A City Destroying Itself, 1965.
16 Website The New York Preservation Archive Project, New York City Landmarks Law. The law was amended considerably in 1973, allowing the protection of "interior" and "scenic" landmarks and establishing a continuous designation process (ibid).
17 Goldstone/Dalrymple, A Guide to New York City, 1976, 20–21.
18 Ellen/McCabe/Stern, Fifty Years, 2016, 2, 20–21.

Figure 4: Among New York's earliest Historic Districts. Brooklyn Heights ...

Figure 5: ... and SoHo (Photos: imke.sta 2017; Beyond My Ken 2011)

Heritage Conservation as a Planning Tool

During the 1960s, American heritage conservation underwent a systematic reorientation. The decisive milestone was the National Historic Preservation Act of 1966, the first piece of federal legislation on heritage conservation in the history of the United States – and very close in time to the events we are concerned with here. As in the case of the German conservation laws that were passed almost a decade later, the National Historic Preservation Act was conceived of as a way of regulating the rush towards modernisation, a counterweight to the planning boom and the demolitions that had devastated so many urban and rural areas in the post-war era. This departure from an object-oriented heritage conservation – in which buildings were evaluated according to their historical and artistic significance – went hand in hand with a redefinition of conservation as socially relevant planning practice, and in particular with a new approach to urban planning, one that found its clearest expression in the concept of the historic district. This model of heritage management law, which can only be comprehended in terms of the specifically American zoning-law tradition, transformed the field of heritage conservation. In the USA, according to one veteran conservationist with an intimate understanding of these matters, heritage conservation is now above all an "environmentally orientated concept of preservation planning".[19]

During the 1960s, many countries undertook a similar reorientation, seeking to grant heritage conservation a new social relevance.[20] Yet the consistency of the American approach, which we shall examine in further detail below, is certainly impressive. In Germany, by contrast, similar conceptions that emerged just slightly later were blocked, and heritage conservation institutions remain trapped to this day in an "antiquarian" tradition that considers questions of planning and development to be outside its remit. Paradoxically, it is precisely the establishment of the "historic urban ensemble" as a technical term in heritage management law in Germany since the 1970s that has weakened the links between conservation and urban planning, while also discouraging citizen engagement. The "ensemble" as a concept, a loaded term as a result of its origin in the traditionalist, not to say nationalist and *völkisch* concept of *Heimatschutz* (literally "homeland protection"), was seen rather as a means of preventing the erection of 'ugly' modern buildings than a contribution to historically informed urban planning.[21] A momentous step forward in this regard was the declaration of the European Architectural Heritage Year in 1975, an acclaimed event which is generally seen as a watershed in the development of effective heritage conservation.[22] But although this did place urban conservation on the agenda, it did not do so as part of urban development and

---

19 Murtagh, Keeping Time, 2006, 86. William J. Murtagh was active in the field for nearly 50 years, working on the National Register of Historic Places administered by the U.S. Department of the Interior and serving as vice-president of the National Trust for Historic Preservation.
20 Cf., e.g., Baumeister/Bonomo/Schott, Cities Contested, 2017 and particularly the chapter by Vinken, Escaping Modernity, 2017.
21 Breuer, Ensemble, 1989.
22 Eidloth/Ongyerth/Walgern, Grundlagen und Grundsätze, 2013, 13, 32.

planning but merely to 'save' buildings of historical value from a contemporary building and planning practice that was – not always unjustly – seen as 'damaging to the environment'.[23] If institutionalized heritage conservation in Germany could recognize in 1975 that "urban and ensemble heritage conservation has long since grown into the central problem and challenge",[24] then this also partly reflected the wish – shared by a broad section of the public – to offer an alternative to this experience of destruction: namely, another kind of city. In particular the "reformist wing" of heritage conservation, with its stronghold in academia, laid great hopes at that time on the possibility of obliging heritage conservation to accept some social responsibility.[25] "Heritage conservation must be much more than a concern to save certain 'islands of tradition' [...]. Heritage conservation today must encompass the living preservation of the entire urban environment, to the extent that it has its origin in history or its positive urban qualities are obvious to everyone: ambience, mixing, centrality, affordability, building on the human scale, variety of form."[26] These are all arguments that had been made a decade earlier in the USA and had led to a reorientation in that country. In Germany, however, the voices calling for a fundamental reorientation remained in the minority.[27] Leading experts considered fundamentally overhauling urban conservation to be "a side-issue within the discipline at best".[28] The tenor of a statement by the Association of State Conservationists (*Vereinigung der Landesdenkmalpfleger*), which was drafted by the then Cologne-based conservationist Georg Mörsch, is typical in this regard. It criticizes "an eagerness more suited to medical emergencies" in "social aspects of urban planning" and "the tendency to understand and accept heritage conservation largely in relation to issues of urban planning". This paper calls into question the basic legitimacy of heritage conservation "to move in areas that are generally considered from the perspective of urban planning" and underlines the priority of the conventional stand-alone monument.[29] The 'academic' heritage conservation that was mobilized against a "short-lived prevalence in public opinion" is revealed again to be a case of experts defending their territory and rejecting more plural and participatory mechanisms for the appropriation of heritage.[30] Above all, however, the insistence on an object-oriented concept of the historic monument (as a 'historical document') limits the social relevance of heritage conservation to 'rescuing' and managing built heritage. By rejecting a role in forward-looking social planning and development activities, state heritage conservation went down a path, enacted in legislation at state level, that echoes down to the present.

In the 1960s, the United States drew different conclusions from a similar set of crises. The destructive potential of technocentric planning became evident earlier there than in Europe. New York was not the only city whose citizens demanded new regulations to stem the ubiquitous demolition work – demands that were fulfilled at the

---

23   Petzet, Zukunft für unsere Vergangenheit, 1975, 7–8.
24   Gebeßler, Altstadt und Denkmalpflege, 1975, 69.
25   Haindl, Denkmalpflege in der sozialen Verantwortung, 1976.
26   Bode, Unser Lebensraum braucht Schutz, 1975, 38.
27   Vinken, Altstadtkonjunktur und Modernefeindlichkeit, 2020.
28   Schmidt, Einführung in die Denkmalpflege, 2008, 68.
29   Mörsch/Vereinigung der Landesdenkmalpfleger, Denkmalpflege 1975, 1976, 87–89.
30   Vinken, Escaping Modernity, 2017, 169–191.

local level in the *New York City Landmarks Law* und and nationally in the *Preservation Act*. The transformation of heritage conservation into a social 'planning tool' that shifted the focus from historic monuments to city neighbourhoods stands at the end of a long and conflict-riven history. As in Europe, heritage conservation in the USA had for many years centred on historic monuments, above all on what are known as *Heroic Places*, locations associated with the founding fathers and the young nation's first president, George Washington. It was only with the *City Beautiful* movement around the turn of the last century that the the value of the city and the landscape in its entirety was acknowledged: the goal of urban planning now became the harmonic development of the whole, including elements such as parks.[31] Against this background, a growing awareness of the visual qualities of monuments can be observed, alongside their historical significance. This paralleled the work of theorists such as Alois Riegl that became typical of the turn-of-the-century Reform movement in architecture in Europe and the traditionalist, regionalist *Heimatschutz* style. The first legislative measures taken in the USA also show that there was growing recognition of urban ensembles and of spatial qualities beyond the mere preservation of objects. In Boston, for instance, the height of the planned Westminster Chambers building was reduced because it limited the visual impact of Trinity Church.[32] Nonetheless, the path from here to urban conservation was by no means direct, nor was the going always easy.

Zoning Laws: Heritage vs. Private Property

In the USA, private property rights have been a particular obstacle to heritage conservation from the start. They enjoy constitutional protection and cannot easily be overturned even in the public interest. The history of urban conservation can be considered a special case within the debate over how urban development should be subjected to public control, i.e. within the history of legislative regulation of urban planning. In Europe, too, we can see a direct connection between legislative efforts to plan and modernize cities and the creation of historic districts.[33] In Basel, for instance, the 'old town preservation zone' (*Schutzzone Altstadt*) was established via the designation of building zones.[34] There is a dialectical relationship between modernizing cities and 'saving' islands of tradition. Meanwhile, in the USA, the origin of urban conservation in the planning – and modernization – of cities is far more obvious: the origin of the historic district can be traced directly to America's zoning laws, which made it possible to encroach upon that country's private property rights.[35]

The first zoning laws in the USA were enacted in California. Pioneering legislation in the 1880s excluded laundries from certain city districts. This rule, which ostensibly aimed to curb certain emissions, was in fact an instance of contemporary racial

---

31 Holleran, Changeful Times, 1998, 110–134.
32 Holleran, Changeful Times, 1998, 174–182.
33 Vinken, Zone Heimat, 2010.
34 Vinken, Zone Heimat, 2010, 73–80, and the essay on Basel in this volume (Chapter 6).
35 Holleran, Changeful Times, 1998, 245–268.

policy that sought to exclude the Chinese population by undermining their sources of income.[36] Nonetheless, the practice succeeded in establishing purely residential (and privileged) areas, undisturbed by industry and commerce. In Los Angeles in 1909 for instance, the German concept of zoning rings, which aimed at a decreasing intensity of use as one moved from the centre to the outskirts of the city, was adapted and put into practice.[37] The controversy over zoning regulations applying to New York's 5th Avenue from 1916 is also famous.[38] Zoning grew in importance as the symptoms of crisis began to proliferate in many US cities after 1900. The flipside of dynamic urban development was that formerly desirable residential areas often became so-called slums. The 'rehabilitation' of historical areas was often initiated using planning regulations. Functional zoning kept industry at arm's length, height regulations protected against overshadowing, and regulations limiting building density made newbuilds unprofitable, thereby putting the brakes on speculation- and development-driven pressure.[39] In Boston, for instance, zoning was seen early on by both conservationists and city planners explicitly as a potent instrument of heritage preservation: "A direct benefit of Zoning [...] will be the protection and preservation of old historical buildings and sites."[40] Yet even in the conservation-friendly atmosphere of the New Deal, no national legislation was passed granting protection to building ensembles, though, at the local level, zoning laws became *the* mainspring of heritage conservation, which was now shifting from being a question of civil society interest to a matter for planning departments.[41] In short, America's historic districts began as areas subject to special planning regulations, where various approaches to planning were synthesized and optimized over time.[42] Particularly in the early days, this was often undertaken in order to promote tourism. The forerunner here was New Orleans, which had been trying to protect its famous French Quarter (*Vieux Carré*) by means of zoning regulations since 1924.[43] The protection scheme that took force in 1936, however, did not have any legal standing at the federal level. Charleston, South Carolina, had designated the Battery area of the city an 'Old and Historic District' as early as 1931 (fig. 6) – and this very first historic district in the USA was also a direct product of local zoning regulations.[44]

---

36   Holleran, Changeful Times, 1998, 257.
37   Mullin, American Perceptions, 1977.
38   Explored in detail in Toll, Zoned American, 1969, 188–196.
39   Holleran, Changeful Times, 1998, 262–267.
40   Quoted in: Holleran, Changeful Times, 1998, 264, Note 62, with reference to: Boston City Planning Board, Zoning for Boston, 34 (no year given, probably 1915).
41   Murtagh, Keeping Time, 2006, 44–45. On the relationship between zoning and area preservation, cf. Holleran, Changeful Times, 1998, 262.
42   Morrison, Historic Preservation Law, 1974, 16–19; Murtagh, Keeping Time, 2006, 87–98; Holleran, Changeful Times, 1998, 265.
43   Morrison, Historic Preservation Law, 1974, 39; Holleran, Changeful Times, 1998, 265 and Note 65; for details on New Orleans: Ellis, Madame Vieux Carré, 2010, and the essay on New Orleans in this volume (Chapter 16).
44   This began with regulations to ban the building of gas stations in the historic city centre. See Murtagh, Keeping Time, 2006, 89. On Charleston, cf. also Weyeneth, Historic Preservation for a Living City, 2000.

Figure 6: Conservation by means of zoning. King Street, Old Charleston (Photo 1910)

Using zoning regulations to protect historic districts remained a topic of legal conflict. Doubts about whether a general ban on alterations such as that enacted in Charleston could be adequately justified on the grounds of public interest – referred to in the sources as "public benefit", "public welfare" or "general welfare" – continued to be expressed for a considerable period. This is probably why the example of Charleston was emulated only with great hesitation: By 1957 there were only eleven historic districts in the whole of the United States.[45] The key barrier to effective urban conservation remains the high degree of protection afforded to private property, which has constitutional status in the USA.[46] For a long time, the transfer of property to be protected to public ownership (with compensation for the former owners) was considered the most legitimate and culturally acceptable form of heritage conservation, following the example of various privately organized societies and groups since the 19th century.[47] Even efforts to turn entire estates and city districts into open-air museums were ultimately based on this approach and required large sums of cash for their realization. For one project of this kind, Colonial Williamsburg, John D. Rockefeller Jr. bought up city lots in secret before creating a historical city in the style of the 18th century.[48] In Charleston, too, the Revolving Fund established by the city government

---

45   Morrison, Historic Preservation Law, 1974, 16.
46   Morrison, Historic Preservation Law, 1974, 20–34, contains detailed sources for the relevant rulings and sources of law.
47   The very first instance being in 1816, when the city of Philadelphia purchased and restored the Old State House to save it from demolition, cf. Murtagh, Keeping Time, 2006, 12.
48   On Colonial Williamsburg, cf. Greenspan, Creating Colonial Williamsburg, 2009; as well as, more critically, Huxtable, The unreal America, 1997, 12–36. On the – underestimated – impact of America's outdoor museums on heritage conservation, cf. Murtagh, Keeping Time, 2006, 75–85.

for the upkeep of the old town's street fronts followed the logic that ownership is a prerequisite for effective preservation. The fund is used to purchase houses deemed worthy of preserving in order to restore their façades and sell them on at a profit. The new owners are to be responsible for the renovation of the interiors, and the profit on each deal is reinvested in the purchase of additional properties.[49]

The success of this model naturally had its limits, just as it was clear that it is only possible and desirable to turn entire city districts into open-air museums in exceptional circumstances, as in Williamsburg. For the protection of building ensembles to be effective, a way needs to be found to place the interests of heritage conservation above those of property owners.[50] And while zoning laws were able to encroach upon private property rights to a previously unheard-of degree in the name of the public interest, this was generally accomplished in the name of some legally uncontentious reason of security, health or economic efficiency. Restrictions in the name of heritage conservation, by contrast, were counted as merely "special cases of aesthetic control", which did not provide an adequate level of justification in the public interest.[51] 'Beauty alone' was for most judges not a sufficient reason for the public sphere to interfere in private property rights. A turning point only came in 1954, when the US Supreme Court ruled the 'attractiveness' of a municipality is a matter of public interest and that beauty is, alongside health and security, a legitimate goal of city planning.[52] The frequently cited *Right of Cities to Be Beautiful* is at the heart of this ruling, which considers this right to be entirely compatible with the constitutionally protected right to private property.[53] The efforts of conservationists to amend New York City's zoning regulation in 1962 to include a clause on "aesthetic zoning" for "historic neighbourhoods", as discussed above, needs to be seen in terms of this change in legal opinion.

At the national level as well, efforts intensified to establish the institutional basis for heritage conservation, and particularly to include heritage areas. The Preservation Act, which was passed in 1966 and remains central to this day, was strongly influenced by the a conference entitled "On Natural Beauty", which was hosted by Lady Bird Johnson, then the First Lady, at the White House. Published by the conference committee with the support of the National Trust for Historic Preservation, the book *With Heritage So Rich* completed the paradigm shift from an object-oriented, preservationist model of heritage conservation to one that understood itself to have an active role in shaping cities and societies: "If the preservation movement is to be successful, it must go beyond saving bricks and mortar. It must go beyond saving occasional historic houses and opening museums. It must be more than a cult of antiquarians. It must do more than revere a few precious national shrines. It must attempt to give a sense of orientation to our society, using structures and objects of the past to establish values of time and

---

49 Murtagh, Keeping Time, 2006, 94.
50 A detailed discussion may be found in Morrison, Historic Preservation Law, 1974, 16, 31–32, 133; Murtagh, Keeping Time, 2006, 87–98.
51 Cf., e.g., the case of Welch v. Swaseyt, cf. Holleran, Changeful Times, 1998, 265.
52 "It is within the power of the legislature to determine that the community should be beautiful as well as healthy, spacious as well as clean, well-balanced as well as carefully patrolled." US-Supreme Court, Berman v. Parker 1954 (348 U.S. 26). Cf.: US-Supreme Court, United States Reports, 1955, 33.
53 Cf. Morrison, Historic Preservation Law, 1974, 26; as well as the preface to H. D. Bullock (ibid.), IX.

place."[54] The conflicts occurring simultaneously in New York over Greenwich Village show that this redefinition was overdue. The proponents of conserving the "historic" neighbourhood of The Village did consider that it possessed value in purely architectural terms, but were far more focused on its value as an organic, human-scale and heterogeneous habitat – environmental heritage in the broadest sense.

Historic Districts: Environmental Heritage

Against this background, the reorientation of American heritage conservation towards environmental heritage is as necessary as it is logical. The term 'environment', which is capable of encompassing both social aspects ('milieu') and spatial ones (cultural or heritage area), represents a new departure in the practice of heritage conservation. After all, the key aim of the National Historic Preservation Act was to provide a legal basis for heritage conservation as a socially relevant practice. In order to achieve this, it seemed essential to include, beyond architectural 'crown jewels' and conventional stand-alone monuments, both vernacular architecture and the lived environments peculiar to specific population groups. Addressing large entities such as housing developments, street facades and historic town centres amounted to a considerable expansion of responsibility for heritage conservation in terms of both scale and types of object. Above all, however, with the emphasis on historic neighbourhoods, the focus now turned to the groups immediately affected by conservation – owners, residents and users – and to those controlling and influencing it.

'Historic District' became a new category of protected object in the National Register of Historic Places. The term was now defined very generally as a geographically definable area, urban or rural, small or large, "possessing a significant concentration, linkage, or continuity of sites, buildings, structures, and/or objects united by past events or aesthetically by plan or physical development".[55] In concrete terms, the new provisions meant that responsibility for planning and rehabilitation in listed historic areas now lay with the Department of the Interior, and effectively with specialist departments established in each state. The political repercussions were significant. When demolitions are planned as part of large-scale government modernization or infrastructure, the Department of the Interior can intervene at the same level. And while municipalities had previously only been able to apply for grants for renovation projects from the Department of Housing and Urban Renewal, which had a strong focus on wholesale redevelopment (demolishing and rebuilding along new plans), the new law meant that state funds were now also available for restoration and rehabilitation. And finally, in the conflict of interests between demolition and conservation, there was now the possibility of appealing to the Department of the Interior's Advisory Council.

The establishment of historic districts as a zoning tool spelled out how the conservation of heritage areas, which would gain ground in the decades to come, would

---

54 Quoted in: Murtagh, Keeping Time, 2006, 50–51. The full text of the document *With Heritage So Rich* from 1966 is available on the Website Archives and Special Collections Library.
55 Quoted in: Murtagh, Keeping Time, 2006, 88.

be undertaken using the existing planning instruments and spatial planning procedures. Many regulatory instruments were subsequently adopted at state and local level. Historic districts were identified via a process of "selective local zoning". This involved updating the usual zoning restrictions to include specific heritage conservation requirements – a practice sometimes referred to as "preservation-oriented zoning".[56] Values such as identity, continuity and beauty, now legally defined as serving the common good, were established by means of zoning regulations as integral parts of municipal planning procedures.

Historic districts are geographically limited and usually defined in a zoning plan. In New York, according to the legal definition, a historic district must be a "distinct section of the city" with a "special character or a special historical or aesthetic interest or value".[57] In most US states, a permit must be issued before any changes are made to the shape, structure, colour, texture or material of buildings within historic districts. Applications to perform construction or demolition work or to make any amendments that affect the exterior of buildings and are visible to the public within the historic district are considered by a specially convened Board of Architectural Review. Public hearings are generally held, and objections may be lodged; infringements are subject to punishment, which may take the form of fines or imprisonment.[58] The regulations concerning a historic district generally encompass highly detailed "guidelines for design", which also apply to extensions, conversions and new construction. The rules for infills can vary widely – from requiring historical reproductions that match exactly in terms of form and colour, to allowing contemporary adaptations of the original style that are generally required to conform in terms of proportions, typology, materials, etc. A degree of heterogeneity may be allowed; however, elements including buildings, rooms, forms and surfaces are required to be old and "cohesive",[59] a term also open to discussion. As with all listed buildings, renovation work carried out in historic districts since 1976 is tax-deductible up to a certain level. This is conditional on the work fulfilling the criteria of 'rehabilitation'. Rehabilitation is defined in the general sense by the 1965 Venice Charter as the restoration of buildings to usability by means of repair or reconstruction work that preserves those parts and features with architectural and cultural significance. Later additions are to be respected, repairs are to be preferred to replacement.

The protection provided by historic-district status applies, as do similar regulations in Europe, strictly to the exteriors of buildings that are visible in public space. Comfort and modern conveniences are explicitly not considered to be incompatible with the preservation of a 'historic' streetscape. On the contrary, in the USA the repair and restoration of exteriors and the modernization of interiors have always been equally important goals in the rehabilitation of historic neighbourhoods. Already in Charleston, where external preservation work was undertaken "with the aim of maintaining or re-

---

56   Murtagh, Keeping Time, 2006, 87–88.
57   Website Administrative Code of the City of New York, 25-301, 25-302.
58   Morrison, Historic Preservation Law, 1974, 19.
59   Murtagh, Keeping Time, 2006, 92.

capturing the sense [...] of the neighborhood identity in potential jeopardy",[60] internal work focused explicitly on the modernization *(rehabilitation)* of living standards. Such an approach is well known in Europe. The renovation of Basel's Old Town in the 1940s was publicized using the slogan *"Brausebad für alle"* ("A shower-bath in every home");[61] the highly acclaimed reconstruction of Warsaw's old town aimed – in line with Stalin's slogan "national in form, socialist in content" – to combine historical reconstructions with modern comforts such as district heating.[62] Similar approaches were also standard in Germany's post-war reconstruction.

It has been noted how, in Europe, the protection of building ensembles often amounts to no more than an aesthetic concern with the 'character' of a town that easily veers into kitsch picturesqueness. The creation of old towns generally goes hand in hand with a radical formal harmonization and homogenization, which continue to betray the historic ensemble's origins in the traditionalist and conservative *Heimatschutz* movement.[63] Here the boundary becomes blurred between a preservation-focused stance, on the one hand, and a questionable, taste-based preference for vaguely historicizing forms on the other. No systematic distinction is made between restoration and augmentation; archaeological reconstruction and free invention; historically informed, formally sensitive complementary building and the propagation of clichés of all kinds. Or, which is even worse, the annulment of this distinction is, if it is not the explicit aim of the measures, at least passively approved of. There has been a real boom in such urban beautification measures in Germany in recent decades, some of which have involved the collaboration of state and local conservation agencies. Emblematic of this are the many remodelings of Mainz's main square *(Marktplatz)*, each more 'historical' then the last,[64] and, more recently, the many old town clones that have cropped up, whether with or without reconstructions – as in Frankfurt am Main or Potsdam, where the lines between reconstruction and postmodern historicism become completely blurred.[65]

These kinds of phenomena are not unknown in the USA. More strongly than is the case in Europe, the American legislation relies on arguments of aesthetic in addition to historical value. Among other things, the landmark ruling *The Right of Cities to be Beautiful* that was mentioned above dealt with the right of cities to regulate advertising billboards. This had been a favourite topic of German civic beautification ever since the traditionalist *Heimatschutz* movement of the early 20th century – and proves just how strong the interest in a picturesque and harmonic cityscape was in the thought of conservationists regarding the historic districts.[66] As in Europe, so too were architects and conservationists in the New World initially united in rejecting what they identified as a

---

60   Murtagh, Keeping Time, 2006, 88. Emphasis added.
61   Vinken, Zone Heimat, 2010, 80–83, 94.
62   According to Andrzej Tomaszewski in a conversation in 2009. Cf. Stalin, Deviations on the National Question, 1942 (1930), 207.
63   For discussion, see several chapters in Enss/Vinken, Produkt Altstadt, 2016.
64   Karn, Geschichte im Rückwärtsgang, 2008; cf. also Glatz, Rekonstruktion der Rekonstruktion, 2008.
65   Vinken, Unstillbarer Hunger, 2013.
66   Morrison, Historic Preservation Law, 1974, 26–35.

'Victorian' historicism, with its large-scale urban expansion projects; both parties were in favour of urban change and modernization, with the difference being that the conservationists wished to preserve 'islands' of architecture from the preindustrial past as historic districts.[67]

Research in the US has so far paid little attention to this issue. Morrison's expositions made it clear that up to the 1960s, aesthetic arguments were used almost exclusively in applying for conservation status and that efforts to regulate focused almost entirely on formal questions – on questions of design rather than preservation. At its heart, this was a matter of defending against destructive interventions, particularly in the interest of tourism and the economy. Legal disputes over whether regulations affecting the formal and visual characteristics of a neighbourhood should also apply to new buildings, or whether only passive 'protection of the surrounding area' should apply, are instructive. In the French Quarter of New Orleans, the rules on advertising and other elements were affirmed to apply to *all* the buildings in the zone, on the basis that the aim was to protect "the antiquity as a whole"; with antiquity being apparently understood as an aesthetic value or a question of appearance.[68] In 1964, in a legal dispute concerning the historic district of Santa Fé, New Mexico, the court rejected a claim based on the stipulation contained in the 1953 zoning law according to which construction had to exhibit "harmony with adjacent buildings, preservation of historical and characteristic qualities, and conformity to Old Santa Fe Style".[69] To date, theorists continue to stress the need for formal homogeneity: "The overall visual impact gives to the viewer an instinctive sense of locality and place"; "nonconforming intrusions", by contrast, would weaken the sense of identity that is rooted in cohesion and homogeneity.[70] The retention of the (often largely homogeneous) population in the neighbourhoods is also reflected in the goal of retaining – or manufacturing – a formal homogeneity.

In the meantime, however, this attitude has met with resistance. In January 2015, the 'case' of Charleston made it onto the front page of *The New York Times*.[71] The city is prosperous and currently experiencing a building boom, thanks in part to the Boeing plant and to a flourishing tourism sector. The latter is concentrated on the historical centre of Old Charleston, which, as already mentioned, was placed under protection as the US's first historic district in 1931. The city, whose reputation is built on the grandeur of its historical buildings, has trouble reaching consensus on how construction should be carried out in the city. Traditionalists block the erection of modern buildings in the historical centre; modernists complain about the poor quality of the historicizing buildings springing up everywhere: "dull boxes dressed up with the occasional row of columns (fig. 7)"[72].

67　Holleran, Changeful Times, 1998, 271.
68　Morrison, Historic Preservation Law, 1974, 47–48.
69　Morrison, Historic Preservation Law, 1974, 34.
70　Murtagh, Keeping Time, 2006, 92.
71　Fausset, Stately Old Charleston, 2015.
72　Fausset, Stately Old Charleston, 2015, A1, A3.

Figure 7: Real estate advertisement for "Old Charleston Cottages" (Photo 2013)

Since every architectural plan in the historic district must also be approved by the Board of Architectural Review, a culture of historical reproductions has developed. The recent appointment to a consulting role of Andrés Duany, an urban planner and architect from Miami, has revived this controversy. Critics fear that Duany – who is an exponent of New Urbanism and associated with the Florida retirement community of Seaside that served as the set for the dystopian film "The Truman Show" – might be seeking to bring about a 'movie-set uniformity' in Charleston as well.[73]

'Movie-Set Uniformity': Sylvan Terrace, NYC

New York also has streets with an artificial – and quite literal – 'movie-set uniformity' that are listed as historic districts. In some cases, the effort to return to the 'historical' streetscape has gone so far that all traces of more recent development has been erased. Sylvan Terrace, a street of wooden row houses built between 1890 and 1902, was listed as a historic district in the 1970s (fig. 8).[74]

---

73 Fausset, Stately Old Charleston, 2015, A1, A3.
74 As part of the Jumel Terrace Historic District, cf. Website Wikipedia, Jumel Terrace Historic District.

Figure 8: Historic District as film set. Sylvan Terrace, New York (Photo: Sailko 2017)

With state support, the ensemble was returned to its 'historical appearance' – though this only concerned the façades, while the backs of the houses often retained their aluminium facing. A report from *The New York Times* in 1989 noted that the occupants felt the city had left them to take care of the high-maintenance wooden façades themselves and wished they could have the weather-resistant metal facing back. At that point, additional funding was found to restore the buildings to the full glory of their original form in perfect detail. When asked whether it was worth replacing so much material for the sake of recapturing a historical version of these buildings, my American colleagues appeared puzzled. The replica was authentic, they argued, in the sense that it was based on historical evidence. According to Andrew Dolkart, the former Director of Columbia University's renowned Historic Preservation programme, nearly every detail has been preserved on at least one of the houses in situ. And the replacement elements, in contrast to the first campaign, do indeed appear to be of high quality and well crafted. The objection that it might be in the best interest of heritage conservation to be able to distinguish between original features and replicas – as the Venice Charter stipulates – is dismissed as European hair-splitting. The economic success of the restoration certainly speaks for itself: "Nearly all of the properties are back to excellent condition, and homes are selling [in 2011, author's note] for nearly a million each."[75] These rows of houses are seen as a piece of authentic old New York and are a popular set for films: both "Bamboozled" (directed by Spike Lee) and the widely viewed television series "Boardwalk Empire" were filmed here. However, comments make it clear that the flawless, stage-set perfection of the reconstructions also undermines the intention of showing an authentic piece of atmospheric old New York. As one worker on a filmset noted in 2011 with irritation "The rows of houses and

---

75   Website Scouting New York, Sylvan Terrace.

cobblestone street are so uniform and perfectly preserved that I'd assumed the whole thing was set aside specifically for film shoots. I had no idea people still lived there."[76]

The enthusiasm for such antiseptically 'original' historical islands is particularly bizarre in a city where many cityscapes can reveal a deeply impressive richness of historical detail that is hard to find in European metropolises. In Brooklyn, that is true of both listed and unlisted neighbourhoods. However, even there, architectural reproductions are now spreading, with the proliferation of more or less successful imitations of the tightly packed brownstones that are so beloved of residents and students of architecture alike. It is undeniable that even in New York's historic districts, a kind of heritage conservation is often favoured that aims at the most complete and homogeneous reproduction of 'historical' conditions. Less value is placed on the distinction between reproduction and original than on the use of the 'right' materials and traditional manufacturing techniques. As long as the – tax-deductible – expense is balanced by the properties' maintaining or increasing their value, the formula appears to be a sustainable basis for the interests of conservationists to meet those of the owners. Especially the argument that established neighbourhoods should be maintained in a stable form (including social stability) and that large-scale new building should be avoided, unites a large cross-section of the population.

Historic Districts and Gentrification

However, this situation can also be described in a less sympathetic way. The architecture critic Ada Louise Huxtable was one of the founding figures of heritage conservation in New York, which emerged from civic protest. Already in 1997, she noted that "preservation, development, and real estate have become a very comfortable ménage à trois".[77] It is a triangular relationship that appears above all to produce one thing: social homogenization and isolation. This is a significant shift in perception, as earlier authors had ascribed the success of the historic districts, particularly in New York, to "belonging", i.e. to continuity and identity in a time of acceleration.[78] Greenwich Village was and still is celebrated as a case where committed citizens successfully fought back against remote urban grand planning, a triumph of the local and the grass roots, a successful effort to save the neighbourhood as a mixed, diverse, 'living' entity from the monotony of the drawing-board. This narrative, which the resistance movement around Jane Jacobs promoted so successfully, is even cited in the formal justification for the conservation status of Greenwich Village. For Harmon H. Goldstone, the director of the LPC for many years, the Village is the very model of "diversity in architecture und variety in social structure". And today, the Greenwich Village Society for Historic Preservation (GVSHP) still has the goal to maintain the "sense of place and human scale that define

---

76 Website Scouting New York, Sylvan Terrace.
77 Huxtable, The unreal America, 1997, 32.
78 Goldstone/Dalrymple, A Guide to New York City, 1976, 23.

the Village's unique community".[79] But the critical voices are multiplying. Many authors have become critical of Jane Jacob's legacy and see the protection of neighbourhoods as historic districts as an expression of the group self-interest of a privileged class (fig. 9).

Figure 9: *The collective egocentrism of privileged classes? Brownstones in Park Slope Historic District, Brooklyn (Photo 2016)*

The sociologist Sharon Zukin sees a direct connection between the authenticity claimed by the Village (and confirmed by its listing as a historic district) and the neighbourhood's rapid gentrification. According to Zukin, Jane Jacobs discovered that the quality of life of public space depends on diversity and density; but in her inability to recognize that authenticity is a social product, she developed an idyllic image of small-town life in the big city, perpetuating the idealized image of the New York block as a microcosmos of social diversity; she was unaware that she was following an aesthetic of gentrification, a rhetoric of authenticity that is significantly responsible for the city's rising property prices:[80] "Jacobs's values – the small blocks, the cobblestone streets, the sense of local identity in old neighbourhoods – became the gentrifiers' ideal".[81]

Looking back on the story of The Village, the picture that emerges is indeed complex. In many respects, The Village remains a single entity and a space apart within the city. The LGBTQ community still has a strong presence and Christopher Street has become a place of pilgrimage. The annual jazz festival reanimates many of the once-pulsating alternative ('Off') performance spaces, which are nonetheless in decline. The image of diversity is barely sustainable: In the heart of the city, those who can afford it find in the Village a privileged life of walkable distances in a historical oasis built on a

---

79 Website Greenwich Village Society for Preservation. Relevant details may be found in the tabs "About Us" and "Resources/Village History" (Thanks to Sophie Stackmann).
80 Zukin, Naked City, 2009, 17–18.
81 Zukin in an interview with the New York Times in 2010. Cf. Powell, Contrarian's Lament, 2010.

human scale, a kind of preserve: Greenwich Village is a prime example of turbo-gentrification, extreme even for Manhattan.[82] According to a 2014 survey by Forbes, the four ZIP code areas that constitute the Village are the wealthiest in the United States,[83] with average property prices of $23,000 US per square metre.[84] Naturally, Madonna and Bob Dylan are among those who live here. A key player in the property sector is New York University, one of the biggest landowners in the city. Detailed empirical studies show that while the Village may be an extreme case, it is far from unique. Similar developments can be observed with regard to many of New York's protected areas, including the above-mentioned historic districts of SoHo[85] and Brooklyn Heights.[86] Residents of New York's historic districts enjoy higher incomes and larger apartments than most of the city's residents, and they also have higher levels of educational attainment – and are very likely to be "non-Hispanic whites".[87]

If conservationists are now quick to point out that property values have, without exception, risen in historic districts, this message remains deeply ambivalent.[88] What is often overlooked here is that this development is, in a certain regard, inevitable, given the way area conservation is based on zoning regulations. Zoning regulations in the USA have always aimed at social homogenization and the stabilization of property prices. When laws for area conservation were being passed in the 1960s, zoning laws were an incredibly controversial topic.[89] In a phase of enormous social upheaval (and class- and race-based conflict), suburbia was the locus where hopes and fears of a loss of status came together. Zoning was the chosen means for keeping property prices stable. Through it, the social homogeneity of neighbourhoods was ensured and the incursion of 'undesirable' segments of the population could be hindered (as had already been achieved with the earliest zoning rules in cities such as Los Angeles, see above). One means by which this was carried out was the definition of minimum lot sizes in a given zone, in order to keep low-income people out of established neighbourhoods. Increasing mobility and uncontrolled growth in cities were thereby translated into a concrete experience that directly affected the majority of people. Zoning was widely discussed, including on the front pages or covers of *The New York Times*, *Wall Street Journal*, *Look and Harper's*, and even on popular entertainment shows on television.[90] Similar debates were also soon held in the urban centres, where the aim was to use zoning regulations to address problems such as urban decay and the decline of traditional residential areas into slums. Alongside rules for the density and height of new buildings, the acquisition of historic district status could lead to a significant level of gentrification in an area; in other words, to rising property values). It cannot be denied that in the USA, zoning

---

82   Sternbergh, Embers of Gentrification, 2007.
83   Carlyle, Most Expensive ZIP Codes, 2014.
84   Website Wikipedia, Greenwich Village, which references in particular the real estate website trulia.com.
85   Shkuda, Lofts of SoHo, 2016; Petrus, From Gritty to Chic, 2003, 52.
86   Osman, Invention of Brooklyn Brownstone, 2001.
87   For extensive figures and statistics: Ellen/McCabe/Stern, Fifty Years, 2016.
88   Murtagh, Keeping Time, 2006, 94.
89   Toll, Zoned American, 1969, 197.
90   Toll, Zoned American, 1969, 294–295.

regulations – an instrument created in the public interest, in the service of health and security – has in boom times largely served the interests of the real-estate market – and private property owners.

Islands of the Blessed?

This is all too evident in NYC, where the real-estate market is prone to frequent overheating. The historic districts listed in the first decade[91] after the NYC Landmark Preservation Commission was established in 1965 included many exquisite properties: they include MacDougal-Sullivan Gardens in the South Village (fig. 10), built from 1844–50 around a common garden in the Greek revival style and home to Bob Dylan and Richard Gere, among others; Treadwell Farm on the Upper East Side, where Kim Novak, Montgomery Clift, Eleanor Roosevelt and Paul Gallico have come and gone; and Turtle Bay Gardens, another reform-driven project of the 1920s with a common garden, where in 2010 Katharine Hepburn's old apartment was available to rent for $27,500 per month.[92]

Figure 10: Island of the blessed. MacDougal-Sullivan Gardens (Photo 2016)

Such 'islands of the blessed' have sprung up in many parts of Manhattan, where the protection of unspoiled, human-scale urban architecture has created a rare and thus highly desirable situation: historical single-family residences with arcadian, semi-private parks designed on the model of historical gardens, and interiors that allow free rein to the individual imagination of total luxury: astronomical prices and glamour guaranteed. The *ménage à trois* of heritage conservation, urban development and the

---

91 For details of the first historic districts listed in New York, cf. Goldstone/Dalrymple, A Guide to New York City, 1976. Comprehensive details are available on the Website New York City's Historic Districts Council.
92 Taylor, Hepburn's former brownstone, 2010, or Website Curbed New York, Hepburn's Turtle Bay House.

property market that Huxtable condemned here reaches truly pornographic levels. The goal of making heritage conservation socially relevant again that was pursued by the reformers of the 1960s achieved a paradoxical fulfilment in some places: by reinforcing social divisions.

The broad picture is a very heterogeneous one. It is indisputable that New York districts like the Village and SoHo only avoided the devastation of large-scale redevelopment thanks to being placed under protection.[93] Rehabilitation of existing fabric means that these areas can be experienced as 'historic' and organically developed. However, the popularity they owe to their positive qualities has also done long-term damage to their established social structures by ushering in turbo-gentrification.[94] At the same time however, in terms of heritage conservation, the historic districts represent enormous achievements. For one thing, listing such an area requires an enormous effort of inventorization. The precise recording of formal and historical details represents a major increase in our store of knowledge, particularly since it also encompasses the history of usage and social structure as well as architectural typology and patterns of urban development. In general, this work of researching and recording is privately financed, at least in part. A further factor, the influence of which cannot be exaggerated, must be appended to this argument. On the whole, the listing of a historic district is initiated by its residents or by private interest groups, and therefore goes hand in hand with significant civic commitment.[95] This complex and at times protracted process involving so many actors provides an – apparently – highly effective platform for articulating and negotiating among all these different interests – economic, cultural and social. The involvement of municipal planning authorities ensures that the requirements of heritage conservation are discussed broadly and have a permanent presence in local government bureaucracies. Overall, historic districts appear to have ensured that conservation issues, which were for too long the preserve of a tiny and highly specialized elite, now reach a wider public. Some of the structural weaknesses of German heritage conservation, such as the distinction between conservation and development planning responsibilities, could be overcome in this way. New York has found sustainable ways both to integrate heritage concerns into other vital fields of urban development and to involve residents in the assessment of value – so often called for but so seldom pursued with any seriousness. The city, the residential district, the village appear here as habitats in which diverse interests are gathered, and in which all questions of their future direction are naturally linked with issues of identity, historical and social character, heritage and history.

It is certainly incontestable that in today's increasingly diverse society, effective and vital approaches to heritage that involve a diverse range of voices are particularly important.[96] Here, the USA has been a trailblazer, thanks in part to the multicultural understanding of heritage that is now dominant there. If the US heritage movement

---

93   Flint, Wrestling with Moses, 2011.
94   Zukin, Naked City, 2009; see also many media pieces, such as Fisher, Tyranny of Nostalgia, 2015.
95   The book by Schmickle, Politics of Historic Districts, 2007, is very illuminating here.
96   Vinken, Pranger von Bahia, 2015.

has shifted from a concern with museum-quality landmarks to become a neighbourhood-based planning process which works hand in hand with a productive mass movement and is planning-, profit- and process-oriented,[97] then this should be welcomed from the point of view of heritage conservation. Already in the 1980s, James Marston Fitch (Columbia University) saw meaningful heritage conservation not as a one-time act of rescue, but as a process which he defined as "curatorial management of the Built World".[98] For all the contradictions of these 'special zones', New York's historic districts represent a culturally acceptable instrument that can manage this transformation – offering scope in which public negotiations over the value of heritage can be fruitfully carried out.

---

97 Murtagh, Keeping Time, 2006, 98.
98 Fitch, Curatorial Management, 1982.

8 Düsseldorf / Germany
Size Matters. Modern Megastructures as Heritage

> The fact that something has grown old now gives rise to the demand that it be made immortal
>
> *(Friedrich Nietzsche)*[1]

The question of how to deal with the large buildings and megastructures of modernism is one that increasingly both urban conservationists and the general public. These 'giants' appear to pose a new challenge for institutions charged with preserving the built environment: On the one hand, they go against the ideal image of the human-scale, mixed-use city that has been re-established as the urban ideal since the 1970s, partly as a result of the work of just such conservationists.[2] Civic initiatives and conservationists vehemently opposed the monofunctional and giganticist planning of the 1960s and 70s, seeking to banish such 'inhospitability' (*Unwirtlichkeit*) from the urban environment and to restore quality of life.[3] European Architectural Heritage Year in 1975 was an important step towards re-establishing the positive values of the historical city with its liveability and traditional use of space in the public consciousness.[4] On the other hand, attitudes towards the buildings of post-war modernism have also changed in recent years. Outside architectural circles, a growing number of people agree that many of the modern 'giants' possess architectural merit and aesthetic value of their own. This supports the aim of conservationists who seek to place a representative selection of buildings from the modernist period under protection; especially since this period is increasingly seen as a completed historical epoch. After all, conservationists now more than ever see it as their task to represent the architectural canon as completely as possible in their lists. Today it is simply the turn of high modernism and brutalism – this is an international phenomenon.[5]

---

1 Nietzsche, Untimely Mediations, 1997 (1873–1876), 75.
2 Vinken, Im Namen der Altstadt, 2016.
3 Mitscherlich, Unwirtlichkeit unserer Städte, 1965.
4 Cf. several chapters in Falser/Lipp, A Future for Our Past, 2015.
5 Glendinning, Postwar Mass Housing, 2008; Escherich, Denkmal Ost-Moderne, 2012/2016.

Figure 1: Lübeck, view from St. Peter's Church (Photo: M. Brix 2014)

The view from St Peter's church in Lubeck (fig. 1) makes abundantly clear, however, that this re-evaluation reveals a fundamental dilemma. This is not merely a matter of dealing with shifting tastes; there is more at stake here than an expansion of the architectural canon. The dilemma of this re-evaluation in the field of conservation lies in the fact that now, buildings are to come under protection which have often had lasting negative and destructive effects on the substance of the city and were often constructed in the face of vehement opposition on the part of the citizenry. Many of the major modernist projects continue to stand quite literally in the way of liveable urban development; they can have a lasting detrimental effect on civic spaces and a negative influence on other buildings and even on protected monuments. Modern megastructures are coming down in part because cities are seeking to reshape and upgrade the space they have available.

An instructive example of this trend is the demolition of the Technical Town Hall (*Technisches Rathaus*) in Frankfurt am Main (fig. 2). Erected in 1972–74 to a design by Bartsch, Thürwächter und Weber, whose winning proposal in 1963 had seen off prominent competitors such as Ernst May, Walter Gropius, Hans Scharoun and Arne Jacobsen,[6] this controversial project, with its rather forbidding 'brutalist' raw concrete surfaces, went ahead in the face of considerable public protests, which were supported by Frankfurt's active squatter movement.

---

6   Müller-Raemisch, Frankfurt am Main, 1998, 56–64, 342–345.

Figure 2: Frankfurt, "Technisches Rathaus" and Dom (Photo: S. Suchanek 2010)

Five houses had to be demolished to make way for the modern Town Hall, one of which dated back to the 16th century. In contrast to some of the high-rises that define Frankfurt's famous skyline, the *Technisches Rathaus* never enjoyed much popularity in the city. It should be noted, however, that the height of the building, which was considered excessive given its historical setting, as well as the fortress-like solidity of the structure were partly the consequence of alterations and expansions to the plans undertaken in 1969 to meet increased requirements for floor space. Consequently, the decision made in 2005 to demolish the building did not initially cause much of a stir. Only when the first competition to design its replacement produced a series of unimaginative and arbitrary mall-like structures did the debate take an unexpected turn. The civic protest movement kindled by the Society of Friends of the City of Frankfurt (formerly Friends of the Old Town: *Altstadtfreunde*), the city's marketing department and an association of local entrepreneurs, and championed politically by the centre-right Christian Democratic Union party, called for the 'recreation' of the Old Town that had been burnt down in 1945.

Erected on the site of the *Technisches Rathaus*, the project known as the *DomRömer-Areal* (fig. 3), a laboratory-generated piece of Old Town, pervaded with reconstructions and authenticated through the inclusion of architectural spolia, has just (2018) been completed.[7] It is a clone of dubious worth, though one that is likely capable of commanding the support of a majority, while barely anyone mourns the fallen giant.

---

7   Cf. Vinken, Geschichte wird gemacht, 2018, and the essay on Frankfurt in this volume (Chapter 12).

Figure 3: Frankfurt, restored Hühnermarkt (Photo: Simsalabimbam 2018)

Düsseldorf's 'Millipede'

The fate of the modern Town Hall in Frankfurt can be contrasted to the case of Düsseldorf's *Tausendfüßler* ('Millipede') (fig. 4). The elevated roadway built in the 1960s between Hofgarten, a public park, and the Dreischeibenhaus high-rise was part of the effort to rebuild Düsseldorf as a modern, car-friendly city.[8]

Figure 4: Düsseldorf, 'Millipede', (Photo: Heinz Gräf 1961)

The project aimed to break up and reorganize traffic flows and, thanks to its stylish design, became a symbol of the city. In the words of the cabaret artist Jürgen Becker, "the

---

8   Droste/Fischer, Düsseldorfer Tausendfüßler, 2015; cf. also Sterl, Tausendfüßler in Düsseldorf, 2015.

Millipede gave the city a shot of roller-coaster".[9] Though the elevated roadway has been protected as a stand-alone monument since 1993, the decision to demolish it was taken in 2012 when it was decided to remodel the central area of the city between Hofgarten and Königsallee as part of the project to construct Daniel Libeskind's new *Kö-Bogen* complex (fig. 5).

Figure 5: *Düsseldorf, "Kö-Bogen" complex (Photo: FSWLA Landschaftsarchitektur GmbH 2013)*

Unlike in the case of the *Technisches Rathaus*, not only did Hessen's state office for the preservation of monuments (*Hessisches Landesamt für Denkmalpflege*) lodge an objection, there were also unexpectedly loud protests and campaigns by citizens in favour of keeping this particular giant, and these ultimately contributed to the election defeat of the city's long-serving mayor. This is all the more astonishing as the plans to which the Millipede fell victim represented a significant revision of the city's post-war planning mistakes and aimed at 'repairing' the city, drawing on a vision of the historical qualities of city centre spaces. Specifically, the connection between Königsallee and the Hofgarten park that was destroyed in the course of post-war reconstruction was to be restored, while Hofgartenstraße was to be rebuilt on a new, curved plan, based on historical precedent. Removing traffic in this area by means of tunnels enabled a redefinition of urban space, as already achieved at the Rheinpromenade. In Düsseldorf as in Frankfurt, a modernist 'giant' was felled in the name of retrospective planning that sought a qualitative restoration of urban life. Lanes of traffic were replaced by urban spaces where people would want to spend time. In Frankfurt, a brutalist block was, without a word of complaint, replaced by a pathetic clone of an old town, while in Düsseldorf, the citizens took to the barricades to oppose the 'repair' of their city and the

---

9   Jürgen Becker on 16 January 2013 in the Neue Ruhr Zeitung, quoted in: Website Düsseldorf Blog, Ein Schuss Achterbahn.

reduction of traffic volume, and to save an elevated expressway. What is impossible to overlook is that modern megastructures – regardless of the quality of the planning that is carried out – often represent a major challenge for the development of liveable cities.

Modernization and Destruction: Giants in the City

When this topic is placed in a broad historical context, it is easy to show that the conflict between megastructures and urban development is nothing new, but it also becomes clear that the fronts have now shifted. The struggle used to be between the modernisers and the conservationists. Paris only became the modern city we know, the capital of the 19th century, as a result of Haussmann's radical reshaping. This was necessary for the creation of effective large-scale systems of order and the series of squares connected by boulevards that became the model for city planners around the world – though many contemporaries mourned the loss of *Vieux Paris*. "The old Paris is gone" wrote Baudelaire in an oft-cited section of *Les fleurs du mal* in 1857: "the form a city takes more quickly shifts, alas, than does the mortal heart".[10] The urban metropolis in particular seems to be inherently dynamic in its development; for modern urban planning, the phenomenon of the city itself is inescapably bound up with continual and wide-reaching destruction.

Le Corbusier already made this explicit, advising that 'surgery', cutting deeply, was necessary for the modernization of the city.[11] Accordingly, in 1925, he proposed replacing the centre of Paris with a monostructural megacity (fig. 6). In line with the principles of his *Ville Contemporaine*, the first ever 'Fordist' design for a city, which was based on a concept of functional zones for diverse activities and a radical reduction in density, the chaotic patchwork of central Paris was to give way to an urban landscape cut through by highways and studded with tower blocks.[12]

Although the functionality of the structure, which was provocatively named after a make of car, was barely called into question, critics focused on what they considered the destruction of the character and identity of the city. Le Corbusier gave a remarkable reply: Change, and even destruction, he insisted, belonged to the history of the city and were constitutive of its progress. The *Plan Voisin* was part of a tradition of great architectural transformations, among which we could already count the Louvre, the Arc de Triomphe and the Eiffel Tower: "That is still Paris" pleaded the caption of an accompanying sketch (fig. 7).[13] The architect prophesied shrewdly that his megastructures would one day be considered aspects of the identity of the global metropolis that is Paris. The *Plan Voisin* would today certainly have been one of those giants born out of destruc-

---

10 Baudelaire, The Flowers of Evil, 1998 (1857), 175.
11 Vinken, Ort und Bahn, 2008, and the essay on *The Crises of the Modern City* in this volume (Chapter 2).
12 On *Ville Voisin*, cf. Le Corbusier, The City of To-morrow, 1987 (1925), 277–289; Le Corbusier, Precisions on the present State, 2015 (1930), 169–214.
13 Le Corbusier, Precisions on the present State, 2015 (1930), 169–214.

tion over which splendid arguments would be exchanged regarding their worthiness for consideration as historic monuments.

Figure 6: "Ville Voisin", Le Corbusier 1925

Figure 7: In the tradition of great architectural transformations? "That is still Paris!", Le Corbusier 1930

Modernization as a consequence of disruptions of scale and structural change, brutality and surgery: Le Corbusier almost enthusiastically associated himself with this tradition – and for many he remains the incarnation of a destructive and ignorant planning mania. In this connection, it should not be forgotten that the earth-shattering experience of aerial bombardment had not stopped most city planners from seeing in the large-scale destruction of so many cities a unique opportunity.[14] And in retrospect it is just as clear that, since the 1960s, modern conservation has found its place in the heart of society by opposing modernist planning and outsized megaprojects and setting itself up as a brave and cunning David in an eternal struggle with the destructive 'giants'.

No better symbol for this struggle between David and Goliath can be found than New York, a city that was long in thrall to modernist planning and yet can also be considered something like the cradle of urban conservation as a civic movement.[15] The conflict crystalized in the 1960s in two prominent protagonists who appeared each to embody one side of thinking about urban planning. On the one side, there is Robert Moses, whose large-scale infrastructure plans and modernization programmes make him something like the Haussmann of New York and of the 20th century.[16] His key opponent was Jane Jacobs, the icon of civic action and advocate of a liveable city, who brought about a transformation in city planning, who invented the use of civic engagement as a weapon, and whose popular book *The Death and Life of Great American Cities*[17] was an early statement of a foundational critique of modernist urban planning policy. The Lower Manhattan Expressway was a key part of Moses' urban highway network that was to cut through Greenwich Village, SoHo and Little Italy. To build it, the heart of alternative and activist New York would have been laid waste and largely rebuilt in the name of 'slum clearance'. Following persistent protests, the city government finally shelved the project in 1964. The move marked a major shift in planning policy – and in conservation: today, the Village and SoHo are Manhattan's largest 'historic districts' by area.[18] Car-friendly, large-scale planning vs. neighbourhoods – that is the same basic conflict that led to the emergence of a conservation movement in Europe.[19] The small-scale, mixed-use city with its organic structures is defended against the hostile giants. In Germany, this conflict has flared up in Frankfurt's Westend, in the Kreuzberg neighbourhood of Berlin, and in Hanover's List district, as well as many other historic areas, particularly those developed during the Wilhelmine period.

Role Reversal: Canon and Heritage

These days, the established roles have changed. To some degree they have even swapped places. Since the dawn of postmodernism, architects and urban planners have developed an interest in the positive qualities of historic architecture. Authors such as Aldo Rossi and Kevin Lynch have brought about a decisive shift in thinking, which is reflected in planning approaches such as critical reconstruction, 'urban repair', and lo-

---

14   Vinken, Zone Heimat, 2010, 124.
15   Gratz, Battle for Gotham, 2010; Flint, Wrestling with Moses, 2011.
16   Ballon/Jackson, Robert Moses and the Modern City, 2007.
17   Jacobs, Death and Life, 1961.
18   Cf. also the essay on New York in this volume (Chapter 7).
19   Vinken, Escaping Modernity, 2017.

cation-sensitive building. The International Building Exhibition Berlin (*IBA Berlin*) 1987 even created a separate 'Old Town' section (*IBA Alt*), which foregrounded the effectiveness of minimal intervention, rehabilitation and revitalisation in place of large-scale planning. In the meantime, German cities including Dresden, Hildesheim, Frankfurt and Potsdam have been outdoing each other in the creation of 'islands of tradition'.[20]

By contrast, conservationists have come to embrace the legacy of radical modernism. After resistance to late modernism's faith in planning culminated in European Architectural Heritage Year in 1975, we have now reached the point predicted by Le Corbusier, at which brutalism and satellite towns, multi-storey carparks and multi-lane expressways – in short, Goliath's legacy – are considered in terms of their heritage value. In a reversal of roles, conservationists are now placing under protection precisely those forms of architecture and structure that are considered the incarnation of state and capitalist arrogance, products of real-estate speculation and planning mania. But if this hostile Goliath against whom David had forged his identity has now mutated into a friendly Gulliver, what happens to David himself?

As I see it, this debate concerns more than merely the normal and predictable expansion of the stock of buildings that are subject to conservation to include an additional epoch. Pressure in this direction is created by a discipline of conservation that understands itself to be a (historical) science. From this perspective, listed structures should portray each past period as fully as possible and provide a base of sources broad enough to enable us to trace all of the various branchings of architectural history. By this logic, a heritage site, conservation site or monument is above all a witness or a source; every design task, every type of building is evidence for one or another epoch and its artistic, historical and social practices and preferences. Of course, urban conservationists have to consider the value and quality of the buildings and structures of the late 20th century – as, thankfully, is now being done again with renewed seriousness. But when it comes to evaluating the giants, it has also become clear that inventorization has to be more than merely a positivistic reflection of architectural history. If built heritage is taken seriously as an identity-forming anchor for the self-reassurance of a society, it becomes clear that this is not a purpose that can be fulfilled using the scientific categories applied by specialist authorities. Cultural heritage and its value can be captured only incompletely using the categories of History and Art History; heritage is more, it is the result of complex societal negotiation processes that are, at heart, processes of acknowledgement, adoption and appropriation.[21]

Processes of Deliberation and Negotiation

Modern megastructures reveal the problems with defining heritage value in a one-dimensional way in terms of historical and scientific criteria more clearly than do most types of monument. The question of historical (local-historical, architectural-historical, technological-historical) value (like 'oldest elevated railway bridge'; 'characteristic

---

20 Vinken, Im Namen der Altstadt, 2016. Cf. also the essay on Frankfurt in this volume (Chapter 12).
21 Franz/Vinken, Monuments – Values – Assessment, 2014.

example of brutalism'; 'early steel-frame building'; 'first skyscraper', 'technologically innovative', etc.) is revealed here to be simply inadequate. The question of what should be acknowledged as heritage from a period whose legacy often involves conflicts of use and frequently turns out to have lingering structural-spatial problems needs to be negotiated on a case-by-case basis in a more widely ranging debate with broader participation. This is likely to involve a discussion of what values are associated with each building beyond its strictly historical significance. Düsseldorfers clearly embraced their elevated highway. But that is not enough by itself to justify its preservation. Even if the structure's value as a historical object is indisputable, even though many citizens are willing to campaign for its preservation, the 'giants' pose certain questions in a more urgent way than do other buildings, simply on account of their scale (fig. 8).[22]

Figure 8: Limiting urban life? 'Millipede' overshadowing public space in Düsseldorf

Often destructive as a result of their monopolization of space, 'large' structures raise questions such as: How are they integrated in urban spaces? Can they even be so integrated? Who and what do they stand in the way of? What qualitative features of urban life do they block, damage or limit?

In Düsseldorf, even the defenders of the Millipede appear to have been surprised at the positive effects its demolition had on the urban space. Not only can the long-destroyed link between the City and Hofgarten park be enjoyed once more, but the new spaces that have opened up have revealed a number of historical monuments that had literally been overshadowed by the elevated highway, including St John's church, which has only been able to exert the effect it was intended to have on the cityscape by its 19th century architects since the Millipede's demolition (fig. 9).

---

22 The significance of scale in architecture has been discussed with great insight by Rem Koolhaas, cf. Koolhaas/Mau, S, M, L, XL, 1995.

Figure 9: Düsseldorf, Demolition of the 'Millipede' next to St. John's Church (Photo: Perlgrau 2013)

This is not a plea to condemn, reject or exclude the legacy of modernism. It is a plea to orient our gaze not towards the object, the giant, but rather to its potentials and problems in terms of space and urban planning. Our goal cannot be to retrospectively memorialize and legitimize structures that have come to be recognized as dead ends in the history of architecture and of urbanism. Only in a few exceptional cases will something that has tangibly harmed the development and quality of life of a city become a part of cultural heritage. At a fundamental level, conservation needs to open itself to qualities and values beyond academic historical categorization and learn to listen to and respect voices from outside its own field. Many people will want to join discussions on the quality of the urban environment, because these are fundamentally matters of quality of life and of sustainability, to which a living heritage ultimately contributes.

Today, the logic of the representative and illustrative canon that guided the approach to inventarization established in the 19th century has reached the limits of its applicability. Establishing a canon always entails value judgements. Heritage is not merely a programmable and objectivizable activity (a simple 'handing on'). To inherit means to accept, to select, to adopt. An unwelcome legacy is something you can fight for, if you can persuade others of its specific value and potential. This reveals once again the dilemma of state conservation programmes, which have to rest on a solid legal basis and work according to rational, scientific criteria – in a field that draws its vitality from emotion and the collective generation of meaning, from the work of memory.

Doing Tradition. Heritage Politics and Identity-Building

9 Cologne / Germany[1]
Islands of Tradition. Heritage Politics from the Nazi Era to Postwar Reconstruction

> Kölle bliev Kölle
> Cologne must remain Cologne
> *(local saying)*

Due to the extensive destruction of German cities in World War II, an examination of their present-day appearance is largely confronted with the products of postwar urban planning and architecture. Even where the rebuilding effort aimed to establish continuity and the decision was made to reconstruct the prewar appearance of a city, the majority of the buildings are substantially new. We may at most distinguish between cities that exemplify a new beginning in urban planning (such as Mainz, Frankfurt, and Hannover) and others that sought to preserve the historic townscape (such as Munich and Nuremberg).[2] In Germany's so-called 'Old Towns' (*Altstädte*), unlike in Italy's, the 'artificial' is accordingly the default register, although many people now prefer to remain unaware of this artificiality. In the following study of continuity in the German rebuilding effort, the focus is on continuities in the guiding principles of urban planning and the conceptions of modernization that shaped the ways planners engaged with historic city centers from the 1920s and 1930s through to the postwar era. As we will see, the conceptions elaborated by Germany's historic preservationists, too, show a striking degree of constancy from the 1920s through the Nazi era to the reconstruction period.

Modernization and the Question of Identity

The war constitutes a watershed moment in the history of Germany's cities; the guiding principles of urban planning, however, evince a great deal of continuity. In a larger

---

1 Translation from the German by Gerrit Jackson with assistance from Johanna Blokker.
2 See Beyme, Der Wiederaufbau, 1987, 175–182; Beseler/Gutschow, Kriegsschicksale Deutscher Architektur, 1988, XLIX–LXV.

historical perspective, the rebuilding effort – which is to say, the phase of urban construction that largely defined the present appearance of German cities – may be described as part of the great conflict surrounding the issue of modernization that began in the 19th century and was largely fought on the battlefield of the European city.[3] The competing urbanistic goals of the different sides in this conflict may be described as either progressive or traditional, but the categorization is superficial. On the one hand, it was a matter of meeting the challenges posed by industrialization and rapid urbanization, of modernizing the city by rebuilding its transportation infrastructure, installing sanitation facilities, and revising its overall structure. On the other, it involved overcoming the feelings of rootlessness and alienation engendered by these transformations, a profoundly disruptive experience which Charles Baudelaire captured as early as 1857 in a much-quoted sentence in his *Fleurs du mal*: "Le vieux Paris n'est plus; la forme d'une ville change plus vite, hélas, que le cœur d'un mortel!"[4] This inversion of the relative paces of change seemed to imperil the city as a self-contained structure which may be experienced as such, as an entity quite literally filled with meaning. During the core period of Modernism, however, the foundational role the city plays for its residents' identity was often effectively ignored or explicitly rejected. Ideas such as continuity and traditionalism ran counter to the era's avant-garde self-conception, which posited that identity flowed from radical contemporaneity (*être-du-temps*). Le Corbusier, for example, planned to rebuild the center of Paris in the spirit of the Athens Charter, the paradigmatic founding document of Modernist urban planning.[5] The city's historic core – which the architect vilified as a "flattened-out and jumbled city", a "maze", "the seventh circle of Dante's Inferno"[6] – would have been razed to make way for an array of functionalist skyscrapers called the *Ville Voisin*. Planners whose perspective was defined by their enthusiasm for technology saw the traditional city as deficient more than anything else, as unsanitary and dangerous, but also as crowded, ugly, and 'unmodern'.

It is characteristic of this attitude that the majority of planners saw the destruction of almost all major cities in Germany by area-bombing as creating a welcome opportunity to impose radically new and forward-looking plans.[7]

"Holy Cologne" with its iconic Rhine riverfront (fig. 1) perished in World War II: on May 31, 1942, more than a thousand bombers of the British Royal Air Force took the city as their target in the first devastating large-scale operation against a major German urban center (fig. 2). In addition to damaging most of Cologne's historic monuments, the attacks destroyed 120,000 apartments and rendered 350,000 people homeless.[8] By the end of the war, 95 percent of the city's Old Town had been ravaged. Of its prewar

---

3   For a detailed discussion, see Vinken, Zone Heimat, 2010.
4   The old Paris is gone (the form a city takes / More quickly shifts, alas, than does the mortal heart). Baudelaire, The Flowers of Evil, 1998 (1857), 175.
5   Tönnesmann, Paris ist tot, 1993. Cf. the essay on The Crises of the Modern City in this volume (Chapter 2).
6   Le Corbusier, The City of To-morrow, 1987 (1925), 280, 284.
7   Vinken, Zone Heimat, 2010, 161–163.
8   Beseler/Gutschow, Kriegsschicksale Deutscher Architektur, 1988, XLVI.

population of over 700,000, no more than 10,000 people remained in the areas on the left bank of the Rhine.⁹

Figure 1: *Veduta of Cologne* (detail), woodcut by Anton von Worms 1531

In 1944, the National Socialist mayor of Cologne, Robert Brandes, mused: "If there is a point to the destruction of our major cities, [... it is that we will have to] define the intellectual foundations on which the planning for the *metropolis of the future* will be based and work toward that great goal [...] Entirely new cities will be built. Existing neighborhoods are at bottom a burden."¹⁰ Even historic preservationists shared the euphoric sense that a new beginning was possible; shortly before the end of the war, Andreas Huppertz expressed the sentiment with particular bluntness, welcoming the ravages of the war as an "opportunity the like of which will probably never arise again" to remake Cologne's urban core, which he described as a "filthy slum" marred by the "lapses in taste" of the late 19th century.¹¹ The mood remained widespread once the war was over; in a programmatic essay entitled "Altstadt und Neuzeit" (Old City and Modern Era), Wilhelm Heilig wrote that the war had effectively "expurgated" what "should long ago have been cleaned up, if in a different and reasonable manner".¹²

Yet the caesura of 1945 also raised the question of the identity of the city with new urgency. In the rubble-filled wasteland of the ravaged cities, the formerly powerful bonds of tradition seemed to have worn thin and in fact threatened to snap. The war generation shared the shocking experience that intimately familiar environments and images might be lost from one day to the next. The architect Hans Hansen, who had been a member of Bruno Taut's avant-gardist *Gläserner Kette* (Chain of Glass), described with precision the changes of perception wrought by the destruction of the war: "Here, in the narrower framework of our home town, all spaces and streets reflected the life of the past, both great and small. We were free to draw from that source without fearing

---

9 Beseler/Gutschow, Kriegsschicksale Deutscher Architektur, 1988, 522.
10 Brandes, Wiederaufbau und Gemeindeverwaltung, 1944, 1.
11 Huppertz, Schönere Zukunft, 1945/1947.
12 Huppertz, Schönere Zukunft, 1945/1947.

Figure 2: Cologne, view of the Rhine riverbank with the Cathedral and the ruins of Groß-St.-Martin (left), photograph by August Sander, 1946

that it would ever be exhausted [...] In 1918, still possessed of a rich and undestroyed world of creative forms, we proposed to renew the realm of the arts 'utterly and without compromise'; now we stand before a world that has truly been destroyed [...] That which we, in the high spirits of youth, once wished to throw on the scrap heap has suddenly become precious, now that we have lost it: *tradition*. Where the eternal principle of living art still shines forth from the devastation, it must be preserved by all means necessary."[13]

Yet what would it look like to tie the plans for the postwar city back to local tradition as an "eternal principle"? Views on this question diverged widely from the very outset. The architect Paul Schmitthenner noted as early as 1943: "Cologne, at least the core, the old town with its famed houses of worship and other valuable old structures, cannot be rebuilt, if by rebuilding we mean the recreation of the former state of affairs. [...] The city needs to be planned from scratch if a new Cologne is to rise that will meet the needs of a new era and be a living structural creation of our time."[14] That same year, the municipal conservator, Hans Vogts, remarked on the same question: "Historical consciousness, which is heavily dependent on the townscape, constitutes [...] an indispensable foundation for future development; its worth cannot be overestimated."[15] To regain its position as the metropolis of the Rhineland, Vogts wrote, Cologne needed to have character, to convey a sense of home and the values associated with it; functional modern buildings were unsuited to this task. From his perspective, the "recovery of the townscape" was the most pressing need the rebuilding effort would have to address.

---

13   Hansen, Gedanken über Grundlage, 1945, 1–2. Italics in the original.
14   Quoted in: Beseler/Gutschow, Kriegsschicksale Deutscher Architektur, 1988, XLVI.
15   Vogts, Betrifft Wiederaufbau, 1943, 2. See Roth, Vorstellung des alten heiligen Köln, 1998, 590.

After the war was over, Cologne was the scene of an especially impassioned debate over the city's identity that drew a great deal of public interest.[16] Not everyone shared the writer and journalist Carl Oskar Jatho's confidence that the *genius loci*, as a spirit slumbering in the city's soil, would guarantee that "future and tradition" would fuse into an "harmonious continuum".[17] The various factions, including Modernist advocates of a new beginning as well as defenders of a reconstructive approach to rebuilding, quickly united behind the consensus slogan "Cologne must remain Cologne" (fig. 3).[18]

Figure 3: "Cologne must remain Cologne". Poster produced by the municipal authorities of Cologne soliciting voluntary participation in the rubble clearance effort, 1945

"Cologne must remain Cologne": that meant – and probably all parties involved were in agreement on this point – building a "modern, viable" city, but also taking care that this new city would be not just any city, that it would still be recognizable as Cologne. The rebuilding of Cologne is thus a paradigmatic example of the double task facing those leading the rebuilding effort in West Germany: the need to make a fresh start – ethically, politically, socially – while safeguarding values such as recognizability and continuity, identity and the sense of home.

---

16 For a detailed discussion, see Vinken, Zone Heimat, 2010, 151–206.
17 Jatho, Urbanität, 1946, 67. See also Jatho, Eine Stadt von Welt, 1958, 99.
18 Heinen, Moderne für die Römerstadt, 1992, 221; Frohn, Vom Trümmerhaufen zur Millionenstadt, 1982, 139–140.

Rebuilding Cologne

Cologne, the only major city to pursue a 'conservationist' rebuilding policy, is regarded as one of the cities that sought to steer a middle course between Modernist construction and traditionalist reconstruction.[19] In 1946, Rudolf Schwarz had been appointed as Cologne's head of general reconstruction planning; Schwarz was an architect with theoretical ambitions who had published numerous essays and treatises engaging the consequences of the radical changes wrought by modernity for architecture and urban planning.[20] Schwarz's genuine contribution to the architectural debate was his attempt to show that the specific quality of the European city derived from its double mission: it had to be both a functional living environment and a place that was literally filled with meaning.[21] Taking up the ideas of organic urban planning, he saw it as one central challenge to overcome the centripetal structure of the city in order to prevent transportation gridlock and relieve congestion in the center. He designed a regional development scheme for Cologne that envisioned a confederation of cities composed of autonomous units arrayed in the manner of interrelated cells.[22] They would represent different urban types – Mülheim, for instance, would again be an industrial city, while the urban core of Cologne would be what Schwarz called the *Hochstadt* or "acropolis" – and would be interconnected by a "double band of transportation", itself a modification of the basic idea of the industrial linear or ribbon city (fig. 4a). These plans assigned a preeminent role to Cologne's urban core or "acropolis".[23] As the site of representation and education, of the collective generation of meaning and communal praxis, the center was to be the "head" of the urban confederation (fig. 4b). In order to maintain the "cellular tissue" of this area as it developed historically, Schwarz sought to preserve the urban layout and elements that lend it structure; major buildings that defined the city's identity were to be reconstructed, while a moderately modernist style would predominate in the remaining area.

Rudolf Schwarz's tenure as head of general city planning was short – he was relieved in 1950 – but many of his goals were implemented in the city center. The historic urban layout with its streets and squares was largely respected; the most important monuments, especially Cologne's famous Romanesque churches, were reconstructed, albeit sometimes in simplified form.[24] The city was given the contemporary face he had envisioned, based on a moderately modern design vocabulary; only the neighborhood around Groß-St.-Martin was reconstructed in a way that recreated its historic appearance.

---

19   Diefendorf, In the Wake of War, 1993, 197–198, 201–202. Other examples of conservationist planning are Münster, Freiburg, Nuremberg, Rothenburg ob der Tauber, and Freudenstadt. See Beseler/Gutschow, Kriegsschicksale Deutscher Architektur, 1988, XLIX–LXV.
20   Pehnt/Strohl, Rudolf Schwarz, 1997.
21   Vinken, Ort und Bahn, 2008. Cf. also the essay on *The Crises of the Modern City* in this volume (Chapter 2).
22   Schwarz, Das neue Köln, 1950.
23   Schwarz, Das neue Köln, 1950, 43–44. Pehnt/Strohl, Rudolf Schwarz, 1997, 116–117.
24   Blokker, (Re)konstruierte Identität, 2011, and Blokker, (Re)Constructing Identity, 2012.

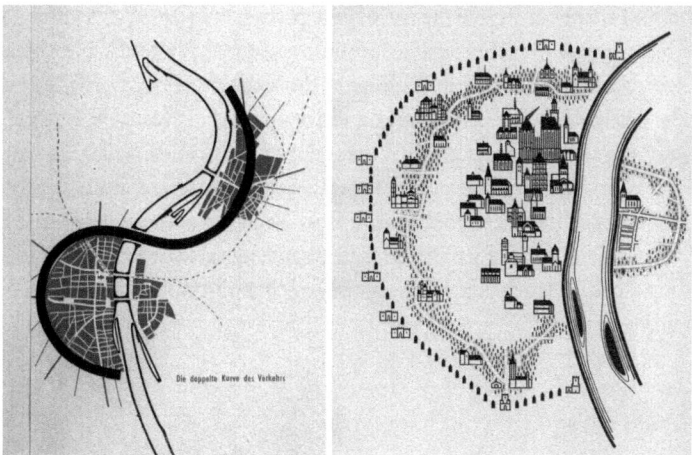

Figures 4 a, b: "The Double Band of Transportation" – "Sacred Cologne", Rudolf Schwarz 1950

An island of tradition: the St. Martin quarter

On the initiative of historic preservationists and champions of native traditions, an image of the old Cologne was recreated in the St. Martin quarter, located on the Rhine riverbank and not far from the cathedral; here, copies and reconstructions of old buildings and new buildings that adapt to their surroundings predominate.[25] Even today, the Fischmarkt square with its narrow houses huddling against the apse of Groß-St.-Martin is popular with photographers (figs 5, 6).

Figures 5, 6: Cologne, Groß-St.-Martin and the Fischmarkt square in 1937 and in 1954

The rebuilding of the St. Martin quarter explicitly aimed to evoke an "image of the Old Town". Buildings and parts of façades were transplanted here from all over the city. New buildings were required to conform to the restrictive regulations stipulated in the

---

25 Roth, Vorstellung des alten heiligen Köln, 1998, 590–594; Schlungbaum-Stehr, Das Martinsviertel, 1991.

bylaw of 1937, which prescribed historically appropriate numbers of storeys, façade designs, and roof shapes as well as the use of lime plaster and slate roof cladding. Because salvaged building components such as portals, decorated keystones and the like were reused, it is virtually impossible to distinguish the reconstructions from the new houses built in the old style.[26] The Alter Markt and Heumarkt squares were restored – with certain compromises – to their original shapes, with mostly new buildings rising along their edges.[27] Besides unambitious adaptive architecture, there are also very accomplished and original instances of the more abstract recourse to tradition that Schwarz had called for (fig. 7).[28] In a parallel process, a considerable proportion of the surviving building stock was torn down in response to economic or functional considerations during redevelopment.[29]

Figure 7: Cologne, the reconstructed Fischmarkt square, 1967

To sum up, the conflict that pitted function against meaning in the city centers of destroyed German cities was resolved in Cologne by means of spatial differentiation; in this regard, the metropolis of the Rhineland is emblematic of the German rebuilding process as a whole. The desire for an experience of continuity and the presence of history was satisfied by means of a placebo of sorts: the creation of a modestly-sized island of tradition set off from the rest of the city. As long as such zones of native tradition were limited to a few streets, even those planners who much preferred the technical and the modern could make their peace with them. Wilhelm Riphahn, for example, a devotee of the ideal of a spacious urban layout with generous green spaces, a city that would accommodate healthy residential areas as well as a highly efficient transportation infrastructure, observed drily that "the goal of preserving Cologne's ancient character is to be achieved by reconstructing the St. Martin quarter (rehabilitation of the Old Town) with the Alter Markt square".[30] His drafts for the Rhine riverfront (fig. 8) show

---

26   Adenauer, Die Pflege der profanen Denkmäler, 1955/1956, 162–163.
27   Beseler and Gutschow have tallied the damage to individual rows of houses; see Beseler/Gutschow, Kriegsschicksale Deutscher Architektur, 1988, 575–596.
28   Roth, Vorstellung des alten heiligen Köln, 1998, 594–595.
29   Adenauer, Die Pflege der profanen Denkmäler, 1955/1956, 173.
30   Riphahn, Grundgedanken zur Neugestaltung, 1945, 7–8.

generously spaced large-format residential buildings in a thoroughly Modernist style; the designation 'preserve of tradition' appears, a little sheepishly, in the margin.

Figure 8: Cologne, reconstruction proposal for the west bank of the Rhine near the Heumarkt square, Wilhelm Riphahn 1947

The concept of the island of tradition had already been proposed in Germany before the end of the war. In Hamburg, for example, which was likewise completely destroyed, planner Fritz Schumacher suggested that "consolidating [surviving buildings and placing them] anywhere [sic!] would allow the creation of an 'Historic Center', however modest".[31] A well-known example is Hannover, which was rebuilt under the direction of Rudolf Hillebrecht as a modern, "car-friendly" city, in complete disregard of existing structures; numerous historic buildings were demolished.[32] As though to compensate for the loss, a small old-town island was created around the reconstructed Marktkirche, including the transplantation of half-timbered houses from all over the city. In Cologne, Municipal Conservator Hanna Adenauer praised these measures in retrospect for having preserved the townscape: "The question of the townscape is of particular significance in Cologne. The staggered arrangement of gables, churches, towers, and walls, which appears in many illustrations dating back as far as Schedel's World Chronicle [...] is familiar to people all over the world. Even now, anyone thinking of Cologne and its Rhine riverfront will vividly remember the sight of the churches and towers from the Cathedral to Groß St. Martin and on to St. Maria Lyskirchen and, between them, the residential buildings of the St. Martin quarter with their pointed gables [...] Out of consideration for the townscape, the city's historic preservationists, fully aware that only some of the buildings are originals, and that the neighborhood as a whole is for the most part a new ensemble more or less created from scratch in the course of the rehabilitation of the Old Town before World War II, insisted on retaining the gable pattern and the height and rhythm of the architectural volumes".[33]

---

31 Quoted in: Beseler/Gutschow, Kriegsschicksale Deutscher Architektur, 1988, XLVIII.
32 Beseler/Gutschow, Kriegsschicksale Deutscher Architektur, 1988, 250–251.
33 Adenauer, Die Pflege der profanen Denkmäler, 1955/1956, 168.

A fateful continuity

There is an intriguing detail to the history of the rebuilding of Cologne that Adenauer mentions only in passing: the fact that the reconstruction of the St. Martin quarter recreated a showcase ensemble first created by a rehabilitation project launched in the 1930s.[34] As Rudolf Schwarz put it succinctly, "the old Cologne that appealed to the tourist and the picture-postcard vendor, between the market squares and the Rhine, did not come into existence until the Nazi period".[35] In today's perspective, this sort of maintenance of a tradition – its advocates were "fully aware", to quote Hanna Adenauer's words, of its implications – would seem positively scandalous. Hans Vogts, who had been appointed Municipal Conservator in 1933, an office he held until 1948, embodied a commitment to continuity in the guiding principles of urban planning across changing political systems that even his successor, Hanna Adenauer, was not ready to abandon. During the postwar rebuilding effort, historic preservationists buried the ideological overtones of the Nazi rehabilitation project and its disgraceful aspects under a blanket of silence. The rehabilitation measures of the time, which operated under the title of "sanitization and decontamination") (*Gesundung und Entschandelung*) aimed to Aryanize areas such as the St. Martin quarter in terms of aesthetics as well as social and "racial hygiene"; their goals were to "eliminate" the "breeding grounds" of "communists", "anti-social elements", and "Jews" and to homogenize the "national body".[36] In Cologne, prostitution was to be expelled from the area in the city center that one observer described as a "slum".[37] "Light-shy" and "unclean elements", Hans Vogts wrote in 1935, were to be kept out in order to prevent "infestation of the remainder of the city" and to protect the population that had roots in the neighborhood.[38] As part of the radical "cleansing" of the area in accordance with the goals of demographic (and 'racial') policies, around two hundred families were resettled to the urban periphery: "With the removal of the inferior elements, the area, whose central location and large open spaces recommend it for the goals of housing policy, is ready to receive honorable members of the German nation."[39]

The reliance of the postwar 'reconstructions' on the results of the Nazi-era rehabilitation project seems problematic even from a preservationist's perspective, since the measures had entailed considerable structural changes.[40] To improve the residents' access to light and fresh air, Vogts had created two new squares, the Eisenmarkt and the Ostermannplatz (fig. 9).

---

34   Schlungbaum-Stehr, Das Martinsviertel, 1991, 36; Menne-Thomé, City-Bildung, 1995, 164.
35   Schwarz, Das neue Köln, 1950, 60.
36   Düwel/Gutschow, Städtebau in Deutschland, 2001, 90–91; Petz, Stadtsanierung im Dritten Reich, 1987, 135–166, especially 152–153.
37   Füllenbach, Die Kölner Altstadtgesundung, 1937, 247.
38   Vogts, Gesundungsmaßnahmen, 1998 (1935), 590; Petz, Stadtsanierung im Dritten Reich, 1987, 141–142.
39   Füllenbach, Die Kölner Altstadtgesundung, 1937, 248.
40   Statistical information on the rehabilitation can be found in Vogts, Die Kölner Altstadtgesundung, 1938, 465; Schlungbaum-Stehr, Das Martinsviertel, 1991, 39; Beseler/Gutschow, Kriegsschicksale Deutscher Architektur, 1988, 575–596.

Figure 9: Cologne, rehabilitation works at the Eisenmarkt square, 1938

The dense ensembles of courtyards surrounded by buildings, some of which dated back to the Middle Ages, had been razed, and the backs of houses redesigned as façades.[41] To achieve a more rational use of the available space, entire rows of houses had been torn down and replaced with apartment buildings. The houses that survived the sanitization project had been modernized throughout; in many instances, no more than parts of the exterior walls and staircases had remained standing. In total, roughly one third of all buildings had been demolished and rebuilt during the 1930s (fig. 10).[42]

By reusing characteristic details and pieces of décor taken from condemned houses, the architects had sought to lend the new buildings an air of the "home-like and unique".[43] Portals, embrasures, or salvaged wall anchors with dates made it almost impossible to distinguish new from rehabilitated houses, especially since even 'faceless' old buildings were enriched by adding such spolia. The old-town atmosphere had been a product of deliberate mimicry and simulation: the "typical Cologne character" of some alleys, Vogts wrote, was "heavily dependent on new buildings".[44] The "decontamination" had turned out to be a radical effort at aesthetic homogenization (fig. 11) whose contradictions and factitiousness were keenly felt by observers even then.[45]

---

41 Vogts, Gesundungsmaßnahmen, 1997 (1936), 171.
42 Wiktorin, Der historische Atlas Köln, 2001, 159.
43 Vogts, Gesundungsmaßnahmen, 1997 (1936), 171.
44 Vogts, Gesundungsmaßnahmen, 1997 (1936), 171.
45 Vogts, Gesundungsmaßnahmen, 1997 (1936), 173.

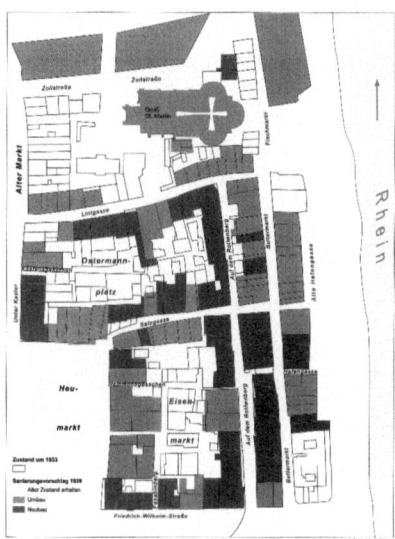

Figure 10: Cologne, redevelopment of the St. Martin quarter, changes between 1933 and 1939 (light gray: modification, dark gray: new construction)

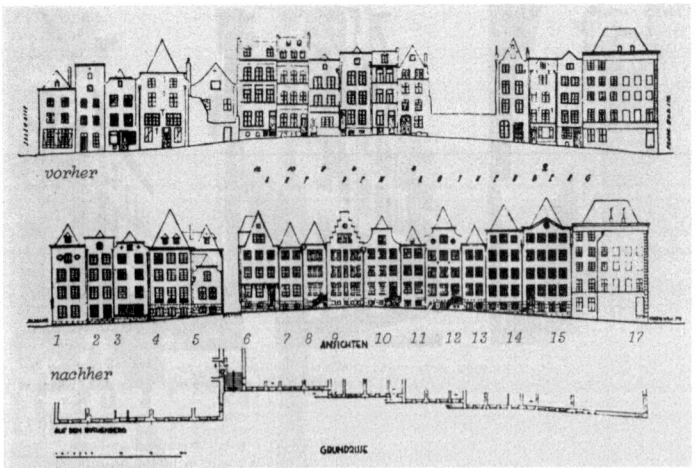

Figure 11: Cologne, Auf dem Rothenberg. Existing building stock (above) and planning, 1940

Vogts had defended the sanitization as a white lie that was necessary "for the benefit of the whole",[46] a prerequisite "if the quality of home-like livability and native tradition is to be preserved in the countenance of the metropolis".[47] Little wonder, then, that the municipal conservator in office during the postwar rebuilding period adopted the principles of Nazi-era sanitization without qualification. In some instances, bombed-out houses that had first been built in the 1930s were carefully reconstructed. The generously spaced structure with its 'intimate' courtyards was consistent with postwar Modernism's hygienic as well as aesthetic ideas. The aesthetic goals the Nazis had championed – to preserve native traditions while establishing visual homogeneity – were likewise pursued with undiminished zeal in the postwar era. Despite its synthetic nature – it is the product of two phases of sweeping rehabilitation – the St. Martin quarter in some ways succeeds as an historic town center. "Even if there is little by way of truly old building stock here, even if many houses are reconstructions of new buildings from the 1930s, locals and tourists alike regard this small neighborhood as Cologne's Old Town (*Altstadt*) par excellence."[48] Hiltrud Kier, who was Cologne's municipal conservator for many years, came to an altogether negative assessment of how the city had been rebuilt, but she praised St. Martin quarter for its old-Cologne-style cozy atmosphere: "Only in a very small area of the old town did the rebuilding effort successfully retain the true small-scale proportions that corresponded to the historic urban layout" – even if this same neighborhood, she noted in 1976, was gradually becoming the "backdrop for an entertainment district."[49] With the blessing of historic preservationists who have yet to dissociate themselves from such fateful continuity, more recent measures have perfected this scenery. Since the 1980s, a growing number of old-town buildings whose aesthetic was informed by the conservative modernism of the 1950s have been replaced by new structures in the 'old Cologne' style that imitate the models of the 1930s.[50]

---

46   Vogts, Gesundungsmaßnahmen, 1997 (1936), 173.
47   Vogts, Gesundungsmaßnahmen, 1997 (1936), 170.
48   Hagspiel, Reflexe, 1994, 82.
49   Kier, Der Wiederaufbau von Köln, 1976, 233.
50   Roth, Vorstellung des alten heiligen Köln, 1998, 594–595. On the current boom in the creation of 'new' Old Towns, see also Vinken, Unstillbarer Hunger, 2013, and the essay on Frankfurt in this volume (Chapter 12).

10 Berlin / Germany
Monumental Revision. A Capital between Ruin and Restoration

> Die DDR hat's nie gegeben
> East Germany never existed
> (graffito on the rubble of the demolished Palace of
> the Republic, Berlin 2008)[1]

In Berlin, it feels like we have been arguing over the demolition of the GDR-era Palace of the Republic and the reconstruction of the old Hohenzollern *Stadtschloss* for a whole generation.[2] The structure of the latter is now standing, and its façades are nearing completion. Is it time to draw conclusions? Not yet: not until the concrete building is occupied and its new functions and uses have settled into their spatial patterns and relationships. But several observations on the consequences of this decision can already be made, and some are quite surprising. The structure, the volume of the royal palace has been restored. Eagles milled by computer-guided lasers now adorn the façades again. It looks Baroque, and yet also quite up-to-date (fig. 1). Is it imposing? In fact, it is surprisingly boring. And very large indeed.

The wing facing the River Spree, originally heterogeneous and asymmetrical, has not been reconstructed 'historically' but rather redone using modern forms, giving it a somewhat *fin-de-siècle* (20th) look (fig. 2). One surprise is the effect that the palace has from a distance. Unter den Linden, the grand old boulevard that previously led rather aimlessly towards the socialist Palace of the Republic – itself quite awkwardly positioned in the urban landscape – once again has perspective and direction. The effects of the *Stadtschloss* reconstruction had been a matter of much speculation as well as anticipation, and the recreation of its façade by Wilhelm von Boddien in 1993/94 made strikingly visible one of strongest arguments for proceeding with the project. What is surprising, however, is the prominence of the reconstructed building's new dome, which will soon

---

1   See below, figure 7.
2   Hennet, Berliner Schlossplatzdebatte, 2005; Flierl, Identitätssuche, 2008.

Figure 1: Reconstructed "Stadtschloss", with baroque ... (Photo G. Vinken 2020)
Figure 2: ... and 'timelessly modern' façades (Photo G. Vinken 2020)

be crowned by the monumental golden cross of the Hohenzollern king Friedrich Wilhelm IV once again.[3] On leaving the Bode-Museum, for instance, at the other end of Berlin's lengthy Museum Island, the dome of the palace is unexpectedly revealed; anyone walking around Berlin these days experiences again and again the emergence of new visual relationships and shifts in the balance of forms and spaces. Often this involves the re-emergence of connections and contexts that were relevant for the structuring and design of the Mitte district as Berlin's monumental urban centre in the 19th and 20th centuries.

By contrast, in the immediate vicinity of the rebuilt *Stadtschloss*, the Prussian mood never really manages to set in. The wound opened up by the demolition of the Palace of the Republic is still too fresh for many. Opposite the new palace's main front, a faded canvas façade printed with the lines of Schinkel's Bauakademie solicits for the reconstruction of that building as well. Although its structural volume is already outlined in the urban space, even the full-scale construction of a sample bay at its northeast corner – the one closest to the *Stadtschloss* – can contribute little, with its look of an off-the-shelf home improvement project, to the arguments for completing this undertaking. The Schinkelplatz, once occupied by East Germany's Foreign Ministry, was reconstructed in 2007/8; there, three gigantic monuments to Prussian heroes – only one of which (Thaer) is a copy – still wait for a 'suitable' setting to take shape around them (fig. 3).

---

3 Made possible thanks to a large, anonymous donation. On the surrounding controversy, see, for instance: Schulz, Humboldt Forum bekommt Kreuz, 2020.

Figure 3: Reconstructed Schinkelplatz with Friedrichswerder Church and canvas façade of the Bauakademie, left (Photo M. Brückels 2010)

It is possible to experience the provisional character of the Schlossplatz, the heterogeneity that swings between ambition and indifference, as charming – but it conceals a genuine scandal. The Friedrichswerder Church to the west of the Schlossplatz, also by Karl Friedrich Schinkel and reopened as the Schinkel Museum in the latter years of the GDR, was evacuated in 2012 and has been officially declared off-limits ever since, having possibly received a mortal wound during the excavation work undertaken in order to create a piece of deeply pseudo-Prussian investor architecture (the neighbouring *Kronprinzengärten*) that was unable to do without underground parking (fig. 4).[4] The profound contradictions evident here have often been remarked upon: a society that wants '*das Schloss*' back and is yet prepared to accept the loss of an original and surviving early example of Schinkel's brick architecture in order to do it.

---

4   See Friedrichswerdersche Kirche, Frankfurter Allgemeine Zeitung, 6 February 2016. By 2020, the danger had been averted, and the museum is set to open again following a costly renovation.

Figure 4: Menaced by new neighbours, empty and closed to visitors for safety reasons. Schinkel's Friedrichswerder Church (Photo K. Kleist-Heinrich 2015)

Ambivalent Attempts at Healing

Yet the second and larger surprise that the resurrected palace holds in store is waiting in the Lustgarten. There, another iconic building by Schinkel, the Altes Museum, again has an architectural complement, and it is now possible once again to experience spatially the self-confidence with which this neo-Grecian marvel referred to its royal neighbour. Here it becomes clear just how permanently the reconstruction of the *Stadtschloss* is changing the character and relationships of space in central Berlin. After the demolition of the original palace, the erection of the Palace of the Republic and many other interventions, the overall feeling here was one of disharmony. The fractured history of the city, the violent exploitation of its spaces and architectures was always evident here; the imposing cityscape of the pre-war years could only be grasped in fragments. Through the cubic volume of the palace's incomplete structure, we are already experiencing a restitution of the space-defining effects generated by Berlin's central monuments, such as Schlüter's Zeughaus or indeed the Altes Museum; an increase in visual power, a calming and also a monumentalization.[5]

Yet the ambivalence of this attempt at spatial healing – 'healing' was always a central part of the case for rebuilding the palace – is also especially evident here. It takes the form of yet another monument that forces itself into the field of vision with renewed force. From a perspective in middle of the Lustgarten, it suddenly becomes very clear who the real winner here is: Berlin Cathedral. As a result of the reconstruction, the Cathedral is now flanked by two lower buildings – palace and museum – of similar proportions (fig. 5).

---

5 Vinken, Räume des Denkmals, 2020 and the essay on The Spaces of the Monument in this volume (Chapter 4).

Figure 5: Magnificence restored. Berlin's "Stadtschloss" with the Cathedral and "Lustgarten" (Mockup photomontage: Franco Stella 2019)

Since, furthermore, the Cathedral's dome is now engaged in an intense dialogue with the dome of the Palace, this preeminent symbol of Wilhelmine power and pomp is now restored to its intended position of spatial dominance. Yet this is a winner that virtually no-one had reckoned with at the start of the reconstruction debate between the Prussia-enthusiasts and the enemies of the Palace – a debate that ultimately had to be decided in the Bundestag. What then has been restored in the centre of Berlin? Whose heritage – what kind of heritage – are we talking about? What narratives are being (re-)established?

The Cathedral of the Hohenzollerns

Berlin Cathedral has had a varied history.[6] Since the founding of the Empire, calls had grown for a suitably grand church that would be the equal of the world's other great Christian houses of worship. In order to build the new cathedral, a project personally supported by Kaiser Wilhelm II, Schinkel's old cathedral, an almost modest component of the Lustgarten ensemble, had to give way. Built after lengthy preliminaries from 1894–1905 according to plans drawn up by Julius Raschdorf, Berlin's new cathedral, which was also to contain the tombs of the Hohenzollerns, is a symbol of the fusion of Protestantism and German Empire – with the head of the latter, the King of Prussia, also functioning as the head and highest representative of the Protestant Church.[7] It is no coincidence that this architectural expression of power, which echoes the forms of the Renaissance and the high Baroque, makes reference to St Peter's in Rome, and

---

6 On the history of its construction and alteration, see: Besier, Zur Geschichte des Wiederaufbaus, 1993 and Schröder, Baugestalt und Raumprogramm, 2002.
7 Wolf, Monarchen als religiöse Repräsentanten, 2004.

does so in a way that can be read as an attempt to outdo the latter: This central church of German Protestantism stood for the merging of nation, religion and empire – an empire in which, since the *Kulturkampf* conflict between the Catholic Church and the Prussian state in the 1870s, Catholics were often made to feel like second-class citizens.[8] The solidarity between the Protestant state church and the state, which was acting in an increasingly aggressive manner both internally (toward socialists and 'ultramontanes') and externally (in the form of nationalism and colonialism) achieved its highest form in the so-called 'German Christians' (*Deutsche Christen*) of the Third Reich, with their 1933 campaign slogan *"ein Volk, ein Reich, eine Kirche"* (One People, One Empire, One Church). In these years the Cathedral served as the backdrop for National Socialist propaganda, such as grand weddings for the new leaders.[9] There is a certain dark humour to the fact that it was the Humboldt Forum – this forcibly democratized copy of the Hohenzollern palace – that enabled this monument to Prussian nationalism to once again exert its strong spatial influence in the centre of Berlin.

Yet Berlin Cathedral, as it stands before us today, has even more to tell. A ruin after the war, for many years it was merely preserved from complete collapse, and renovation only began in 1975. At the same time, the nearly untouched apse at the north end of the church, known as the *Denkmalskirche*, was demolished for ideological reasons, because it was considered the 'hall of honour of the Hohenzollerns'. This caesura in the history of the building is particularly evident in the dome, which has been radically simplified and possesses a remodelled crown. The Cathedral's congregation and the Monument Authority of the city of Berlin are to be thanked for this, as in 2008, when the restored dome needed renovation, loud calls for the dome to be rebuilt in its entire Wilhelmine glory, boosted by the general sense of renewal and restoration, were rejected on the grounds that the Cathedral was a listed building.[10]

Meanwhile, the interior tells a different and simpler story, as the Cathedral has been restored to create a seamless whole – the result of a series of costly campaigns driven by the zeal for a historical 'completeness' that was not disheartened by the loss of much of its interior decoration and furnishings. For instance, seven of the eight dome mosaics needed to be entirely remade using the surviving drawings.[11] In a similar way, All Saints' Church in Wittenberg (also a central location for nationalist conservatives' evocation of the unity of throne and altar) was subject to an uncritical and unreflecting restoration as part of the celebrations marking the 2017 anniversary of the start of the Protestant Reformation.[12] In line with this pattern, Munich's *Haus der Kunst* is now also to be largely restored to its 'original' condition. It is a monumental structure by Hitler's favourite architect, Paul Ludwig Troost, and a "manifestation of the National Socialist views of art and the world [...], a party slogan made of stone."[13] What drives those responsible to

---

8   Borutta, Antikatholizismus, 2010, 412.
9   Website Berliner Dom, Drittes Reich.
10 Hein/Pletl, Streit um die Kuppel, 2008.
11 Schnitzler, Restaurierung des Berliner Doms, 2013.
12 Reichelt, Erlebnisraum Lutherstadt Wittenberg, 2013, particularly 61–77.
13 Görl, Was vom Wahnsinn blieb, 2016, 36.

repeat word for word, to retrace letter by letter the aesthetic of dominance expressed at these sites?

Standing in Berlin's Lustgarten, it becomes clear that our debates over architectural monuments remain fixated on the values of the 19th century, namely authenticity and aesthetics. When we focus on the documentary character of built heritage, we draw attention to the layered nature of historical evidence and to an authenticity that is ideally grounded in materiality. When, on the other hand, our focus is the monument, then our lines of argument are guided by artistic value, visual power, integrity. The key questions of heritage politics are only marginally glimpsed: Who is trying to achieve what with these deletions, reinterpretations, restagings? What kinds of memory-work are being carried out or obstructed here? Which narratives are being established, and which suppressed? The question of justice or, put in political terms, the question of power, is suspended in this conception of cultural heritage; meanwhile, in contexts such as the postcolonial debates taking place internationally, race, class and gender have long been recognized as central questions in the struggle for identity and heritage.[14] For a moment, all this was present in Berlin as well: in the struggle over the two palaces – the socialist Palace of the Republic and the *Stadtschloss* – which was debated and finally decided in Germany's national parliament. The Berlin debates also taught us that these questions cannot be answered in isolation with regard to a single structure. In reconstructing the Palace, did we even consider whether we wanted to restore the Cathedral's place as the dominant symbolic building in central Berlin? But the resulting shifts in signification certainly cut deep. Before the rebuilding of the Palace, this Cathedral, which was saved in almost miraculous fashion from the destruction of the war and from ideologically motivated neglect, was another building entirely. It stood there with its war wounds, fire-blackened, its simplified dome and its somewhat ill-fitting neo-Art-Deco crown, next to the overbearing mirrored façades of the pompous Palace of the (socialist) Republic: two entirely unequal brothers, yet both in a certain sense unfortunate. That was a different story altogether (fig. 6).

---

14 Readers in search of enlightenment are directed to the texts selected for the most recent English-language anthology on Cultural Heritage: Smith, Cultural Heritage, 2007; above all the texts by Stuart Hall, David C. Harvey, Joe Littler/Roshi Naidoo, Sharon Sullyvan and Dolores Hayden.

Figure 6: Fading memories. Participants in the Whitsun meeting of the state youth organisation FDJ, with Palace of the Republic and Cathedral, 1979 (Photo R. Kaufhold)

From Monument to Heritage

The revaluations and transformations of Berlin's monumental centre that I have sketched here, and which came about as a direct result of the reconstruction of the Hohenzollern palace, raise fundamental questions regarding the conservation of historic monuments. Yet the conceptual apparatus of architectural conservation is in no position to deal effectively with the questions thus raised, not even by means of the detour via 'urban conservation'. In contrast to the concept of architectural monument (*Baudenkmal, monument historique*) which has been established in Europe since the 19th century, the notion of cultural heritage has the advantage of being deeply rooted in fundamental human cultural practices, in processes of cultural transmission and adoption that are common to all cultures – albeit to varying degrees. These days, the fact that heritage has been (and continues to be) leveraged to generate racist and nationalist ideologies of exclusion is less important than the notion of a worldwide 'human heritage', as has been exploited with particular success by UNESCO. Already in the French Revolution, however, which created the *monument historique* out of the bankrupt mass of the *Ancien Régime*, processes of adoption and reinterpretation were supplied with ammunition not only by the idea of national greatness, but also by a vision of humanity's common cultural heritage.

Figure 7: "East Germany never existed". Graffito on the rubble of the demolished Palace of the Republic. In the background, the cathedral (Photo: Arno Burgi 2008)

The concept of architectural heritage (*Denkmal* in German), as fascinatingly as it oscillates between commemoration and documentation,[15] appears in the meantime to have become bogged down in fruitless debates between substance and image, memory and history, in terms of both its analytical power and its ability to build connections with international discourses.[16] The turn towards the production of memory, towards identity politics and narratives of identity, to post-national and transcultural identities, to performance and performativity, encoding and decoding, mapping and remapping: all of this appears to get short shrift in the very German debate over commemoration and documentation – and this turn was taken firmly in the name of the concept of 'heritage'.[17] And this although the decisive reorientation was the brainchild of a German-speaking author, namely the Austrian art historian Alois Riegl, who emphatically shifted the terms of the debate over values in conservation theory towards the pole of reception.[18] A frequently overlooked consequence of this move from an object-oriented understanding of monuments to one based on reception and appropriation is that the field of architectural conservation has been able to profit from inclusion in the broader and more general field of heritage – and I hesitate to write 'cultural heritage', as this concerns far more than culture, which is in any case extremely difficult to distinguish from other inheritable objects. In the philosophical tradition, heritage and inheritance are intimately connected with the concept of work.[19] For Hegel, it is the work of the mind which ensures that that which is transmitted no longer remains bound to the past: "To receive this inheritance is also to enter upon its use […] that which is received is changed [by the work of the mind], and the material worked upon is both enriched

---

15   For further discussion, see Euler-Rolle, Am Anfang war das Auge, 2010.
16   Vinken, Pranger von Bahia, 2015 and the essay on Salvador da Bahia in this volume (Chapter 15).
17   The 2007 anthology by Smith that I mentioned above, Cultural Heritage, covers all these terms, while, significantly, Alois Riegl is the sole representative of the German *Denkmal* tradition.
18   Euler-Rolle, Stimmungswert, 2005.
19   Willer, Kulturelles Erbe, 2013, 161–162, 165–166.

and preserved at the same time".[20] The social aspect, and also the question of power ("who has the right to speak?" and "whose heritage is it?"), can be better articulated using a definition of heritage of this kind.

The near ruin of Berlin's last Schinkel church says more about power relations in Berlin than we would like to admit. And Berlin's damaged centre: has it now been healed by means of this moderately reactionary Prussian stage-setting? Has it been repaired by the reinterpretation of a deeply ideological architecture of representation – the Berlin Cathedral – as a *Gesamtkunstwerk* and its rehabilitation to a position of absolute (and unanswered?) spatial dominance? By adopting the concept of heritage, it becomes easier to understand all that we have lost with the Palace of the Republic (fig. 7): the manifestation of ruptures, of losses, of violence and salvation in the centre of Berlin – and, to a certain extent, the Cathedral as well.

---

20 Hegel, Lectures on the History of Philosophy, 1892 (1817), Introduction, 3.

11 Palermo / Italy
A Dark Legacy. Surviving through Remembering

> Il Titolo della Città è di Felice
> The Title of the City is The Happy One
> (*Francesco M. E. Gaetani, 1754*)[1]

Heritage Value – from Object to Process

Why do we talk about heritage values? At heart we are less concerned with discussing the conditions under which a historical artefact can be considered to possess "value", so that it can be listed and preserved as a monument, than with providing an ethical basis for the work we perform as conservationists (in a very broad sense) for society. In more general terms, we are concerned with establishing the current and future relevance of heritage conservation in a heterogeneous field of diverse heritage practices. At times, we may also be called to examine whether the concepts that we use, that have come down to us – concepts such as 'nation' and 'society' – can still carry the burden placed upon them by the members of what we might describe as increasingly diverse heritage communities. Can the discomfort that Wilfried Lipp identified around the debate over values in the field of heritage conservation[2] be brought into connection with this shift in the debate over values outlined here? The series of "thresholds" that Lipp hypothesizes is easy to read as a story of weakening and decline in which the monument – from its start as mythos charged with nationalist resonances – is tamed, to become mere historical evidence, then successively democratized and globalized, until it finally experiences complete dematerialization. Equally, however, one could conceive of the shifts analysed so perceptively by Lipp as a necessary precursor for the restoration of vitality and civic potency to a form of heritage conservation, considered as a specific heritage practice – a vitality and potency that it doubtlessly possessed through much of the 19th and 20th centuries.[3]

---

1 Gaetani, Della Sicilia Nobile, 1754–1775, I/1754: 30.
2 Lipp, Heritage Trends, 2014.
3 Vinken, From Monument to Heritage, 2018.

The challenges are huge for a new heritage conservation: one that that seeks to overcome the concept of the monument rooted in archaeology that was established in the 19th century – the idea of a monument that possesses "artistic and historical value" – and to confront the necessity of a concept of heritage that takes a social perspective, such as that of Critical Heritage Studies.[4] Awareness of the pitfalls of inclusive and hegemonic constructions of identity has grown, and the ideological production that was heritage conservation's twin and constant companion (when it acted, for instance, as the herald of national cultural heritage)[5] is now, thanks to postcolonial studies, subject to theoretical scrutiny; nevertheless, in practice, the danger that heritage politics are yoked to ideological ends has by no means disappeared, as the global growth in heritage-formations employing nationalist, racist, and other exclusive identitarian narratives shows. The ruling house of Saudi Arabia is currently seeking to cement its claim to represent all the people of that country by undertaking wholesale destruction of the holy sites of non-Sunni Muslims such as the Marabouts. Poland's right-wing nationalist government is propagating an interpretation of the Holocaust in which Polish national identity is exclusively associated with the victim role. China, India and many other states are trying to prevent the articulation of cultural or religious diversity – and this random selection of examples could continue indefinitely.

To analyse such processes, it is less important to discuss the quality and value of the cultural assets that are threatened by destruction, reinterpretation and suppression than it is to analyse existing power relations and the goals and rationales of relevant actors. Heritage politics can hardly be analysed in terms of the internationally established criteria of quality, integrity or authenticity. Although questions of materiality are also important, when layering, diversity and ruptures are more likely to signify socially negotiated heritage than are purity, reconstruction or simulation, the focus in the evaluation of heritage-figurations should be directed at the processes rather than the objects themselves.[6] The decisive question remains: "Who has the right to speak?" In other words: which groups are even able to articulate their conceptions of heritage? To what extent are processes of heritage making, implementation and canonization subject to mechanisms of hegemony, censorship and oppression? A reorientation of the value debate against this background seems imperative.

As a lengthy research visit to Palermo again made very apparent to me, heritage conservation can only be conceived of in connection with societal processes and negotiations over heritage, memory and identity. In the Sicilian capital, which so long appeared to be in a state of permanent bondage to the mafia, heritage conservation works as part of a diverse heritage movement that has literally become a lifeline for an urban population whose very existence is at stake.

---

4 On the shift from an archaeological and object-oriented notion of cultural heritage to one founded in the social sciences and focused on actors, cf. Smith, Cultural Heritage, 2007; Eriksen, From Antiquities to Heritage, 2014.
5 Glendinning, The Conservation Movement, 2013.
6 Ashworth/Graham/Tunbridge, Pluralising Pasts, 2007.

The Redemption of Palermo

In recent decades, the historical centre of Palermo has experienced a true resurrection.[7] The port city was destroyed twice in the 20th century. In the Second World War, allied bombers destroyed more of Palermo than of any other Italian city. Some 150,000 of the city's residents remained homeless for years, living in ruins or caves. The city was devastated for a second time during its post-1945 reconstruction (the "scempio" or Sack of Palermo, as it is still known in Sicily), which was orchestrated by a conspiratorial combination of local politics, the construction industry and organized crime that sought to bypass all applicable laws and planning regulations to siphon off aid money flowing from a range of sources. As a result, the historical centre remained in an abject state until the 1980s, with ruins standing cheek-by-jowl with crumbling *palazzi* and wasteland sites lined with oversized new buildings (Fig. 1).

Figure 1: Death, destruction, decay. Albergheria quarter in Palermo (Photo: G. Vinken 2019)

After the war, the population of the historic districts fell from 200,000 (1946) to just 20,000 (1996).[8] The devastated districts were full of poverty and crime and lacked infrastructure; they had collapsed into a no-go area at the heart of the dynamic and dysfunctional sprawl that is this city of over a million souls.

The redemption of the historic centre of Palermo is inseparably tied up with the struggle against the mafia. The low point in terms of humiliation and powerlessness was

---

7   On the rehabilitation of the old town, cf. Di Benedetto, La città che cambia, 2000; Di Benedetto, Restoration and Re-Use, 2000; Prescia, Restauri a Palermo, 2012.
8   The historic low came in 2001, when only 21,500 residents remained; by 2008, the number of people making their home in the historic centre had risen again to 27,000, which included 5,500 foreigners. Cf. Söderström, Urban Cosmographies, 2009, 90.

the murder of General Carlo Alberto Dalla Chiesa in 1982, which inaugurated a period of energetic effort on the part of the state to combat organized crime and the ubiquitous corruption. An anti-mafia movement was formed in Palermo which would change the city forever. It was supported by broad sections of the population and took tangible form when local elections were won by non-corrupt politicians around reformist mayor Leoluca Orlando.[9] Today, the entire area – at 240 hectares, likely the largest historic town centre in Europe with 158 churches, 55 monasteries and convents, and over 400 aristocratic residences – is protected.[10] In order to break with established customs in the building trade and with old elites, Orlando consciously appointed renowned specialists from outside Palermo to oversee the rehabilitation: Pier Luigi Cervellati, the lead architect in the restoration of Bologna, as well as Leonardo Benevolo, Italo Insolera and others.[11] The *Piano Particolareggiato Esecutivo Centro Storico* (P.P.E. Centro Storico) that they developed took effect in 1993, following the return of the reformist mayor to office after a series of political intrigues had temporarily cost him his position, leading him to break with the established parties.[12] The ambitious goal was to restore the old city's population to at least 50,000 and to bring back the middle class, while avoiding the gentrification and commercialization that had, despite the best intentions, occurred in Bologna: there, those with low incomes had been driven out and the rehabilitated historic town centre – meanwhile cleaned-up and stylish – was now firmly controlled by the wealthy.[13]

The rehabilitation of the historic centre was generously supported with EU funds and matching money was provided by the city, the region and the Italian state.[14] With the founding of the Office for the Historic City Centre (*Ufficio Centro Storico*), Palermo now had, for the first time, an effective heritage conservation department and the ability to make use of modern restoration techniques.[15] After the restoration of several large prestige projects and public buildings, the focus was then placed on the most badly damaged buildings, which were purchased, restored and sold for residential use. In return for observing conservation regulations, new purchasers received financial support from the authorities. In 1999, work was being undertaken on 200 churches, monasteries/convents and palazzi; during this period, some 90 billion lire went to support over 360 individual projects.[16] Significant attention was paid to building up infrastructure. Paving and lighting were restored according to historical models (Fig. 2).[17]

---

9   For the general history of the anti-mafia movement in Palermo: Schneider/Schneider, Reversible Destiny, 2003.
10 Di Benedetto, Restoration and Re-Use, 2000, 13.
11 Schneider/Schneider, Reversible Destiny, 2003, 240–243.
12 Di Benedetto, Restoration and Re-Use, 2000, 25–26; Prescia, Restauri a Palermo, 2012, 10–138.
13 Schneider/Schneider, Reversible Destiny, 2003, 247.
14 Di Benedetto, Restoration and Re-Use, 2000, 27–28.
15 Prescia, Restauri a Palermo, 2012, 75; Di Benedetto, Restoration and Re-Use, 2000, 27–39.
16 Di Benedetto, Restoration and Re-Use, 2000, 28.
17 Di Benedetto, La città che cambia, 2000, II:689–696.

Figure 2: "Restauro in Corso". Fontana del Genio, Palermo (Photo: G. Vinken 2019)

Considerable progress has since been made. Quarters such as Kalsa have been successfully turned around. The middle class and the tourists are back, and with them, amenities such as restaurants and shops. The traces of gentrification, which are certainly present, may be considered here as normalization – in the sense of the heterogenization of formerly homogeneous slums. Other districts, such as Capo and Alberghia, continue to exhibit significant problems with both buildings and infrastructure: tenantlessness and dereliction can still be seen here, indeed ruins and wasteland may even be seen on main roads. The urban fabric of Palermo, which reflects hundreds of years of social polarisation (the frequently absentee major landowners from church and aristocracy on the one hand, an impoverished underclass on the other), has proven to be a very different obstacle than in Bologna.[18] A major problem remains the restoration of the 400 palazzi, some of which go back to Norman times and are among the city's most valuable buildings. Most of these are not inhabited by their owners, but fractionally subdivided and owned by multiple people; others have been abandoned and are in a state of ruin. One reason for the slow progress is the high barriers set up by the city authorities to deter speculation. These restrict subsidy applications to people who have lived in a property for at least ten years.[19] In practice, the widely divergent interests of owners are extremely hard to coordinate.[20] Critics have also complained about the generally reconstructionist approach taken in the so-called *Cervellati Plan*. This project is guided by an image of the "historic" city as it appeared in 1870. The plan aims at (partially) reconstructing badly damaged and lost buildings on the basis of historical plans

---

18 Schneider/Schneider, Reversible Destiny, 2003, 248–251.
19 Schneider/Schneider, Reversible Destiny, 2003, 248–249.
20 Cannarozzo, Riqualificazione, 1996, 40–41.

and pictures, and requiring the remaining structures to be replaced with new buildings that conform typologically, while "intrusive" modern buildings are to be torn down.[21] The strongest source of criticism of these specifications has been the faculty of architecture at the University of Palermo, which has recently been increasingly vocal in its support for the buildings of the 1950s.

Reappropriating the City

In any case, the balance between restoration and revitalization is highly impressive, especially when one looks beyond the technical discourse of heritage conservation. The architectural measures have been integrated in a process that has seen the city reappropriated by its citizens, with the support of a broad range of actors. The reformers around Mayor Orlando should be given credit for orchestrating a grassroots cultural and social politics, a heritage politics that aimed at providing an alternative based on cultural heritage and new opportunities for identification, to contrast with the apparently irrevocable stigmatization of Palermo as the capital of the mafia. The city's government itself initiated a broad package of measures, but focused above all on involving a broad cross-section of the population and providing the many groups of actors with scope to bring forward their own initiatives.

The variety of activities carried out can only be roughly outlined here. One aspect was the deliberate framing by the city authorities of the restoration of historic buildings as a symbol of a new politics. A particularly symbolic event was the reopening of the Teatro Massimo, celebrated on its hundredth anniversary in 1997. Formerly one of the largest opera houses in Europe, it had been closed for "temporary" renovation in 1974 and had stood rotting away ever since, a monument to corruption (Fig. 3).[22]

A similar effect was achieved by means of the uncovering and restoration of the ruins of Santa Maria dello Spasimo, a long-deconsecrated church that had been completely hidden from view (Fig. 4).[23] Typical of this project, as of so many others, was the high level of engagement on the part of numerous volunteers and the subsequent public use of the building as a multi-purpose cultural space. In many other cases, too, expensive restoration work that was funded by the state went hand in hand with the transfer of usage rights to private bodies in the culture sector. Prominent examples include the Chiesa di Montevergini, which has been used as a theatre since 2005, or more recently the anti-mafia memorial set up in a centrally located *palazzo* by the *Centro Siciliano di Documentazione "Giuseppe Impastato"* (CSD Giuseppe Impastato), the first formally incorporated anti-mafia initiative. By such means, numerous symbolically charged points of reference for civic initiatives and the development of the surrounding districts were created.

---

21 Schneider/Schneider, Reversible Destiny, 2003, 240–243.
22 Di Benedetto, La città che cambia, 2000, I:453–492.
23 Di Benedetto, La città che cambia, 2000, I:261–274.

Figure 3: Open again after decades of agony. Teatro Massimo, Palermo (Photo: G. Vinken 2019)

Figure 4: New centre of urban culture. Santa Maria dello Spasimo, Palermo (Photo: G. Vinken 2019)

One key precondition for this reappropriation of the city by its citizens was the rapidity with which the civic authorities recognized the significance of public spaces. A new department in the civic administration was established to deal only with public green spaces. It was overseen by Letizia Battaglia, who had gained fame as a result of her photographic documentation of mafia crimes. Joint private-public initiatives cleaned up public squares, terraces were created for use by restaurants, and in 1995 Palermo's intersecting main axial roads, the Via Vittorio Emanuele und and the Via Maqueda (Fig. 5), were closed to motor traffic (if only temporarily at first).[24]

Figure 5: Now closed to motor traffic. Via Maqueda, Palermo (Photo: G. Vinken 2019)

These and other similar measures have been very well received, as not only have they improved the quality of life in the old town, but they also stand for a conscious effort to win back areas that had previously been abandoned to organized crime, and for the reclamation of public space by an autonomous civic society.

The most concise example of how heritage politics and urban planning can create new opportunities for identification is provided by the district around the Piazza Magione. According to plans made in the 1960s, an expressway (the *Asse Stazione-Porto*) was to be built from the harbour that would have sliced right through the old city and the botanic gardens. Fourteen city blocks had been demolished before the project was stopped at the *Convento della Sapienza*, which now stands isolated in middle of the Piazza Magione.[25] In 2000, the piazza was redesigned to expose the foundation walls of the destroyed houses and show the historical layout of this part of the city. A memorial plaque explains the historic structure and commemorates Judge Giovani Falcone ("to whom we all owe a debt of gratitude"), a victim of mafia murder who grew up in the area.

---

24 Examples are given in Di Benedetto, Restoration and Re-Use, 2000, 180–219.
25 Di Benedetto, La città che cambia, 2000, II:673–678, with reconstruction of the pre-war state.

Figure 6: Banner commemorating Paolo Borsellino and Giovanni Falcone in front of the school at the Piazza Magione in Palermo (Photo: G. Vinken 2019)

A banner that was affixed to a fence at the side of the piazza on the 25th anniversary of the assassination of Falcone and his comrades-in-arms states that the city authorities will hold a ceremony each year to commemorate the murder (23rd May 1992) (fig. 6).[26] The piazza was long a popular meeting place for the city's youth and remains a central site for the reaffirmation of the organized civic anti-mafia movement.

Heritage as a Survival Strategy

It is indeed impossible to understand Palermo's recent heritage formations without the anti-mafia struggle, which is a common point of reference for the various actors. The events known as the *Palermo Spring* were made possible thanks to broad civic engagement and the ability of the anti-mafia activists to overcome the divide that had split Italian society in the Cold War.[27] While there were numerous protest movements, campaigns and initiatives at the start, there was no coordinated remembrance or heritage politics. Following the murder of Dalla Chiesa in 1982, the first anti-mafia monument was erected, the *Monumento Ai Caduti Nella Lotta Contro La Mafia*, which expressly positioned itself in the tradition of monuments to the fallen.[28] Yet this martial monument was never really accepted by the people. Initiatives such as the renaming of streets in the

---

26 Website La Repubblica Palermo, slideshow.
27 For a long time, the struggle against the orthodox left and the "red scare" united Giulio Andreotti's middle class *Democrazia Cristiana* party and the church and allowed even cooperation with organized crime to be seen as the lesser evil. Cf. Schneider/Schneider, Reversible Destiny, 2003, 49–80.
28 On the events that lead up to this, cf. Schneider/Schneider, Reversible Destiny, 2003, 175, 195.

late 1980s by means of signs memorializing the victims of the mafia, which inscribed public space as part of the anti-mafia movement, were more popular.[29] Only with the murder of two prominent mafia hunters, Paolo Borsellino and Giovanni Falcone, in 1992 were the social conditions in place for a broad public culture of remembrance. This was then able to achieve its full potential with the institutional and civic engagement that followed the re-election of Leoluca Orlando as mayor in 1993. If Palermo used to be *the* city of the mafia, today it is impossible to overlook the symbols of the anti-mafia movement. When approaching the city from the harbour, one is greeted by a more than life-size mural of Borsellino und Falcone, who are honoured as martyrs. When leaving the city on the *autostrada* to the international airport – which is named after the two mafia hunters – one passes two monumental obelisks that mark the site of the assassination of Falcone, and, a short distance away, the hut from which the bomb that killed all five occupants of the car was detonated, and on which the painted slogan "NO MAFIA" can be seen from a considerable distance. And the last thing one might see when going through airport security is a poster of Borsellino and Falcone with the catchy slogan "*insieme per non dimenticare*": united so as not to forget.

The current phase is characterized by the close interlinking of heritage politics and other commemorative practices, which often seek the broad involvement of the population. Schools play a particularly important role. The project *Palermo apre le Porte*, which, based on a successful project in Naples, encourages school classes to "adopt" monuments, to ensure regular opening times and to act as guides at specific times. By 1999, 73 schools were already participating, and by 2007 over 70 percent of "adopted" monuments had been restored.[30] As in similar projects, there are multiple effects. Opening the long-neglected landmarks, which had often been forgotten about, is an important engine for the reappropriation of the city. The main goal is a form of re-education in which the children are taken off the streets and offered alternatives to a life of crime, but also to give them a sense of pride and ownership of a shared heritage.

The branding of urban space by means of murals (*murales*) of varying sizes is also part of the city's efforts to grant Palermo a new identity. Whether painted officially or unofficially, the murals include not only anti-mafia themes, but also religious and popular motifs.[31] The *murales* are extremely popular and are now not only promoted officially but also by word of mouth. This is a tangible attempt to oppose the branding of Palermo as the city of the mafia with a broad politics of commemoration that makes use of and reinterprets a variety of resources from history. The city's revered patron saint, Rosalia, who once saved Palermo from the plague, has been repurposed to provide divine protection from the mafia: first through reorganization of her feast day in July in accordance with historical models – in the 18th century it was a multi-day spectacle that attracted visitors from around the world, and today it is again the city's main festival – but also through the creation of a monumental mural depiction of her in the public space. To this image has been added the figure of an "African Saint", San Benedetto il

---

29 Schneider/Schneider, Reversible Destiny, 2003, 181.
30 Troisi, Schools adopt monuments, 1998.
31 There are many good sources available online; for a selection of the most spectacular, *Murales* cf. Rotolo, Cinque nuovi murals, 2018.

Moro (fig. 7), as an expression of a culture of welcoming; less well-known until now, he has acquired real popularity and significance at a moment when Italy's government is attempting aggressively to close the country's borders to migrants from the south – migrants who make up nearly 20 percent of the population in this part of Palermo.[32]

Figure 7: Mural of San Benedetto il Moro by Igor Scalisi Palminteri in Palermo (Photo: G. Vinken 2019)

These are only a few highlights of the diverse cultures of commemoration that Palermo's civic authorities are orchestrating and promoting. They are working to reconcile the city with its rich history and to popularize a range of alternative narratives. Classical formats of heritage politics and heritage conservation are being combined with intangible, experimental and ephemeral formats; the official and the institutional are combining with the voices of individual communities and actors. The frequently described transformation of cultural heritage from an area of antiquarian interest to one of immediate social concern may be experienced here in paradigmatic form. Heritage-formations thus take on a new force and relevance, in the face of which a heritage conservation field that has typically focused on its own professional concerns must attempt to assert itself anew. The field's contribution as an academically informed specialist discipline is indispensable in this connection, as Palermo again shows. The values conservation identifies and conveys must, however, hold their own in a multi-vocal process of appropriation and interpretation; more concerted efforts to involve citizens in its institutional processes – not just by transmitting information on heritage sites and objects, but by engaging the public in dialogue and exchange – would be constructive in both a pragmatic and a fundamental sense for the goal of greater sustainability.[33] The valuation of heritage can never be a matter only for experts: heritage is not, to adapt one of

---

32 On several occasions recently Orlando has expressed his vehement opposition to the Salvini government's treatment of foreigners. Cf. Affaticati, Widerstand gegen Salvini, 2019.
33 Selitz/Vinken, Kommunales Denkmalkonzept, 2017.

Alois Riegl's expressions, a mere "passion for art and history",[34] but rather, as Derrida puts it,[35] an activity that is deeply and intimately linked with individual existence and social processes of identity formation and negotiation.

---

[34] Riegl, Neue Strömungen, 1905, 95.
[35] Derrida, Specters of Marx, 1994 (1993), 67–68.

12 Frankfurt / Germany[1]
Clone City. An Insatiable Thirst for Authenticity

> It is a cultural irony – but an economic fact – that this thirst for 'authenticity' can now be slaked only by forgeries.
> (Jean Baudrillard)[2]

The historic centre of Frankfurt unfolds as a tale of destruction and neglect, grand designs and shifting interpretations. For conservationists, it is a tragedy in several acts – specifically in the post-war period. By contrast, Frankfurt's earlier history is quite typical. Overcrowding, impoverishment and neglect in the 19th century were followed by modernization initiatives featuring large-scale edifices and cross-cutting boulevards. Around 1900, Braubachstrasse and Domstrasse were forced through in the immediate vicinity of the Römerberg. Frankfurt's Altstadt, it is often forgotten, was already an island before the devastation of the war. It is now over 70 years since the centre of Frankfurt was bombed to rubble. In the meantime, on the insular plot between the *Römer* and the *Dom* (cathedral) with which we will mostly be concerned, a wide variety of urban development schemes have been dreamt up. They have rarely attempted to do justice to the meaning of this place at the heart of the city.[3] A quite scandalous torpor led to this central location being used as a carpark well beyond the immediate post-war years. Then, in the early 1970s, the Römer area was subject to the construction of a huge, three-storey underground garage. There followed, along Braubachstrasse, the erection of the *Technisches Rathaus* (Technical Town Hall), a piece of brutalist high-rise architecture by Bartsch, Thürwächter und Weber.[4] However, this attempt to install a landmark in a city that had dedicated itself to architectural modernism during its reconstruction and was seeking to position itself as a city of skyscrapers failed (fig. 1).

---

[1] The title is a quote from Jean Baudrillard; cf. Baudrillard, The System of Objects, 1996 (1968), 84.
[2] Baudrillard, The System of Objects, 1996 (1968), 84.
[3] Müller-Raemisch, Frankfurt am Main, 1996; Pötschke, Dreißig Häuser sind keine Altstadt, 2007.
[4] Brutalism, it is important to remind the non-specialist, in the field of architecture, has nothing to do with "brutality" – it owes its name to "béton brut", literally "raw concrete", a reference to the honest materiality of modern exposed concrete architecture.

Figure 1: View from the cathedral (Dom) over the historic center of Frankfurt with the three ornamented gables of the old Town Hall ("Römer"), the modern City Administration Building ("Technisches Rathaus", foreground right) and the "Kunsthalle Schirn" museum of art, all seen against the skyline of the modern central business district (Undated photograph, prior to 2010)

While the Frankfurt skyline is widely accepted to be the city's most important marketing icon and is the foremost symbol of the city's identity for many residents, there was – unsurprisingly – little opposition when the decision was made to tear down the unpopular modern Town Hall. The City of Frankfurt has approved the demolition of incomparably more significant examples of modern high-rise architecture in recent decades.

The dimensional caesura that the *Technisches Rathaus* established in the heart of Frankfurt (see also fig. 2 in chapter 8) was made irreversible by future projects such as the postmodern *Schirn Kunsthalle* (1983–1986, architects: Architekturbüro BJSS). The construction towards the Römerberg that was planned to be carried out together in parallel with the construction of the Schirn was conceived of as 'city repair' (*Stadtreparatur*) in the sense in which this concept became popular in Germany following the Berlin International Building Exhibition in 1987, and spatially is not without sophistication. The remodelling of Frankfurt's most important city square, the Römerberg, led to a reconstruction debate that was lively enough to even affect the local elections. As the pet project of then Mayor Walter Wallmann (CDU), the eastern side of the square that

Frankfurters refer to proudly as their '*gute Stubb*' (colloquially: front parlour) was reconstructed in half-timbering (fig. 2) and now exudes more postcard charm than ever before, a precedent that we will come back to.

Figure 2: *The eastern side of the Römerberg, reconstructed in half-timbering 1981–84. (Photo: G. Vinken 2019)*

We will complete this prehistory by considering the *Haus am Dom*. Built from 2004 to 2006 between the Cathedral and the *Technisches Rathaus*, whose demolition had already been agreed, on plans drawn up Jochem Jourdan, it functions as a counter-argument to the fever for reconstruction. It transcends questions of taste to demonstrate the potential of modern architecture when the task is to create accents in a heterogeneous area by reflectively referencing the typology of the town house and the historic city centre. Today, the *Haus am Dom* is a rather bewildered onlooker at the current building site and has the appearance of an unintentional blow-up image.

DomRömer Quarter

The most recent act in the variety show being performed in the heart of Frankfurt oscillates between parody and soap opera. It concerns the construction of what is known as the *DomRömer* Quarter on the plot cleared for this purpose by the demolition of the *Technisches Rathaus* (fig. 3, 4).

Figure 3: Cleared to build a "historic" town center. Demolition of the "Technisches Rathaus" (Photo: Sarah Bonnert, 2011)

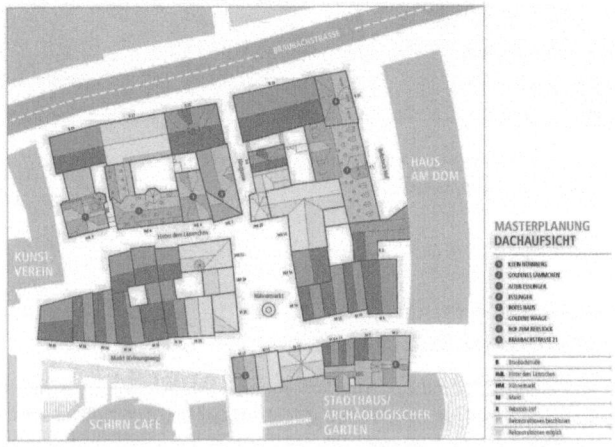

Figure 4: New roofscape. Blueprint for the DomRömer Quarter on the same area, DomRömerGmbH 2012

In objective terms, this project concerns the rebuilding of a mid-sized city centre area with small units and at medium density, with occasional replicas of houses destroyed in the war (fig. 5, 6).[5]

---

5   Marek, Rekonstruktion und Kulturgesellschaft, 2009, 53–98; cf. also Hansen, Die Frankfurter Altstadtdebatte, 2008 and Bideau, Fallstudie Frankfurt, 2011. I am grateful for pointers received from Sarah Bonnert, who wrote her dissertation at Offenbach University of Art and Design on this topic and has created several artworks focusing on the redesign of the area. Her website collates numerous documents, photographs and other information, cf. Website Alte Stadt aus neuen Häusern.

Figures 5, 6: The brand-new "Altstadt" – finally inaugurated: Visitors in the "DomRömerAreal" 2019 (Photos: G. Vinken)

The public interest that this project received over many years and which made architecture an election issue in Frankfurt once again doubtlessly has something to do with the dazzling effect of the term *Altstadt*. The now commonplace habit of referring to the *DomRömer* Quarter using this expression draws together various fantasies and hopes and focuses them on this city centre district: the return of the old Frankfurt that was lost, the possibility of healing by means of architectural reconstruction. The idea that the *DomRömer* Quarter could bring back Frankfurt's old town has been the emotional mainspring of the debate for years. Yet the idea of rebuilding a central part of the city, one that happened to be in public ownership, did not initially generate any unusual ideas. The most important piece of land in the city would become the home of the usual sort of thing: a modern, densely built city-centre district, with shops, offices and a few apartments – business as usual (fig. 7). Only the cookie-cutter ordinariness, the faceless 'niceness' of the proposals that won the 2005 design competition generated a real buzz around proposals – already existing – to reconstruct along historical lines. One key means to ensuring that the old town became firmly established in the public image supply was the online publication of digital models (fig. 8).[6] The calls to "rebuild the historic old town" grew ever louder, until ultimately one of the major parties – the centre-right CDU – aligned itself firmly with the proposal.

The reconstruction debate was led by the *Altstadtforum* (Old Town Forum), which was founded in 2004.[7] It brought together various pressure groups: the Society of Friends of the City of Frankfurt (created in 1966 as the successor to the Friends of the Old Town, *Bund tätiger Altstadtfreunde*, which dated back to 1922), the Frankfurt Retail Association (*Einzelhandelsverband Frankfurt*), the city-marketing group City Forum ProFrankfurt e.V.,

---

6   Website Wikimedia Commons, Virtuelles Altstadtmodell Frankfurt am Main. Sadly, the original, interactive website with the digital city model (http://www.virtuelle-altstadt.de/das-altstadtmodell.html) is not currently operational.

7   Website AltstadtForum Frankfurt.

Figure 7: Inhospitable modernism: winning design in the 2005 competition for a concept to replace Frankfurt's "Technisches Rathaus" (KPS Architekten Engel / Zimmermann)
Figure 8: Digital Old Town. The reconstructed Hühnermarkt (HHVISON, DomRömerGmbH 2013)

and the agency EQUIPE Marketing GmbH. While the 'Friends of Frankfurt' originally called for the pre-war city to be reconstructed as closely as possible, a compromise has since been reached: the new development will respect the lines of the pre-war streets and the volumes of historic buildings "for the most part". As things stand,[8] the plan is to build nearly 40 new houses, guided by the old volumes, including at least eight 'true' reconstructions of historic buildings. The project's principal contractor is the City of Frankfurt am Main itself, represented by DomRömer GmbH, which is owned in full by the city. The chair of the Design Committee (*Gestaltungsbeitrat*) is the architect Christoph Mäckler, a co-founder of the Dortmund-based German Institute for the Art of Urban Design, who has plenty of other business in Frankfurt, including the new airport terminal and highrises such as the Opernturm and Tower 185. "DomRömer GmbH [...] is responsible for developing, planning and completing the DomRömer district. DomRömer GmbH is also responsible for marketing and selling the new houses and apartments – via the establishment of leaseholds."[9] In other words, the houses will be built by a developer and the individual plots preferably granted to private investors on long-term leaseholds. According to the guidelines for the development of the site of the former *Technisches Rathaus* produced by the City Planning Department: "In the spirit of city repair, a quarter is to be developed with the high density and small scale typical of a traditional old town. The historical network of lanes and squares is to be largely rebuilt [...]. The characteristics of the former old town should be recognisable on the façades and roofs of the other buildings." The design guidelines specify that façades should reflect "historical features", locally typical structural elements and "natural stone from the local region".[10] A public competition for designs was announced in November 2010, and a high-calibre jury of experts selected a further 38 agencies to submit designs alongside

---

8   This text was originally written in 2013, before the completion of the DomRömer Quarter (2012–18), which closely followed the plans discussed here.
9   Website DomRömer Frankfurt.
10 Website Stadtplanungsamt Frankfurt am Main, Leitlinien für die Gestaltung.

the 18 participants who were invited to submit. In March 2011, the winning entries were put on display in the German Architecture Museum.

A high-quality video produced by the city was released in spring 2012 – appropriately enough at Cannes[11] – aiming to give an impression of the form and flair of the new city district. It shows young people strolling through the streets, window-shopping, and visiting a café. We wander down narrow lanes, stand on the rebuilt *Hühnermarkt* in front of the 1895 monument to local poet and proud Frankfurter Friedrich Stoltze (*"[...] un es will merr net in mein Kopp enei: wie kann nor e Mensch net von Frankfort sei!"*),[12] which is to be transferred from its current location behind St. Catherine's church. The film shows the familiar spaces of a mid-sized European city. Long 'tracking shots' along the digital façades show a pleasant mixture of replicas and contemporary architecture, most of the latter featuring more or less subtly historicizing forms. There is a deliberate avoidance of the spectacular, we are rather shown the familiar pattern of historical layers: The atmosphere of a lively city centre, where tradition and timeless style, homely streetscapes and international brands, the local and the global are skilfully synthesized. Designed on the drawing board and created by a single developer, the project is presented here as a model of the city of the future: equally the perfect backdrop for leisure and consumption and a source of identity – even if (and maybe this is only an effect of the digital rendering?), despite the meticulously animated bubbling fountain, it comes across as almost uncannily sterile. The *DomRömer* Quarter is promoted as a successful synthesis of two quite different tendencies. Redeeming a postmodern promise, it is simultaneously inclusive and exclusive. On the one hand, it satisfies the popular demand for restoration and historical reconstruction and thus reinforces the related populist condemnation of 'modernity' as cold and impersonal. On the other hand, the project draws on the concept of "city repair" and thus focuses on a more exclusive architectural conception, namely the debates of postmodern theory and "critical reconstruction".

Reconstruction

The first reading, which seeks to consider the *DomRömer* Quarter as a (partial) rebuilding of the historic center of Frankfurt that was destroyed in the war, relies on the rhetoric of recovery, or even continuity. For the 'Friends of Frankfurt', this is about nothing less than "regaining" the central reference point of Frankfurt's identity. "The area between the Main and the former Braubach, on the one side, and between Fahrgasse and Römerbergsenke, on the other, is the primordial cell of the city. That is where the Carolingian Palace stood, whose remains can be seen in the Archaeological Garden and whose chapel was the precursor of the Cathedral. Around the palace, a settlement formed. The market street ran through it, from east to west, forming the route later taken by kings and emperors following their election and coronation."[13] The *AltstadtForum* website describes

---

11   Website DomRömer Frankfurt, marketing trailer.
12   "And I can't wrap my head around it / How can someone not be from Frankfurt?" (written in the Frankfurt dialect).
13   Website Freunde Frankfurts.

the loss of this "primordial cell" as follows: "[...] Before its destruction in the war in May 1944, Frankfurt's old town was one of the most beautiful gothic old towns in Germany. More than 1,200 buildings, most of great historical interest, fell victim to a terrible hail of bombs [...] Now, following the demolition of the 'Technisches Rathaus' in 2010, more than 65 years after the destruction, Frankfurt has, for the first time, a chance to reconstruct some 30 historic houses, thereby regaining a valuable part of its old town."[14]

Typically, this 'regaining' is presented here without further context together with a tale of ruin that befell the city like a terrible storm (a "hail of bombs"). Also typical is the historical carelessness of describing the old town as 'Gothic' (just as Dresden is always Baroque), which overlooks 500 years of continual renewal and destruction – as well as the heritage conservation measures and the aesthetically-driven urban interventions of the immediate pre-war period. Also typical of this world view is the suggestive positioning of modernism as the continuation of the destruction: according to this logic, the *Technisches Rathaus* is one more disturbance, and its demolition offers a chance at redemption, healing, recovery. From this perspective, it is simply not apparent that the desire to "recover" the old town is a radical devaluation of the historical. For if (nearly) every part of this "valuable old town" was created in 2012 or later, then the simple fact of being old (or "age-value", to borrow a turn of phrase from the great conservation theorist Alois Riegl)[15] cannot be considered the defining feature of the historical. The arguments in favour of the value of the new old town use the magic words authenticity, integrity, and continuity, which UNESCO established as the criteria for World Cultural Heritage.

Authenticity

In the terminology of its proponents, the *DomRömer* Quarter is not being built on the concrete roof of an underground car park, as is in fact the case, but in a fictitious historical topography. "In line with a master plan adopted by the city council in September 2007, 30 houses will be erected there by 2013 on the streets Alter Markt, Hühnermarkt and Hinter dem Lämmchen. The best documented houses – Goldene Waage, Rotes Haus, Klein Nürnberg, Goldenes Lämmchen, Alter Esslinger, Junger Esslinger and perhaps also Haus Rebstock – will be reconstructed. The other houses, whose specifications still need to be elaborated, should, through their individual character, detailed façades, the use of local natural stone and the remains of the houses that were destroyed, resemble the old buildings in form. Additional reconstructions are also possible, in accordance with the goal of forming an appropriate and desirable ensemble. [...] Ground elevations will be restored to historical levels."[16] Only the final sentence touches upon the complex problem of creating a reconstruction on this particular site. The new area has to come to terms with the fact that the topography has completely changed since the war: with the *Schirn Kunsthalle* and its entrance (the monumental 'table' that functioned as an

---

14 Website AltstadtForum Frankfurt.
15 Riegl, The modern Cult of Monuments, 1982 (1903).
16 Website AltstadtForum Frankfurt.

abstract marker of the entrance has already had to make way), with the excavations in the archaeological zone (and the plan to build the Stadthaus on top of this has already come under fire because it would block the view of the Cathedral), and above all with the brute fact of Frankfurt's metro system, whose ramps and entrances can hardly be relocated. Already the "original level" of this reconstruction is barely more than a lazy compromise. In the diction of the Friends of Frankfurt, what is being built here is not a few rows of houses following pre-war street alignments, but rather buildings that are actually "on *am Alten Markt*, on the *Hühnermarkt*, on *Hinter dem Lämmchen*". Confirmed by the ubiquity of digital renderings, historical plans and photos, the old topography of the city has long been the reality overlaid on the wasteland that the demolitions left behind. And the coronation route, which never really existed in name, is already included in every tourist brochure and will probably soon grace street signs.

The same is true of the quant-yet-exotic old Frankfurt names of the houses that are to be replicated – *Goldenes Lämmchen, Alter Esslinger, Junger Esslinger, Klein Nürnberg*: thanks to the constant repetition, everyone is now familiar with them. In these names, at least, there is an authentic transmission of the historical. To build is now to repeat that which is known by name; the evocatively recapitulated name becomes the band linking the townhouses that were destroyed and their mocked-up revenants. *Altstadt* boosters even like to suggest a certain continuity of use: "There has been much interest in taking an apartment, opening a shop or a restaurant in one of the reconstructed houses. One of those making such inquiries is Frank Albrecht, whose chain of perfume stores can be traced back to a business founded in 1732 in the house known as Würzgarten (Markt). Ernesto Melber and his daughter want to open a café in the house 'Zum Esslinger'; they are descendants of Georg Adolf Melber, who was married to the sister of Goethe's mother and ran a dry-goods retail business out of the same building. The young Goethe often spent time there [...]. Clearly, not only this house but the entire area will doubtless become a major attraction for both locals and tourists."[17] Since it is impossible to provide a direct descendant of Goethe's mother's sister to live in every house, the *AltstadtForum* has taken on the task of "supporting the efforts of the publicly owned *DomRömer GmbH* in its efforts to find suitable investors for this area of such importance". It is also "looking for 30 Frankfurters who would like to invest in a piece of the old town"[18] Thirty Frankfurters! Does that mean, no 'outsiders' need apply? Are investors from neighbouring Offenbach excluded? Do immigrants need to prove their 'assimilation'? Once more, in the name of the old town, an exclusive and alienating ingroup designation with xenophobic undertones is used, as is always the case with local patriotism.[19]

The city's official marketing video for the project, which we have already mentioned, tries to evoke the old town in another way. As a strolling female visitor flicks through the pages of a historical guide to the city, the black and white photos are overlaid with

---

17 Website AltstadtForum Frankfurt.
18 Website AltstadtForum Frankfurt, details in the section "Aktion 30 Frankfurter".
19 The website has recently been amended to include the following definition of a Frankfurter: "We consider a Franfurter to be anyone who lives here or who loves Frankfurt", cf. Website AltstadtForum Frankfurt, in the section "Aktion 30 Frankfurter".

colour views of the replica buildings. The *DomRömer* Quarter is explicitly presented as the resurrection of the ruined old town. In another scene, there is a further invocation of material authenticity. A couple stop again and again to look at historical details, gazing in wonder at things like the richly decorated door surrounds and lion's head keystones of the reconstructed *Haus zur goldenen Waage*, where architectural fragments that have survived in museums are to be incorporated in the reconstruction (fig. 9).

Figure 9: New half-timbering and authentic spolia – Reconstruction of "Zur Goldenen Waage" (HHVISON, DomRömerGmbH 2013)

The design specifications that have already been produced recommend the use of such spolia "wherever historically or aesthetically possible".[20] After the war, many architectural fragments were indeed recovered and squirreled away in the city's archives.[21] The fact that these can now be used in 'meaningful' ways has persuaded many a once critical observer.[22] As attractive as the prospect of fetching the sometimes exquisite late Mediaeval and Renaissance fragments from storage and putting them on public display appears: when incorporated in the 'correct' or, as is mostly the case, the 'wrong' building, these genuine fragments complete the planned pastiche in a way that blurs the boundary – so vital from the perspective of heritage conservation – between original and copy. The practice of reusing recovered fragments from buildings that have been demolished

---

20   Website Stadtplanungsamt Frankfurt am Main, Leitlinien für die Gestaltung.
21   A detailed online catalogue of all the spolia that survive has since been developed, cf. Website Spolien der Frankfurter Altstadt.
22   Bartetzko, Aus Alt mach Neu, 2007.

or destroyed in new buildings is familiar from many old town restorations.²³ In the name of a homogenizing cityscape grooming, a certain degree of deception is, if not deliberately pursued, at least passively condoned.

Postmodern *Heimatschutz*

From the perspective of the *Heimatschutz* movement, a late 19th and early 20th century conservation tendency rooted in romantic nationalism, architecturally accurate replicas of destroyed buildings are always a guarantee of architectural quality. According to this logic, new buildings – always a second-best solution for the supporters of reconstruction – have to be subject to the strictest possible set of design regulations in order to limit the damage they do. In the *DomRömer* Quarter, new buildings are subject to regulations that normally – and quite rightly – apply only to historic districts. Strict conditions regarding scale and volume, typology and materiality seek explicitly to prohibit any outbursts of modern formal language. However, the German term *Stadtreparatur*²⁴ (literally "city repair") that is often used in this regard is misleading. It suggests a reference to concepts from urban planning and architecture that belong to a debate first held in the 1960s by the circle around Aldo Rossi. At that time, architecture was looking for a way out of the inhospitable dead-end street that functionalist modernism had become. By turning to the *site* in its historical stratification, to its typologies and materialities, it was hoped that a richer, 'site-specific' architecture could be developed. In Germany, these ideas inspired the highly fertile Berlin IBA (1977–87), which was guided by the concepts of "careful urban renewal" and "critical reconstruction".²⁵ And it is no coincidence that it was in Berlin, at an international building exhibition that is conventionally conceived of as a means to showcase the architecture of the future, that a part of the event was dedicated to the revitalization of old buildings (*IBA-Altbau*). The approach that was first realized here went hand in hand with a fundamental shift of perspective that returned the historic city to the centre of attention and rehabilitated it as a touchstone for contemporary architecture. Hans Stimmann's *Planwerk Berlin* – a comprehensive urban design plan for the city – which sought to rein in the city's uncontrolled post-unification growth, yet lacked conceptual depth and exhausted itself mostly in formalist promises of punctuated "stone" façades, etc. The search for the "city beautiful" that was also pursued in the German Institute for the Art of Urban Design in Dortmund (where Hans Stimmann worked alongside Christoph Mäckler) points in the same direction. Anointed once again as a model, the historic city is above all consulted as a versatile repertoire of forms for deployment. Existing structures are rarely subjected to systematic analysis in their heterogeneity, which would be a precondition for a site-specific building practice and individual city repair.²⁶

---

23   Meier, Spolien, 2021, in particular 65-70.
24   Website Stadtplanungsamt Frankfurt am Main, Dom-Römer-Areal.
25   Bauausstellung Berlin GmbH, Internationale Bauausstellung Berlin, 1987.
26   Löw/Vinken, Anpassung und Wirkung, 2012.

In Frankfurt, too, site-specific thinking is entirely alien to the *DomRömer* project. The textures of central Frankfurt, the scale and organization of the existing urban spaces around the *DomRömer* Quarter are too heterogeneous to enable the evocation of a credible 'old-town' architecture. The *Technisches Rathaus*, on top of whose underground garage the new district is being built, was flanked not only by the Dom and the Römer, but was also, and far more tangibly, the neighbour of the postmodern *Schirn Kunsthalle* and Braubachstraße, which only sliced through the old street plan in 1900 – and was further embedded in an architectural mix typical of Frankfurt's post-war regeneration, a combination of true urbanism and looser, almost suburban construction. Towards the Main river, the characteristic city centre pattern of block-perimeter buildings with inner courtyards gives way to two-storey terraced houses with front gardens and balconies. The reminiscences of local heritage in the *DomRömer* Quarter are not the result of analysis of and reflection on the existing structures, typologies and forms in their historical stratifications, but are rather entirely the expression of a will for restoration and reconstruction on the part of the city's planners. In Frankfurt, Aldo Rossi's call for a return to place and history has been reduced to a sheer formalism, a kind of postmodern *Heimatschutz* aesthetic.

Despite the narrow and uninspiring specifications in the call for entries, the competition generated some eminently respectable results.[27] *Morger+Dettli* (Markt 30), for instance, designed a naked façade of unquestionable modernity. The references to the "gothic" half-timbered house, evident, for instance, in the steep angle of the roof and the successively protruding storeys, attractively contrasts to the abstract simplicity of the stone façade. As an (ironic?) concession to the original specifications, the half-timbered façade of the replica opposite is reflected in the building's large windows. Naturally, this façade, which is entirely lacking in old-world charm, is not featured in the film. The bulk of the designs, however, are compliant: pragmatic variations on more or less non-specific historical motifs; synthetic finger exercises in urban façade design that risk little and have little to gain. The hermaphroditic nature of the designs is everywhere more than evident. Behind historicist façades are revealed beautiful floor plans, refined halls and stairways and light effects that no half-timbered house can provide. And, naturally, many addresses have direct access to an underground garage. Only a few of the selected agencies have genuinely attempted to create high-quality contemporary architecture in dialogue with historical typologies and structures, and not just to fill gaps.

Frankfurt's old town development is not 'city repair', is not the evolution of the city's unique character using the means of contemporary architecture. It is rather the creation of a 'zone of tradition' as a compromise between identity formation and the demands of the market. In this regard, the formation of the *AltstadtForum* out of representatives of retail, city marketing, and heritage conservation has proved a success; the opportunities to exploit the houses have been considerably enhanced as a result of the new building's more flexible floor plans compared to the total replica that was originally called for. If one looks for precedents for this pleasing and slick, clean and safe (and hence very non-urban) 'zone of tradition', there are two directions where surprising

---

27 The press also reviewed the process positively, as in the extensive report in the *Frankfurter Rundschau* newspaper by Göpfert/Michels, Kein Egotrip eines Architekten, 2012.

connections can be made: on the one hand, with the 'making' of the old town, namely with the homogenizing restoration projects undertaken since the 1930s and with post-war reconstruction, and, on the other, with the 'historically themed architecture' that has blossomed internationally since the 1980s.

Islands of Tradition

The rehabilitation and restoration of historic city centres in Europe has always had a double goal: the 'reintegration' of slums in the economic cycle, and the creation of aesthetically homogeneous historic districts.[28] Indeed, earlier projects, such as the "recovery and demutilation" (*Gesundung und Entschandelung*) of the area of Cologne around Great St Martin's church that was carried out under Nazi rule, reveal clear parallels to the most recent project in central Frankfurt. Situated near the Cathedral and directly on the River Rhine, the *Martinsviertel*, which continues to enjoy popularity as the historic quarter of the severely bombed city, was created in the 1930s by means of large-scale reconstruction.[29] In this context, *Gesundung* (healing, recovery) meant the creation of new squares and targeted demolition to enable the circulation of air and facilitate 'hygienic' modernization, while *Entschandelung* (demutilation) encompassed cityscape beautification measures such as the dismantling of intrusive Wilhelmine façades and billboards. Large-scale demolitions and gap-filling by means of pseudo-historical buildings, whose numbers far exceeded those of the houses that remained or were restored, created a homogeneous island of 'Old Cologne' tradition.[30] Strict building regulations meant the architects involved were required to refer back to the 'timelessly simple' traditional form of 'typical' Cologne houses, without a more specific historical reference point. Requirements included slate roofs and window and door surrounds of "rhenish cut stone".[31] As in Frankfurt today, the area was to retain its "unique local character" via the application of spolia from condemned buildings.[32] Portals, embrasures, borrowed anchor plates indicating the year of construction meant it could sometimes be hard to tell new and restored buildings apart, especially since older buildings that "lacked character" were also enriched with spolia.[33] In some cases, entire façades were relocated. Old town character is the conscious result of mimicry and simulation: as the conservationist responsible, Hans Vogts, put it, for instance, the "typical Cologne character" of the extended Kastellgäßchen would "depend more on new building".[34]

It is a bitter irony that precisely this synthetic old-town quarter, whose creation was in part the result of nationalist and racist policies, was rebuilt after the war as an 'island of tradition' (*Traditionsinsel* was then a technical term among city planners in

---

28 Vinken, Zone Heimat, 2010; Vinken, Kampf um die Mitte, 2011.
29 Cf. the essay on Cologne in this volume (Chapter 9).
30 Schlungbaum-Stehr, Das Martinsviertel, 1999; Vinken, Zone Heimat, 2010, 137–206.
31 Petz, Stadtsanierung im Dritten Reich, 1987, 151.
32 Examples are included in Vogts, Gesundungsmaßnahmen, 1997 (1936), 171.
33 Houses on the *Buttermarkt* with reused anchor plates in the form of numbers indicating years were later mistakenly listed as historic monuments, Schlungbaum-Stehr, Das Martinsviertel, 1999, 42.
34 Vogts, Gesundungsmaßnahmen, 1997 (1936), 171.

Germany). "With respect for the cityscape, taking into consideration the fact that only a limited number of houses are originals, and that, for the most part, this is a city district that was more or less newly created in the course of old-town rehabilitation before the Second World War with the use of old architectural features, the city's conservation authorities maintained the gabled contours of the rooflines as well as the height and rhythm of the built volumes", as Hanna Adenauer, the head of Cologne's conservation department explained at the time.[35] In Cologne, which had prescribed itself a moderately modern reconstruction, this kind of identity-confirming measure was also able to generate consensus. "The rebuilding of the area around Great St. Martin's (restoration of the old town) with the old market will make it possible to preserve what is original and unique about Cologne",[36] as even such a technocratic modernist planner as Wilhelm Riphahn saw fit to comment. Riphahn's proposal to rebuild the city's Rhine front in a modernist style would in fact have turned the old town into a truly isolated island of tradition in a quite alien environment (see figure 8 in chapter 9 on Cologne in this volume).

The *DomRömer* Quarter is one of a series of urban construction projects, both pre- and post-war, that aimed to use 'islands of tradition' as anchors of identity for cities that were undergoing modernization. For Hamburg, which was completely destroyed by aerial bombardment and, as far as he was concerned, unrebuildable, the planner Fritz Schumacher proposed in 1944 "joining together [surviving buildings] somewhere to create a 'historic centre' however modest."[37] The case of Hanover is more familiar. After severe destruction during World War II, it was rebuilt as a modern "car-friendly" city under Rudolf Hillebrecht, with no regard for existing structures. Many of the few surviving historic buildings were even demolished in the process.[38] As if to compensate, an 'island of tradition' was created out of relocated half-timbered houses around the *Marktkirche*. It is striking that, after 1945, in the most ruthlessly modernized cities – and that certainly includes Frankfurt – similar decisions were reached even many years after the war: as in Hildesheim, where from 1986 the reconstruction of the famous *Knochenhaueramtshaus* (Butchers' Guild Hall), which garnered a great deal of attention at the time, the 'dismantling' of the modern market square and the erection of a 'historic' ensemble were carried out consecutively, so in Dresden, where following the reconstruction of the *Frauenkirche*, the fake Baroque Dresden is currently extending its tentacles at the *Neumarkt*.

These entirely artificial 'islands of tradition' have, as is easily seen in Frankfurt, a compensatory function. In many regards, the *DomRömer* Quarter was able to refer back directly to a precedent from just 20 years previously: the aforementioned reconstruction of the buildings on the eastern side of the Römerberg.[39] After lying in ruin for years, the reconstructed row of half-timbered houses is today one of the city's most well-loved landmarks (see above, fig. 2). The proponents of the *DomRömer* project referred explicitly

---

35   Adenauer, Die Pflege der profanen Denkmäler, 1955/1956, 168.
36   Riphahn, Grundgedanken zur Neugestaltung, 1945, 7–8.
37   Quoted in: Beseler/Gutschow, Kriegsschicksale Deutscher Architektur, 1988, XLVIII.
38   Beseler/Gutschow, Kriegsschicksale Deutscher Architektur, 1988, 250–251.
39   Burgard, Frankfurt und der Retrotaumel, 2007.

to this project: "The reconstruction on historical lines of the eastern side of the Römerberg (Samstagberg) and the restaurant *Zum Schwarzen Stern*, which was concluded in 1983, corresponds to the wishes of the Friends of Frankfurt. It also shows that, when the right level of commitment is present, reconstruction is possible."[40] Of course, this project – like all undertakings of its type – also subjected its historical model to embellishment and modernization. Examples of embellishment include freely designing half-timbered façades where none had been visible before, as, apart from the building at the northern corner, all the structures destroyed in the war had been faced with plaster or slate. And modernization includes raising the ground level on which the new houses were built by a metre or so in order to retain the underground garage that had been build in the meantime – a case of palpable interference in the subtle evolution of the historic square. And, of course, modernization also means making sure that "historical façades" conceal floor plans that offer a generous rate of return: by breaking up the traditional unity of the town house into separate floors; by removing entrances to newly constructed annexes in the rear, which was necessary to enable the creation of shops and modern apartments behind the half-timbered frontages.

The *DomRömer* Quarter thus belongs to a tradition, well-established in Germany, of old-town clones and simulations, which have enjoyed a revival since the advent of postmodernism. Where the old town had once possessed a certain historicity, and where this had once given a basis to claims for its authentic and historical character, the most recent debates in Frankfurt show forcefully that the connection between "old town" and "old" has been entirely dissolved. DomRömer GmbH has even used the slogan "We are planning the old town", and an audience member at a panel discussion expressed her hope that "the mayor might soon be able to formally dedicate the old town". Road signs advertising the presence of a "historic old town", which until now have appeared pleonastic (as in the infamous "free gift") could in the future be augmented by new signs alerting the traveller to the location of a newly built "old town".

Historicizing theme-architecture

At the point where the old town has become completely decoupled from any concept of age itself, it becomes clear how close this project is to another branch of real estate – one that has also enjoyed great international success since the onset of postmodernism, namely historicizing theme-architecture. It has its origins in the consumerist realms of the amusement park and the casino; icons of themed architecture include Las Vegas with its Bridge of Sighs, Eifel Tower and Pyramids, and, of course, Disneyland's Main Street U.S.A., where America's small-town utopian dream recurs ad infinitum. And yet these themes have also been present in the real world for some time now. Shopping malls now compete with outlet villages built on organically irregular, vaguely historical patterns. In many of Germany's "Outlet Villages", behind façades similar to those of Disney's Main Street U.S.A., the deep stores of multinational corporations line up in rows (fig. 10).

---

40   Website Freunde Frankfurts.

Figure 10: Brave old world that has such consumers in it – Outlet Village near Berlin (Photo: G. Vinken 2017)

Of course, here we find ourselves on a completely different architectural and aesthetic level from the *DomRömer* Quarter. The pastiche architecture of the outlets consists of a limited number of simple elements, historical references are reduced to a bare minimum, and details alluding to city life are merely sketched in. Comparable, however, is the attempt to generate a sense of comfort and the consumption-friendly effect of these small-scale urban spaces that imitate organic structures, that are safe – and somehow familiar.

Everywhere, themed architecture is successfully capitalizing on vaguely historical, easily recognizable architectural forms. The spatial and aesthetic revival of the idea of neighbourhoods organized like small towns or along pre-industrial lines emerged in the USA in the 1980s as New Urbanism. It was opposed to the devastation of landscapes and the waste of resources as a result of urban sprawl.[41] This movement proposed to establish a new, denser and more traditional architecture in contrast to the anonymity and formless spread of the suburbs. Themed architecture was particularly successful at the higher end of the property market, for instance in the Florida town of Seaside, which provided the set for the film "The Truman Show", and the city of Celebration, founded by The Walt Disney Company itself. Perhaps the most spectacular example of historically themed planning in Europe was established near Dorchester in England by Leon Krier from 1993, with the personal support of Prince Charles. Poundbury is a large suburban development with an "organic" street plan and a dense building pattern that follows decorous pre-industrial lines (fig. 11).

---

41 Talen, New Urbanism and American Planning, 2005 *or* Katz, The New Urbanism, 1994.

Figure 11: 'Olde English' suburb: Poundbury, Dorchester (Photo: R. Dorrell 2010)

A middle-class suburb in the form of a traditional English town, it is currently undergoing considerable expansion as a result of high demand. It is telling that the proponents of reconstruction in Frankfurt see this artificial clone of old England, one that involves no "reconstruction" whatsoever, as a model. On their website, they refer to Leon Trier's project as a successful example of traditionalist, "antimodern" architecture.[42] Nor is it surprising that the centrally steered city planning authorities of China's boomtowns are aware of this successful approach. Around Shanghai, a city of 18 million people, numerous satellite towns are being constructed as part of the *One City. Nine Towns* project, not only in the old English style, but using a broad palate of European themed architectural styles. However, the attempt to found a "New Amsterdam" built around canals in northern China has since collapsed, along with the investors' prospects of a return on their outlay, as this pattern of living proved unsuited to meeting key needs of Chinese life.[43]

Dieter Hassenpflug coined the word "citytainment" to describe these Chinese satellite towns built in traditional European styles.[44] In Frankfurt's city centre, a 'luxury' feel-good 'historic' district is currently being built at a cost of 100 million euros, with a pre-industrial small-town flair, on a human scale and with a familiar set of experiences on offer. Is this still the "thirst for authenticity" that the French philosopher Jean Baudrillard suggested in 1968 could "be slaked only by forgeries"?[45] Frankfurt's old town is a homogeneous, familiar and almost certainly highly profitable newly constructed city district. The old town here is nothing more than an architectural pattern that can be invoked anywhere and at any time to reproduce a certain atmosphere. It is not that the

---

42 Website Freunde Frankfurts.
43 Hassenpflug, Der urbane Code, 2008.
44 Hassenpflug, Citytainment, 2000.
45 Baudrillard, The System of Objects, 1996 (1968), 84.

authentic cannot be distinguished from a simulation; however, that distinction appears to be largely insignificant for both the public perception and for building and planning policy. Baudrillard called this kind of situation, where the distinction between the real and the simulation was no longer relevant, "hyperreal".[46] If the challenges of the present can overwhelm us from time to time, if the new is sometimes confusing, or if our urban heritage seems too burdensome or too expensive then there is now an alternative we can all agree on: let's build a lovely new old-town clone.

---

46   Baudrillard, Simulacra and Simulation, 1994 (1981), chapter "The Hyperreal and the Imaginary", 12–14.

Reclaiming Heritage. Conflict, Contestation, Canonization

13 Palermo / Italy
Appropriations. The Canonization of the City in Early Travel Literature

> Panormus conca aurea suos devorat alienos nutrit
> Palermo the golden dell, devours her own and feeds the foreigners
> (inscription on the "Genius of the City" in the Palazzo Pretorio)[1]

The history of modern Palermo was long characterized by corruption and destruction: after the city suffered worse devastation than any other Italian city in the Second World War, the mafia-dominated construction industry brought about a second wave of destruction, referred to within the city as the "sacco" (sack) or "scempio" (massacre).[2] In the meantime, however, Arab-Norman Palermo has been canonized as UNESCO World Heritage (fig. 1): "Located on the northern coast of Sicily, Arab-Norman Palermo includes a series of nine civil and religious structures dating from the era of the Norman kingdom of Sicily (1130–1194): two palaces, three churches, a cathedral, a bridge, as well as the cathedrals of Cefalú and Monreale. Collectively, they are an example of a social-cultural syncretism between Western, Islamic and Byzantine cultures on the island which gave rise to new concepts of space, structure and decoration.

They also bear testimony to the fruitful coexistence of people of different origins and religions (Muslim, Byzantine, Latin, Jewish, Lombard and French)".[3] Looking back, this award, for all that it may appear justified today, was far from inevitable. Early travellers

---

[1] Unless stated to the contrary, all translations from German, French, Latin and Italian sources are by Graeme Currie.
[2] Schneider/Schneider, Reversible Destiny, 2003, 14.
[3] Website UNESCO, Arab-Norman Palermo, where we also find the following: "The monuments that comprise this 6.235-ha serial property include the Royal Palace and Palatine Chapel; Zisa Palace; Palermo Cathedral; Monreale Cathedral; Cefalù Cathedral; Church of San Giovanni degli Eremiti; Church of Santa Maria dell'Ammiraglio; Church of San Cataldo; and Admiral's Bridge."

Figure 1: Arab-Norman heritage. Mosaics in the Capella Palatina (Photo: G. Vinken 2019)

to Sicily were interested largely in Classical antiquity, while the Arab-Norman monuments (and those from the period of Hohenstaufen rule) were long neglected. One of the pioneer travellers, for instance, Baron von Riedesel, recording his visit to Monreale Cathedral, "passes over the Gothic mosaic work, about which the Sicilians make such a fuss".[4] In contrast to mainland Italy, which, as far south as Naples, had been the goal and the climax of the Grand Tour, Sicily was not 'discovered' until the advent of Neoclassicism, when Johann Joachim Winckelmann encouraged a new perspective on the ancient world. For German travellers in particular, Sicily was not simply an extension of the journey through Italy. At a time when the 'motherland' was an inaccessible part of the Ottoman Empire, they looked towards places such as Syracuse, Agrigento, Selinunte and Segesta for authentic contact with 'the Greek world'.[5] Only with the Historicism of the 19th century do we see a revaluation of the monumental landscape, one that established the Middle Ages as a key point of reference for the narratives of national heritage that emerged in countries such as England, France and Germany.[6] The shift in taste and significance that this brought about is vividly obvious in the criticisms that later travellers made of their predecessors. Even the sainted Goethe, who visited Sicily as early as 1787 and documented his impressions in the widely read *Italian Journey*[7] was not immune to the criticisms of a later, more historically aware generation. In 1854, for

---

4   Riedesel, Reise durch Sicilien, 1965 (1771), 23. On the discovery and reception of Sicily's Arab-Norman architecture, see Meier, Die normannischen Königspaläste, 1994, 6–11.

5   See Osterkamp, Geschichte der deutschen Sizilienwahrnehmung, 1987, 146. It was architects in particular who took up Winckelmann's mission "to go to the source": Schinkel visited the island in 1804, von Klenze in 1823–24, as did Hittdorf and others.

6   Osterkamp, Geschichte der deutschen Sizilienwahrnehmung, 1987, 150.

7   Goethe, Italian Journey, 1982 (1816/17).

instance, the author and historian Adolf Stahr called "Goethe's description of Palermo and its environs [...] very unsatisfactory". He noted that when Goethe travelled to Monreale, he mentioned the "foolish rococo fountains" but not the "marvel of the majestic cathedral with its colossal splendid columns, its giant mosaics, its grand arches, elaborate bronze doors, and finally, could not even say that he had seen the fabulous beauty of the marvellous cloister, in whose columned halls an entire world of Christian art lives".[8] While, according to Stahr, Goethe describes in full detail even "monumental extravagances" such as the "daring" fountain (Fontana Pretori) or the monstrous Villa Palagonia, "wonderful buildings" such as the Martorana, the Cappella Palatina (see above, fig. 1) or the cathedral with its mosaic artworks go unmentioned.[9] In fact, Goethe's itinerary during his visit to the island was entirely conventional for the time.[10] What is surprising about Stahr's description, however, is that he himself does not mention the cathedral's monumental porphyry sarcophagus, constructed for the Norman Roger II for his burial site in Cefalú and brought to Palermo by Frederick II.[11] This Hohenstaufen emperor's tomb was to become a place of pilgrimage at the high water mark of German patriotism that followed the defeat of Napoleon, as it allowed the Germans in Sicily to "dream of both: of the spiritual beauty of Greek humanity and of the power of mediaeval imperiality".[12] This was how Cosima Wagner recorded her visit: "Sublime impression, 'What kind of people are they, who build such a thing?' R[ichard] calls out. The cloister is charming."[13]

In the 18th century, visitors were less prone to speculate about the Normans and the Staufer than they were to consider ancient heroes and gods with Homer and Virgil. Nevertheless, especially in the early years, the expectations and interests of visitors varied significantly. The first modern traveller to Sicily, Karl Graf von Zinzendorf, visited the island in 1764–65 with a political and economic agenda as Councillor of Commerce (*Kommerzienrat*), in which capacity he was expected to gather concrete facts about economic, political, military and geographical matters.[14] In 1767, another pioneer, Winckelmann's pupil Baron von Riedesel, eagerly sought out traces of the Greeks, undertaking archaeological explorations and surveys in emulation of his teacher and role model.[15] Patrick Brydone, whose widely read travelogue was to influence the expectations of early travellers, journeyed as the mentor and companion of two aristocrats in the tradition of the Grand Tour,[16] this physicist's side-trip to Sicily was encouraged by Hamilton, the English ambassador in Naples, who was also a famous volcanologist, and it offered

---

8   Stahr, Tage in Palermo, 1986 (1845), 158–159.
9   Osterkamp, Sizilien Reisebilder, 1986, 158–159. Elsewhere, Osterkamp notes correctly that by the time of its publication – in 1817, almost three decades after his time in Sicily – Goethe's *Italian Journey* already represented a contrasting standpoint to the patriotic Mediaevalism of the Romantics. Osterkamp, Geschichte der deutschen Sizilienwahrnehmung, 1987, 149–150.
10 Osterkamp, Geschichte der deutschen Sizilienwahrnehmung, 1987, 148–149.
11 Rader, Die Kraft des Porphyrs, 2009, 43.
12 Osterkamp, Geschichte der deutschen Sizilienwahrnehmung, 1987, 150, 152.
13 Quoted in: Osterkamp, Sizilien Reisebilder, 1986, 174–175.
14 Zinzendorf, Mémoire, 1773 (1766).
15 Details below.
16 Brydone, A Tour through Sicily and Malta, 1774 (1773), I:137.

the further prospect of an ascent of Etna.[17] Brydone's approach to antiquity still drew largely on antiquarian (book) learning.

An examination of the genesis of Palermo's heritage-figurations is also particularly interesting because the city offered the classically educated travellers of the late Enlightenment relatively little of relevance. The anecdote handed down by one such visitor, Johann Gottfried Seume, in this regard is revealing. Seume, who, in contrast to his wealthy contemporaries, made the journey from Leipzig to Syracuse on foot, used a mule (with muleteer) to travel around the island's interior. On an adventurous ride from Palermo to Agrigento, he met muleteers from "all parts of the island" who easily guessed that the foreigner wanted "to visit their antiquities". "Then a quarrel arose [...] concerning the advantages of their home towns in matters of antiquity. The muleteer from Agrigento listed the temple and other marvels and the antiquity of his town; the muleteer from Syracuse mentioned the theatre, the quarries and the ear [of Dionysius, author's note]; the muleteer from Alcamo named Segesta." Seume's muleteer, meanwhile, who was from Palermo, "listened with regal patience and said – nothing".[18]

Part 1: Knowledge Transfer: The Learned Sicilians and the Foreigners

If Palermo didn't offer any Greek heritage – then what did it have? How and in what form did the city's heritage come into view? If earlier literature largely focused on reconstructing 18th-century Palermo from historical descriptions or examining questions of intertextuality,[19] the focus of research today has shifted considerably under the influence of post-colonial theory. The history of travel, on which so much has been published that it is barely possible to gain a complete overview, has also taken on board themes such as race, class and gender.[20] The field now questions the experience of alienness and the "situation of the other" as a key aspect of travel[21] and has turned its attention to the circulation of knowledge and to questions of agency.[22] Particularly when it comes to heritage formations, the question "who has the right to speak?" or "whose heritage is it?" is central.[23] The power imbalance in relation to questions of interpretation in the early phases of the appropriation of heritage in Palermo is evident: the insertion of Sicily's heritage into the European context was carried out in line with the cultural knowledge and aesthetic standards of (northern) European elites. In a certain regard, the focus of contemporary research still reflects this power imbalance by continuing to give a central role to the writings of travellers and their reception, particularly Goethe's *Italian Jour-*

---

17 Smecca, Three travel writers, 2009, for Brydone 47–101, here 47.
18 Seume, Spaziergang, 2003 (1802), 124–125.
19 On the travel literature of the 18th century: Tuzet, La Sicile au XVIIIe siècle, 1955. Cf. also Wuthenow, Die erfahrene Welt, 1980.
20 E.g. Maurer, Neue Impulse, 1999.
21 Möller, Situationen des Fremden, 2016.
22 Mackenthun/Nicolas/Wodianka, Circulation of Knowledge, 2017.
23 Ashworth/Graham/Tunbridge, Pluralising Pasts, 2007; Rampley, Identity in Central and Eastern Europe, 2012; Vinken, Das Erbe der Anderen, 2015.

ney, which has been scrutinized in the most exhaustive detail.[24] While this focus does grant a place to local elites, on whose information and work the knowledge of the early travellers' very much depended, the local knowledge communities are nonetheless only revealed in outline.[25] There is also a lack of detailed examinations of the earlier topographic and historical literature, something that this chapter can at best only attempt to patch up in places.

This contribution to understanding the genesis of Palermo's heritage-figurations therefore follows a twofold plan. It examines the appropriation of the city by foreigners, while inquiring at the same time into processes of evaluation and meaning-making. In a city that has little to offer the expectations of the cultural canon, there will be a particular focus on evaluating the monumental landscape via the questions of what can be seen, described, praised and criticized. The emphasis here will be less on intertextual questions ('What did Bartels adopt from Brydone?") or matters of cultural difference ("How do the English, the Germans travel?") than the attempt to analyse early travelogues against the background of local interpretative frameworks. Furthermore, a more precise look at contemporary topographic and historical works of Sicilian authorship provides an opportunity to work out what the state of knowledge was in the late 18th century and what explicit or immanent categories of evaluation were dominant in the discourse of local knowledge elites with regard to heritage-figurations. To gain an insight into local voices and sentiments, it is necessary to re-read familiar texts in view of the guiding questions: What sources, what contacts are mentioned? How are local elites and the inhabitants of the city viewed with regard to heritage? What dissonances can be detected between local evaluations and those of the visitors? Is it maybe even possible to discern a variety of heritage communities?

Topography and Cityscape

If Palermo offered little in the way of ancient sites, the city was by no means without interest (fig. 2). On the contrary, many early travellers made liberal use of superlatives. Goethe, for instance, enthuses about "the contours of Monte Pellegrino [...], the most beautiful promontory in the world", the purity of the contours of the city and the landscape, the harmony of sky, earth and sea.[26] Because of its location, but also its layout and amenities, Palermo is considered one of the "first cities of Europe"; it has been called "one of the most beautiful cities" in the world.[27] Travellers who say this are adopting a topos that is deeply rooted in the local literature, where Palermo is referred to as "Paradiso della Sicilia [...,] Conca di Oro, [...], Città [...] Felice" (Sicily's paradise, Golden dell, happy City).[28]

---

24 On Goethe in Sicily, cf. Cometa, Il romanzo dell'architettura, 1999; Meier, Ein unsäglich schönes Land, 1987; cf. also Osterloh, Versammelte Menschenkraft, 2016; Zilcosky, Learning How to Get Lost, 2017; Spelsberg, I patrimonio culturale, 2011; Hirdt/Tappert, Goethe und Italien, 2001.
25 This is discussed, for instance, in Faber/Garms-Cornides, Entdeckung Siziliens, 2005. Cf. Pahnke, Spaziergang durchs papierne Jahrhundert, 2018.
26 Goethe, Italienische Reise, 1988 (1816/17), 230–231 (3 April 1787).
27 Bartels, Briefe über Kalabrien und Sizilien, 1787–1792.
28 Gaetani, Della Sicilia Nobile, 1754–1775, I/1754: 15, 22, 30. Cf. Leanti, Lo stato presente della Sicilia, 1761, I:65.

Figure 2: "Spaziergang in Palermo" (A stroll in Palermo), Franz Ludwig Catel, oil on canvas, 1846

Palermo, by far the largest and most important city on the island, which, since the loss of its independence, was ruled by viceroys from 1412 until 1816, was also the island's ecclesiastical capital and seat of its archbishop.[29] With 100,000–200,000 inhabitants – numbers vary[30] – Palermo was, alongside Naples (ca. 300,000) and Rome (ca. 160,000) one of the largest Italian cities.[31] Reached from Naples by means of a short – though not entirely easy – sea journey, Palermo was where most travellers began their visits to Sicily. With its streetlights, promenades and numerous cafés, it did not need to shirk comparison with the city of Vesuvius. Yet the contrast to the rest of Sicily came as a shock. On the one hand, the urban "hothouse", with an abundance of everything, a confusing "labyrinth", full of "heterogeneous things",[32] on the other, the impassable and impoverished countryside, exploited to enable the luxury of the capital: "It is hard to believe that one is in the same country, where the condition of the nation is closer to a state of barbarism than one of culture."[33] It is telling that outside the city the only streets that were firm and fit for traffic were those to nearby Monreale. Travelling any further was correspondingly difficult – on horseback for the privileged, but for most, by mule on narrow paths. Wealthy travellers such as Zinzendorf or Brydone reached their goals mostly by ship and restricted their overland travel on the island to a minimum.

---

29 Since 1734, the Kingdom of Sicily had been ruled in a personal union with the Kingdom of Naples by a subsidiary line of the Spanish Bourbons; the king resided in Naples.

30 Leanti gives a figure of 102,105 inhabitants (Leanti, Lo stato presente della Sicilia, 1761, I:52), Gaetani 140,000 (Gaetani, Della Sicilia Nobile, 1754–1775, I/1754: 18); Riedesel mentions "supposedly 150,000, but more like 120,000" (Riedesel, Reise durch Sicilien, 1965 (1771), 22), Bartels 200,000 (Bartels, Briefe über Kalabrien und Sizilien, 1787–1792, III/1792: 540).

31 Zern, Die Entdeckung Siziliens, 2014, 90.

32 Bartels, Briefe über Kalabrien und Sizilien, 1787–1792, III/1792: 476, 521–522, 540, 550. Cf. also Goethe, Italienische Reise, 1988 (1816/17), 229–230 (3 April 1787).

33 Bartels, Briefe über Kalabrien und Sizilien, 1787–1792, III/1792: 475–477.

Zinzendorf's Mémoire and the Topographic and Historical Literature

From the 16th century, the Spanish had built Palermo into a splendid princely seat; the mediaeval city walls had been expanded to create regular bastions, adorned with magnificent gates. The urban plan, organized by two grand main thoroughfares intersecting in a cross, was striking in its regularity; an additional accent was lent by the new harbour with its long *molo*, completed in 1590. As evidenced by numerous extant *vedute*, Palermo had already assumed its iconic cruciform layout by 1700 (fig. 3).[34]

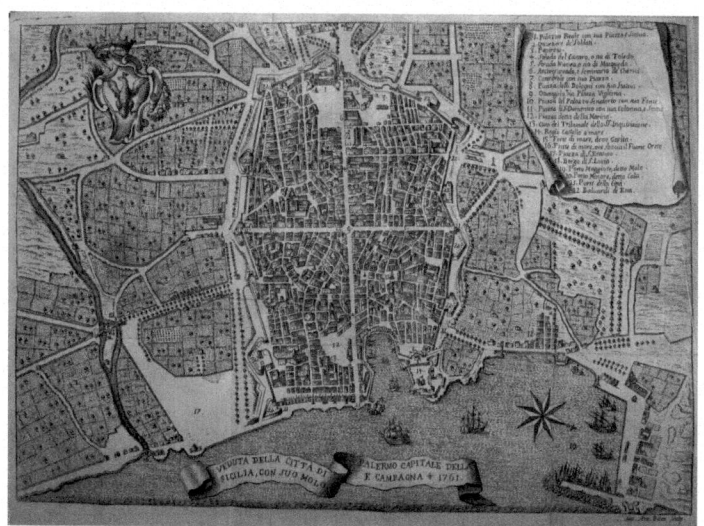

Figure 3: Inscription of a cross. Plan of Palermo, engraving by Antonio Bova, 1761

A concise description of the city was given by the first of the modern travellers, Karl Graf von Zinzendorf, scion of a landed family from Lower Austria who journeyed throughout Europe and the Habsburg monarchy in 1763–76 in his function as Counsellor of Commerce – one of his objectives being to strengthen the Habsburg presence in the Mediterranean.[35] First published in French in 1766, his *Mémoire sur le Royaume de Sicile*[36] is rather unique, as already mentioned, in that it is the result of a narrowly interpreted political mandate, namely to gather detailed information on finances and trade, political structures and other matters for his superior Kaunitz, the Austrian State Chancellor. In the *Mémoire*, Zinzendorf devotes some 30 pages to Palermo, where he spent eleven days.[37] We will find the key elements of his description of the city echoed in the writings of most travellers: the beautiful location on a small gulf surrounded by high mountains; the two well-planned main streets that "adorn the city so beautifully": Along

---

34 A good overview is provided by Cesare, Raffigurazioni, 2008.
35 For details of Zinzendorf's trip to Sicily, see Faber/Garms-Cornides, Entdeckung Siziliens, 2005, 346. On his biography ibid., 343–345.
36 Zinzendorf, Mémoire, 1773 (1766). Cited after the edition from Lausanne of 1773, which also contains a French translation of Riedesel's travel journals as well as Hamilton's description of Etna.
37 Faber/Garms-Cornides, Entdeckung Siziliens, 2005, 347.

the main axis, the Via Cassaro or Toledo (today's Corso Vittorio Emanuele), grandly rebuilt in 1564; along the short axis, the Via Nuova or Maqueda, laid out in 1609, and the point where they meet, inspired by the Quattro Fontane in Rome, an octagonal square decorated with fountains and called Ottangolo or Quattro Canti.[38]

Figure 4: Poorer than Rome? Palermo, Fontana Pretoria (Photo: G. Vinken 2019)

Zinzendorf goes on to detail the following sites – in this order: many fountains, including the one in front of the Senatorial Palace (Fontana Pretoria), which is remarkable for its beauty and architecture, fig. 4); more squares, including the one in front of the Royal Palace with the statue of Philip IV, and the Piazza Bologni with the statue of Charles V; the promenades, said to be far better than those of Naples, especially the seafront (La Marina). The cathedral is described as "very richly decorated, with beautiful columns of oriental granite, a tabernacle of lapis lazuli, columns of jasper and porphyry; the sepulchres of Emperors Henry VI & Frederick II, both of porphyry".[39] The Jesuit and Theatine churches are also "très riches", and an additional 13 churches (meaning parishes) are mentioned, eight monasteries for men and five for women, 71 convents, 18 schools (conservatoires) "for poor girls and two for poor boys", eight hostels, etc.[40] The old harbour, he notes, is now only for boats (barques), while the new harbour lies outside the city and has the beautiful mole from 1590 and a lighthouse. The description closes by mentioning that many noble residences may be found outside the city, at Monte Pellegrino and in La Bagaria. Details are also given of the city government, trade, customs, etc.

---

38   Zinzendorf, Mémoire, 1773 (1766), 301.
39   All from Zinzendorf, Mémoire, 1773 (1766), 301–302.
40   Zinzendorf, Mémoire, 1773 (1766), 302–303.

At first glance, this deliberately dry text, which seeks to assemble relevant 'facts', appears to be of little relevance to the matter of our inquiry. This report, which lies somewhere between information-gathering and economic and military espionage, mostly refrains from making evaluations.[41] In her overview, Hélène Tuzet calls the *Mémoire* "barely travel writing", and not without cause.[42] Yet the normative character of the text reveals clearly what was really important to the author. He may not have been interested in tourist attractions in the conventional sense, but he was looking for anything worth reporting, for "curiosities" in a literal sense. What is clear is that Zinzendorf could not have put together his *Mémoire* in such a short time without a significant amount of preliminary work. Very little concrete and up-to-date information about Sicily was available in northern Europe at the time – which may have been one of the reasons for this journey of discovery. Winckelmann, for instance, advised Riedesel to prepare by reading an older text, the *Siciliae Antiquae libri duo* by the German geographer and historian Philipp Clüver from 1619. In view of Zinzendorf's working methods, which appear to have involved composing his reports at least in part before setting off,[43] relevant sources of information may have included not just the local network of educated people, who served travellers to Sicily as contacts and expert guides (of which we shall have more to say below), but above all recent historiographic and topographic studies. In his *Mémoire*, Zinzendorf names, alongside two older printed volumes,[44] two further Sicilian authors, namely Vito Maria Amico and the Marquise de Villabiancha.[45] In addition, there are, as we shall see, clear reasons to suppose that Zinzendorf also consulted the volume *Lo stato presente della Sicilia* by Arcangiolo Leanti, which was published in Palermo in 1761, close to the time of his visit to Sicily.[46] A comparison of the *Mémoire* with the contemporary local authors mentioned above is revealing, particularly with respect to the choice of objects and their evaluation. When analysing Zinzendorf's work in terms of the contemporary Sicilian topographic and historical authors, we are not concerned with precisely accounting for the internal links between these texts, which are largely compilatory in character. The aim is rather to grasp how Palermo's monumental landscape is portrayed, and whether a more or less established canon of curiosities had already become established, in relation to which the observations of Zinzendorf and the other early travellers could then be placed.

The three texts to be compared are very different in terms of their aims and scope. It is all the more remarkable that one can answer the question of whether there was

---

41 Faber/Garms-Cornides, Entdeckung Siziliens, 2005, 346. On determining the text's genre, also 348–349.
42 Tuzet's verdict is harsh; in her view, the report has "rien d'un récit de voyage" (Tuzet, La Sicile au XVIIIe siècle, 1955, 8). Zinzendorf's journals and correspondence, which, however, remain unpublished to this day, could give a different picture.
43 Faber/Garms-Cornides, Entdeckung Siziliens, 2005, 349, Note 38.
44 Faber/Garms-Cornides, Entdeckung Siziliens, 2005, 34, Note 64, with reference to Fazello, Baruta, Monitore, Caruso. Source for this indications is the manuscript of Zinzendorf's *Mémoire* in the State Archives of the City of Vienna/Hofkammerarchiv (HKA Vienna, Hs. 302), 347–419, here 383–384.
45 Cf. the manuscript of Zinzendorf's *Mémoire* (as in note 44), 360, 383–384.
46 Leanti, Lo stato presente della Sicilia, 1761. Also noted without further explanation by Faber/Garms-Cornides, Entdeckung Siziliens, 2005, 354, Note 64.

an established canon in the affirmative simply on this narrow basis, also noting that Zinzendorf, as we shall see, reproduced this canon to a very large extent. Francesco Maria Emanuele e Gaetani, from whom Zinzendorf borrowed his entire section on organs of government and administration, was a senator and a historian. His Magnum Opus *Della Sicilia Nobile* was an attempt to compile a comprehensive overview of the Sicilian nobility.[47] His account is preceded by general historical and geographical information gathered from older sources, which in structure and style resemble those given by Zinzendorf. Then, following a typographical-historical overview, he introduces the capital city and a selection of major sites. Palermo is dealt with relatively briefly, and here too there are many points of agreement with Zinzendorf, including a nearly identical ordering of the sites of interest and monuments.[48] Both authors list historical monuments and items of modern infrastructure and technological achievements together, including the molo with its lighthouse and the extensive streetlighting, which in Gaetani's eyes, is comparable with that of the most distinguished cities in Europe, such as Paris, London, Vienna and Venice – a formula that is repeated almost word forward in Leanti.[49] Occasional deviations in detail and variations in numbers show that Gaetani was not Zinzendorf's only source.[50] Some passages of Zinzendorf's report read like a straightforward response to Gaetani. Where the latter, full of local patriotism, describes the Fontane Pretoria (see above, fig. 4) as "one of the most distinguished in Europe", Zinzendorf plays the well-travelled connoisseur, noting that Palermo possessed neither the money nor the artists to create such beautiful fountains as those in Rome.[51]

There are far fewer points of agreement in the description of Palermo with the *Lexicon topographicum Siculum* of Vito Maria Amico, which Zinzendorf also names as a source. By far the best known work of this Benedictine monk of noble heritage, who studied at the University of Catania,[52] the body of this text consists of an alphabetical gazetteer of Sicily; In terms of Palermo, Amico does name broadly similar aspects as Gaetani and later Zinzendorf, yet he places them in a different, less rigid order.[53] Far more significant for our purposes is the publication by the Benedictine Abbot Arcangiolo Leanti (fig. 5) of *Lo stato presente della Sicilia*,[54] which is elaborately illustrated with some 40 large etchings by Antonio Bova.[55]

---

47   Gaetani, Della Sicilia Nobile, 1754–1775. The 1st and 2nd volumes deal with Palermo.
48   Gaetani, Della Sicilia Nobile, 1754–1775, I/1754: 14–31.
49   Gaetani, Della Sicilia Nobile, 1754–1775, I/1754: 20; Leanti, Lo stato presente della Sicilia, 1761, I:65.
50   Cf., for instance, the unsystematic list of parishes and religious institutions. Gaetani, Della Sicilia Nobile, 1754–1775, I/1754: 18–19.
51   Gaetani, Della Sicilia Nobile, 1754–1775, I/1754: 17; Zinzendorf, Mémoire, 1773 (1766), 302.
52   On his biography, cf. Zapperi, Vito Maria Amico, 1960.
53   Amico, Lexicon topographicum siculum, 1855/1856 (1757–1760).
54   Leanti, Lo stato presente della Sicilia, 1761.
55   On Bova cf. Augello, La Sicilia, 1983.

Figure 5: Local knowledge elite. Abbot Arcangiolo Leanti, engraving by Antonio Bova, 1761

Much of Zinzendorf's description of the city reads like a shortened version of this book, published by the historiographer and co-founder of the palermitan Accademia degli Ereini, which is far more detailed and includes some astonishingly precise figures on history and architectural history, presented in the same broad plan and order.[56] Comparing the arrangement of the etchings in Leanti's publication with the order of Zinzendorf's description reveals even more striking similarities. Zinzendorf's description appears to be based on the book's 16 *vedute* of Palermo. Even his description of the plan of the city, as I have already mentioned, can be read as a verbal description of the cityscape by Bova that is found in Leanti's book (fig. 2). The highly distinctive view of the Quattro Canti should also be mentioned here, where the artist has chosen a point of view from which, in an apparently forced perspective, both city gates are visible at the end of the two grand streets (fig. 6) – and this detail is stressed in the Councillor of Commerce's otherwise sober report: "[...] where towards the four gates, we have the most beautiful view in the world".[57] Zinzendorf's praise of the city's beautiful promenades (including specifically the *Marina*), which he claims are far superior to those of

---

56 Here, too, the figures occasionally vary. Leanti names 13 parishes, including one that follows the *rito greco*, 46 convents, six hostels, twelve *Compagnie et Confraterie*, including three noble convents, 23 nunneries, including 18 conservatori di Fanculle (Leanti, Lo stato presente della Sicilia, 1761, I:52); by contrast Zinzendorf lists 13 churches (meaning parishes), eight monasteries and five nunneries, 71 convents, 18 "conservatoire pour les pauvres filles & deux pour les garcons pauvres", and eight hostels, one of which is brand new. Zinzendorf, Mémoire, 1773 (1766), 302–303.
57 Zinzendorf, Mémoire, 1773 (1766), 301.

Naples,[58] can also be understood as reflecting Leanti's publication, whose first image of Palermo is of the coastal promenade, the *Marina* that later travellers sought out with so much enthusiasm (fig. 7).

Figure 6: "*Le plus beaux coup d'oeil du monde*". Palermo's "Quattro Canti", engraving by Antonio Bova, 1761

Figure 7: *The centre of Palermo's social life. Marina and Porta Felice*, engraving by Antonio Bova, 1761

---

58 Zinzendorf, Mémoire, 1773 (1766), 302.

Contrasting Evaluations: The Sicilian Authors

Though brief, the sketch given here of the texts by Sicilian authors as they relate to Palermo gives a clear initial impression of the way in which the monumental landscape of the city was perceived by the local intellectual elite, at a time before travelers began to exert an appreciable effect on the canon through their own writings. Zinzendorf's *Mémoire* assumed the body of knowledge and – with respect to Palermo's monumental landscape – evaluative categories of the authors named here. The Sicilian texts also cover a range of topics taken up by many later travellers, even if they did not find their way into the Austrian Councillor of Commerce's brief *Mémoire*. The Feast of Santa Rosalia, which after Brydone was to become one of the main attractions for travellers to Sicily, is also highlighted by local authors: Gaetani, for instance, describes the festival of several days' duration "with such sublime pomp that perhaps there is no greater in the Catholic Church".[59] Zinzendorf's occasional comments on everyday life, such as the dense population of the city, the magnificent coaches (*équipages*) of the nobles or the numerous social gatherings (*assemblées*)[60] are apparently too obvious for the local authors to mention, but are reproduced in subsequent travelogues.[61]

Although local authors of this period focus on a widely varying range of topics, if we examine their evaluation of monuments and historical architecture in detail we can speak of a broad consensus. In general, the learned Sicilians place great emphasis on material artefacts. The monuments and their history, which are generally associated with specific events, dynasties and dates, are significant to the extent that they demonstrate the great antiquity and importance of Palermo and Sicily as a whole. Gaetini, for instance, begins his description of the capital with a detailed account of the (few) ancient remains within and outside the walls, as they demonstrated that Palermo could be counted "among the most ancient and principle cities of Sicily".[62] In this, however, the various historical epochs are given significantly different evaluations. According to Gaetani, the Romans granted Palermo civic immunity (*immunità*), Vandals and Goths confirmed this and the Saracens consolidated it; the Normans made Palermo into their capital and held coronations there – from the Ruggieri to the Bourbon Charles III – and the Staufer do not even make an appearance in this context.[63]

It is not surprising that Greek antiquity is also an important point of reference for these Sicilian authors, even if their ranking is somewhat unusual. The city with the strongest connotations of 'Greekness' is certainly Syracuse, once "one of the most important cities in Europe",[64] the largest and most powerful city of the ancient Greek world with – according to Amico – over a million inhabitants.[65] Not only is the history of the city expanded upon in appropriately extensive detail (it being described as,

---

59 Gaetani, Della Sicilia Nobile, 1754–1775, I/1754: 22. Zinzendorf, who did not witness the event, also omits to mention it.
60 Zinzendorf, Mémoire, 1773 (1766), 303.
61 The *équipages*, for instance, are a major theme for several authors, including Brydone, A Tour through Sicily and Malta, 1774 (1773), II:238–242, 318–320.
62 Gaetani, Della Sicilia Nobile, 1754–1775, I/1754: 16.
63 Gaetani, Della Sicilia Nobile, 1754–1775, I/1754: 22.
64 Gaetani, Della Sicilia Nobile, 1754–1775, I/1754: 60.
65 Amico, Lexicon topographicum siculum, 1855/1856 (1757–1760), II/1856: 504.

among other things, the "home of Archimedes" and "flower of the Greeks"), the "most precious ancient monuments" (*memorie*) are also depicted.⁶⁶ Many of the "remarkable structures" and anecdotes that later circulated among the travellers are found in an earlier form in the local literature (often drawing on even earlier sources). For instance, in describing the Ear of Dionysius, Gaetani mentions the cave's famous echo and the experiment with the pistol shot, which no later traveller would think to leave out.⁶⁷ The authors are certain that there is a large and international interest in 'Greek' Syracuse: Both Gaetani and Leanti name as their source a local "eruditissimo letterato",⁶⁸ Conte Cesare Gaetani, on whom the "oltramontani" travellers would rely: "He is responsible for the number of oltramontani visiting Syracuse to admire the very precious ancient monuments that remain there".⁶⁹ Gaetani's description of the temple of Agrigento is also full of local pride. He claims that visitors from all the world visit it "with surprise and amazement". Its size is said to exceed every other comparable site "[...] that he had seen in Greece before or after".⁷⁰ By contrast, Leanti's description of Agrigento is very brief and fails entirely to mention the Greeks by name.⁷¹ He lists the most important ancient cult sites of the island – cursorily – only in the second volume of his monograph, tellingly in connection with an overview of religious institutions, specifically the pagan cults.⁷² The local authors provide nothing like an overview of the Greek remains and demonstrate no ambition to explore remote ruins or gather archaeological observations. The Sicilian authors are concerned with significant towns and their histories, not with archaeological sites.

Nonetheless, the fields of interest and knowledge of the Sicilian experts are significantly broader than those of the travellers. They are familiar with the basic outline of the Arab history of the island and value it.⁷³ In Palermo, they are wrongly believed to have built the Palazzo di Maredolce, the summer palaces La Zisa and La Cuba (and sometimes even the Palatine Chapel), which formerly stood before the city, all of which were in fact not built until the Norman period. The Norman monuments are themselves often called magnificent, beautiful etc., and sometimes described in great detail. In Palermo, it is the Palatine Chapel with its "intarsia floors of finest marbles and design", its "dome with various figures from ancient mosaics", that evokes admiration: "In sum, this court chapel (Regia capella) deserves, in good faith, to be counted among the best which are

---

66   Leanti pays particularly thorough attention to Syracuse (Leanti, Lo stato presente della Sicilia, 1761, I:125–133); cf. Gaetani, Della Sicilia Nobile, 1754–1775, I/1754: 59–62.
67   Gaetani, Della Sicilia Nobile, 1754–1775, I/1754: 60.
68   Gaetani, Della Sicilia Nobile, 1754–1775, I/1754: 60.
69   Leanti, Lo stato presente della Sicilia, 1761, I:128–129. For more on Cesare Gaetani della Torre (who should not be confused with Francesco Maria Emanuele Gaetani whom we have cited above) and his importance for travellers and local authors including Swinburne, Comte de Borch, Torremuzza, Villabianca, Schiavo, Amico and Hamilton cf. Cannarella, Profili di siracusani illustri, 1958.
70   Gaetani, Della Sicilia Nobile, 1754–1775, I/1754: 31. Cf. Amico, Lexicon topographicum siculum, 1855/1856 (1757–1760), II/1856: 513–515.
71   Leanti, Lo stato presente della Sicilia, 1761, I:79–80.
72   "Culto in tempo de Gentili", Leanti, Lo stato presente della Sicilia, 1761, II:365–369.
73   Cf. Amico, Lexicon topographicum siculum, 1855/1856 (1757–1760), II/1856: 261.

in Italy, and perhaps outside of it."[74] But Leanti also considers the mediaeval cathedral – behind its elaborate Baroque enclosure – to merit an engraving (fig. 8). It is therefore hardly surprising that he also mentions the Cathedral of Monreale, which he calls one of the most beautiful churches in all of Europe, whose "eccellenti architetture" with its marble pillars, mosaics and bronze doors arouses "the wonder of strangers".[75] In his extensive account, Amico even describes the cloister (*patio*), with "216 colonette".[76]

Figure 8: Mediaeval majesty. View of Palermo Cathedral, engraving by Antonio Bova, 1761

The Staufer and their remains, which have been part of the standard tourist itinerary since the 19th century, are less evident in the descriptions of the early travellers. In 18th century Palermo, Friedrich II was at least associated with the expansion of the city walls[77] and efforts to create an "erudie Accademie".[78] Gaetani, who goes through all the Kings of Sicily in chronological order, does not spend much time on this member of the Staufer dynasty, yet he does know to report that the emperor was laid to rest in a "tumulo di porfiro" in Palermo.[79] In his description of the cathedral, Gaetani is able to give an accurate account of many members of the Norman and Staufer dynasties who are buried here.[80] Amico and Leanti also mention "the gorgeous porphyry tombs of kings

---

74 Leanti, Lo stato presente della Sicilia, 1761, I:58; Amico calls it "excellent for its mosaics" (Amico, Lexicon topographicum siculum, 1855/1856 (1757–1760), II/1856: 250, 259), Gaetani knows that the mosaic works were commissioned by King Roger (Gaetani, Della Sicilia Nobile, 1754–1775, I/1754: 17).
75 For full details, see, for instance, Leanti, Lo stato presente della Sicilia, 1761, I:71–72, here 72.
76 Amico, Lexicon topographicum siculum, 1855/1856 (1757–1760), II/1856: 169–173, here 171.
77 Amico, Lexicon topographicum siculum, 1855/1856 (1757–1760), II/1856: 262.
78 Gaetani, Della Sicilia Nobile, 1754–1775, I/1754: 25.
79 Gaetani, Della Sicilia Nobile, 1754–1775, I/1754: 325–326.
80 Roger I (instead of II) and many relatives, Henry VI and Constance Frederick II, and Constance of Aragorn, and others (Gaetani, Della Sicilia Nobile, 1754–1775, I/1754: 17–18). It had been known for a long time that many Normans and Staufer were buried here. The graves were identified and

and princes",[81] "the four famous royal porphyry urns"[82] as sites of interest. Zinzendorf, by contrast, did not personally visit the site; nonetheless he knew of the two porphyry tombs of the emperors Henry VI and Frederick II.[83] Later travellers generally had other interests. Riedesel (see below) did not think the tombs were worth mentioning, and even Goethe ignored the cathedral and the imperial graves, while Brydone did at least mention the tombs of the Norman Kings "some of them near 700 years old, and yet of very tolerable workmanship".[84]

Naturally, these differences also depend in part on the intended readerships of the texts. The aim of the learned Sicilians, whose books were generally dedicated to the ruling (Spanish) Viceroy, was to emphasize Sicily's age, power and importance.[85] Leanti's splendid volume is illustrated largely with *vedute* and the most impressive (mostly recent) palaces, churches and statues from the period of Spanish rule. In chapter IV, Economy and Trade, he presents a panel showing, alongside salt production and oyster farming, the complex equipment involved in tuna fishing, which was to become an enthusiastic topic for travellers' accounts.[86] Antiquity is of marginal importance here. It is no coincidence that in Agrigento only the (modern) harbour is pictured; in Catania, alongside the Basilica della Collegiata, the university and the Palazzo Senatorio, the cathedral, whose – quite obviously – ancient origins as a temple of Minerva are indeed, however, noted with pride. Only two of the many Greek monuments are honoured with illustrations, the amphitheatre in Syracuse and the well-preserved temple at Segesta (fig. 9).[87]

With regard to the Middle Ages, whose monuments were highly regarded within Sicily, we can also observe significant differences in how they are evaluated by local people and by visitors. Travelling on his political mission, Zinzendorf assumes the position of a kind of intermediary. In his – rather tentative and conventional – judgments, he generally goes along with his Sicilian authors and considers it self-evident that the large Arab-Norman monuments as well as the cathedral of Monreale – "remarkable for its age & for its richness of marble, porphyry & ancient mosaics"[88] – are worth highlighting as "curiosities" (*Merkwürdigkeiten*) – evaluations that later 18th century travellers would not share. The contrast is even greater with respect to Baroque and Late Baroque forms,

---

labelled as early as the 16th century by canon Roger Paruta, cf. The present state of Sicily and Malta, modern travellers, 1788, 137. But only since the porphyry sarcophagi were opened in 1771/72 during a thoroughgoing Classicist renovation of the church has it been possible to assign the tombs with any certainty to individual rulers, who include, in Henry VI and Frederick II, two emperors that the Germans would later revere so highly. For full details: Bartels, Briefe über Kalabrien und Sizilien, 1787–1792, III/1792: 691–692.

81   Leanti, Lo stato presente della Sicilia, 1761, I:60.
82   Amico, Lexicon topographicum siculum, 1855/1856 (1757–1760), II/1856: 252.
83   Zinzendorf, Mémoire, 1773 (1766), 301–302.
84   Brydone, A Tour through Sicily and Malta, 1774 (1773), II:256.
85   As with many books published abroad, these were also subject to censorship; a number of authors avoided this by publishing in more liberal jurisdictions such as the Netherlands or Switzerland.
86   Saline, Pescagione de' Coralli, e de' Tonni in Trapani. Leanti, Lo stato presente della Sicilia, 1761, I: pl. 33 on 165.
87   Leanti, Lo stato presente della Sicilia, 1761, I: pl. 31 and II: pl. 34, pl. 35.
88   Zinzendorf, Mémoire, 1773 (1766), 292.

Figure 9: A pagan place. Temple of Segesta, engraving by Antonio Bova, 1761

which, without exception, gave foreign travellers cause to engage in extended mockery of the Sicilians' "bad taste". As we shall see, alongside the standards of taste of northern Neoclassicism, a powerful narrative was also set up that contrasted ancient greatness with the decline and corruption of the present, a point of view that was naturally alien to the Sicilian authors.

Part 2: Appropriations: The Pioneer Travellers

From the 1760s, international travellers became increasingly aware of Sicily. Following the publication – belatedly and via a roundabout route – of Zinzendorf's *Mémoire*,[89] there followed in short order many travelogues, mostly by English, German and French authors, more than 20 In the 18th century alone.[90] There were shifts in emphasis: texts by local authors, which had a limited reach and were only of interest to a specialist readership were joined by new travel writing that targeted an educated international public and described the new destination with increasing accuracy and detail. How the view of Palermo subsequently changed is the topic of the following section, which sketches out the process by which a new canon of appraisal and taste was generated.

Baron von Riedesel, or the Greek

The Pioneers of modern travel to Sicily are the archaeologist Johann Hermann von Riedesel (1767) and the physicist Patrick Brydone (1770). The volume that Baron von Riedesel published in 1771 in the form of a series of letters, *Reise durch Sicilien und Großgriechenland* (A Journey through Sicily and Magna Grecia),[91] is the very first piece of

---

89 For details, see Faber/Garms-Cornides, Entdeckung Siziliens, 2005, 348–351.
90 There is an overview in Tuzet, La Sicile au XVIIIe siècle, 1955, 9–16.
91 Riedesel, Reise durch Sicilien, 1965 (1771).

travel writing on Sicily in the narrow sense.[92] The book was quite well known for a while in Germany, not least because Goethe recommended it several times in connection with his travels to Italy,[93] but internationally, Riedesel's report was soon overshadowed by the extraordinarily successful book *A Tour through Sicily and Malta* by Brydone (printed in 1773), which would soon be translated into several languages.[94]

Riedesel's mission to Sicily had a single purpose: he was largely concerned with documenting the island's Greek remains for his mentor Winckelmann.[95] Winckelmann himself gave a concrete impulse by publishing previously unseen material on Agrigento, based on a survey by the Scottish architect Robert Mylne.[96] Riedesel, scion of a much branched Hessian noble family, had joined Winckelmann in Rome in 1762 while the latter was employed as the Papal antiquary, and had received a very thorough year-long education in classical antiquity. Following the rediscovery of Paestum in 1746, Winckelmann (who was likely the first German to visit the temples on the site) had become convinced that it was vital to carry out a systematic survey of Magna Graecia – the ancient Greek colonies in southern Italy – and Riedesel was happy to fulfill this wish using the means at his disposal. He had in fact planned to undertake the journey to Sicily together with Winckelmann, who also wanted to write a foreword to the book on the island that his pupil intended to publish, but these plans had fallen through. From 1765, Riedesel undertook a highly unusual six-year journey of discovery through the Mediterranean on his own, which took him to Italy and Sicily, Greece and Asia Minor as well as Constantinople, Spain and Portugal.[97] His subsequent book *Reise durch Sicilien und Großgriechenland*, which was published anonymously in Switzerland in 1771, is dedicated to Winckelmann, who had died three years earlier and who often seems to be the fictive addressee of the text.[98]

Riedesel's route was indeed based on the location of ancient sites. His report is certainly at its most detailed and liveliest when he is listing and describing Greek antiquities with the greatest possible precision. As an empiricist, who – as did Winckelmann – believed in archaeological research as the basis of knowledge production, Riedesel focused on the remains of ancient buildings in their materiality, while precise knowledge of the relevant written sources is also assumed.[99] From Segesta, Riedesel reported

---

92   Osterkamp, Riedesels Sizilienreise, 1992; Tuzet, La Sicile au XVIIIe siècle, 1955, 28–33, though this is now obsolete.
93   Though Goethe also still read Homer's Odyssey, cf. for full details Osterkamp, Riedesels Sizilienreise, 1992, 105–106.
94   Tuzet, La Sicile au XVIIIe siècle, 1955, 10.
95   For details of Riedesel: Osterkamp, Riedesels Sizilienreise, 1992, 93–106; cf. also Osterkamp, Geschichte der deutschen Sizilienwahrnehmung, 1987 and, for a general overview, Arthur Schulz's foreword to his edition of Riedesel 1965: Schulz, Riedesels Reise, 1965, 7–18.
96   Winckelmann, Anmerkungen über die Baukunst, 1968 (1759). Cf. Osterkamp, Riedesels Sizilienreise, 1992, 96, Note 4.
97   Thereafter also to England, Scotland and Ireland, Osterkamp, Riedesels Sizilienreise, 1992, 94–95. On Riedesel's life, see also Faber/Garms-Cornides, Entdeckung Siziliens, 2005, 345.
98   Osterkamp has examined the extent to which Winckelmann's expectations and commission influenced the travelogue. Osterkamp, Geschichte der deutschen Sizilienwahrnehmung, 1987 as well as Osterkamp, Riedesels Sizilienreise, 1992.
99   Osterkamp, Riedesels Sizilienreise, 1992, 99. Cf. also Bernauer, Von Griechen, 2006, 22–23.

enthusiastically on "one of the best preserved temples of the older Doric type, like the temples of Pest (Paestum), which you have visited".[100] His report contains precise archaeological descriptions complete with measurements and detailed comparisons with other temples, given together with chronological considerations.[101] The cities of Catania and Girgenti/Agrigento are described in particular detail – including brief observations of the remains of the ancient walls and the use of antique spolia in newer buildings, the ancient street surface with traces of ancient ruts, etc.[102] In Agrigento, which was already enjoying the attention of the international community,[103] Riedesel encouraged 100 scudi to be spent annually for the upkeep of the temple.[104] The various collections of vases, coins, etc. are also described in fairly great detail. In Syracuse, the archaeologist visited all the important sites, such as the famous and much discussed Ear of Dionysius (complete with echo), and the so-called well under the Church of Saint Phillip the Apostle (actually a mikveh, whose classical origins Riedesel rightly calls into question).[105] Ingeniously drawing together textual criticism and archaeological observations, he reconsiders the assessment of many sites, for instance when he declares correctly – here revising Pancrazi – that the so-called Tomb of Theron in Agrigento is in fact not Greek but Roman.[106]

For the circle around Winckelmann, the 'discovery' of Sicily was a consequence of a reassessment of Greek antiquity. Riedesel's goal was to document the little-researched remains of the ancient Greek world, to classify them and to assign them their place in history. Yet Riedesel did not write a specifically archaeological treatment of Sicily but rather something that was very much a travelogue:

> "since you allow me, my dearest friend, to share with you my remarks on the journey I have completed in Sicily and the Kingdom of Naples, so be prepared to hear a variety of things, and not only concerning antiquity but rather all manner of objects. You know [...] that I have a number of bees in my bonnet, [and] [...] so this is how I wish to share with you all my observations."[107]

The fact that this book was translated so quickly into English and French bears witness to the broad interest that existed in Riedesel's account of Sicily.[108] His interest was by no means focused only on antiquity but also quite naturally on the architecture, painting and sculpture of more recent periods. Furthermore, the text is full of short

---

100 Riedesel, Reise durch Sicilien, 1965 (1771), 24.
101 Riedesel, Reise durch Sicilien, 1965 (1771), 24–25; he followed the same procedure, for instance, in Selinus/Selinunte, which he describes as "entirely torn down" (ibid., 28).
102 Riedesel, Reise durch Sicilien, 1965 (1771), 29–40.
103 Riedesel reports, among other things, that an Englishman had had himself interred in one of the temples. Riedesel, Reise durch Sicilien, (1771), 34.
104 Riedesel, Reise durch Sicilien, 1965 (1771), 37.
105 Riedesel, Reise durch Sicilien, 1965 (1771), 48.
106 Riedesel, Reise durch Sicilien, 1965 (1771), 35.
107 Riedesel, Reise durch Sicilien, 1965 (1771), 21.
108 Tuzet, La Sicile au XVIIIe siècle, 1955, 28. Schulz noted that the later travelogues from Greece and Turkey, when he was no longer in Wickelmann's service, have all the character of "modern" travel writing and give less space to antiquity. Schulz, Riedesels Reise, 1965, 16.

historical anecdotes and, with the sharpened eye of the experienced traveller and would-be diplomat for essential matters, including social and economic affairs. From Palermo, Riedesel reported among other things that the price of bread was fixed and that most of the city's income came from the trade in corn or the taxation of the same,[109] but he also noted the "great liberty" of the "Dames" whose men had started "to become ashamed of their natural jealousy".[110] Remarks on the fertility and beauty of the landscape and the meanness of the monks was soon to become a permanent feature of the literature on Sicily: "if a good government could establish order, equality and justice here, this would be the happiest corner of the earth".[111] Just like so many of his successors, ascending Etna gave Riedesel cause to philosophize about creation and the meaning of life.[112] The description of the country and its population provided as an appendix draws on Winckelmann's climate theory and also shows a strong interest in the possible ongoing influence of the heritage of Greece in terms of physiognomy, customs and cuisine.[113] Compared to this idealized image of antiquity, the modern world appears unfree and weak: "In short, the climate, the soil of the country, and the fruit of the same are as abundant as they ever were; but the golden liberty of Greece, the people, the power, the glory and the good taste are no longer to be found in them as they once were".[114] Syracuse in particular is frozen in an image that will soon be established as the topos of ancient greatness and current misery.[115]

On 17 March 1767, Riedesel reached Palermo by ship. On 30 March, he departed for Segesta. In keeping with his class, he travelled on horseback, in the company of soldiers "inflicted" upon him by the King to protect against bandits.[116] What did Winckelmann's pupil see in these two weeks? What did he consider worth reporting from the capital? In the first place: there are only a few pages, and although he concedes that one can "spend one's time well in Palermo",[117] it is also telling that Riedesel avoids the round-about return journey to Palermo along the north coast from Messina, as "there is nothing particularly remarkable on this side of Sicily" and sails straight for Reggio.[118]

Immediately upon arrival in Palermo, he finds it small but populous and less attractive than he expected. The city is crossed by two "beautiful" main streets and the only city "in all Italy to be illuminated at night at public cost".[119] Apart from that, he finds the museum collections – of the Jesuits or at Saint Martin's Convent outside the city – relatively unremarkable. The young German considers the four porphyry sarcophagi in the

---

109   Riedesel, Reise durch Sicilien, 1965 (1771), 23.
110   Riedesel, Reise durch Sicilien, 1965 (1771), 74.
111   Riedesel, Reise durch Sicilien, 1965 (1771), 39.
112   Riedesel, Reise durch Sicilien, 1965 (1771), 61–62. While dismissing the observation, ascribed to Fazellus, that the inhabitants there are particularly savage and wild, which Brydone will continually cite: Brydone, A Tour through Sicily and Malta, 1774 (1773), I:63.
113   Riedesel, Reise durch Sicilien, 1965 (1771), 72–75.
114   Riedesel, Reise durch Sicilien, 1965 (1771), 74.
115   E.g. Riedesel, Reise durch Sicilien, 1965 (1771), 52.
116   Riedesel, Reise durch Sicilien, 1965 (1771), 24.
117   Riedesel, Reise durch Sicilien, 1965 (1771), 74.
118   Riedesel, Reise durch Sicilien, 1965 (1771), 72.
119   Riedesel, Reise durch Sicilien, 1965 (1771), 22.

cathedral to be Roman spolia since they are "not quite in the Greek style but too beautiful for the age of the Kings that lie buried in them" – whose names he remarkably omits to give. Riedesel reports with the self-confident attitude of a connoisseur and an explorer: a painting of the Angelo Custode in San Francesco d'Assisi that is "falsely claimed to be by Rafael", he calls "a beautiful piece, with good draughtsmanship and colouring"; in "San Francesco di Paolo, before the city, are two wonderful paintings which no man sees or values" and which he ascribes to Veronese. He considers the local people and the local elite to be no help at all in this regard: "all knowledge of painting appears to have entirely vanished in Palermo: I found no-one who was in a position to provide me with information about the best paintings".[120]

In view of the shortness of the text, the accumulation of expressions that bear witness to an elite desire to create distance is striking. Not only does the existing body of knowledge fail to live up to the expectations of Winckelmann's pupil, he also comes across evaluative categories that he cannot comprehend and considers to be uneducated and emotional: Of the statues in the cathedral by Ghagini, considered the "Sicilian Michel Angelo", "much fuss" is made; in the cathedral at Monreale, which is "worth visiting because of two porphyry caskets", he "passes over", as already noted, "the Gothic mosaic work, about which the Sicilians make such a fuss";[121] the "description of all the special churches and palaces" he leaves to "others who might possess more patience to write".[122]

Here we should note Riedesel's self-imposed restriction to "essential things" and to say nothing of popular destinations: "Just as I remained silent on Saint Rosalia of Palermo, so will I do the same with the Madonna di Trapani and other miracle-working Saints in all Sicily".[123] In Monreale, Riedesel asked (with regard to the supposedly ancient porphyry sarcophagi) "that I be forgiven for pausing here a moment"; none of the other Arab-Norman monuments are worthy of a line from the elite art connoisseur. This attitude can only be ascribed to some extent to a conscious narrowness – his dedication to Winckelmann's project.[124] It is far more an articulation of an aesthetic judgement that is highly aware of a sense of distinction regarding the "fuss" and "bother", the "terrible taste" of the uninitiated, at the very forefront of which Riedesel places the native population. In the rejection of the lavishly decorative Sicilian Baroque, assessments of taste can also be heard that would soon become fixed elements in the repertoire of travellers to Sicily.

It is interesting to note that Riedesel apparently consulted a completely different set of sources from someone like Zinzendorf. Winckelmann's protégé refers to ancient sources (Diodorus Siculus, Virgil, etc) with particular frequency. He also regularly cites the literature recommended by his teacher – now often somewhat dated – including the *Siciliae Antiquae libri duo* by the German geographer and historian Philipp Clüver

---

120 Riedesel, Reise durch Sicilien, 1965 (1771), 22.
121 Riedesel, Reise durch Sicilien, 1965 (1771), 23.
122 Riedesel, Reise durch Sicilien, 1965 (1771), 22.
123 Riedesel, Reise durch Sicilien, 1965 (1771), 26.
124 Osterkamp ascribes the neglect of monuments such as Castel del Monte to "Winckelmann's instructions", Osterkamp, Riedesels Sizilienreise, 1992, 96.

(1619),[125] the work of the Dutch classical philologist Jean Philippe d'Orville,[126] and the two volumes by the Theatine Guiseppe Maria Pancrazi on antiquities in Agrigento.[127] Riedesel appears to have had no interest in the contemporary historiographical authors that were Zinzendorf's main source. The situation was quite different regarding the local experts, with whom Riedesel had occasional intensive exchanges. In the manner of noble travellers of the time, Riedesel set off on his travels with appropriate recommendations and contacts. Most of the time, he was the guest of local members of his class, preferring those who shared his research interests. Catania was the unexpected highlight of the young German's journey, as a friendship developed between him and his host, Ignazio Paternò Castello, Prince of Biscari (fig. 10).

Figure 10: Patron and archaeologist. Ignazio Paterno, Prince of Biscari, engraving ca. 1789

The Prince, a prominent patron of the arts and an archaeologist, proved a highly knowledgeable guide for Riedesel, and had himself undertaken minor excavations. According to Riedesel, he was at the time preparing an exhaustive publication on all

---

125 E.g. at Agrigento, Riedesel, Reise durch Sicilien, 1965 (1771), 35–36.
126 D'Orville, Jacobi Philippi D'Orville Sicula, 1764. The Journey to Sicily upon which this book was based had already taken place in 1726/28; published posthumously.
127 Pancrazi, Antichità siciliane, 1751/1752; cf. Riedesel, Reise durch Sicilien, 1965 (1771), 30–31.

the ancient monuments of the city, with numerous engravings.[128] Above all, however, the Prince put together the first significant collection of antiquities on the island, for Riedesel, "one of the most complete and most beautiful that exists in Italy and perhaps (without exaggeration) the world".[129] Riedesel also found support in Agrigento, visiting the sites in the company of a Roman scholar who had made his home there, Ettore Barone di St. Anna.[130]

The first contrasts to Zinzendorf become clear at this point. The latter is interested in gathering positive knowledge about the island. When it comes to the question of what is remarkable, worth seeing or of significance he remains relatively conventional in the sense that he largely follows local standards. His brief *Mémoire* has been little appreciated as a text but frequently used as a concise source of information.[131] Riedesel not only marks the beginning of an age of specialization, whose audience is an international group of elite connoisseurs with an interest in archaeology. The standard of knowledge and taste invoked here explicitly distances itself from a traditional canon of knowledge and values. Idolizing Greece, banishing the Middle Ages and condemning the Late Baroque establishes new standards. In the process, a set of profoundly differing heritage communities emerges more clearly – communities that barely refer to a common heritage and that reveal irreconcilable constructs of identity: on the one hand, an international elite of specialists with a background in classical and Enlightenment thought, in search of the origins of Western culture; and on the other, diverse local cultures of memory that are bound up in various ways with complex, long-lasting processes of regional identity-formation and self-narration.

Patrick Brydone: "Gay and Buffy" Palermo

The most successful book on Sicily, however, was written by another: the Scot Patrick Brydon, whose *A Tour through Sicily and Malta* (1773) is considered a milestone of modern travel literature and was responsible for Sicily's popularity.[132] The success of this travelogue, published in epistolary form, can be seen in the speed at which it was reprinted (seven times in England alone) and translated into various languages.[133] Brydone, who had enjoyed an excellent education and was a trained physicist, travelled in the tradition of the Grand Tour as a tutor to young English gentlemen. Accordingly, in Sicily he moved in noble circles and saw little of the island's interior since he reached his destinations (Palermo, Catania and Etna, Messina, Syracuse, Agrigento, etc) by boat. His

---

128   Riedesel, Reise durch Sicilien, 1965 (1771), 54, 56. For details of Riedesel's biography and his meetings with other travellers: Guzzetta, Per la gloria, 2001, the publication project is mentioned on page 18. Ignazio Paternos book, which is however largely without illustrations, was not published until 1781: Paterno, Viaggio per tutte le antichità della Sicilia, 1781.
129   Riedesel, Reise durch Sicilien, 1965 (1771), 56; Riedesel reports that the antique epigraphs in the collection were being published by Prince Torremuzza in Palermo (ibid., 57–58). In Catania, he had contact with other scholars at the university, including Leonardo Gambino (ibid., 64).
130   According to Riedesel, the Barone had "produced the drawings and most of the descriptions in Pater Pancrazi's study", cf. Riedesel, Reise durch Sicilien, 1965 (1771), 33.
131   On the reception of the text, Faber/Garms-Cornides, Entdeckung Siziliens, 2005, 354, Note 65.
132   Brydone, A Tour through Sicily and Malta, 1774 (1773); cf. Tuzet, La Sicile au XVIIIe siècle, 1955, 33–34.
133   Smecca, Three travel writers, 2009, 49.

account of the ascent of Mount Etna (possibly fictional) and of the sunrise as viewed from the crater would exert a strong influence on the narratives of later writers; he also gave a detailed report of weather phenomena and air pressure.

The strength and 'modernity' of Brydone's writing lie in the fact that he does not compose his accounts from a specific perspective – as does Zinzendorf – or in pursuit of a specific interest – like Riedesel – but rather reports on sites of interest and curiosities in a way that is both learned and entertaining. Many other guides have followed his lead in providing lively accounts of Sicily's history, climate, character and customs.[134] It is nonetheless surprising that even recent commentators on his work such as Joseph Farrell still want to see him as an Enlightenment figure who rejected absolutism and tyranny and united within himself a scientifically informed scepticism towards Catholic religion with a critical and irreverent knowledge of antiquity.[135] Nevertheless, the interest in "living people"[136] that Farrell invokes is limited – entirely encompassed within the colonial viewpoint – to picturesque, rustic or mocking anecdotes. When Brydone talks about the Sicilians, he refers, of course, to people of standing.[137] Brydone's main interest, particularly in Palermo, is in the aesthetic world, the *beau monde sicilien*, whose life he describes with glee and a strong sense of caricature, exaggeration and gossip. The ordinary folk are here a mixture of savages, apes, beasts – amusing yet dangerous. In this way, Brydone makes the figure of the brigand as a noble and chivalrous desperado into a fixture of the island's folklore. He is well aware of cultural differences and propagates them out of a feeling of superiority: For instance, with regard to a 17th century author (Borelli) who expressed his regret that so many of Catania's antique monuments had been destroyed in the 1669 eruption of Etna, Brydone commented that contemporary Sicilians in contrast "do not value their island half so much for having given birth to Archimedes or Empedocles, as to St Agatha and St Rosalia".[138]

Brydone is no archaeologist, but he is always interested in making connections between visible monuments and relevant ancient sources, thereby "allowing the ruins to speak". He is aware of Diodorus Siculus, Pliny and Strabo, Homer and Virgil, as well as Milton and Pope. For him, "philosophical" is an insult, a synonym for speculative – and stupid.[139] In Agrigento, for instance, where he largely relied on information from the Prince of Torremuzza, he demonstrated not only a healthy scepticism with regard to local traditions but also great ignorance at the possibilities of the burgeoning field of archaeological building research: "We have seen a great many old walls and vaults that little or nothing can be made of. They give them names, and pretend to tell you what they were, but as they bear not the least resemblance of these things now, it would be no

---

134 For the historical and statistical details, he drew upon older Italian authors such as Massa, Guarneri, Carrera and above all – as did e.g. Zinzendorf – on Tommaso Fazello's *De Rebus Siculis Decades Duae*, Palermo 1558.
135 Farrell, Enlightenment traveller, 1991, 294–297.
136 Farrell, Enlightenment traveller, 1991, 294.
137 Tuzet, La Sicile au XVIIIe siècle, 1955, 36, 46.
138 Brydone, A Tour through Sicily and Malta, 1774 (1773), I:127.
139 Brydone, A Tour through Sicily and Malta, 1774 (1773), I:185.

less idle to believe them than to trouble you with their nonsense."¹⁴⁰ Brydone's reception among those of his contemporaries who were schooled in Winckelmann's methods was correspondingly negative.¹⁴¹

Indeed, the Palermo one encounters in Brydone's report is remarkably different, a city, shimmering in its wealth and its splendour, full of gallant adventurers, colourful social gatherings and festive events. We hear about the Viceroy's elegant court and his beautiful porcelain services, their dining habits, entertainment rituals and *conversazioni*,¹⁴² the Anglomania of the young nobles, and the taboo they placed on moving through the city on foot.¹⁴³ The opera is described in one very long letter, complete with knowledgeable critiques of various singers and much juicy gossip.¹⁴⁴ According to Brydone, Palermo's 'must-see' destinations are the Feast of Santa Rosalia,¹⁴⁵ the Capuchin Catacombs,¹⁴⁶ the spectacularly "ugly" and "senseless" Villa Palagonia in Bagheria,¹⁴⁷ and the *Marina*'s gallant hustle.¹⁴⁸ At Monte Pellegrino – "to pay our respects to St. Rosalie, and thank her for the variety of entertainments she has afforded us, it is one of the most fatiguing expeditions I ever made in my life" – he is not content with descriptions of coin collections but enthuses in the grotto – as Goethe also will later – about the statue of Rosalia "of most exquisite workmanship [...]. I never in my life saw one that affected me so much".¹⁴⁹ The view of Palermo from the mountain is commended extensively and the region is praised, echoing the ancient literature, as Garden of Eden, Conca d'Oro, Aurea Valle, Hortis Siciliae, etc.¹⁵⁰ By contrast, the monuments in the city are touched upon astonishingly briefly and almost in passing, comparable perhaps to how our travel guides, after giving us hotel, shopping and party tips, add a brief run-down of sites considered "unmissable". Brydone calls the cathedral "a very venerable Gothic building",¹⁵¹ the Palace Chapel "is entirely encrusted over with an-

---

140 Brydone, A Tour through Sicily and Malta, 1774 (1773), I:189. Cf. also Letter XXIX: "We have now had time to enquire a little into some of the antiquities of the island, and have found several people, particularly the prince of Toremuzzo, who have made this the great project of their study. However, I find we must wade through oceans of fiction, before we can arrive at any thing certain or satisfactory." Brydone, A Tour through Sicily and Malta, 1774 (1773), II:289.
141 On Johann Heinrich Bartels' critique of Brydone, for instance, see below.
142 Brydone, A Tour through Sicily and Malta, 1774 (1773), II:213. He describes the city's nobles as better educated than their neighbours; the conversation was often about politics and history, but most of all about poetry, because, as he states, knowledge of other matters remained at a basic level.
143 Brydone, A Tour through Sicily and Malta, 1774 (1773), II:238–242, 318–320; for more on the Anglomania, see Bartels, Briefe über Kalabrien und Sizilien, 1787–1792, III/1792: 539.
144 Brydone, A Tour through Sicily and Malta, 1774 (1773), II:325–323.
145 Brydone, A Tour through Sicily and Malta, 1774 (1773), II:258–260.
146 Brydone, A Tour through Sicily and Malta, 1774 (1773), II:228–230.
147 In great detail in Letter XXII (Brydone, A Tour through Sicily and Malta, 1774 (1773), II:221–226). Later travellers established this narrative of the Villa Palagonia as a "temple of folly [...] of whimsical taste" (nonetheless wort visiting). Cf. The present state of Sicily and Malta, modern travellers, 1788, 151–152.
148 Brydone, A Tour through Sicily and Malta, 1774 (1773), II:212–213.
149 Brydone, A Tour through Sicily and Malta, 1774 (1773), II:297.
150 Brydone, A Tour through Sicily and Malta, 1774 (1773), II:298–299.
151 Brydone, A Tour through Sicily and Malta, 1774 (1773), II:256.

cient mosaic"[152] – that is more or less all that is described of Palermo's monuments, entirely conventionally, with little interest in historical details, and often remarkably uninformed. With regard to Monreale, Brydone mentions, as one might well expect, the main street with its magnificent fountains, the mosaics in the cathedral, and the porphyry sarcophagi "of Sicily's first kings".[153]

Brydone's success rests upon a colonial gaze that he casts – with virtuosic choreography – on a strange, exciting, amusing and challenging environment, and the promise of variety and amusement mixed with class- and gender-specific doses of adventurous thrill and cultural pedagogy. In contrast to most of his contemporaries, this 'mentor' is cautious about passing judgement himself on the quality of the architecture and art he sees. This is revealed by the comparison with an English bestseller in the field of travel literature, a book that aimed to combine Brydone's account with those of other travellers to create a comprehensive travel guide.[154] In this work, one notes that a general judgement regarding the 'bad style' and 'bad taste' of Sicilian art had become established. Palermo's many statues are "in general executed in a very bad style", the cathedral is large but "defective in elegance" (the same is said word for word of the Royal Palace); the ornamentation of the city's churches is "disposed in the worst taste imaginable".[155] The mediaeval monuments are also almost universally condemned on grounds of taste; Monreale "is built in the Gothic stile in an extremely bad taste [...]", etc.[156]

Houël's Voyage pittoresque: Images of "Good Taste"

In the pioneering phase of Sicilian tourism, in particular, we can therefore see that the canon of the island's built heritage was very much in a state of flux. Nevertheless, regardless of how strongly they were guided by their – very different – special interests, Zinzendorf's and Riedesel's descriptions are each – though again in very different ways – embedded in local traditions and discourses. With Brydone, however, we see the island becoming largely incorporated in the colonial discourse of the Grand Tour. While Brydone was himself not a man of the arts (or the burgeoning field of empirical archaeology) and largely refrained from passing personal aesthetic judgements on the monuments, those who came after him would settle firmly on a transmontane-Classicist consensus of "bad taste" with regard not just to the Sicilian Baroque but to all of the island's creations. Furthermore, the Arab-Norman (and Staufer) monuments that the Sicilian authors had unambivalently accepted as heritage increasingly fell under aesthetic suspicion.

The entry of Sicily into the canon of travellers and ultramontane connoisseurs is eminently visible in the "picturesque" travel books that began to appear. The two most elaborate were published as richly illustrated folio volumes in Paris, namely the four-

---

152   Brydone, A Tour through Sicily and Malta, 1774 (1773), II:257.
153   Brydone, A Tour through Sicily and Malta, 1774 (1773), II:257.
154   The present state of Sicily and Malta, modern travellers, 1788.
155   The present state of Sicily and Malta, modern travellers, 1788, 134, 138, 140.
156   The present state of Sicily and Malta, modern travellers, 1788, 159; one exception is the supposedly 'Saracen' Zisa Palace (ibid., 164).

volume *Voyage Pittoresque des Isles de Sicile, de Malthe et de Lipari*[157] by Jean-Pierre Houël from 1782 and the five-volume *Voyage pittoresque ou Description des royaumes de Naples et de Sicile* that was edited by Jean-Claude Richard de Saint-Non and published in 1785/86.[158] The more homogeneous of the two monumental publications that determined the expectations of travellers is the one published by the draughtsman, painter and engraver Jean-Pierre Houël, who created all the illustrations – 264 large-format etchings based on his own drawings – following a long stay on the island.[159] The complete title, *Voyage Pittoresque des Isles de Sicile, de Malthe et de Lipari, où l'on traite des Antiquités qui s'y trouvent encore; des principaux Phénomènes que la nature y offre; du Costume des habitants, & de quelques usages*,[160] outlines the undertaking quite precisely: the book displays scenic ruins and heroic or bucolic landscapes, coins and statues, but also activities and customs such as haymaking and anchovy preparation, local people in costume and armed brigands, famous places like the Ear of Dionysius complete with a gunshot/echo test (Plate CLXXXIII): an image cycle that confirmed and canonized the writings of Brydone and others. Numerous plates with detailed plans, sections, views and details of ancient monuments bear witness to the travellers' archaeological interest (fig. 11).

Most of the city views and street scenes are of Messina, often showing a procession or the feast day celebration of a saint (procession for the Feast of the Assumption in Messina; procession in front of the cathedral in Syracuse; Feast of St Agatha in the Cathedral of Catania); in Palermo, which is otherwise treated quite shabbily, naturally the Feast of St Rosalia is portrayed. The text is compiled from older books, Houël mentions Riedesel and Brydone by name. A fixed canon of places to be visited can now be observed, together with an increasingly fixed set of aesthetic judgements. The comments on Palermo[161] follow the well-trodden path and visit the well-known sites. Relatively detailed descriptions are given of the Capuchin Convent with its famous Catacombs, "at the same time hideous & ridiculous, appalling & disgusting",[162] and above all the Feast of St Rosalia, which lasts for several days and to which people stream from all of Sicily and the Kingdom of Naples, including "every" tourist: "a delightful spectacle[…] the public joy makes one happy".[163] There is also an engraving of the banana tree in the Archbishop's palace – the Archbishop, described as having an artistic temperament and well educated, is also an enthusiastic gardener – a fixed item on the itinerary of nearly every visitor to Palermo.

---

157 Houël, Voyage Pittoresque, 1782–1787.
158 Saint Non, Voyage pittoresque, 1781–1786. Sicily is the subject of the last two half volumes, which were published in 1785/86. Lit.: Lamers, Il viaggio nel Sud, 1995; Bernauer, Die Voyage pittoresque des Abbé de Saint-Non, 2004.
159 On his life and journey to Sicily: Pinault, Voyage en Sicile, 1990, 12–18; Pantano, Jean Houël, 2003, 17–56. For a general overview, cf. also Tuzet, La Sicile au XVIIIe siècle, 1955, 93–111.
160 "Picturesque journey to the Isles of Sicily, Malta and Lipari, where we discuss the Antiquities that can still be found there; the main phenomena that nature offers; the Costume of the inhabitants, & some of their customs".
161 Houël, Voyage Pittoresque, 1782–1787, I/1782: 62–78.
162 Houël, Voyage Pittoresque, 1782–1787, I/1782: 71.
163 Houël, Voyage Pittoresque, 1782–1787, I/1782: 75.

Figure 11: The canonizing gaze. Ancient capital and sarcophagus in Monreale Cathedral, engraving by Jean Houël, 1782

If we compare this production of images with the work of the Palermitan Leanti of only a few years earlier, the shift in evaluation is tangible. Assessments of significance are now usually accompanied by aesthetic evaluation. The Arab-Norman monuments are excluded from the aesthetico-ethical exemplary function of the monumental. Houël justifies their blanket exclusion in terms of his intention "to search for ancient beauties which can serve as a model for the progress of the arts, & not to collect crude objects, which are only sad proofs of their decadence, & which can only satisfy a sterile curiosity".[164] Some of the mediaeval monuments are at least mentioned as sites worth seeing, including the Palace Chapel and the Martorana.[165] Whereas the cathedral, which was quite neglected at the time, appeared to Houël "as of a strong and heavy Gothic taste [...]; the whole ridiculous",[166] by contrast, the painter was excited by the cloister in Monreale: "one of the finest of its kind that has ever been built".[167] The verdict *mauvais goût* cannot always be predicted: the Renaissance fountain in front of the Senatorial Palace (fig. 4), which in Houël's mind causes "confusion" as a result of its disparate proportions, is yet

---

164 Houël, Voyage Pittoresque, 1782–1787, I/1782: 60. Tuzet notes that Saint Non (op. cit.) came to a far more positive evaluation of mediaeval buildings, such as the Palace Chapel of Palermo or the cathedral of Monreale and also includes numerous images of these structures, cf. Tuzet, La Sicile au XVIIIe siècle, 1955, 285–286.
165 Houël, Voyage Pittoresque, 1782–1787, I/1782: 63, 66.
166 Houël, Voyage Pittoresque, 1782–1787, I/1782: 64.
167 Houël, Voyage Pittoresque, 1782–1787, I/1782: 60.

an "ingenious ensemble [...] whose conception is unique and felicitous";[168] the porphyry sarcophagi in Monreale (which were considered to belong to classical antiquity) exhibit, by contrast, "bad taste";[169] for Houël, the Baroque fountains on the road to Monreale are even worth an engraving (Plate 37).[170] But Palermo's major buildings, on this all travellers now agree, were not built in eras that demonstrated "good taste", and the Sicilian Baroque is considered particularly tasteless, or, put in a friendlier way, an expression of the love of a backward people for the decorative.[171] The colonial arrogance of the Grand Tour is now linked to the aesthetic and moral arrogance of Classicism and the Enlightenment: Sicily's entry into the canon of heritage of the enlightened world took place under the aegis of an aggressive and elitist assessment and the disenfranchisement of the local heritage culture.

Bartel's Letters – Paternalistic Protestant Interpretative Hegemony

This thesis can be demonstrated with reference to one of the most extensive pieces of Sicilian travel writing by a German during this period, the three-volume *Briefe über Kalabrien und Sizilien* (Letters on Calabria and Sicily) that Johann Heinrich Bartels published in Göttingen after a lengthy stay in Sicily starting in 1787.[172] Bartels, who was later to rise to prominence as a Senator in Hamburg and eventually the city's Mayor, travelled to Italy after completing his degree in Theology and Oriental Languages at Göttingen.[173] His expressly stated goal was to gather "strict truths" without prejudice.[174] Alongside his own observations, he relied upon "information from knowledgeable men". He singled out two of his informants for particular praise: though his book does not contain many engravings, he did find space for portraits of Ignazio Paterno, Prince of Biscari (fig. 10),[175] and Landolina Nava from Syracuse, two important contacts for nearly all travellers to Sicily at the time.[176] Yet Bartels' extensive bibliography tells a different story, also revealing vividly just how rapidly the body of available knowledge was growing.[177] He begins by reviewing all the existing travelogues – and is particularly critical of Brydone for his "old wives' tales" and incorrect details, while praising writers including Riedesel, Houël and Swineburne.[178] The two Sicilian authors he names, however, are not particularly suitable for use by travellers, according to Bartels. While Ignazio

---

168   Houël, Voyage Pittoresque, 1782–1787, I/1782: 65.
169   Houël, Voyage Pittoresque, 1782–1787, I/1782: 60.
170   Leanti also gives the fountain a plate (Leanti, Lo stato presente della Sicilia, 1761, I: pl. 8) and even gives a bibliographical reference for its interpretation (ibid., 55–56).
171   As does Zinzendorf (Zinzendorf, Mémoire 1773 (1766), 302). Houël also considers the Oratorio di San Filippo Neri to be "moderne, de bon gout" (Houël, Voyage Pittoresque, 1782–1787, I/1782: 67).
172   Bartels, Briefe über Kalabrien und Sizilien, 1787–1792. Sicily is dealt with in volumes 2 and 3. For details of Bartels cf. Bernauer, Von Griechen, 2006.
173   Martelli, Oltre la capitale, 2012.
174   Bartels, Briefe über Kalabrien und Sizilien, 1787–1792, II/1789, XII; III/1792 and passim.
175   Engraving after Antonius Zacco, 1781.
176   Both are in the endpapers; in some editions, the portrait of Paterno is bound at page 240.
177   A comprehensive overview of the literature is included in volume 2 before the letters from Sicily (Roman numerals: III–XXIII); supplemented in volume 3 with a list of everything published in the meantime. Bartels, Briefe über Kalabrien und Sizilien, 1787–1792, III/1792: 13–36.
178   Cf. also Bernauer, Von Griechen, 2006, 18–19, 23–24.

Paterno[179] does provide a useful overview sites of interest, his endless, meandering descriptions are, in Bartels' view, only helpful to people who have already seen the objects in person;[180] and though Domenico Sestini,[181] a Florentine by birth, who was for time the librarian of the Prince of Biscari in Catania, provides reports that Bartels considers to be thorough and extensive, the German author states that one looks in vain for "information of ancient remains, the character, way of life, customs, manufacturers, arts, trade, and industry of the Sicilians."[182]

Naturally, Bartels produces a wealth of new observations, details and clarifications. For instance, he reports comprehensively on Sicily's publishing houses and educational institutions. However, reading his letters on Palermo, it becomes clear that, despite their considerable length at over 250 pages, he largely recapitulates the conventional form of description, visit the well-known sites, repeats standard evaluations or his own variations thereupon – in short, reproduces the view of the foreigner with increasing canonicity, as do all the travellers in this phase in greater or lesser detail: the overall situation, the cityscape is described as generally magnificent; the two main streets, as so often before, as "two of the most beautiful thoroughfares that perhaps any city can offer".[183] The *Marina*, where "the Palermitan dispenses with his status and his class ends the evening under extinguished torches without strife or envy in a spirit of light playfulness",[184] the Capuchin Catacombs, where the dead are decked out like "puppets of wire and plaster",[185] and the country seat of the Princes of Palagonia, a grotesque "monument to disorientation"[186] are established attractions for all travellers.

Sites that are actually worth seeing, and this is already a topos, are limited in number;[187] the "material is quite infertile", cataloguing it "unnecessary micrology".[188] Bartels' aesthetic standards come as no surprise, "Roger's dark chapel" (the Capella Palatina) (fig. 1) is large and imposing, "yet one looks for beauty in vain";[189] "of the cathedral [in Monreale, author's note] I will say nothing; I saw it in the twilight [...]there was effort in its construction but in an age when Oriental taste had permeated the rules of Greek simplicity."[190] Naturally, the Baroque comes off particularly badly: The Quattro Canto (fig. 6) is a testament to bad taste, shows a lack of feeling for large beautiful forms,

---

179   Paterno, Viaggio per tutte le antichità della Sicilia, 1781.
180   Bartels, Briefe über Kalabrien und Sizilien, 1787–1792, II/1789, XIX–XX. In another section of this volume, Bartels gives a detailed description of the mourning rituals held for the prince, who had died shortly before his arrival n Catania in 1786 (ibid., 238–258).
181   Cf. Lettere Del Signor Abate Domenico Sestini, 1779–1784.
182   Bartels, Briefe über Kalabrien und Sizilien, 1787–1792, II/1789, XIX.
183   Together with the observation that these are the backdrops for social life and that clergymen, when they make themselves seen at all, appear out of place, though in the narrow alleyways, where the people live, the church is in charge. Bartels, Briefe über Kalabrien und Sizilien, 1787–1792, III/1792: 548–549.
184   Bartels, Briefe über Kalabrien und Sizilien, 1787–1792, III/1792: 552.
185   Bartels, Briefe über Kalabrien und Sizilien, 1787–1792, III/1792: 629.
186   Bartels, Briefe über Kalabrien und Sizilien, 1787–1792, III/1792: 718–720.
187   Bartels, Briefe über Kalabrien und Sizilien, 1787–1792, III/1792: 607–608.
188   Bartels, Briefe über Kalabrien und Sizilien, 1787–1792, III/1792: 677.
189   Bartels, Briefe über Kalabrien und Sizilien, 1787–1792, III/1792: 678.
190   Bartels, Briefe über Kalabrien und Sizilien, 1787–1792, III/1792: 671–672.

and, instead, a childish love of whittling.[191] Bartels includes among the "lifeless memorabilia" many churches: "tasteless pomp, which even when it abounds with gold, silver and gemstones always remains boring, boring to regard, with no nourishment for the soul and the heart, and boring to describe", "far from the key principles of simplicity" "playful" architecture "without truth", without naturalness (fig. 12).[192]

Figure 12: "Tasteless pomp, with no nourishment for the soul and the heart"? Palermo, Santa Caterina (Photo: G. Vinken 2019)

Here the critique of Sicilian Baroque fuses with the topos of the superficial decoration-obsessed Sicilian: he "[...] loves the gaudy, [...] loves the caricature, the exaggeration [...]", "appropriate simplicity and scale, those are things that do not harmonize with his character".[193] The Sicilian "national character" is located in the enthusiasm for the exuberant and exaggerated, the brightly coloured, outwardness, superficiality and inconstancy.[194] And the yardstick for the "cultural level" of a nation is its "artistic taste"; aesthetics and ethics are conflated: "Artistic taste and a real feeling for the good, the true, and the beautiful always progress at the same tempo as learning and cultures". The cultural level of a nation is thus easy to determine, and Sicily is still at the stage of "the Bremen Roland", in other words it is a place where the uncouth Middle Ages has never been killed off.[195]

---

191   Bartels, Briefe über Kalabrien und Sizilien, 1787–1792, III/1792: 534.
192   Bartels, Briefe über Kalabrien und Sizilien, 1787–1792, III/1792: 689 (given as 896 as a result of a typesetting error).
193   Bartels, Briefe über Kalabrien und Sizilien, 1787–1792, III/1792: 513.
194   Bartels, Briefe über Kalabrien und Sizilien, 1787–1792, III/1792: 536–538.
195   Bartels, Briefe über Kalabrien und Sizilien, 1787–1792, III/1792: 708.

Nevertheless, Bartels' view of Sicily and the Sicilians is far from entirely negative.[196] In his final letter from the island, he writes that he had spent "a happy time" among the "noblest people" in the "most blessed country of Europe".[197] Under the heading of "character", his first thoughts are of the Sicilians' honesty and gregariousness (such as that of the local bankers) and their ability to retain dignity even in the deepest misery. And the traveller from Hamburg praises the beggars and workers of Palermo for their fire, insight into human nature, sense of liberty and decency – only then, in almost the same breath, to condemn their deep immorality, intemperate debaucheries, quarrelsomeness and love of play, bigotry and propensity for prostitution and pimping.[198] The "vainglorious and grandiose" "natives" need, according to the missionary-minded Freemason, a "proper education" and "knowledge of what is decent" if "they are to grow into a nation".[199] For this, it should not come as a surprise, Bartels considers that the best sources of help and orientation are external: the best of the Sicilian artists, such as Ignazio Marabitti, had studied in Rome;[200] Bartels praises Palermo's public library (located in the former Jesuit College), which had been established and was still run by the German Theatine monk Pater Sterzinger, and where there was also a school and a museum: the whole thing "bundled together by tasteless clerics with no knowledge of art".[201]

Although Bartels also reports on many reform efforts and initiatives being undertaken by the learned of Sicily, his verdict of a lack of culture and backwardness also applies to the Palermitan elites. Nevertheless, he describes them as easy-going and welcoming; the nobles include "educated people", some of whom had spent considerable time abroad; French manners and language were however the exception; French was spoken rarely and then only when strangers were present. Bartels repeatedly complains at the boastfulness and pomposity of the people he talks with;[202] learned conversations are rare and restricted to the topic of Sicily; foreign authors are largely unknown; even members of the most elite circles had little knowledge of geography or history; one encountered much wealth exhibited without a trace of artistic taste: here and there small collections, paintings, antiquities, but nothing to compare with Rome: "There are only a few Biscaris in Sicily, though many would claim to be what he is".[203] In particular, Bartels thought there was a lack of intellectual exchange.[204] Nor, in his view, were learned circle particularly well educated;[205] learned Palermitans might be perceptive and have

---

196 Bernauer goes so far as to call Bartels "one of the first to attempt to travel through the Mezzogiorno without presuppositions". Bernauer, Von Griechen, 2006, 29.
197 Bartels, Briefe über Kalabrien und Sizilien, 1787–1792, III/1792: 833.
198 Bartels, Briefe über Kalabrien und Sizilien, 1787–1792, III/1792: 578–583.
199 Bartels, Briefe über Kalabrien und Sizilien, 1787–1792, III/1792: 627.
200 Bartels, Briefe über Kalabrien und Sizilien, 1787–1792, III/1792: 709–710.
201 Bartels, Briefe über Kalabrien und Sizilien, 1787–1792, III/1792: 617.
202 Bartels, Briefe über Kalabrien und Sizilien, 1787–1792, III/1792: 596–597.
203 Bartels, Briefe über Kalabrien und Sizilien, 1787–1792, III/1792: 603–604.
204 Bartels, Briefe über Kalabrien und Sizilien, 1787–1792, III/1792: 612.
205 On the learned people of the island in detail Bartels, Briefe über Kalabrien und Sizilien, 1787–1792, III/1792: 694–704.

excellent deductive powers and good memories,[206] yet – with a few exceptions, such as the Prince of Torremuzza – they were generally deficient in scholarship.[207] For Bartels, the academies were insignificant;[208] there was a lack of political support, infrastructure,[209] international contacts: the "frenzy of the passions keeps the spirit shackled here".[210]

In this Protestant-paternalistic and self-satisfied Enlightenment worldview, interpretive hegemony lies entirely with the educated traveller from the North: in Agrigento, Bartels found people who "in gazing on the proud monuments of former greatness are not filled with new courage – but rather look upon them, yawn and fall asleep".[211] He considers the local experts, stuck in their own traditions and interpretative standards, to be "ignorant". The elitist Bartels would dearly like to overlook this and explain that the figures on the *Marina* are "exaggerated, tasteless, and far removed from pure Greek simplicity" by means of the "degeneracy of taste of the masses"; "but it provokes real displeasure when one is led by men who are generally considered knowledgeable in the arts to similar caricatures and forced to listen to hours of the most detailed praise and constant admiring exclamations. Unfortunately, this was often my fate, and I would therefore like to declare in general that, of all Italians, the Palermitans are those with the least correct artistic taste and whose eyes may only be captivated by caricatures. Individual exceptions do not contradict this general remark!"[212]

If, with Elizabeth Bronfen, we understand the Enlightenment to be an "invention of the night", this is a vivid example.[213] Only with the establishment of aesthetic and moral norms, could 'the Greek' become an international cultural standard to aspire to – and Sicily a 'developing country'. Goethe, too, whose itinerary in Palermo during his visit to Sicily appears to have been largely conventional, may also be included in this development without further ado.[214] In terms of the various heritage communities, this development, which reached a kind of conclusion in Bartels' generation, is ambivalent. On the one side, an increasingly homogeneous class of connoisseurs emerged as a new heritage community, establishing an ever more rigid and codified canon of heritage according to the norms of taste, understanding of history and evaluative categories of the "enlightened" world; they heavily filtered local traditions and interpretations and

---

206 Bartels, Briefe über Kalabrien und Sizilien, 1787–1792, III/1792: 694.
207 Bartels, Briefe über Kalabrien und Sizilien, 1787–1792, III/1792: 705. The Prince of Torremuzza (actually Gabriele Lancillotto Castello) appears not to have received him. Nonetheless, Bartels did get to know many scholars and poets personally (ibid., 699).
208 Bartels, Briefe über Kalabrien und Sizilien, 1787–1792, III/1792: 704–708.
209 The island's only university was in Catania; the institutions in Palermo and Messina were closer in level to superior high schools, and did not have the right to award doctorates (Bartels, Briefe über Kalabrien und Sizilien, 1787–1792, II/1789: 271); according to Bartels, book printing and publishing were also underdeveloped (ibid., 261–262).
210 Bartels, Briefe über Kalabrien und Sizilien, 1787–1792, III/1792: 70.
211 Bartels, Briefe über Kalabrien und Sizilien, 1787–1792, III/1792: 549.
212 Bartels, Briefe über Kalabrien und Sizilien, 1787–1792, III/1792: 555.
213 Bronfen, Tiefer als der Tag, 2008.
214 Goethe, who has already been more than exhaustively researched (Goethe, Italian Journey, 1982 (1816/17)) was not considered here and is not particularly useful in considering this question.

treated them with scepticism. Sicily was no different, and 'northern'-influenced evaluative categories and traditional local meanings increasingly drifted apart. Parts of the elite joined the internationalized heritage community, which weakened their connections to local categories of evaluation; the mediators who were aware of local tradition were looked down upon by the international *connoisseurs*. The cultural heritage of the 'ordinary people' was increasingly unarticulated. Similar developments may also be seen, for example, in the countries of the Maghreb, where the society became divided into entirely separate heritage communities that are barely able to communicate with each other, for instance with respect to the heritage of the Classical Mediterranean world or of Islam.[215]

In any case, the value judgements of 'ordinary people' in the 18th century are hard to grasp, as they rarely achieved written form. One of the few extensive sources in this regard is Johann Gottfried Seume, mentioned at the start of the chapter, who, in contrast to his wealthier contemporaries, travelled on foot and by mule, and thus had extensive contact with all kinds of people.[216] The debate around the claim that the small room in the Ear of Dionysius was originally built as a "eavesdropping spot" (*Lauscheplätzchen*) is revealing in this regard, a belief that Seume claims that the "philistines of Syracuse" shared. Almost admiringly, he notes that the ordinary citizens do not want to let archaeologists and other experts take away "their pretty romance", conceding that "for a citizen of Syracuse" their reasoning is "not terrible".[217] Even the Sicilian muleteers, Seume calls, half in jest, "very strong antiquarians, though they do not always grasp the matter very exactly".[218] His muleteer regularly offered his services as a guide: "'I know everything, my lord, I know all the wonders' he told me with an apodictic urgency that one could no more argue against than the infallibility of the Pope. Since I knew quite well most of what I wanted to see, I had nothing against the kind-heartedness of the lad, a boy of about 19 years of age."[219] In another passage, Seume also makes fun of the 'knowledge' of his muleteer, who tells him "with utter conviction" – and in this passages Seume artfully mocks the Sicilian dialect: "'this is the temple of St. Gregory; that Madonna is ancient', and to the non-believers *anathema sit*. [...] He preferred above all to show me carefully all the monasteries and to tell me how rich they are" – to which the Protestant and arch anti-Catholic Seume commented that he wished "they were pigsties".[220] Here everything collides vividly: mentalities, forms of knowledge, and heritage concepts. The anecdote about the muleteers who get into a quarrel "concerning the advantages of their home towns in matters of antiquity" has already been mentioned, whereby the one from Palermo had to remain silent, owing to his home town's lack of such monuments. This passage is also revealing in terms of the local evaluations.[221] The significance of the Temple of Agrigento, the theatre, quar-

---

215 Vinken, Das Erbe der Anderen, 2015.
216 Seume, Spaziergang, 2003 (1802), e.g. 135–136, 138–139.
217 Seume, Spaziergang, 2003 (1802), 150–151.
218 Seume, Spaziergang, 2003 (1802), 125.
219 Seume, Spaziergang, 2003 (1802), 128.
220 "Kischt' è il tempio di san – Gregoli; Kischta Madonna è antica'", Seume, Spaziergang, 2003 (1802), 132. Italics in the original.
221 Seume, Spaziergang, 2003 (1802), 124–125.

ries and the "Ear" in Syracuse, the theatre – where Alcibiades was said to have spoken – and the university of Catania seemed indisputable to the muleteers. Yet the muleteer from Alcamo, who brought up the temple in Segesta, is subject to derision: "You swell with pride", says the muleteer from Catania to the one from Alcamo, "with your miniature Margarethe temple, which isn't even really yours".[222] According to Seume, this mockery was not only a reference to the fact that Segesta did not belong to the municipality of Alcamo, but above all that the temple is dedicated to an unchaste goddess (Venus/Aphrodite). "You must know, for the Sicilians, Margarethe is a name of an easy, venal woman; that was no special incense for the mother of the honourable hero of the Aeneid."[223] Here, the voice of the muleteer introduces a contemporary morality to the story, one that passes judgement on an 'immoral' monument: a *ressentiment* that, in contrast to those of the learned travellers, is by no means rooted in aesthetics.

---

222 Seume, Spaziergang, 2003 (1802), 124–125.
223 Seume connects the mocking name *Margaretentempelchen* with the Goddess Venus/Aphrodite, the mother of Aeneis, to whom, according to local tradition, the temple in Segesta was supposedly dedicated. The negative connotations of the name Margaret(h)e are also recorded elsewhere. Cf. Heckscher, Anadyomene in the Mediaeval Tradition, 1956, 9–10. According to tradition – later disproved by coins that were found – Segesta was originally *Acesta* (= unchaste woman), cf. Roscher, Lexikon der griechischen und römischen Mythologie, 1884, 143.

14 New York / USA
Sharing Heritage? Heinrich Heine in the Bronx

> Ich weiß nicht, was soll es bedeuten, dass ich so traurig bin.
> I don't know what it can mean that I am so sad
> (Heinrich Heine)[1]

That heritage conservation is, as Alois Riegl put it, "largely a matter of feeling",[2] is something that one understands best when abroad. For instance, when a visitor to New York, or more precisely, to a poorly planned and rather sprawling area of the Bronx, is surprised to stumble over a shining white fin-de-siècle monument, whose lines appear strangely familiar, and which on closer inspection is revealed to be a monument to someone extremely familiar: namely, to Heinrich Heine, unveiled here in 1899 as a somewhat belated commemoration of his hundredth birthday (fig. 1). At this point at the latest, a warm feeling sets in, especially when the visitor is from Germany, admires Heine and has lived for a while in Düsseldorf, making this a meeting of not just spiritual fellow travellers but of fellow citizens. A matter of feeling, to be sure, and as we will see, also a complex case of sharing heritage.

Sites, Traces. The Spaces of the Monument

The statue rises white above the fountain's pool, perched high above, the siren Lorelei combs her hair, while three naked mermaids, personifications of Poetry, Satire and Melancholy stretch out at her feet. The familiar fin-de-siècle lines, the monument's thoroughly European style generate a sudden shock of recognition that reverberates off the surrounding structures and in turn makes them seem quite alien. The extremely tidy park that has clearly been renovated very recently is still ringed by the large residential blocks that reveal their bourgeois history, even more so now that an even more hesitant gentrification is increasingly causing the traces of the ghetto to fade out of

---

1   Heine, Song of the Lorelei, 2015 (1824).
2   Riegl, Neue Strömungen, 1995 (1905), 232.

Figure 1: The restored Lorelei Fountain near Yankee Stadium (Photo: J. Henderson 2010)

sight; opposite stands the monumental Bronx County Courthouse from 1931–34, recalling the architecture of Fascism in spite of itself. Behind that is visible the legendary Yankee Stadium, which gave the South Bronx a decisive development boost when it was opened in 1923 and remains a place of pilgrimage for fans of America's national pastime. And in the middle of all this: Heinrich Heine, or more precisely, the Lorelei Fountain that is dedicated to the poet's memory. Why here? What and who brought Heine to the Bronx – with what feelings was he received? And what was his fate in this foreign land? Some brief research reveals this site to be a kind of culmination of much that is characteristic of current debates surrounding monuments: alienness and rejection, appropriation and reinterpretation – and also the potential to arouse emotions and provoke conflict that is inherent to monuments and is possibly the most important source of their value.[3]

The history of this monument is certainly a story of feelings: love and admiration, but above all hatred and malice. The strange familiarity of the Lorelei Fountain may be put down to the fact that it was created by a German artist, the Berlin sculptor Ernst Gustav Herter.[4] It was originally supposed to stand in Düsseldorf, the poet's city of birth. A committee had already been formed to realize the monument in 1887, and early on, the project enjoyed the support of the city council and prominent admirers of Heine. The Austrian empress known to history only as 'Sissi' promised her financial support for the project and personally proposed the choice of sculptor.[5] But a hate campaign

---

3 Dolff-Bonekämper, Gegenwartswerte, 2010.
4 All statements concerning the history of the Heine monument are, where not otherwise indicated, drawn from: Schubert, Kampf um das erste Heine-Denkmal, 1990.
5 The Empress later withdrew from the project, supposedly for political reasons. In 1891, she had a monument to Heine erected on Corfu.

soon formed in opposition to the project, a campaign which, led by anti-Semites and 'Pan-Germanists', had an impact that stretched far beyond the city (fig. 2). "Blood is indeed a very special fluid. [...] Heine is a Jew through and through, not a real German; [...] the prototype of modern, degenerate Jewry. Which [...] nowhere in the world thrives more happily than in Germany."[6] A focal point for this dispute was the newly funded journal *Kunstwart*, which led the philosopher Friedrich Nietzsche, an admirer of Heine, to cancel his subscription. In 1893, the Düsseldorf town council finally withdrew its offer to have the monument erected in the *Hofgarten* – significantly, its place was taken by a memorial for the dead of the 1870–71 Franco-Prussian War. Further attempts to realize the project in Frankfurt am Main and Mainz also fell victim to the poisonous atmosphere.[7]

Figure 2: "The Dispute Over the Heine Monument". Caricature from "Der wahre Jacob", Otto Marcus 1895

A surprising solution finally came in the form of an offer from New York, where the German community volunteered to give the Heine monument a home. Led by the Arion Verein, a German choral group, an initiative was founded in 1893 to raise money via charity bazaars and theatre evenings to transport the monument to New York.[8]

---

6   Xanthippos (Pseudonym of the poet Franz Sandvoß), Was dünkt euch um Heine? Ein Bekenntnis, Leipzig 1888, quoted in: Schubert, Kampf um das erste Heine-Denkmal, 1990, 251 (author's translation).
7   The first monument to Heine in Germany was only unveiled in 1913 (in Frankfurt). On the fate of the early Heine memorials cf. Bergmann, Die Loreley, 2006.
8   Reitter, Heine in the Bronx, 1999, 329.

The original plan was to place the fountain in Manhattan's Central Park, with the inscription *"IHREM GROSSEN DICHTER DIE DEUTSCHEN IN NEW YORK"* (To their great poet, from the German community in New York).[9] Yet Heine's cause did not run entirely smoothly in the New World either. The prominent location could not be secured, supposedly on artistic grounds: *The New York Times* described the monument as an "example of academic mediocrity, worthy of erection, but not worthy of erection as our chief municipal ornament."[10] Anti-Semitic arguments may have played a role here, too.[11] In any case, Heine was banished to the periphery. In 1899, the "Lorelei Fountain" was somewhat belatedly unveiled "in a wasteland on the outskirts of the city, surrounded by swamps and desolate empty lots."[12] The first monograph on the monument called the remote location in the Bronx an "ingenious hiding-place".[13] Nonetheless, in the coming decades, with the construction of the Grand Concourse – modelled on Paris's Champs Elysees – a glamorous centre of Jewish life in New York would be constructed, centred – in the 1920s and 30s – on the Bronx.

Sharing Heritage – Appropriation and Its Limits

The inauguration ceremony was a thoroughly emotional event. The sculptor, who was in attendance, wrote of an "imposing ceremony" attended by between four and six thousand people: "All the German societies with their flags stood around the monument to their best-known and best-loved poet and showed him their gratitude for his work. It must have been satisfying for his friends to see that it was he of all people, a man who had been branded as unpatriotic and un-German in the Fatherland, who was able to unite Germans abroad to a collective affirmation of their sentiments".[14]

The New York Times stressed that no German flags were to be seen, though American ones were in evidence.[15] Nonetheless, the reporter found the statue "disappointing" – and un-American: the main figure did not accord with the American image of Lorelei, he wrote, but was rather reminiscent of Brünhilde.[16] In his speech, Randolph Guggenheimer, President of the City Council, praised Heine as, among other things, a torchbearer for modernity, and the erection of the monument in New York as an expression

---

9   Schubert, Kampf um das erste Heine-Denkmal, 1990, 267.
10 Quoted in: Gray, Sturm und Drang, 2007.
11 Yale Professor Jeffrey Sammons speculates on the possible role of anti-Semitism, cf. Website The Bronx Ink, Lorelei Fountain. Such suspicions are shared by Stefan Elfenbein, who wrote in the Berliner Zeitung newspaper, referring to "Aufbau", the newspaper of Jewish emigrants – though this was not established until 1934: "Naturally the anti-Semitic tendency was concealed out of shame [...]. The monument could only be erected following forceful protests by the Jewish intellectual Carl Schurz." Elfenbein, Die Lorelei in der Bronx, 1999.
12 Elfenbein, Die Lorelei in der Bronx, 1999.
13 Kahn, Rudolf, Der Kampf um das Heine Denkmal, Leipzig 1911, 39–40, quoted in: Schubert, Kampf um das erste Heine-Denkmal, 1990, 267.
14 Kahn, Rudolf, Der Kampf um das Heine Denkmal, Leipzig 1911, 39–40, quoted in: Schubert, Kampf um das erste Heine-Denkmal, 1990, 267.
15 Heine Monument Unveiled, The New York Times, 9 July 1899.
16 Heine Monument Unveiled, The New York Times, 9 July 1899.

of American values – namely of tolerance, liberty and warm cosmopolitanism, while narrow-minded Germany could not forget that Heine was a Jew.[17]

But the appropriation of Heine's commemoration in the form of the Lorelei Fountain came up against limits even in the 'free and cosmopolitan' New world, including some that had not existed in the German debate. In puritan New York, the monument posed less of a political than it did a moral problem. The 'obscene' nudes are said to have already played a role in the debate about where the monument should be erected.[18] Iconoclastic attempts at destruction soon targeted the memorial, and as early as January 1900, one of the female figures – Poetry – was beheaded. In the court case that followed, women belonging to the Christian Association of Abstinence described the monument as "indecent",[19] while the Christian Temperance Union called it a "pornographic spectacle".[20] Because of continuing vandalism, the monument had to be placed under police protection. In 1940, it was banished to the northern end of the park.

Figure 3: The mutilated Lorelei Fountain (Photo: Phyllis Cohen 1986)

---

17 Heine Monument Unveiled, The New York Times, 9 July 1899.
18 Elfenbein, Die Lorelei in der Bronx, 1999.
19 The New York Heine Memorial in Court, in: Berliner Tageblatt, no. 92, 20 February 1900, quoted in: Schubert, Kampf um das erste Heine-Denkmal, 1990, 268.
20 Reitter, Heine in the Bronx, 1999, 330.

Even after the South Bronx had become a slum, the fountain remained a favourite target for attacks and vandalism. Heads and arms were broken off, faces and breasts defaced. The motivations for such attacks – anti-German or anti-Semitic, hatred of high culture, of (white, naked?) women – can only be a matter of speculation. In 1975, the fountain, which was covered with layer upon layer of graffiti, was considered the monument most affected by vandalism and destructive rage in the entire city (fig. 3).[21] Yet – in terms of their potential to disturb and to destroy – these traces are also evidence of a kind of appropriation, albeit one that is thoroughly ambivalent. Photographs, probably taken sometimes in the 1990s, captured a completely new version of the Lorelei, transformed by unknown persons into a Black woman in a brilliant red dress.[22]

Where there is hate, there is also love: Hermann Klaas, a dentist from Düsseldorf made a name for himself as the "Heine scrubber" by regularly cleaning the monument of graffiti on his own initiative.[23] When the New York City Council launched the successful *Adopt-a-Monument Program* for 20 particularly at-risk monuments in 1987, the Lorelei Fountain was the only one not to find sponsors. Only after Johannes Rau, Minister President of the German state of North Rhine-Westphalia, became involved did it prove possible to raise 700,000 US dollars, mostly from private donors, and on July 8 1999, Heine's monument – restored and partially rebuilt – was returned to its original site and ceremonially unveiled for a second time[24] – to surprise travellers with unexpected wanderlust, alienness and joy.

---

21 Schubert, Kampf um das erste Heine-Denkmal, 1990, 267–268.
22 This version and images of the restoration can be viewed at Website The Bronx Ink, Lorelei Fountain.
23 Ein Heine-Schrubber in New York, FOCUS Magazin, 16 September 1996.
24 See Sammons, Restoration of the Heine Monument, 1999.

15 Salvador da Bahia / Brazil
Whose Heritage? Globalization and Local Practices in the Pelourinho District

> They Don't Care About Us
> (Michael Jackson)[1]

From Historic Monument to Heritage

Historic buildings and places are very popular these days. The most high-profile sites, in particular, are enjoying record visitor numbers. Above all, the sites that have received UNESCO's 'World Heritage' label are proving to be absolute tourist magnets. Interest in the classic "historic monument", by contrast, seems to be declining rapidly. My colleague Marion Wohlleben reports from Switzerland that the concept of architectural monument (*Denkmal* in German) is indeed in the process of falling out of use, while the tendency today is to speak of cultural heritage (*Kulturgut, Patrimoine culturel*).[2] In this shift, we can perhaps see signs of a deeper transformation, whose significance cannot yet be determined. Concepts such as heritage, patrimony and "place of memory" represent the reversal of a restriction of the concept of historic monument that has obtained over the last century, particularly in the German-language debate. This restriction   which had momentous consequences – culminated in the concept of a historic monument being reduced from the symbolically charged and identity-formative *monument historique* of its origins in the French Revolution, to a mere historical document.[3] The historic building that we protect today, in accordance with a value that is legally defined and certified by experts, is above all *evidence* of a certain epoch, a particular style, a historic way of life or mode of production. The architectural monument has thus been tamed as an exemplar of a closed canon. The sum total of such monuments is imagined as a built archive of history. Wherever the productive appropriation of cultural heritage is replaced by the archivization of buildings as historical examples,

---

1   Michael Jackson, song title from his album *HIStory – Past, Present and Future Book I*, 1995.
2   Wohlleben, Gibt es ein neues Verständnis, 2014.
3   Euler-Rolle, Stimmungswert, 2005.

heritage conservation loses relevance and the ability to create attachment. Why we preserve certain buildings, what they mean for us, where they touch our feelings, and what the significance of all this may be for us – these are questions that a narrow concept of the historic monument is systematically incapable of answering.[4] Here the concept of heritage truly opens new prospects. Monuments represent the past, but heritage is something we have to make our own – in a certain sense, therefore, it lies ahead of us.[5] Johann Wolfgang Goethe already recognized this connection when he gave Faust the line "What from your father's heritage is lent / Earn it anew, to really possess it!"[6] Legitimate heritage is more than merely the transmission of things of value. The true heir of a rare violin, we might say, is whoever can play it. For Georg W. F. Hegel, heritage is closely associated with the concept of work.[7] The work of the mind is necessary before the inheritance received is no longer of the past: "To receive this inheritance is also to enter upon its use [...] that which is received is changed [by the work of the mind], and the material worked upon is both enriched and preserved at the same time".[8] The French philosopher Jacques Derrida took this thought further. For Derrida, heritage is not about having or receiving something or being enriched by means of some bequest, rather: "the being of what we are is first of all inheritance"; heritage is never a "given"; it is always a "task".[9] Here, inheriting and heritage are inextricably interwoven with human existence – they are intimately connected with our being and our search for identity. Conceiving of inheritance as active acquisition and appropriation means, in the particular context of cultural heritage, that heritage objects not only have to be worked up and worked on by professionals and academics, but also, and above all, that their meaning must be worked out and worked through by society.

Applying scientific methods to trace the contradictions in society so as to bring them to bear fruitfully on a debate about historic monuments is a major challenge for a discipline that is traditionally less focused on processes of appropriation and conflicts over interpretation than it is on technical questions of material preservation. UNESCO, whose World Heritage Convention made a decisive contribution to popularizing the heritage concept, has only hesitantly accepted this challenge. In the text adopted in 1972, the potential for conflict and the ambivalences of heritage appropriation are covered up by incantatory formulas of 'the world's heritage' and 'for all the peoples of the world'; as usual, the vision is proclaimed of a common legacy that it is our task to preserve and pass on.[10] The World Heritage label has even led to the intensification of the conflicts between normative, Western-influenced conceptions of heritage and local processes of meaning-making; i.e. between that which the List identifies as worthy of the 'outstanding cultural value' brand and that which is locally understood and accepted

---

4   Vinken, Amt und Gesellschaft, 2014, 22–25.
5   Willer/Weigel/Jussen, Übertragungskonzepte, 2013, especially Willer, Kulturelles Erbe, 2013.
6   "Was Du ererbt von deinen Vätern hast, erwirb es um es zu besitzen." Originally in part 1 from 1808, 682/3, here cited after this Translation: Goethe, Faust, 1963 (1808/1832), 329–330.
7   Willer, Kulturelles Erbe, 2013, 161–162, 165–166.
8   Hegel, Lectures on the History of Philosophy, 1892 (1817), Introduction, 3.
9   Derrida, Specters of Marx, 1994 (1993), 67–68.
10 Website UNESCO, Convention Concerning the Protection.

as heritage.[11] In Salvador da Bahia, the development taken by the centre of the city since its listing as World Heritage has also been deeply ambivalent.

Colonial City as World Heritage Site

With its three million residents, Brazil's first capital, Salvador da Bahia, or, Bahia, as the locals refer to it, is still the third-largest city in the country. The historic city centre, which was developed in the 17th and 18th centuries during the heyday of Brazil's sugar cane plantations, is considered the largest surviving colonial city in the New World and was elevated to UNESCO World Heritage status in 1985.[12] The heart of the old city, the district known as the *Pelourinho* ('the Pillory') was for a long time dilapidated and impoverished. But it has been thoroughly restored since the 1970s in a series of internationally funded campaigns (fig. 1).[13] Today, Bahia's old town is one of the most important tourist attractions in the poverty stricken northeast of Brazil and a major economic factor for the economically underdeveloped city.

Figure 1: *World Heritage as homogenisation. Pelourinho district (Photo: G. Vinken 2014)*

How one evaluates this rehabilitation and renewal programme depends on which questions one asks and which criteria one applies. Sociologists and local activists rightly complain that the rights of the local population have been systematically ignored dur-

---

11 Ashworth/Graham/Tunbridge, Pluralising Pasts, 2007, 1–2.
12 Website UNESCO, Historic Centre of Salvador de Bahia.
13 For a first important contribution to the topic see the sociological dissertation by Craanen, Altstadtsanierung, 1998.

ing various major restoration campaigns over the decades.[14] Before rehabilitation, the Pelourinho had suffered a fairly typical fate. The once genteel residential area gradually became a slum. By the 1930s, it was home to the city's largest red-light district. Some of the two- and three-storey townhouses were occupied by more than a hundred people, living crammed together in subdivisions separated by makeshift cardboard partitions. A spiral of poverty, exploitation and underinvestment sustained this decline. Ultimately, an increasing number of houses began to collapse.[15] The renovation and restoration measures carried out since the 1970s were largely financed by UNESCO and the World Bank and went hand in hand with a more-or-less systematic policy of resettlement. Particularly in the early stages, many residents were thrown out of their homes without appreciable compensation, while later they were often rehoused in concrete silos on the periphery. The rehabilitation transformed the Pelourinho into a commercial district with a tourist infrastructure. Ground floors these days are generally given over to business; the floors above are often empty. In 1995 around a million tourists visited the Pelourinho – in the meantime this number has likely risen.

While the project was a disgrace in terms of social policy, it might also be called an economic success story. If this is the case, why was the organization that funded it – which was after all a UN agency – unable to secure higher standards of welfare for the population? Moreover, the restoration work came nowhere close to meeting international heritage conservation standards. The aim was to return the colonial quarter to its "original state", eliminating all later additions. On top of that, only the façades were to be restored, and the new occupants were given more or less free rein to model the interiors for their own purposes. Even the façades were refurbished or sometimes completely reconstructed with a lack of concern for historical accuracy and in a generic colonial style (fig. 2).[16]

None of that can be reconciled with the standards of the authoritative Venice Charter (1964). Economic regeneration was combined with homogenizing beautification measures – a kind of synthetic cityscape grooming – of the kind that has long been practised in Europe and still has many devotees.[17] Anyone who is interested in learning about how life was lived in colonial Brazil, you will be disappointed by this stage set, which, for all its picturesque colourfulness, remains sterile. The same goes for anyone with an interest in the urban slums of the 20th century, with their complex relationship networks and precarious spaces, as described so vividly by Jorge Amado in his Bahia Novels. In many regards, the restored Pelourinho appears as a regrettable product of a globalization process in which both an architectural pearl of the colonial age and the interests of its residents were sacrificed for the profits of the tourism industry in the name of World Heritage. Is this a case of the city not so much embracing its heritage as betraying and selling it?

---

14   Craanen, Altstadtsanierung, 1998, 6–10, 34–41.
15   Craanen, Altstadtsanierung, 1998, 21–29.
16   Craanen, Altstadtsanierung, 1998, 34–41.
17   Vinken, Zone Heimat, 2010; see also Vinken, Patrimônio Cultural e Globalização, 2010.

Figure 2: Facadism and gentrification. Houses in the Pelourinho district (Photo: G. Vinken 2014)

UNESCO World Heritage vs. Africanità

In answering this question, the criteria used by experts are barely relevant. Cologne Cathedral, more deeply anchored in the self-image of that city's residents than anything else save perhaps their annual Carnival tradition, was reviled by most art historians on its completion as a hulking fake, the desecration of a mediaeval monument. Georg Dehio, one of the spokesmen of modern conservation ideology, reacted to the neo-Gothic completion, which, he said, could not awaken "the old art" "to real life", with the words of Jesus: "Let the dead bury their dead!" (Matthew 8:22).[18] On the other hand, Cologne Cathedral, which was reconceptualized as a "national monument" following the liberation from French occupation, is a particularly vivid example of permanent processes of social reinterpretation and appropriation. Conceived by patriotic proponents of a free, united and republican Germany, the project was concluded under Prussian rule in the spirit of restoration:[19] against the will of the liberals who, as Heinrich Heine's famous *Germany: A Winter's Tale* shows, had only scorn for the completion of the cathedral, an undertaking they considered to be backward-looking.[20]

What significance, what importance does the Pelourinho district have for Bahia's self-perception? Colonial monuments, in particular, are subject to widely varying evaluations, depending on whether one's forebears can be counted on the side of the per-

---

18 Dehio, Geschichte der deutschen Kunst, 1930, 40–41.
19 Nipperdey, Kölner Dom als Nationaldenkmal, 1983.
20 Heine, A Winter's Tale, 1986 (1844), caput IV, 35–39, here 37–38.

petrators or the victims.[21] Salvador da Bahia was not only the first capital of the Portuguese colony from the 16th to the 18th century, the city was also the fulcrum of the slave trade in South America. Around 40 percent of all the enslaved people carried off from Africa, some four to five million in total, were disembarked at Bahia and sold at its slave market. The Pelourinho – where many former slaveowners used to live and whose name is derived from the central square where enslaved women and men were often publicly tortured and put on show for minor offences – appears at first glance to be ill suited to function as a space of memory and collective heritage; especially in a city like Bahia, where the proportion of residents of African descent is unusually high for Brazil.

However, an initial survey of opinion in Bahia, carried out by a team of cultural theorists and sociologists, shows that the historic centre is a strong point of reference in the consciousness of the city's inhabitants and a key component of even regional identities: on the mythical map of Brazil, Salvador da Bahia, more than any other city, symbolizes the African roots of Brazilian society.[22] In this connection, it is significant that Salvador da Bahia is essentially a Brazilian domestic tourist destination, with nearly 80 percent of the tourists that visit the city being Brazilian.[23] Bahia's Black heritage is manifested above all in two ubiquitous intangible phenomena: capoeira and the bajanas. Capoeira is a combination of martial art and dance whose origins have been traced to Nigeria. Bahia considers itself the home of capoeira (fig. 3).[24] As with all customs – think of Carnival or Mardi Gras – capoeira is a product of layers of reappropriation and transformation. As a martial art practised in Brazil by enslaved men since the 18th century, it plays a legendary role in the history of Black resistance. And it certainly later played a role as an urban martial art – and was banned until 1937. Capoeira's revival as a popular phenomenon is associated with the Black Power movement of the 1960s. Today, it is taught in sport clubs and dance schools throughout the city and displays can be seen on the streets of Bahia. It is important to note that, in contrast to the USA, where Black Power was a phenomenon that sought distance from the white mainstream, Brazil's Black heritage is very much accepted by the mainstream and represents a figure of consensus.[25]

---

21 Di Giovine, The heritage-scape, 2008; Lagae, From Patrimoine partagé, 2008.
22 Löw, Schwarzsein als kollektive Praxis, 2010.
23 Website Governo da Bahia/Secretaria da Cultura e Turismo.
24 Almeida, Capoeira, 1986.
25 Löw, Schwarzsein als kollektive Praxis, 2010, 142–144.

15 Salvador da Bahia – Whose Heritage?   239

Figure 3: The (martial) art of resistance. Capoeira demonstration in Bahia (Photo: A. M. Teles Zimerer 2014)

Figure 4: Central to identity and religion. A bajana selling acarajé (Photo: R. Pozzebom 2008

The bajanas are also a permanent feature of Bahia's cityscape (fig. 4) – white-robed women with white turbans, offering their famous street food – acarajé. This delicacy, a kind of croquette of ground beans, shrimp and spices, also has its origins in Africa. The bajanas owe their valued position in society in part to their links to Candomblé, a polytheistic underground religion that was likewise imported from West Africa and was forbidden for many years. The bajanas were originally a kind of holy women – their "office" is still passed down from mother to daughter – while the sale of street food was used to finance the forbidden religion. Now, of course, the bajanas are an integral part of the city's brand image, appearing as sculptures on fountains, as souvenirs, even as a special Bahia Barbie doll. In fact, the city government now insists that acarajé sellers wear traditional clothing. Yet although the religious significance of the street food vendors is in the process of declining, the buying and eating of acarajé remains a practice that is loaded with layers of symbolism: the African delicacy is still the food of the Candomblé gods, and is still prepared by women who traditionally considered themselves as the intermediaries to the divine; it is 'living heritage' in the best and most literal sense.[26]

Processes of Purification and Homogenization

The old town of Salvador da Bahia, this much can be said, is a space of continuous re-enactment of a self-conscious and nostalgic Africanità – and Bahia in particular feels itself called to be the custodian of this heritage, which has been modernized out of existence in Africa itself.[27] Against Bahia's colonial backdrop, a mixed population secures its Black heritage, a nation celebrates itself, drawing pride from knowing that its great diversity has given rise to something new and unique. If our task in each instance is to reappropriate our heritage through active work, then the reinterpretation of the colonial quarter that grew up in the shadow of the pillory into a figure of consensus evoking an imagined Africanità must be considered a happy development. It is therefore all the more regrettable that this wealth of built heritage has been largely reduced to a scenic backdrop, its complexity and contradictions homogenized in response to a primary concern with the city's outward image. On my return to Salvador da Bahia four years later in 2014, the negative consequences of this programme of heritage conservation in the service of superficial scenic effects are unmistakable. A walk through the old town confirms the ongoing 'purification' and homogenization of the district as the backdrop for an increasingly manufactured tourism industry (fig. 5).

The immaterial Black heritage, by contrast – the music and especially the dance groups – appears to have moved to the neighbouring districts that have not yet been rehabilitated. When attending the conference "Berlim/Salvador: Reapropriação urbana entre marketing e autoafirmação"[28] I was alarmed to note – in sharp contrast to another conference held in 2010[29] – that the restoration of the old town was discussed without any mention of the Pelourinho's Black roots; now all the talk was about an open-air shopping mall and similar commercial ideas. Clearly, with the creation of a homogeneous district full of picture-postcard colonial architecture, a manifold heritage

---

26 Löw, Schwarzsein als kollektive Praxis, 2010, 150–152.
27 Löw points out the growth of the number of African-Americans visiting Brazil in search of their roots, many of whom fly to Salvador de Bahia, cf. Löw, Schwarzsein als kollektive Praxis, 2010 and also Pinho, African-American Roots, 2008.
28 Reappropriation of the City between Marketing and Self-Assertation (Goethe-Institute Salvador da Bahia, 3–4 April 2014).
29 *Salvador-Hamburgo - Passado e Presente da Globalização*, Salvador da Bahia (Instituto Cultural Brasil-Alemanha) 2010.

landscape has been starkly reduced. One could go so far as to say that the broad understanding of heritage has been diminished here by its architecturalization (specifically, by affixing the complex heritage-formations of the Pelourinho quarter exclusively to its colonial architecture): the colourful façades of the houses now pose as "monuments" of the colonial period, while the complex appropriations of the Black heritage that were once found in the Pelourinho have been squeezed out into other areas of the city. Not a great report card for a World Heritage Site. Processes of heritage appropriation are of vital significance for the identity of communities – locally, nationally and generally. UNESCO (and other professional actors in the field) should not seek to harmonize or streamline processes of heritage appropriation. The goal must rather be to secure the many-layered nature of this heritage, to preserve and to tolerate its complexity and inconsistency.

Figure 5: Backdrop for a manufactured tourism industry? Pelourinho district today (Photo: C. Vinken 2014)

16 New Orleans / USA
Contested Heritage. African-American Culture in a Southern City

> Our Heritage – Your Playground
> (R.F. Langford)[1]

The destruction of New Orleans by Hurricane Katrina in August 2005 was experienced as an existential catastrophe that raised the question of the city's identity once again with renewed urgency. As well as causing untold material damage – on August 31, some 80 percent of the city was under metres of water[2] – this was above all a humanitarian catastrophe that probably took some 1,200 lives and left countless numbers of people injured and traumatized.[3] Most New Orleans residents were evacuated, under conditions that were sometimes chaotic, and the consequences continue to be felt to this day: "The population [...] fell from 484,674 before Katrina (April 2000) to an estimated 230,172 after Katrina (July 2006) – [...] a loss of over half of the city's population. By July of 2014, the population was back up to 384,320 – 79% of what it was in 2000."[4] One of the oldest and most culturally vibrant cities in the South appeared to be facing a watery doom; a city, furthermore, whose urban character and density appears to Europeans to be astonishingly un-American; one whose centre had also attracted the attention of conservationists early on and whose central French Quarter was one of the first Historic Districts to receive official protection in the United States.[5] An initial review of the city's recovery efforts by a team of conservationists concluded that institutionalized heritage preservation has in this case proven to be of limited value for cataloguing, safeguarding and saving the city's heritage, because, in brief, there is a major discrepancy between what is locally considered significant and what is labelled

---

1   Langford, Our Heritage – Your Playground, 1983.
2   Plyer, Facts for Features, 2016.
3   Bialik, We Still Don't Know, 2015. New Orleans alone accounted for almost 1,000 of these fatalities (see previous footnote).
4   Plyer, Facts for Features, 2016.
5   For an overview of the early history of New Orleans, see: Ellis, Madame Vieux Carré, 2010, especially the first three chapters, 3–140.

or listed as cultural heritage on the various registers of monuments.[6] "Whose heritage" we may again ask, is being protected and maintained using public funds? And who gets to decide? What, in the desperation of catastrophe, is abandoned? And how could this situation perhaps be improved? The fundamental question that the catastrophe involuntarily and radically throws up is as follows: Can the heritage of a city, beyond its built heritage and its monuments, ever be effectively addressed by means of institutional protection measures and, if so, by whom and how?

Today, 15 years after Katrina, we can still say without hesitation that New Orleans remains a monumental city, a city of monuments. More than perhaps any other city in the USA, it has been able to maintain its distinct appearance.[7] These days, it is again possible to experience a dense, vibrant city with a European feel in whose centre, the *Vieux Carré* or French Quarter, the regular layout, the street grid of the colonial city (from 1718) remains, and where townhouses with richly decorated iron balconies on all sides evoke the antebellum golden age (1820 to 1861) (fig. 1).[8]

Figure 1: *Antebellum nostalgia in the French Quarter (Photo: G. Vinken 2020)*

Other districts in the city also have atmospheric streets and attract not only lovers of architecture: the grand mansions of the English-speaking landed bourgeoisie in the Garden District, popular neighbourhoods such as the Faubourg Marigny – a centre of the city's musical life – or neighbouring Bywater, with its picturesque single-storey

---

6   Morgen/Morgen/Barrett, Finding a Place, 2006.
7   Documented comprehensively in: Campanella, An Architectural Geography, 2016.
8   Some 60 percent of the city's housing stock was built in this period. On the architectural structure of the French Quarter cf. Campanella, An Architectural Geography, 2016, especially 135.

Figure 2: Well-maintained neighbourhoods, colourful houses, Marigny (Photo: G. Vinken 2020)

Shotgun Houses, now a valued aspect of the city's branding[9] – all are well-appointed and mostly well-kept neighbourhoods that reveal few signs of damage at first glance (fig. 2). Moreover, they are almost entirely listed as Historic Districts.[10] This is certainly a comfort for visitors who arrive with their heads full of the images that flashed around the world in 2005. Nevertheless, the case of New Orleans in particular raises with great urgency a question that has been formulated throughout this book with respect to many case studies and from various perspectives: What is the relationship between heritage as defined by legal protection instruments and the heritage that determines the identity of the city? This text argues from various angles that the treatment of New Orleans' Black heritage perpetuates historical and social injustice to this day and that, moreover, this legacy affects not only the legacy of a particular heritage community but, via marginalization, neglect and corruption, means that a key voice in the American heritage narrative remains largely unheard.

Gentrification, Displacement, Destruction

The necessity of treating *all* discourse concerning cultural heritage as political was made particularly clear by the after-effects of Hurricane Katrina on New Orleans. Much has

---

9   For a typology and on the origins: Campanella, An Architectural Geography, 2016, 149–154.
10   Indeed, large portions of central New Orleans have been classified as Historic Districts since the late 70s. For basic information, see the map at Website HDLC, Historic District Maps, and for details, see Hawkins, City of New Orleans, 2011.

been written about the race and class bias evident in the city's destruction, the rescue effort and the reconstruction.[11] Fifteen years after that devastation, it is easy to see that the outlook for African-American heritage formations in particular has worsened since Katrina, that structures, sites and communities which were often forged with great difficulty under conditions of historical adversity and inequality have been thinned out and eroded, for an overall situation we can best describe as mixed and where occasional aspects are truly catastrophic. There can be no doubt that the process chosen for compensating flood victims enormously accelerated the process of gentrification in many neighbourhoods.[12] The class bias, which in this case is always also a racial bias, is conspicuous, and has led to immeasurable and probably irreversible destruction.[13] The problem is that financial compensation was based on the estimated current value of houses and land. As a consequence, the wealthy in their comparatively middle-class districts, whose property was evaluated correspondingly highly, received a considerable sum. In such areas, therefore, nearly all the houses have been repaired and are now habitable. It is probably also easy to demonstrate that listing as a Historic District (HD) intensified this trend. I have indicated elsewhere that the designation of HDs as zones with a special legal status intensifies social and ethnic homogenization.[14] Furthermore, it has been shown that every single HD in the United States, without exception, demonstrates above average growth in property values.[15] The situation is very different in the poor – often Black – districts, where the 'dangerous' location, poor infrastructure and lack of domestic amenities led to the market value of properties being given such a low estimation that the restitution payment was often not sufficient to pay for the renovations necessary to make the property liveable again.[16] Many Black families, whose property, often their only noteworthy possession, had protected them from sinking into misery and homelessness, are now completely impoverished. They have only been able to find a roof over their heads far from the centre of the city and the neighbourhoods they have always called home. This leads to the irrevocable destruction of social and cultural bonds and hence the possibility of articulating and developing autonomous heritage formats – particularly, as we shall see, because these tend to be weakly institutionalized and public funding is the exception. This is made clear by contrasting two neighbouring districts, both located on the river just south of the city centre.

Bywater, which, like the French Quarter, the Faubourg Marigny and parts of the Lower Garden District, was largely spared the ravages of the flood, was long a mixed lower-middle-class district until artists and urban trendsetters began to flock to the area in the late 1990s.[17] Today it is full of trendy B&Bs and cafes where lactose-free coffee, gluten-free snacks and vegan sandwiches, the latest achievements of Western

---

11 Above all Robert Campanella in the chapter "Gentrification and Its Discontents: Notes from New Orleans" in Campanella, Cityscapes of New Orleans, 2017, 65–71.
12 Ehrenfeucht, Restructuring Public Landscapes, 2016.
13 Moskowitz, How to Kill a City, 2017, on New Orleans 13–68.
14 Cf. the essay on New York (Chapter 7) in this volume.
15 Murtagh, Keeping Time, 2006, 94; Vinken, Vorbild Amerika, 2017, 261–262.
16 Peter Moskowitz details the ways in which the Black population was systematically driven out or prevented from returning, cf. Moskowitz, How to Kill a City, 2017, 45–68.
17 Campanella, Cityscapes of New Orleans, 2017, 3–14.

civilization, are delivered to a mostly young, white clientele. The wave of gentrification that the flood brought in the form of a mass influx of "urban creatives" has almost completely pushed out the poor population, and particularly African-Americans. The number of African-American residents fell from 61 percent in 2005 to 31 percent in 2015, while the number of children declined by two-thirds. Household incomes in the neighbourhood also rose sharply but very unequally: for white residents, the median income increased by more than $10,000, but for African-American residents it rose by only $1,000.[18] Today, Bywater, alongside the neighbouring district of Faubourg Marigny, is one of the most popular destinations for tourists visiting the city. With its almost perfectly preserved historical housing stock, colourful buildings in a synthetic Franco-Spanish colonial style with Caribbean elements as well as many locally typical shotgun houses, it appeals to both urban dwellers and travellers. When, while we were unloading our car, a young African-American woman in a party mood passed, holding a loud debate across the street with her boyfriend, our landlady felt she had to apologise for the situation and emphasize that this was a reputable street: "It is not normally like that around here." Since 1993, much of Bywater (some 120 blocks) has been listed as a HD.[19]

On the other side of the industrial canal that was dredged in the early 20th century, one enters a different world: the legendary Lower Ninth Ward, or what remains of it. Lying somewhat lower than neighbouring Bywater, much of this large neighbourhood, formerly home to many prominent African-Americans, including jazz legends and other prominent musicians, writers and artists, was flooded by Katrina. Sites of pilgrimage, such as the house of rock and roll legend Fats Domino, who himself was for a while thought to have perished during Katrina, were destroyed in the flood. Fifteen years after Katrina, the remains of his grand piano, which was hauled from the rubble, is displayed in the entrance hall of the Louisiana State Museum as the first exhibit in the permanent exhibition on "Living with Hurricanes: Katrina & Beyond". Much of the neighbourhood, however, remains a depopulated and deserted wasteland, criss-crossed by a grid of decaying streets (fig. 3).

Lacking the means to rebuild, residents are slow to return; the lots are overgrown and have begun to appear in environmentally conscious travel guides such as Lonely Planet as "a walk on the wild side": "The popular narrative of the Lower 9th [Ward] is that it was devastated after Katrina, and this is true – but what is left is less urban wasteland, and more reclaimed nature. Those who wanted to move back to the neighborhood are already here [...]. In between the homes that are now occupied, one can find miles of empty lots and jungle-esque overgrowth. In many ways, the neighborhood is doing better than similarly hit areas – celebrity and media attention has at least brought money and volunteers. For all the talk of 'bringing the Lower 9th back,' what's here now is likely to be what will be here for the foreseeable future."[20] Given the sense of despair that is

---

18   Ehrenfeucht, Restructuring Public Landscapes, 2016, 380.
19   Website City of New Orleans, HDLC: Bywater Historic District.
20   Website LonelyPlanet, New Orleans.

Figure 3: Reclaimed nature? The Lower Ninth Ward (Photo: Irina Vinnitskaya 2013)

everywhere palpable and the irreversible displacement of nearly all the neighbourhood's original residents, such statements can only appear totally cynical.[21]

What has been lost in terms of sites of identity formation and cultural heritage can today only be understood by referring to written records. Only very few cultural institutions are still fighting to survive. One example, standing on its own at the side of the street, is the privately owned "House of Dancing Feathers" (1317 Tupelo St, currently closed),[22] whose initiator, Curator and Director Ronald Lewis, has turned his home into a museum. The exhibition is dedicated to the *Social Aid and Pleasure Clubs*, which "can be traced back to 19th century benevolent societies that provided health care and burial services for their members."[23] These African-American clubs were central institutions of Black identity in the city for centuries, and were interwoven in numerous ways not only with the history of Black music and celebratory practices, but also with protest and resistance and the struggle for self-determination. They remain significant today above all thanks to the Second Line parades and Mardi Gras street carnivals.[24] The exhibits include many of the colourful and fantastic costumes of the Mardi Gras Indians, an African-American tradition of dressing up as Native Americans that has become quite well known outside the city in recent decades (fig. 4).

---

21 For a more detailed overview of the situation, see, for instance: Landphair, The Forgotten People of New Orleans, 2007; Lindahl, Legends of Hurricane Katrina, 2012; Rich, Jungleland, 2012.
22 Website House of Dance and Feathers; Breunlin/Lewis, The House of Dance and Feathers, 2010.
23 Website House of Dance and Feathers, Marching Cultures.
24 Sublette, The World that made New Orleans, 2008, 293–311.

Figure 4: Black heritage. Mardi Gras Indians (Photo: Lombana 2012)

A good insight into how "the Indians" see themselves is given by Michael Pietrzyk's 2019 documentary film "All on a Mardi Gras Day", which was successfully shown at a number of film festivals (including the 2019 Berlinale).[25] One important act of identity formation is the creation of these celebrated costumes, with their countless beads and feathers, by hand and at great material cost. They hark back to spiritual practices and should not be dismissed as 'mere folklore'. Following the crisis that threatened the city's very identity, forms of intangible heritage such as the Second Line parades and the Indians experienced an unmistakable resurgence, though some commentators suggested that the parades became not only more popular but also whiter.[26] It is bitterly ironic that the protagonists in these parades, as the film *All on a Mardi Gras Day* also makes clear, have been driven from the districts where they traditionally lived by economic factors and now find themselves forced to survive on the periphery of the city, far from their cultural roots. It is not only social and cultural connections built up over many years that have been lost. What is being suppressed, marginalized and abandoned to destruction are cultural expressions of a unique aspect of America's living heritage. New Orleans, as most researchers agree, is incomparable in terms of the heterogeneity and breadth of its heritage landscape. Yet again it is revealed just what a one-sided vision of this variety is generally propagated; destruction or, at best, ignorance of New Orleans' African-American heritage – perhaps the city's most precious treasure – is a thread woven through the city's history. Rescue efforts after Katrina did not change this pattern but rather intensified it.

---

25   Website ShortsblogBerlinale, An Interview with Michal Pietrzyk.
26   Ehrenfeucht, Restructuring Public Landscapes, 2016, 382. Cf. Gotham, Authentic New Orleans, 2007, 181–187.

Contested Heritage

As Katrina made clear, the uniqueness, the specificity, the 'legacy' of New Orleans cannot be reduced to the city's buildings and physiognomy. New Orleans is a monument to the colonial age and the early Republic, and a vital depository of urban and architectural history, but it is also and above all the unique centre of African-American culture and identity.[27] Indeed, the mainstream narratives on the history of the city were long deaf or even hostile towards the specificity and historical vitality of its Black communities, whose history goes back to the 18th century. New Orleans is the place where, as a result of specific circumstances, earlier and more strongly than almost anywhere else in the USA, a genuinely Black syncretic culture developed. This is most evident in the African-influenced percussion-based form of music-making that found mainstream expression in the form of jazz and went on to create one of the foundations of all rock and pop music. In the city's lively and diverse music scene, as well as in its funeral practices, parades and Mardi Gras street carnival – more details of which are included below – Black heritage is reclaimed and continues to exist as lived experience.[28] This rich heritage is extremely significant for several reasons, a significance that reaches beyond those who maintain this culture and the relevant heritage communities. Related to the hybrid post-colonial cultures of Central and South America, and particularly the Caribbean world, it is a special and unique culture in the 'White Anglo-Saxon Protestant'-dominated USA.[29] New Orleans has always had a special position in the heritage landscape of the United States.[30] It is a palimpsest of three colonial empires: founded by France in 1712, ceded to the Spanish in 1766 and purchased, together with the rest of Louisiana, by the United States in 1803. Established on the Gulf of Mexico at the mouth of the Mississippi, populated by French exiles, such as prisoners and prostitutes but also by exiled French Canadians (Cajuns), for a long time the city was French-speaking (and Roman Catholic); the most 'southern' city in the United States, the most 'northern' outpost of the Caribbean.[31] For historically and in terms of economic geography, New Orleans was, until well into the 19th century, part of the Caribbean world that had been colonized, shaped and exploited by Spain, first in the form of silver mines, and then by means of tobacco and sugar plantations. The centre of gravity in the Gulf region was Havana; and the Spanish influence in New Orleans became even more manifest when Louis XV ceded the colony to the Spanish, who integrated it tightly into their economic zone and legal system, while the rest of North America became increasingly English. Well into the 20th century, the city on the Gulf was, alongside New York, the most important port of entry for immigrants to North America, a city of exchange, of hybridization. And finally, though no less significantly, for more than a century, it was

---

27   Hall, Africans in Colonial Louisiana, 1992, 157, 275–315.
28   Sublette, The World that made New Orleans, 2008, 293–311.
29   Ette/Müller, New Orleans and the Global South, 2017, considers the city in the context of the Global South.
30   Ostendorf, The Mysteries of New Orleans, 2016.
31   Ostendorf, The Mysteries of New Orleans, 2016, 108–109.

a centre of the inhuman and criminal practice of slavery, to which the city owed its material wealth.

Black Creoles, Free People of Colour: Africa-American Communities in New Orleans

Historically and structurally, New Orleans' Black communities are thus distinct from those of other American cities.[32] This rests in part on the legal status of the enslaved population. In the area of the Caribbean that was dominated by Spain, in contrast to slaves' status under English law (and also in distinction to the French *Code Noir*), they had the right to purchase their freedom, to own property and to establish their own households and families; weekends were partially free of work, which relieved the plantation owners of the burden of providing for their slaves, as the enslaved peoples were able to provide for themselves by means of their own gardens and markets. Since many of the enslaved Blacks possessed specialized skills, for instance in the trades, that were lacking in the hybrid 'white' population, a Black economy was able to develop early on.[33] Only with the introduction of a plantation economy (sugar cane, cotton), with the corresponding need for more intense work, and the sharp growth of the slave economy in the late 18th and early 19th centuries did these rights come under increasing pressure. An important and lasting effect of this situation, unique in the USA, was the existence of large numbers of Free People of Colour. It was their unique economic and social situation that made possible a degree of economic independence and the development and transmission of autonomous cultural and social practices, as recent research has shown. This enabled the unique historical flowering of an African-American culture within the USA.[34] If we discount the Spanish military, at the end of the 18th century, there were more Black than white people in New Orleans, and for every two enslaved people, there was one free Black person; among women, the ratio of slaves to free folk was even lower at 718:538.[35] One peculiarity that is often noted in this respect is the *plaçage*, a French colonial tradition whereby a white man would take a second, African-American wife with whom he would establish a second family. These were set up in their own houses around the city; as a rule, they were emancipated and could keep their own slaves.[36] In line with the racist social codes of the time, the second wives were often light-skinned mixed-race "quadroons". This practice was one of the important drivers of creolization; the "Black Creoles" of New Orleans (as they were known in contradistinction to the white

---

32 For background: Hall, Africans in Colonial Louisiana, 1992.
33 Sublette, The World that made New Orleans, 2008, 113.
34 The unusually homogenous ethnic make-up of New Orleans' Black population should also be noted here. Virtually all the enslaved Africans brought to New Orleans between 1720 and 1732 originated in the sub-Saharan "Senegambia". Later, ethnic groups from Congo were in the majority. Cf. Hall, Africans in Colonial Louisiana, 1992, 159–161; Sublette, The World that made New Orleans, 2008, 106–108.
35 Figures for 1791: Sublette, The World that made New Orleans, 2008, 111.
36 Sublette, The World that made New Orleans, 2008, 111. There is a private museum dedicated to the Free People of Color in New Orleans: the Musée de f.p.c. (Website Le Musée de f.p.c.).

colonists, who referred to themselves as "Creoles") were, until the abolition of slavery, the largest group of free Black people on the American continent.[37]

In other American cities, the situation was quite different: enslaved people were kept in barracks on plantations and generally did not share a common language, origin or culture. Via an aggressive practice of 'breeding' and selling enslaved people, a systematic effort was undertaken to suppress the establishment of family groups and cultural or social infrastructures. With increasing Americanization, however, the comparatively better situation in New Orleans came under intense pressure. The prohibition on the import of slaves enacted by President Jefferson in 1808 led to the growth and heterogenization of Black communities in New Orleans. Alongside the 'privateers', who hijacked cargoes of enslaved Africans headed for Cuba and smuggled them into the city in large numbers,[38] there was also growth in the numbers of English-speaking slaves traded domestically within the USA, above all from the breeding farms of Virginia, whose 'excess' slaves were now sold in the Deep South – a business model that ultimately owes its existence to the 1808 import ban.[39] The population growth that went alongside Americanization (in 1840 the city had 10,000 inhabitants; by 1840 there were 102,000), and which consisted mostly of so-called 'Anglo-Americans' (in fact foreign-born 'whites') led to the development of an increasingly harsh racial regime and the ethnic division of the city.[40]

After the Civil War, this pattern intensified as a result of the huge influx of freed slaves from the North, and conflicts arose between the often well-educated French-speaking (and Catholic) 'creoles of colour' and the Protestant and usually illiterate Blacks from the North who settled in the north of the city.[41] Just how alien the social life of New Orleans had to appear to travellers from the North is well documented. Visitors recorded their shock at the 'racially mixed' social life, the Sunday balls and ubiquitous music, and the custom of *plaçage*, which meant 'mixed-race' couples and families would appear openly in public.[42] Particularly scandalous were the mass public African-American rallies and dances accompanied by music and percussion on Congo Square: "African slaves [...] who [...] rock the city with their Congo dances".[43] These events were only finally suppressed in 1851, and had continued on Sundays following the general ban on mass gatherings of Blacks and an explicit prohibition in 1835.[44] The dance and music events

---

37   Ostendorf, The Mysteries of New Orleans, 2016, 111–112. Creolization here refers to race mixing; Black Creoles, Creoles of Color established themselves as a distinct group in contrast to the French colonists, who identified as Creoles.
38   Sublette, The World that made New Orleans, 2008, 263–270.
39   On the "slave-breeding industry" cf. Sublette, The World that made New Orleans, 2008, 220–239.
40   As late as 1820, only some 1/8 of the population was English-speaking (Sublette, The World that made New Orleans, 2008, 266); the 'Anglo-Americans' settled above all in the west of the city, in what is today the Central Business District and in the western part of the Garden District; the Creoles in the French Quarter and in Tremé; Marigny and Baywater were mixed, Ostendorf, The Mysteries of New Orleans, 2016, 112–113.
41   Ostendorf, The Mysteries of New Orleans, 2016, 113.
42   Sublette, The World that made New Orleans, 2008, 273–274.
43   Sublette, The World that made New Orleans, 2008, 271–288, the quote is from 276.
44   Sublette, The World that made New Orleans, 2008, 286.

have their roots in Caribbean custom.⁴⁵ As long as Francophones had the upper hand in New Orleans, Black music (ultimately influenced by population groups with origins in Senegal and Congo) could also be found there of the kind also found in Cuba, Jamaica and the Antilles. This music, featuring drums and banjos, was of incalculable value for the development of jazz, rock and pop.⁴⁶ From the start, the form of music practised by African-Americans had a role in the formation of identity and in politics. It was associated with spiritual concepts and certainly represented a vigorous form of cultural resistance. It must therefore be included alongside other syncretic practices such as the popular form of voodoo practised around New Orleans, which was celebrated outside the city and marketed as a tourist attraction as early as 1870.⁴⁷

A Biased View: Heritage, Tourism and Racism

New Orleans' Black heritage, which stands in a line stretching back to the founding of the city, has inestimable political significance in two regards. On the one hand, it provides a necessary corrective to the American founding myth. The dominant American narrative of a nation whose origin lies in revolution (Equality, Liberty, Fraternity) and the wars of independence against the English, French and Spanish is here counterposed with aspects of US history that are frequently suppressed but are structurally central to the process of American nation-building, namely violence, exploitation and repression. Following the large-scale eradication of the continent's indigenous population, this was most conspicuously manifested in the enslavement and disenfranchisement of and ongoing discrimination against African-Americans. At the same time, with its diverse and flourishing cultural achievements, New Orleans possesses a tradition of alternative bodies of knowledge. This prevents Black heritage from being reduced to misery, powerlessness and speechlessness – extremely powerful traumas that are reproduced in the memory of slavery and, loaded with racism, all too often lead to new forms of discrimination and denigration.

Today, the city's African-American heritage is subject to a double threat: the threat stemming from marginalization, exclusion and extinction (as can be seen, for instance, in the reconstruction of the city following Katrina), and the threat of cultural exploitation by the white mainstream.⁴⁸ The way New Orleans both presents itself and is perceived is, to this day, extremely one-sided. In the USA, New Orleans is considered to be "deeply compromised and [...] strongly energized", to stand for sex and drugs, corruption and crime.⁴⁹ The city has long been considered a site of transgression and the

---

45 Sublette, The World that made New Orleans, 2008, 274.
46 According to Sublette, the banjo, fiddle and semitonal music were brought by Senegalese and related early Islamic ethnic groups, while the drum and brass-dominated style of music that dominates the entire Caribbean is linked to Congo. Sublette, The World that made New Orleans, 2008, 275-281.
47 Sublette, The World that made New Orleans, 2008, 285.
48 Cf. Gotham, Authentic New Orleans, 2007.
49 Ostendorf, The Mysteries of New Orleans, 2016, 107–108.

ideal destination for a white middle class keen to experience its supposed permissiveness on a timeout from the constraints of a puritan Protestant existence. The backdrop for these small acts of escapism is provided by an antebellum architecture that appears to Northerners as colourful and colonial, spiced with the omnipresent colonial French (Creole and Cajun) food and infused with an exotic 'blackness', whose lines of perspective converge on sex and jazz (fig. 5).[50]

Figure 5: Heritage as a brand. Tourists in the Vieux Carré (Photo: G. Vinken 2020)

This image of the city, familiar from 1001 tourist brochures, was in no small part the co-creation of the heritage conservation establishment. Indeed, New Orleans' preservationist movement long remained trapped in antebellum nostalgia, something that J. Mark Souther describes in his inspirational text on the disneyfication of the Vieux Carré. He illustrates this with reference to the ballroom of the Catholic school for African-American girls, Saint Mary's Academy, which was threatened in the 1960s by plans to build a new hotel. Martha Robinson (1888–1981), a women's rights activist and one of the leaders of the heritage movement in the 1960s (and herself the descendant of slave owners) identified the ballroom (falsely) as one of the places where the legendary "Quadroon Balls" had been held, arguing that it was vital to preserve it as "the scene of some of the most glorious social events in the history of the city".[51] The gulf between this conception and that of the African-American community appears to be insurmountable. For the latter, such dances, at which meetings were arranged between plantation owners and Afro-Creole women, understandably evoke painful memories of slavery and oppression. This was no doubt exacerbated by the fact that racist

---

50   Long, Rethinking the Notion of Sexually Liberal New Orleans, 2019; Gotham, Authentic New Orleans, 2007, 138–139.
51   Souther, The Disneyfication of New Orleans, 2007, 807.

segregation made dialogue on heritage issues that transcend the boundaries of class and ethnicity appear illusory for so long. From the very start, the Vieux Carré/French Quarter was formed as a place of "white memory", in an image that provided few points of identification for the Black population.[52]

In terms of architectural history, New Orleans' showcase district, the Vieux Carré, is a remarkable example of colonial building, the syncretic amalgamation of Creole-French, Spanish-Caribbean right up to Victorian forms.[53] Its reception as a historical "tout ensemble" of antebellum Southern magnificence is of course also the result of heritage-making processes. The rescue – better termed the invention – of the Vieux Carré in the early 20th century is already typical of the preferences of a particular – white, English-speaking – educated class, a specific mixture of elite charitable clubs and the artists and bohemians that increasingly settled in the rundown city centre.[54] It was on their initiative that the first efforts to purchase and renovate threatened houses were carried out. The granting to the Vieux Carré of the status as one of the first Historic Districts in the United States enabled extensive restoration, but (following a change the law in 1940) also a harmonizing historicization. The latter included, for instance, the demolition of many buildings that were considered "out of character". The result was to establish the Vieux Carré as a marker of authenticity – with major consequences.[55] While the modernist mainstream did penetrate the French quarter in the 1960s, with the erection of car parks and supermarkets, and even plans for high-rises,[56] at the same time, the first comprehensive inventory of the district was carried out by Tulane University (1961–66).[57] Since around 1980, the city has increased its efforts to create an icon with as few 'blemishes' as possible, erecting numerous 'pastiches' of historical-themed architecture, including many luxury hotels built in the antebellum style with the 'typical' iron balconies.[58]

The construction of a standardized cultural image by means of tourism can be seen on many levels in New Orleans.[59] In order to establish an antebellum quarter for consumption by tourists, every 'problematic' aspect of heritage was systematically banished.[60] In the 1960s, therefore, the plan was to drive out the strip clubs, red-light bars and alcoholic excesses from the French Quarter, which was, in the words of Mayor Victor H. Schiro (1961–70) to become clean and safe, a "Coney Island-like *fun spot*" for the

---

52 Souther, The Disneyfication of New Orleans, 2007, 807.
53 Full details in: Campanella, An Architectural Geography, 2016, 139–154.
54 Cf. Gotham, Authentic New Orleans, 2007, 85–89; Ellis, Madame Vieux Carré, 2010, 22–35.
55 Gotham, Authentic New Orleans, 2007, 85–94.
56 Souther, America's Most Interesting City, 2003, 119–120.
57 The first comprehensive study on the historic Vieux Carré is based largely on these findings: The Vieux Carré Historic District Demonstration Study, 8 vols (ed. Bureau of Governmental Research (BGR) for the City of New Orleans, New Orleans 1968. Cf. Campanella, Geographies of New Orleans, 2006.
58 Souther, The Disneyfication of New Orleans, 2007, 807; Campanella, An Architectural Geography, 2016, 137.
59 For details, Gotham, Authentic New Orleans, 2007, especially 69–94.
60 Details in: Souther, America's Most Interesting City, 2003. Cf. Ellis, Madame Vieux Carré, 2010, 133–152.

middle class.⁶¹ The fact that a 2/3 scale copy of the French quarter was opened by Disney in its Southern California theme park in 1966 may have played a role, influencing visitors to expect the original to be a homogenized district for tourist consumption in which the social conflicts that continue to exist – and thus the real heritage of the city – had to be hidden.⁶² In many regards, it can also be shown that tourism has contributed structurally to racial discrimination and segregation.⁶³ Nor did this change significantly with the end of formal segregation. The 1984 Louisiana World Exhibition is considered rather to have intensified the standardization of the New Orleans tourist experience under the label "most authentic city", with the city's uniqueness becoming its stylized selling point: striking a careful balance between the image of a vibrant and permissive metropolis and the needs of middle-class tourists for security, cleanliness and predictability.⁶⁴ In this way, according to Souther, the white elite "rescued" the French Quarter, marginalizing and destroying other districts of the city in the process. While it proved possible to generate civic engagement to prevent the construction of Robert Moses's Riverside Expressway, which would have cut the French Quarter off from the river, Interstate 10 was nonetheless driven through the neighbouring Tremé district, the "cradle of the black community". Neighbourhoods such as Tremé, which also encompasses the legendary red-light district of Storyville, were considered slums and threatened by programmes of urban renewal and redevelopment in which impoverished residents were frequently resettled elsewhere.⁶⁵

Between Marginalization and Exploitation

Similar processes of reducing, excluding and homogenizing heritage can also be observed with respect to intangible heritage, for instance, in the reception of Black music. With the boom in tourism in the 1970s, New Orleans was branded the "Birthplace of Jazz".⁶⁶ The rise of this style of music and improvisation, which was developed by African Americans and has a complex relationship to forms of African music and dance,⁶⁷ is indeed inseparably connected with New Orleans, and particularly with the above-mentioned red-light district of Storyville, where a professional Black music scene was able to develop. After the suppression of Storyville in 1917, many of the leading figures on the jazz scene were forced to leave the city. At the same time, jukeboxes meant there was less call for live acts; by World War II, jazz had largely disappeared from New

---

61   Souther, America's Most Interesting City, 2003, 120. Italics in the original.
62   Souther, America's Most Interesting City, 2003, 2003, 120–126; Gotham, Authentic New Orleans, 2007, 143–145.
63   Gotham, Authentic New Orleans, 2007, 80–85.
64   Gotham, Authentic New Orleans, 2007, 133-141; Souther, America's Most Interesting City, 2003, 128–129.
65   On Storyville, cf. Long, The Great Southern Babylon, 2004.
66   On New Orleans' mythic role in jazz, cf. Knauer, Do You Know What It Means, 2017.
67   This thesis is at the heart of Ned Sublette's stimulating book, Sublette, The World that made New Orleans, 2008, especially 271–292.

Orleans.[68] The tightening of segregation laws (Jim Crow) also made it harder for professional Black artists to make a living. The jazz renaissance only came about with the opening of Preservation Hall in 1948 as a new centre for live acts. Yet this, too, was soon to be captured by the mainstream and the tourism industry in the form of Dixieland.[69] In 1956, Louis Armstrong was forced to leave his home city when a new law prohibited Black and white musicians from appearing on stage together.[70]

The status of New Orleans' African-American heritage remains highly ambivalent to this day. Precisely because it does not fit within the narrative of mainstream society, it is an important selling point and is exploited for (white) tourism and portrayed accordingly – cut to size, reduced. At the same time, the Black community has itself been increasingly developing a self-awareness about this heritage, one in which questions of self-determination, rehabilitation and justice play a central role. In the USA, as in all post-colonial societies that are divided by racism and social conflict, discussions about cultural heritage always raise issues of power. If it is hard to reach consensus on the interpretation of a history characterized by violence and exploitation, and if an unresolved legacy such as that of slavery and its consequences divides different heritage communities – often irreconcilably – then institutionalized heritage designation processes inevitably reflect more or less exactly the distribution of power in society.

Figure 6: A parade for the white middle class. Louis Armstrong Park (Photo: G. Vinken 2020)

---

68 Souther, America's Most Interesting City, 2003, 118, 122–123.
69 Souther, America's Most Interesting City, 2003, 124–125.
70 Souther, America's Most Interesting City, 2003, 125.

To this day, the Black history of the city remains dramatically underrepresented. It is a tragedy how even its central sites have been neglected. Louis Armstrong's birthplace was torn down in the 1960s to make way for a police headquarters – and Armstrong Park was laid out, fake and sterile, created for white middle-class tourists (fig. 6).[71]

Figure 7: A lively colourful scene? Monument at Congo Square (Photo: G. Vinken 2020)

Congo Square, often mentioned as an early hot-spot of Black heritage practices, is now a little frequented annex of the park. A single memorial portraying Black dancers and musicians is all that remains to remind of the historical significance of this place, and it can do little to counter the establishment view that exoticizes a romantic image of the "lively, colourful scene" (fig. 7). Few of the relevant sites of memory, such as the New Orleans Jazz National Historical Park, the Eagle Saloon Building or Congo Square are included in the National Register of Historic Places.[72] Even the Louisiana African-American Heritage Trail, which was established in 2008 by the State of Louisiana and includes some 26 sites, appears rather randomly thrown together and includes only five locations within the city itself: besides Congo Square, the others are all schools and churches.[73] The most visited museum in the city is the World War II Museum, an ostentatious structure that opened in 2000 to tell a heroic story and that has been designated by Congress as America's National World War II Museum. The second largest museum in New Orleans is the New Orleans Museum of Art (NOMA), which was founded as early as 1911, and which, thanks to generous donations, contains a marvellous collection of art situated in an extensive sculpture park. The Louisiana Jazz Museum, which after many

---

71   Souther, America's Most Interesting City, 2003, 134–135.; Souther, The Disneyfication of New Orleans, 2007, 808.
72   Cf. Website Wikipedia, National Register of Historic Places.
73   Website LouisianaTravel, African American Heritage Trail.

changes of management is now again run by the State of Louisiana, appears currently to be in a state of transition and gives a distinctly underfunded impression. Nonetheless, the History of Music section contains several rooms that deal with the origins of jazz and the significance of African-American percussion styles and Second-Line drumming for the development of jazz (and popular music generally). New Orleans' main Mardi Gras exhibition (in The Presbytère Museum) is still trapped in a very 'white' perspective: the ambivalence of the Zulu parades, for instance, which provided one way for 'black faced' African-American groups to participate in (white) Mardi Gras events during segregation in the early part of the 20th century, is barely mentioned,[74] while the conspicuous fact that Mardi Gras was long used to drive racial segregation is entirely ignored.[75] The establishment in Tremé in 1996 of the New Orleans African American Museum (NOAAM), which is funded by the city, is certainly a major step forwards. Built on the land of a former plantation, it has found a new use for one of the best preserved 'Master's Houses' in the city.[76] In a neighbourhood where a particularly high number of 'Free People of Colour' used to live and which is still an important centre of Black life, the location is well chosen. It is near other important historic African-American sites, such as Saint Augustine church, one of the oldest African-American Catholic parishes in the nation.[77] Close by, the Backstreet Cultural Museum keeps alive the Black tradition of Mardi Gras and Mardi Gras parades with displays including many of the hand sewn costumes of the 'Indians' (fig. 8).[78]

This is a small, poorly funded, private institution that relies on a great deal of personal initiative and engagement.[79] It provides yet further evidence that a cultural sector that relies heavily on private sponsorship disadvantages contested and marginal cultural heritage in particular. Especially in a city like New Orleans, it makes sense to rethink the idea of heritage in terms of concepts such as a "sense of place".[80] In the medium term, greater financial support from local government, the State of Louisiana or the federal government would no doubt help to initiate a broad societal discourse and to ensure that appropriate attention is paid to precarious bodies of heritage.

---

74   Souther, America's Most Interesting City, 2003, 117–118. On the Zulu Parades cf. Smith, Things You'd Imagine, 2019.
75   Gotham, Authentic New Orleans, 2007, 89–94.
76   Website NOAAM, History.
77   Sublette, The World that made New Orleans, 2008, 304–311.
78   Website Backstreet Cultural Museum. The future of the museum appears uncertain since death of the founder and curator, Sylvester Francis, on 1 September 2020 (Website Obits, Sylvester Francis).
79   It is with great regret and sadness that I heard that the museum's founder and curator, Sylvester "Hawk" Francis, who guided us through the museum so expertly, died on 1 September 2020.
80   Morgen/Morgen/Barrett, Finding a Place, 2006.

Figure 8: Hidden treasures. Sylvester Francis (1946 – 2020) in the Backstreet Museum he founded (Photo: G. Vinken 2020)

Decolonization: Toppling Statues

The vigour of conflicts over the interpretation of history and heritage is apparent in the Black Lives Matter movement, which places itself squarely in the lineage of postcolonial struggles. Conflicts over Confederate monuments that have been simmering for some time aim at the revision of national and local heritage politics and target the racist context that is explicitly or implicitly invoked by the incriminating statues. In New Orleans, following a 2017 decision by the city's government, four of the controversial monuments were removed,[81] and a further three were torn down by activists this year (June/July 2020).[82] The website of the most important activist group *Take Em Down NOLA* (slogan: "Take down all symbols of white supremacy") details many more for future consideration. The profound entanglement of heritage politics and ongoing discrimination is also evident with respect to monuments that appear at first glance to be innocuous. The Ninth Ward Victory Arch (238 Burgundy Street), erected in 1919 and dedicated to local veterans of World War I is considered perhaps the first permanent monument of this kind in the USA. It only reveals its racist message on closer examination (fig. 9).

---

81   Le Blanc, Cost of removing Confederate monuments, 2017; New Orleans baut Bürgerkriegsdenkmale ab, Süddeutsche Zeitung, 18 December 2015.
82   Website TakeEmDownNOLA, The Symbols.

Figure 9: Segregation to the grave and beyond. Ninth Ward Victory Arch (Photo: G. Vinken 2020)

The fallen soldiers are shown as still segregated in death, with 'whites' on the front and 'blacks' on the back of the arch, which was placed in its current position in 1951. Articles published to commemorate its unveiling over 100 years ago appeared not to consider this fact worth mentioning[83] – and it is still passed over in silence in contemporary online registers of war memorials.[84]

The most emotional conflict concerns another monument, the equestrian statue of Andrew Jackson on the city's main square, right in front of the Vieux Carré (fig. 10).[85] Entirely different narratives of American history collide here, as do diverse conceptions of heritage values and heritage politics. Andrew Jackson, the 7th President of the United States (1829–37), is considered by many in New Orleans to be a revolutionary hero for commanding US forces at the decisive Battle of New Orleans, the last great battle between the British and the Americans, which cemented the former colony's independence. Like most of the early American presidents, Jackson was a slave owner.[86] What is more controversial, however, is the role he played in the displacement, disenfranchisement and extermination of Native Americans when he broke with the policy of his predecessors, who had sought to conclude treaties at least with the 'Five Civilized Tribes'.[87] The extent of the controversy around the figure of Jackson is revealed vividly

---

83 For example in *The Time-Picayune*, New Orleans, Louisiana, 9 November 1919 (sect. 3, p. 3, col. 3), cf. Website RootsWeb, To Commemorate Services of Men who served in War.
84 Website RootsWeb, The Victory Arch in Macarty Square; or Website Louisiana Digital Library, The Ninths Ward's Tribute.
85 Website TakeEmDownNOLA, Past Actions.
86 Cheathem, Andrew Jackson, 2011.
87 Zinn, A People's History, 1980, 149–170.

by the decision taken under President Obama to replace Jackson's portrait on the $20 bill with that of Harriet Tubman, an African-American icon of the abolitionist movement. President Trump not only reversed this decision, but also gave a prominent place to a portrait of the infamous Indian hater and racist Jackson in the Oval Office.

Figure 10: Scourge of the Indians, Slave Owner. Andrew Jackson's Monument at Jackson Square (Photo: G. Vinken 2020)

The Andrew Jackson monument also reveals a clash of perspectives at the level of theory. The main square in New Orleans, previously known as the Place d'Armes, was modelled on the Place des Vosges in Paris. The square was rebuilt on a grand style in 1850, and the equestrian statue of Jackson was positioned at its centre in 1856.[88] In the view of the conservationists, the square, now renamed in Jackson's honour, is certainly,

---

88 As one of four copies of the original by Clark Mills in Washington D.C., cf. Website Wikipedia, Equestrian statue of Andrew Jackson.

given its historical and architectural significance, a heritage ensemble of the highest rank. It was declared a National Historic Landmark in 1960 (the highest category of monument, of which there are today only 58 in the whole State of Louisiana)[89] "for its central role in the city's history, and as the site where in 1803 Louisiana was made United States territory pursuant to the Louisiana Purchase".[90] In 2012 the American Planning Association designated Jackson Square "one of the Great Public Spaces in the United States".[91] This reveals the long shadow of a conservation movement with its roots in the 19th century that was committed to – supposedly universal – cultural and historical values, and which has trouble to this day in effectively taking account of central questions of social order such as race, class, gender (and religion). The unreflected perpetuation of a standard of nationalist, 'white' historiography in which the heroic monument is a central symbol is today being challenged on several fronts.[92] Before Jackson Square was redesigned as a grand urban plaza, it was the place of execution of criminals and 'rebellious' slaves. In a broader sense, the heroic equestrian statue keeps the ambivalences and racist brutality of the wars of independence out of sight. In the famous battle, African-Americans and Native American warriors fought on both sides. Many 'privateers', who were deeply implicated in the illegal import of enslaved persons, also fought on the side of the US troops. An indirect consequence of the American victory at New Orleans was to enable the conquest of nominally Spanish Florida, which had until then been a refuge for Native Americans and escaped slaves. From 1815, their villages were systematically destroyed, and survivors were often returned to slavery.[93] For many, the emancipation that the wars of independence stand for in the American national narrative led to increased unfreedom, degradation and death. It therefore appears indispensable that these aspects of history are not just taken up in academic discourses; there also needs to consideration of how to present them in public space, implementing appropriate measures. This is because, ultimately, it is not a matter of statues of generals and presidents but of memory and remembrance, of the identity of a nation and the right to self-determination of its constituent parts. It is about pride and tradition, but also trauma and injustice, which culminate in a legitimate demand for a new heritage politics.

---

89 Website National Park Service, List of National Historic Landmarks.
90 "Jackson Square" on Website National Park Service, List of National Historic Landmarks, and Website National Park Service, NHL nomination for Jackson Square.
91 Website American Planning Association, Jackson Square.
92 On this dispute, include the legal aspects, cf. Mock, The Fight to Remove, 2016.
93 Sublette, The World that made New Orleans, 2008, 269.

References

Adams, The Spectacular State, 2010
Adams, Laura L., *The Spectacular State. Culture and National Identity in Uzbekistan*, Durham 2010.

Adell, Between Imagined Communities, 2015
Adell, Nicolas, et al., eds, *Between Imagined Communities and Communities of Practice. Participation, Territory and the Making of Heritage* (Göttingen Studies in Cultural Property - Göttinger Studien zu Cultural Property 8), Göttingen 2015, https://www.univerlag.uni-goettingen.de/handle/3/isbn-978-3-86395-205-1 [accessed 5 March 2021].

Adenauer, Die Pflege der profanen Denkmäler, 1955/1956
Adenauer, Hanna, Die Pflege der profanen Denkmäler in Köln, in: Rheinischer Verein für Denkmalpflege und Heimatschutz, ed., *Die Heimat lebt – Vermächtnis und Verpflichtung*, Neuß 1955/1956, pp. 159–173.

Affaticati, Widerstand gegen Salvini, 2019
Affaticati, Andrea, Widerstand gegen Salvini: "So etwas gibt es in einer Diktatur", in: *n-tv Politik*, 5 January 2019, https://www.n-tv.de/politik/Interview-mit-dem-Buergermeister-von-Palermo-Leoluca-Orlando-So-etwas-gibt-es-in-einer-Diktatur-article20797872.html [accessed 28 June 2019].

Almeida, Capoeira, 1986
Almeida, Ubirajara G., *Capoeira. A Brazilian Art Form*, 2nd ed., Berkeley 1986.

Amico, Lexicon topographicum siculum, 1855/1856 (1757–1760)
Amico, Vito M., *Lexicon topographicum siculum in quo Siciliae urbes, opida, cum vetusta tum extantia montes, flumina, portus adiacentes insula ac singular loca describuntur, illustrantur*, 3 vols, Catania 1757–1760, quoted after reprint *Dizionario topografico della Sicilia di Vito Amico*, 2 vols, Palermo 1855/1856, https://books.google.it/books?id=uzABAAAAQAAJ&dq=inauthor%3A%22Vito%20Maria%20Amico%22&hl=it&pg=PA3#v=onepage&q&f=false **[vol. 1: 1855; accessed 5 August 2020]**, https://books.google.it/books?id=WVTEXPJC

ZewC&printsec=frontcover&hl=de&source=gbs_ge_summary_r&cad=0#v=onepage&q&f=false [vol. 2: 1856; accessed 5 August 2020].

Anziferow, Die Seele Petersburgs, 2003 (1922)
Anziferow, Nikolai P., *Die Seele Petersburgs* (original title: Duša Peterburga, 1922), translated by R. von Maydell, Munich/Vienna 2003.

Arbeitsbeschaffungsbehörden, Altstadt heute und morgen, 1945
Arbeitsbeschaffungsbehörden des Kantons Basel, ed., *Altstadt heute und morgen. Ausstellung der projektierten Massnahmen für die Sanierung der Altstadt von Basel, Kleines Klingental, 23. September – 31.Oktober 1945* (exhibition catalogue), Basel 1945.

Ashworth/Graham/Tunbridge, Pluralising Pasts, 2007
Ashworth, Gregory J./Graham, Brian/Tunbridge, John E., *Pluralising Pasts. Heritage, Identity and Place in Multicultural Societies*, London/Ann Arbor 2007.

Augello, La Sicilia, 1983
Augello, Teresa, *La Sicilia nelle incisioni del Bova*, Palermo 1983.

Augé, Non-Places, 1995 (1992)
Augé, Marc, *Non-Places. Introduction to an Anthropology of Supermodernity* (original title: Introduction à une anthropologie de la surmodernité, 1992), translated by J. Howe, London 1995.

Ballon/Jackson, Robert Moses and the Modern City, 2007
Ballon, Hilary/Jackson, Kenneth T., eds, *Robert Moses and the Modern City. The transformation of New York*, London/New York 2007.

Bartels, Briefe über Kalabrien und Sizilien, 1787-1792
Bartels, Johann H., *Briefe über Kalabrien und Sizilien*, 3 vols, Göttingen 1787–1792, https://reader.digitale-sammlungen.de/de/fs1/object/display/bsb10466282_00007.html [vol. 1: 1787; accessed 5 August 2020], https://reader.digitale-sammlungen.de/de/fs1/object/display/bsb10466283_00007.html [vol. 2: 1789; accessed 5 August 2020], https://books.google.it/books?id=okdCAAAAcAAJ&printsec=frontcover&hl=de&source=gbs_ge_summary_r&cad=0#v=onepage&q&f=false [vol. 3: 1792; accessed 5 August 2020].

Bartetzko, Aus Alt mach Neu, 2007
Bartetzko, Dieter, Aus Alt mach Neu. Plädoyer für eine wahrhaft alte Altstadt, in: Deutscher Werkbund Hessen, ed., *Standpunkte. Zur Bebauung des Frankfurter Römerbergs*, Frankfurt a.M. 2007, pp. 52–55.

Bauausstellung Berlin GmbH, Internationale Bauausstellung Berlin, 1987
Bauausstellung Berlin GmbH, ed., *Internationale Bauausstellung Berlin 1987, Projektübersicht* (exhibition catalogue), Berlin 1987.

Baudelaire, The Flowers of Evil, 1998 (1857)
Baudelaire, Charles P., *The Flowers of Evil* (original title: Les Fleurs du mal, 1857), translated by James McGowan, New York 1998 (1993).

Baudrillard, Simulacra and Simulation, 1994 (1981)
Baudrillard, Jean, *Simulacra and Simulation* (original title: Simulacres et Simulation, 1981), translated by S. F. Glaser, Ann Arbor 1994.

Baudrillard, The System of Objects, 1996 (1968)
Baudrillard, Jean, *The System of Objects* (original title: Le Système des objets, 1968), translated by J. Benedict, London/New York 1996.

Baumeister/Bonomo/Schott, Cities Contested, 2017
Baumeister, Martin/Bonomo, Bruno/Schott, Dieter, eds, *Cities Contested. Urban Politics, Heritage, and Social Movements in Italy and West Germany in the 1970s*, Frankfurt a.M./New York 2017.

Bell, Redefining National Identity, 1999
Bell, James, Redefining National Identity in Uzbekistan: Symbolic Tensions in Tashkent's Official Public Landscape, in: *Ecumene*, 6/2 1999, pp. 183–213.

Benevolo, History of Modern Architecture, 1971 (1960)
Benevolo, Leonardo, *History of Modern Architecture* (original title: Storia dell'architettura moderna, 1960), vol 1: The tradition of modern architecture, Cambridge 1971.

Bergmann, Die Loreley, 2006
Bergmann, Rudij, Die Loreley steht in der Bronx. Heine-Denkmäler gibt es in Amerika, in Afrika – und seit 1981 sogar in seiner Heimatstadt Düsseldorf, in: *Jüdische Allgemeine*, 16 February 2006, http://www.juedische-allgemeine.de/article/view/id/5259 [accessed 8 February 2016].

Berking/Löw, Die Eigenlogik der Städte, 2008
Berking, Helmuth/Löw, Martina, eds, *Die Eigenlogik der Städte. Neue Wege für die Stadtforschung* (Interdisziplinäre Stadtforschung 1), Frankfurt a.M./New York 2008.

Berking, Skizzen zur Erforschung der Stadt und der Städte, 2008
Berking, Helmuth, "Städte lassen sich an ihrem Gang erkennen wie Menschen" – Skizzen zur Erforschung der Stadt und der Städte, in: Berking, Helmuth/Löw, Martina, eds, *Die Eigenlogik der Städte. Neue Wege für die Stadtforschung* (Interdisziplinäre Stadtforschung 1), Frankfurt a.M./New York 2008, pp. 15–32.

Bernauer, Die Voyage pittoresque des Abbé de Saint-Non, 2004
Bernauer, Markus, Die Voyage pittoresque des Abbé de Saint-Non und die 'Entdeckung' Süditaliens, in: Müller-Tamm, Jutta/Ortlieb, Cornelia, eds, *Begrenzte Natur und Unendlichkeit der Idee*, Freiburg i.Brsg. 2004, pp. 61–79.

Bernauer, Von Griechen, 2006
Bernauer, Markus, Von Griechen, Wilden und Naturkatastrophen. Johann Heinrich Bartels revidiert die Tradition der Süditalien-Literatur, in: Bijon, Béatrice/Clavaron, Yves/Dieterle, Bernard, eds, *Le Mezzogiorno des écrivains européens*, Saint-Étienne 2006, pp. 17–29.

Berndt, Chorin, 1997
Berndt, Iris, Chorin. Die Zeichnungen Karl Friedrich Schinkels vom Kloster, in: *Brandenburgische Denkmalpflege*, 6/1 1997, pp. 31–42.

Beseler/Gutschow, Kriegsschicksale Deutscher Architektur, 1988
Beseler, Hartwig/Gutschow, Niels, *Kriegsschicksale Deutscher Architektur. Verluste, Schäden, Wiederaufbau. Eine Dokumentation für das Gebiet der Bundesrepublik Deutschland*, vol. 1, Neumünster 1988.

Besier, Zur Geschichte des Wiederaufbaus, 1993
Besier, Gerhard, Zur Geschichte des Wiederaufbaus des Berliner Doms, in: *Jahrbuch für Berlin – Brandenburgische Kirchengeschichte*, 59/1993, pp. 188–207.

Beyme, Der Wiederaufbau, 1987
Beyme, Klaus von, *Der Wiederaufbau: Architektur und Städtebaupolitik in den beiden deutschen Staaten*, Munich 1987.

Bialik, We Still Don't Know, 2015
Bialik, Carl, We Still Don't Know How Many People Died Because Of Katrina, in: *FiveThirtyEight*, 26 August 2015, https://fivethirtyeight.com/features/we-still-dont-know-how-many-people-died-because-of-katrina/ [accessed 13 January 2021].

Bideau, Fallstudie Frankfurt, 2011
Bideau, André, Fallstudie Frankfurt – Altstadt Reloaded, in: *Arch+ 204*, 2011, pp. 100–103.

Blokker, (Re)konstruierte Identität, 2011
Blokker, Johanna M., (Re)konstruierte Identität. Zum Wiederaufbau der romanischen Kirchen Kölns nach dem Zweiten Weltkrieg, in: *Geschichte in Köln*, 58/2011, pp. 211–228.

Blokker, (Re)Construction Identity, 2012
Blokker, Johanna M., *(Re)Constructing Identity. World War II and the Reconstruction of Cologne's Destroyed Romanesque Churches, 1945–1985*, Ann Arbor, 2012.

Bockrath, Städtischer Habitus, 2008
Bockrath, Franz, Städtischer Habitus – Habitus der Stadt, in: Berking, Helmuth/Löw, Martina, eds, *Die Eigenlogik der Städte. Neue Wege für die Stadtforschung* (Interdisziplinäre Stadtforschung 1), Frankfurt a.M./New York 2008, pp. 55–82.

Bode, Unser Lebensraum braucht Schutz, 1975
Bode, Peter M., Unser Lebensraum braucht Schutz, Denkmalschutz – eine Kampagne der 'Aktion Gemeinsinn' zum Denkmalschutzjahr, in: Deutsches Nationalkomitee für das Europäische Denkmalschutzjahr, ed., *Eine Zukunft für unsere Vergangenheit: Denkmalschutz in der Bundesrepublik. Europäisches Denkmalschutzjahr 1975*, Munich 1975, pp. 38–56.

Boerlin, Denkmalschutzrecht Basel Stadt, 1974
Boerlin, Paul H., et al., Denkmalschutzrecht im Kanton Basel-Stadt, in: *Freiwillige Basler Denkmalpflege 1972–73*, 1974, pp. 23–67.

Boesiger/Girsberger, Le Corbusier, 1999
Boesiger, Willy/Girsberger, Hans, *Le Corbusier 1910–65*, Basel/Boston/Berlin 1999.

Borutta, Antikatholizismus, 2010
Borutta, Manuel, *Antikatholizismus. Deutschland und Italien im Zeitalter der europäischen Kulturkämpfe* (Bürgertum Neue Folge. Studien zur Zivilgesellschaft 7), Göttingen 2010.

Brandes, Wiederaufbau und Gemeindeverwaltung, 1944
Brandes, Robert, *Wiederaufbau und Gemeindeverwaltung luftkriegsbetroffener Städte*, 8 August 1944 (Historical Archive of the City of Cologne/Historisches Archiv der Stadt Köln, Acc 229/426).

Brandi, Teoria del Restauro, 1963
Brandi, Cesare, *Teoria del Restauro*, Rome 1963.

Breuer, Ensemble, 1989
Breuer, Tilmann, Ensemble – ein Begriff gegenwärtiger Denkmalkunde und die Hypotheken seines Ursprungs, in: Mörsch, Georg/Strobel, Richard, eds, *Die Denkmalpflege als Plage und Frage. Festgabe für August Gebeßler*, Munich/Berlin 1989, pp. 38–52.

Breunlin/Lewis, The House of Dance and Feathers, 2010
Breunlin, Rachel/Lewis, Ronald W., *The House of Dance and Feathers: A Museum by Ronald W. Lewis*, New Orleans 2010.

Brock, Inszenierung und Vergegenwärtigung, 1997
Brock, Bazon, *Inszenierung und Vergegenwärtigung. Ästhetische und religiöse Erfahrung heute* (lecture at symposium), Munich 1997, https://bazonbrock.de/werke/detail/?id=134&sectid=1450#sect [accessed 2 August 2019].

Bronfen, Tiefer als der Tag, 2008
Bronfen, Elisabeth, *Tiefer als der Tag gedacht. Eine Kulturgeschichte der Nacht*, Munich 2008.

Brönnimann, Basler Bauten, 1973
Brönnimann, Rolf, *Basler Bauten 1860–1910*, Basel/Stuttgart 1973.

Brydone, A Tour through Sicily and Malta, 1774 (1773)
Brydone, Patrick, A Tour through Sicily and Malta. In a series of letters to William Beckford, Esq. of Somerly in Suffolk, 2 vols, Dublin 1773, quoted after reprint 1774, https://books.google.it/books?id=yhHnPpTBcDMC&printsec=frontcover&hl=de&source=gbs_ge_summary_r&cad=0#v=onepage&q&f=false [accessed 5 August 2020].

Burckhardt, Altstadtsanierung, 1945/1946
Burckardt, Lukas, *Altstadtsanierung* (State Archives of the City of Basel/Staatsarchiv Basel. StA BS BD-Reg A 801/1 – 1945–46).

Burgard, Frankfurt und der Retrotaumel, 2007
Burgard, Roland, Frankfurt und der Retrotaumel, in: Deutscher Werkbund Hessen, ed., *Standpunkte. Zur Bebauung des Frankfurter Römerbergs*, Frankfurt a.M. 2007, pp. 8–12.

Burggraf, Der öffentliche Raum, 2012
Burggraf, Götz, Der öffentliche Raum in Taschkent, in: Meuser, Philipp, ed., *Architekturführer Usbekistan*, Berlin 2012, pp. 121–155.

Buttlar, Denkmalpflege statt Attrappenkult, 2011
Buttlar, Adrian von, et al., eds, *Denkmalpflege statt Attrappenkult. Gegen die Rekonstruktion von Baudenkmälern – eine Anthologie* (Bauwelt Fundamente 146), Basel/Berlin/Boston 2011.

Campanella, Geographies of New Orleans, 2006
Campanella, Richard, *Geographies of New Orleans. Urban Fabrics Before the Storm*, Baton Rouge 2006.

Campanella, An Architectural Geography, 2016
Campanella, Richard, An Architectural Geography of New Orleans' French Quarter, in: Antenhofer, Christina, et al., eds, *Cities as Multiple Landscapes. Investigating the Sister Cities Innsbruck and New Orleans* (Interdisciplinary urban research 21), Frankfurt a.M./New York 2016, pp. 133–165.

Campanella, Cityscapes of New Orleans, 2017
Campanella, Richard, *Cityscapes of New Orleans*, Baton Rouge 2017.

Cannarella, Profili di siracusani illustri, 1958
Cannarella, Giuseppe, *Profili di siracusani illustri*, Syracuse 1958.

Cannarozzo, Riqualificazione, 1996
Cannarozzo, Teresa, Riqualificazione e ricupero del centro storico, in: Cannarozzo, Teresa, ed., *Palermo tra memoria e futuro. Riqualificazione e recupero del centro storico*, Palermo 1996, pp. 23–71.

Carlyle, Most Expensive ZIP Codes, 2014
Carlyle, Erin, America's Most Expensive ZIP Codes 2014: Behind The Numbers, in: *Forbes*, 8 October 2014, https://www.forbes.com/sites/erincarlyle/2014/10/08/americas-most-expensive-zip-codes-2014-behind-the-numbers/#5be2f4b36e7e [accessed 13 May 2020].

Cesare, Raffigurazioni, 2008
Cesare, Barbera A., *Raffigurazioni, vedute e piante di Palermo dal sec. XV al sec. XIX*, Caltanissetta 2008.

Cheathem, Andrew Jackson, 2011
Cheathem, Mark R., Andrew Jackson, Slavery, and Historians, in: *History Compass*, 9/4 2011, pp. 326–338.

Choay, The Invention, 2001
Choay, Françoise, *The Invention of the Historic Monument* (original title: L'Allégorie du Patrimoine, 1992), translated by L. M. O'Connell, New York 2001.

Chukhovich, Building the Living East, 2012
Chukhovich, Boris, Building the Living East, in: Architekturzentrum Wien, ed., *Soviet Modernism 1955–1991: Unknown History* (exhibition catalogue), Vienna 2012, pp. 214–231.

Cometa, Il romanzo dell'architettura, 1999
Cometa, Michele, *Il romanzo dell'architettura. La Sicilia e il grand tour nell'età di Goethe*, Rome 1999.

Comment, Basler Arbeiter-Zeitung, 24 September 1945
Comment of the newspaper *Basler Arbeiter-Zeitung* of 24 September 1945, no. 223, on the occasion of the opening of the exhibition "Altstadt heute und morgen" 1945 (State Archives of the City of Basel/Staatsarchiv Basel. StA BS BD-Reg A 801/1 – 1945–56).

Craanen, Altstadtsanierung, 1998
Craanen, Michael, *Altstadtsanierung am "Pelô". Die sozialen und politischen "Grenzen" städtischer Integration in Salvador/Brasilien* (diss., University of Bielefeld 1998), http://www.baufachinformation.de/literatur.jsp?dis=2004069006478 [accessed 25 May 2020].

Dadabaev, Community life, 2013
Dadabaev, Timur, Community life, memory and a changing nature of mahalla identity in Uzbekistan, in: *Journal of Eurasian Studies*, 4/2013, pp. 181–196, https://www.sciencedirect.com/science/article/pii/S1879366513000183 [accessed 25 June 2020].

Dehio, Geschichte der deutschen Kunst, 1930
Dehio, Georg, *Geschichte der deutschen Kunst. Des Textes zweiter Band: Das späte Mittelalter von Rudolf von Habsburg bis zu Maximilian I. Die Kunst der Gotik*, Berlin/Leipzig 1930.

Dehio, Denkmalschutz und Denkmalpflege, 1988 (1905)
Dehio, Georg, Denkmalschutz und Denkmalpflege im neunzehnten Jahrhundert (1905), reprinted in: Wohlleben, Marion/Mörsch, Georg, eds, *Georg Dehio und Alois Riegl – Konservieren, nicht restaurieren. Streitschriften zur Denkmalpflege um 1900* (Bauwelt Fundamente 80), Braunschweig 1988, pp. 88–103.

Derrida, Specters of Marx, 1994 (1993)
Derrida, Jacques, *Specters of Marx. The State of the Debt, the Work of Mourning and the New International* (original title: Spectres de Marx : l'état de la dette, le travail du deuil et la nouvelle Internationale, 1993), translated by P. Kamuf, New York/London 1994.

Di Benedetto, La città che cambia, 2000
Di Benedetto, Guiseppe, ed., *La città che cambia. Restauro e riuso nel Centro Storico di Palermo*, 2 vols, Palermo 2000.

Di Benedetto, Restoration and Re-Use, 2000
Di Benedetto, Guiseppe, ed., *Restoration and Re-Use of Palermo's Old City* (publication with English, French, Spanish and German parallel text), Palermo 2000.

Dieckmann, Tausend und eine Macht, 2014
Dieckmann, Christoph, Tausend und eine Macht, in: *Die Zeit*, no. 20, 8 May 2014, https://www.zeit.de/2014/20/usbekistan-zentralasien/komplettansicht [accessed 25 June 2020].

Diefendorf, In the Wake of War, 1993
Diefendorf, Jeffry M., *In the Wake of War: The Reconstruction of German Cities after World War II*, New York/Oxford 1993.

Di Giovine, The heritage-scape, 2008
Di Giovine, Michael A., *The heritage-scape. UNESCO, World Heritage, and Tourism*, Lanham 2008.

Dolff-Bonekämper, Gegenwartswerte, 2010
Dolff-Bonekämper, Gabi, Gegenwartswerte. Für eine Erneuerung von Alois Riegls Denkmalwerttheorie, in: Meier, Hans-Rudolf/Scheurmann, Ingrid, eds, *DENKmalWERTE. Beiträge zur Theorie und Aktualität der Denkmalpflege. Georg Mörsch zum 70. Geburtstag*, Berlin/Munich 2010, pp. 27–40.

D'Orville, Jacobi Philippi D'Orville Sicula, 1764

D'Orville, Jacobi P., *Jacobi Philippi D'Orville Sicula, quibus Siciliae veteris rudera, additis antiquitatum tabulis, illustrantur. Edidit, et commentarium ad numismata sicula, 20. tabulis aeneis incisa ... orationem in auctoris obitum, et praefationem adjecit Petrus Burmannus secundus*, Amsterdam 1764.

Droste/Fischer, Düsseldorfer Tausendfüßler, 2015

Droste, Manfred/Fischer, Hagen, eds, *Der Düsseldorfer Tausendfüßler. Die Auseinandersetzung um den Erhalt der Hochstraße und um die Kö-Bogen-Planung*, Düsseldorf 2015.

Düwel/Gutschow, Städtebau in Deutschland, 2001

Düwel, Jörn/Gutschow, Niels, *Städtebau in Deutschland im 20. Jahrhundert: Ideen – Projekte – Akteure* (Teubner Studienbücher der Geographie), Stuttgart/Leipzig/Wiesbaden 2001.

Ehrenfeucht, Restructuring Public Landscapes, 2016

Ehrenfeucht, Renia, Restructuring Public Landscapes in Gentrifying New Orleans, in: Antenhofer, Christina, et al., eds, *Cities as Multiple Landscapes. Investigating the Sister Cities Innsbruck and New Orleans* (Interdisciplinary urban research 21), Frankfurt a.M./New York 2016, pp. 371–390.

Eidloth/Ongyerth/Walgern, Grundlagen und Grundsätze, 2013

Eidloth, Volkmar/Ongyerth, Gerhard/Walgern, Heinrich, Grundlagen und Grundsätze der städtebaulichen Denkmalpflege, in: Eidloth, Volkmar, et al., eds, *Handbuch Städtebauliche Denkmalpflege*, Petersberg 2013, pp. 13–52.

Ein Heine-Schrubber in New York, FOCUS Magazin, 16 September 1996

Ein Heine-Schrubber in New York, in: *FOCUS Magazin*, no. 38, 16 September 1996, https://www.focus.de/politik/deutschland/profile-ein-heine-schrubber-in-new-york_aid_1 59860.html [accessed 30 July 2020].

Elfenbein, Die Lorelei in der Bronx, 1999

Elfenbein, Stefan, Die Lorelei in der Bronx, in: *Berliner Zeitung*, 13 July 1999, http://www.berliner-zeitung.de/archiv/an-heinrich-heine-erinnert-in-new-york-jetzt-wieder-ein-brunnen--der-vor-hundert-jahren-an-dieser-stelle-schon-einmal-feierlich-eingeweiht-wurde-die-lorelei-in-der-bronx,10810590,9666214.html [accessed 1 February 2016].

Ellen/McCabe/Stern, Fifty Years, 2016

Ellen, Ingrid G./McCabe, Brian J./Stern, Eric E., *Fifty Years of Historic Preservation in New York City*, 2016, http://furmancenter.org/files/NYUFurmanCenter_50YearsHistoricPres NYC_7MAR2016.pdf [accessed 13 May 2020].

Ellis, Madame Vieux Carré, 2010

Ellis, Scott S., *Madame Vieux Carré. The French Quarter in the Twentieth Century*, Jackson 2010.

Enss/Vinken, Produkt Altstadt, 2016
Enss, Carmen M./Vinken, Gerhard, eds, *Produkt Altstadt. Historische Stadtzentren in Städtebau und Denkmalpflege*, Bielefeld 2016.

Eriksen, From Antiquities to Heritage, 2014
Eriksen, Anne, *From Antiquities to Heritage. Transformations of Cultural Memory* (Time and the World: Interdisciplinary Studies in Cultural Transformations 1), New York/Oxford 2014.

Escherich, Denkmal Ost-Moderne, 2012/2016
Escherich, Mark, ed., *Denkmal Ost-Moderne*, 2 vols (Stadtentwicklung und Denkmalpflege 16/18), Berlin 2012/2016.

Ette/Müller, New Orleans and the Global South, 2017
Ette, Ottmar/Müller, Gesine, eds, *New Orleans and the Global South. Caribbean, Creolization, Carnival* (Potsdamer inter- und transkulturelle Texte 17), Hildesheim/Zurich/New York 2017.

Euler-Rolle, Stimmungswert, 2005
Euler-Rolle, Bernd, Der "Stimmungswert" im spätmodernen Denkmalkultus – Alois Riegl und die Folgen, in: *Österreichische Zeitschrift für Kunst und Denkmalpflege*, 59/1 2005, pp. 27–34.

Euler-Rolle, Am Anfang war das Auge, 2010
Euler-Rolle, Bernd, "Am Anfang war das Auge" – Zur Rehabilitierung des Schauwerts in der Denkmalpflege, in: Meier, Hans-Rudolf/Scheurmann, Ingrid, eds, *DENKmalWERTE. Beiträge zur Theorie und Aktualität der Denkmalpflege. Georg Mörsch zum 70. Geburtstag*, Berlin/Munich 2010, pp. 89–100.

Faber/Garms-Cornides, Entdeckung Siziliens, 2005
Faber, Eva/Garms-Cornides, Elisabeth, Die 'Entdeckung' Siziliens zwischen Kreuzfahrt, Kommerzreise und Grand Tour. Zinzendorf versus Riedesel, in: Babel, Rainer/Paravicini, Werner, eds, *Grand Tour. Adeliges Reisen und europäische Kultur vom 14. bis 16. Jahrhundert* (Beihefte der Francia 60), Ostfildern 2005, pp. 341–354.

Falser/Lipp, A Future for Our Past, 2015
Falser, Michael/Lipp, Wilfried, eds, *Eine Zukunft für unsere Vergangenheit. Zum 40. Jubiläum des Europäischen Denkmalschutzjahres (1975–2015). A Future for Our Past. The 40th anniversary of European Architectural Heritage Year (1975–2015). Un Avenir pour Notre Passé. 40e Anniversaire de l'Année Européenne du Patrimoine Architectural (1975–2015)*, Berlin 2015, https://www.icomos.de/icomos/pdf/41610-133750-1-sm.pdf [accessed 7 November 2020].

Falter, Grünflächen der Stadt Basel, 1984
Falter, Felix, *Die Grünflächen der Stadt Basel. Humangeographische Studie zur Dynamik urbaner Grünräume im 19. und 20. Jahrhundert unter besonderer Berücksichtigung der Kleingärten* (Basler Beiträge zur Geographie 28), Basel 1984.

Farrell, Enlightenment traveller, 1991
Farrell, Joseph, Patrick Brydone. Enlightenment traveller, in: *Viaggiatori stranieri in Sicilia, Viaggio nel sud*, 1/1991, pp. 291–305.

Fausset, Stately Old Charleston, 2015
Fausset, Richard, In Stately Old Charleston, the New Buildings on the Block Are Struggling to Fit In, in: *The New York Times*, 24 January 2015, pp. A1, A3.

Fehl/Rodríguez-Lores, Die Stadt wird in der Landschaft sein, 1997
Fehl, Gerhard/Rodríguez-Lores, Juan, *Die Stadt wird in der Landschaft sein und die Landschaft in der Stadt. Bandstadt und Bandstruktur als Leitbilder des modernen Städtebaus* (Stadt, Planung, Geschichte 19), Basel/Berlin/Boston 1997.

Fehl, Stadt-Umbau, 1995
Fehl, Gerhard, "Stadt-Umbau" muß sein! In: Fehl, Gerhard/Rodríguez-Lores, Juan, eds, *Stadt-Umbau. Die planmäßige Erneuerung europäischer Großstädte zwischen Wiener Kongreß und Weimarer Republik* (Stadt, Planung, Geschichte 17), Basel/Berlin/Boston 1995, pp. 11–40.

Fisher, Tyranny of Nostalgia, 2015
Fisher, Anthony L., The Tyranny of Nostalgia Is Making Cities Unaffordable, in: *The Observer*, 24 February 2015, http://observer.com/2015/02/the-tyranny-of-nostalgia-is-making-cities-unaffordable/ [accessed 15 October 2016].

Fitch, Curatorial Management, 1982
Fitch, James M., *Historic Preservation: Curatorial Management of the Built World*, New York 1982.

Flierl, Identitätssuche, 2008
Flierl, Bruno, Identitätssuche am Ort Mitte Spreeinsel in Berlin, in: Sigel, Paul/Klein, Bruno, eds, *Konstruktion urbaner Identität. Zitat und Rekonstruktion in Architektur und Städtebau der Gegenwart*, Berlin 2006, online publication 2008, http://schlossdebatte.de/?p=247 [accessed 27 February 2020].

Flint, Wrestling with Moses, 2011
Flint, Anthony, *Wrestling with Moses: How Jane Jacobs Took on New York's Master Builder and Transformed the American City*, New York 2011.

Foucault, Different Spaces, 1998 (1967)
Foucault, Michel, Different Spaces (1967), in: Faubion, James D., ed., *Michel Foucault. Aesthetics, Method, and Epistemology* (Essential Works of Foucault 2), translated by R. Hurley, New York 1998, pp. 175–185.

Frank, Wall memorials and heritage, 2016 (2009)
Frank, Sybille, *Wall memorials and heritage. The Heritage Industry of Berlin's Checkpoint Charlie* (original title: Der Mauer um die Wette gedenken. Die Formation einer Heritage-Industrie am Berliner Checkpoint Charlie, 2009; diss., Technical University of Darmstadt 2008), translated by J. Spengler, New York/London 2016.

Franz/Vinken, Monuments – Values – Assessment, 2014
Franz, Birgit/Vinken, Gerhard, eds, *Denkmale – Werte – Bewertung. Denkmalpflege im Spannungsfeld von Fachinstitution und bürgerschaftlichem Engagement / Monuments – Values – Assessment. Heritage conservation between professional institutions and popular engagement* (Arbeitshefte des AK Theorie und Lehre der Denkmalpflege e.V. 23), Holzminden 2014.

Friedrichswerdersche Kirche, Frankfurter Allgemeine Zeitung, 6 February 2016
Friedrichswerdersche Kirche. "Zerstörung mit Ansage", in: *Frankfurter Allgemeine Zeitung*, 6 February 2016, http://www.faz.net/aktuell/feuilleton/sorge-um-schinkels-friedrichswerdersche-kirche-in-berlin-14055532.html [accessed 25 February 2020].

Frohn, Vom Trümmerhaufen zur Millionenstadt, 1982
Frohn, Robert, *Köln 1945 bis 1981: Vom Trümmerhaufen zur Millionenstadt. Erlebte Geschichte*, Cologne 1982.

Füllenbach, Die Kölner Altstadtgesundung, 1937
Füllenbach, Wilhelm, Die Kölner Altstadtgesundung, in: *Bauamt und Gemeindebau*, 19/24 1937, pp. 247–249.

Gaetani, Della Sicilia Nobile, 1754–1775
Gaetani, Francesco M. E., *Della Sicilia Nobile, Opera di Francesco Maria Emanuele e Gaetani Marchese di Villabianca*, 5 vols, 1754–1775, https://archive.org/details/bub_gb_FMcOAAAAQAAJ/page/n3/mode/2up [accessed 8 August 2020].

Gamper, Die Natur ist republikanisch, 1998
Gamper, Michael, *"Die Natur ist republikanisch". Zu den ästhetischen, anthropologischen und politischen Konzepten der deutschen Gartenliteratur im 18. Jahrhundert*, Würzburg 1998.

Gebeßler, Altstadt und Denkmalpflege, 1975
Gebeßler, August, Altstadt und Denkmalpflege. Die Beispielstädte in der Bundesrepublik Deutschland, in: Deutsches Nationalkomitee für das Europäische Denkmalschutzjahr, ed., *Eine Zukunft für unsere Vergangenheit: Denkmalschutz in der Bundesrepublik. Europäisches Denkmalschutzjahr 1975*, Munich 1975, pp. 57–70.

Glatz, Rekonstruktion der Rekonstruktion, 2008
Glatz, Joachim, Die Rekonstruktion der Rekonstruktion. Fallbeispiel Mainzer Markt, in: *Die Denkmalpflege*, 66/1 2008, pp. 28–33.

Glendinning, Postwar Mass Housing, 2008
Glendinning, Miles, ed., *Postwar Mass Housing* (Docomomo Journal 39), Paris 2008.

Glendinning, The Conservation Movement, 2013
Glendinning, Miles, *The Conservation Movement: A History of Architectural Preservation. Antiquity to Modernity*, Abingdon/New York 2013.

Goethe, Faust, 1963 (1808/1832)
Goethe, Johann W. von, *Faust. Tragedy in Two Parts* (original title: Faust I, 1808, Faust II, 1832), translated by B. Taylor, London 1963.

Goethe, Italian Journey, 1982 (1816/17)
Goethe, Johann W. von, *Italian Journey* (original title: Italienische Reise, 1816/17), translated by W. H. Auden and E. Mayer, San Francisco 1982.

Goethe, Italienische Reise, 1988 (1816/17)
Goethe, Johann W. von, *Italienische Reise* (1816/17), Munich 1988.

Goldstone/Dalrymple, A Guide to New York City, 1976
Goldstone, Harmon H./Dalrymple, Martha, *History Preserved. A Guide to New York City Landmarks and Historic Districts*, New York 1976.

Göpfert/Michels, Kein Egotrip eines Architekten, 2012
Göpfert, Claus-Jürgen/Michels, Claudia, Kein Egotrip eines Architekten, in: *Frankfurter Rundschau*, 23 January 2012, https://www.fr.de/frankfurt/spd-org26325/kein-egotrip-eines-architekten-11334024.html [accessed 3 June 2020].

Görl, Was vom Wahnsinn blieb, 2016
Görl, Wolfgang, Was vom Wahnsinn blieb, in: *Süddeutsche Zeitung*, no. 252, 31 October / 1 November 2016, p. 36.

Gotham, Authentic New Orleans, 2007
Gotham, Kevin F., *Authentic New Orleans. Tourism, Culture, and Race in the Big Easy*, New York/London 2007.

Goziev, Mahalla, 2015
Goziev, Saidbek, *Mahalla: traditional institution in Tajikistan and civil society in the West*, Frankfurt a.M. et al. 2015.

Gratz, Authentic Urbanism, 2003
Gratz, Roberta B., Authentic urbanism and the Jane Jacobs legacy, in: Neal, Peter, ed., *Urban Villages and the Making of Communities*, London 2003, pp. 16–29.

Gratz, Battle for Gotham, 2010
Gratz, Roberta B., *The Battle for Gotham. New York in the Shadow of Robert Moses and Jane Jacobs*, New York 2010.

Gray, Sturm und Drang, 2007
Gray, Christopher, Sturm und Drang. Over a Memorial to Heinrich Heine, in: *The New York Times*, 27 May 2007, https://www.nytimes.com/2007/05/27/realestate/27scap.html [accessed 28 July 2020].

Greenspan, Creating Colonial Williamsburg, 2009
Greenspan, Anders, *Creating Colonial Williamsburg. The Restoration of Virginia's Eighteenth-Century Capital*, 2nd ed., Chapel Hill 2009.

Gurlitt, Handbuch des Städtebaues, 1920
Gurlitt, Cornelius, *Handbuch des Städtebaus*, Berlin 1920.

Guzzetta, Per la gloria, 2001
Guzzetta, Giusepp, Per la gloria di Cantania: Ignazio Paternò Castello Principe di Biscari, in: *Agorà*, VI/a/2/2001, pp. 12–19, https://www.academia.edu/3165768/G_Guzzetta_Per_la_gloria_di_Catania_Ignazio_Patern%C3%B2_Castello_Principe_di_Biscari [accessed 8 August 2020].

Hagspiel, Reflexe, 1994
Hagspiel, Wolfram, Reflexe – Die nationalsozialistische Stadtplanung von Köln und ihre Widerspiegelung im heutigen Stadtbild, in: Matzerath, Horst, ed., *Versteckte Vergangenheit: Über den Umgang mit der NS-Zeit in Köln*, Cologne 1994, pp. 73–84.

Haindl, Denkmalpflege in der sozialen Verantwortung, 1976
Haindl, Erika, Denkmalpflege in der sozialen Verantwortung – ein Wandel beginnt sich abzuzeichnen. Ein Versuch einer Literatur-Analyse, in: Greverus, Ina-Maria, ed., *Denkmalräume – Lebensräume* (Hessische Blätter für Volks- und Kulturforschung 2/3), Giessen 1976, pp. 263–277.

Halbwachs, Das kollektive Gedächtnis, 1950
Halbwachs, Maurice, *Das kollektive Gedächtnis* (original title: *La mémoire collective*, 1950), Frankfurt a.M. 1950.

Hall, Africans in Colonial Louisiana, 1992
Hall, Gwendolyn M., *Africans in Colonial Louisiana. The Development of Afro-Creole Culture in the Eighteenth Century*, Baton Rouge 1992.

Hansen, Die Frankfurter Altstadtdebatte, 2008
Hansen, Astrid, Die Frankfurter Altstadtdebatte. Zur Rekonstruktion eines gefühlten Denkmals, in: *Die Denkmalpflege*, 66/1 2008, pp. 5–17.

Hansen, Gedanken über Grundlage, 1945
Hansen, Hans, *Gedanken über Grundlage und Ziel des Wiederaufbaus unserer Stadt*, 25 August 1945 (Historical Archive of the City of Cologne/Historisches Archiv der Stadt Köln, Acc 229/426 [Denkschriften]).

Harrison, Understanding the Politics, 2009
Harrison, Rodney, ed., *Understanding the Politics of Heritage*, Manchester 2009.

Harrison, Critical Approaches, 2013
Harrison, Rodney, *Heritage: Critical Approaches*, London/New York 2013.

Hartung, Hauptstadtinszenierung, 2012
Hartung, Klaus, Hauptstadtinszenierung und asiatisches Leben, in: Meuser, Philipp, ed., *Architekturführer Usbekistan*, Berlin 2012, pp. 75–94.

Harvey, Heritage Pasts, 2001
Harvey, David, Heritage Pasts and Heritage Presents: temporality, meaning and the scope of heritage studies, in: *International Journal of Heritage Studies*, 7/4 2001, pp. 319–338.

Hassenpflug, Citytainment, 2000
Hassenpflug, Dieter, Citytainment oder die Zukunft des öffentlichen Raums, in: Matejovski, Dirk, ed., *Metropolen. Laboratorien der Moderne*, Frankfurt a.M./New York 2000, pp. 308–320.

Hassenpflug, Der urbane Code, 2008
Hassenpflug, Dieter, *Der urbane Code Chinas*, Basel 2008.

Hawkins, City of New Orleans, 2011
Hawkins, Dominique M., ed., *City of New Orleans Historic District Landmarks Commission Design Guidelines*, Philadelphia 2011.

Heckscher, Anadyomene in the Mediaeval Tradition, 1956
Heckscher, William S., The "Anadyomene" in the Mediaeval Tradition: (Pelagia - Cleopatra - Aphrodite) a Prelude to Botticelli's "Birth of Venus", in: *Nederlands kunsthistorisch jaarboek (NKJ)/Netherlands Yearbook for History of Art*, 7/1956, pp. 1–38.

Hegel, Lectures on the History of Philosophy, 1892 (1817)
Hegel, Georg W. F., *Lectures on the History of Philosophy* (1817), translated by E.S. Haldane, vol. 1, London 1892.

Heidegger, Building Dwelling Thinking, 1971 (1951)
Heidegger, Martin, Building Dwelling Thinking (1951), in: *Poetry, Language, Thought*, translated by A. Hofstadter, New York/London 1971, pp. 141–160.

Heine, A Winter's Tale, 1986 (1844)
Heine, Heinrich, *Deutschland. A Winter's Tale – A not so sentimental journey* (original title: Deutschland. Ein Wintermärchen, 1844), translated by T. J. Reed, London 1986.

Heine, Song of the Lorelei, 2015 (1824)
Heine, Heinrich, *Lied von der Loreley / Song of the Lorelei* (1824), translated by T. Thomson (incomplete, 2015), https://lyricstranslate.com/de/loreley-lorelei.html#songtranslation [accessed 5 January 2021].

Heine Monument Unveiled, The New York Times, 9 July 1899
Heine Monument Unveiled, in: *The New York Times*, 9 July 1899, https://www.nytimes.com/1899/07/09/archives/heine-monument-unveiled-accepted-on-behalf-of-the-city-by-president.html [accessed 30 August 2020].

Heinen, Moderne für die Römerstadt, 1992
Heinen, Werner, Köln: Moderne für die Römerstadt, in: Beyme, Klaus von, ed., *Neue Städte aus Ruinen: Deutscher Städtebau der Nachkriegszeit*, Munich 1992, pp. 217–230.

Hein/Pletl, Streit um die Kuppel, 2008
Hein, Rainer L./Pletl, Steffen, Streit um die Kuppel des Berliner Doms, in: *Die Welt Online*, 1 January 2008, https://www.welt.de/regionales/berlin/article1508448/Streit-um-die-Kuppel-des-Berliner-Doms.html [accessed 27 February 2020].

Helmig/Matt, Inventar Basler Stadtbefestigung, 1989
Helmig, Guido/Matt, Christoph P., Inventar der Basler Stadtbefestigung: Planvorlage und Katalog. 1. Die landseitige Äussere Grossbasler Stadtmauer, in: *Jahresberichte der Archäologischen Bodenforschung des Kantons Basel-Stadt*, 1989, pp. 69–153.

Hennet, Berliner Schlossplatzdebatte, 2005
Hennet, Anna-Inés, *Die Berliner Schlossplatzdebatte im Spiegel der Presse*, Berlin 2005.

Hirdt/Tappert, Goethe und Italien, 2001
Hirdt, Willi/Tappert, Birgit, eds, *Goethe und Italien* (Studium universale 22), Bonn 2001.

Holleran, Changeful Times, 1998
Holleran, Michael, *Boston's "Changeful Times". Origins of Preservation and Planning in America*, Baltimore/London 1998.

Houël, Voyage Pittoresque, 1782–1787
Houël, Jean-Pierre-Laurent, *Voyage pittoresque des isles de Sicile, de Malte et de Lipari, ou l'on traite des antiquites qui s'y trouvent encore; des principaux phenomenes que la nature y offre; du costume des habitants, & de quelques usages*, 4 vols, Paris 1782–1787, https://arachne.uni-k oeln.de/arachne/index.php?view[layout]=buchseite_item&search[constraints][buchsei te][searchSeriennummer]=369107&view[section]=uebersicht&view[page]=0 [accessed 15 August 2020].

Huppertz, Schönere Zukunft, 1945/1947
Huppertz, Andreas, *Schönere Zukunft der kölnischen Kunstdenkmäler durch schöpferische Denkmalpflege*, 1945/1947 (Historical Archive of the City of Cologne/Historisches Archiv der Stadt Köln, Acc 2 [Oberbürgermeister], no. 1313 [Denkschriften 1945–1947]).

Huse, Le Corbusier in Selbstzeugnissen, 1976
Huse, Norbert, *Le Corbusier in Selbstzeugnissen und Bilddokumenten*, Reinbek 1976.

Huse, Deutsche Texte, 1984
Huse, Norbert, ed., *Denkmalpflege. Deutsche Texte aus drei Jahrhunderten*, Munich 1984.

Huxtable, The unreal America, 1997
Huxtable, Ada L., *The unreal America. Architecture and Illusion*, New York 1997.

Jakobi, Die Heimatschutzbewegung, 2005
Jakobi, Verena, Die Heimatschutzbewegung und die Entdeckung des Ensembles, in: Scheurmann, Ingrid, ed., *ZeitSchichten. Erkennen und Erhalten – Denkmalpflege in Deutschland. 100 Jahre Handbuch der Deutschen Kunstdenkmäler von Georg Dehio* (exhibition catalogue), Munich/Berlin 2005, pp. 120–123.

Jacobs, Death and Life, 1961
Jacobs, Jane, *The Death and Life of Great American Cities*, New York 1961.

Jatho, Urbanität, 1946
Jatho, Carl O., *Urbanität: Über die Wiederkehr einer Stadt*, Düsseldorf 1946.

Jatho, Eine Stadt von Welt, 1958
Jatho, Carl O., *Eine Stadt von Welt: Köln vordem und hernach*, Cologne 1958.

Jordan, Transforming Paris, 1995
Jordan, David, *Transforming Paris. The Life and Labors of Baron Haussman*, New York 1995.

Juneja, Mobile Heritage, 2015
Juneja, Monica, Wanderndes Erbe und die Kräfte der Erinnerung / Mobile Heritage and the Powers of Memory, in: Vinken, Gerhard, ed., *Das Erbe der Anderen. Denkmalpflegerisches Handeln im Zeichen der Globalisierung / The Heritage of the Other*.

Conservation Considerations in an Age of Globalization (Forschungen des Instituts für Archäologische Wissenschaften, Denkmalwissenschaften und Kunstgeschichte 2), Bamberg 2015, pp. 9–18.

Kainrath, Die Bandstadt, 1997
Kainrath, Wilhelm, *Die Bandstadt. Städtebauliche Vision oder reales Modell der Stadtentwicklung?* Vienna 1997.

Kalinovsky, Laboratory of Socialist Development, 2018
Kalinovsky, Artemy M., *Laboratory of Socialist Development: Cold War Politics and Decolonization in Soviet Tajikistan*, Ithaca/London 2018.

Karg, Die Landschaftsgestaltung, 1987
Karg, Detlef, Die Landschaftsgestaltung Peter Joseph Lennés am Kloster Chorin, in: Institut für Denkmalpflege: Arbeitsstelle Berlin, ed., *Denkmale in Berlin und der Mark Brandenburg. Ihre Erhaltung und Pflege in der Hauptstadt der DDR und in den Bezirken Frankfurt/Oder und Potsdam*, Weimar 1987, pp. 287–302.

Karn, Geschichte im Rückwärtsgang, 2008
Karn, Georg P., Geschichte im Rückwärtsgang. Eine Fotodokumentation der Nordzeile des Mainzer Marktplatzes von 1978 bis 2008, in: *Die Denkmalpflege*, 66/1 2008, pp. 34–38.

Katz, The New Urbanism, 1994
Katz, Peter, *The New Urbanism – Toward an Architecture of Community*, New York 1994.

Kemp, Kunstwerk und Betrachter, 1988
Kemp, Wolfgang, Kunstwerk und Betrachter: Der rezeptionsästhetische Ansatz, in: Belting, Hans, ed., *Kunstgeschichte: Eine Einführung*, 3rd ed., Berlin 1988, pp. 240–257.

Kemp, Gesammelte Aufsätze, 1995
Kemp, Wolfgang, ed., *Alois Riegl. Gesammelte Aufsätze. Mit einem Nachwort zur Neuausgabe von Wolfgang Kemp*, Berlin 1995.

Kier, Der Wiederaufbau von Köln, 1976
Kier, Hiltrud, Der Wiederaufbau von Köln, 1945–75: Eine Bilanz aus kunsthistorischer Sicht, in: Arbeitskreis Städtebauliche Denkmalpflege der Fritz Thyssen Stiftung, ed., *Die Kunst, unsere Städte zu erhalten*, Stuttgart 1976, pp. 231–248.

Kirshenblatt-Gimblett, From Ethnology to Heritage, 2004
Kirshenblatt-Gimblett, Barbara, *From Ethnology to Heritage. The Role of the Museum* (conference SIEF keynote), Marseilles 2004, https://www.researchgate.net/publication/238714489_From_Ethnology_to_Heritage_The_Role_of_the_Museum [accessed 5 February 2021].

Knauer, Do You Know What It Means, 2017
Knauer, Wolfram, "Do You Know What It Means...". The Myth Called New Orleans in Jazz History, its Origin and its Influence on Jazz up to the Present Day, in: Ette, Ottmar/Müller, Gesine, eds, *New Orleans and the Global South. Caribbean, Creolization, Carnival* (Potsdamer inter- und transkulturelle Texte 17), Hildesheim/Zurich/New York 2017, pp. 201–218.

Knoblauch/Löw, The Re-Figuration, 2020
Knoblauch, Hubert/Löw, Martina, The Re-Figuration of Spaces and Refigured Modernity – Concept and Diagnosis, in: *Historical Social Research*, 45/2 2020, pp. 263–292, https://doi.org/10.12759/hsr.45.2020.2.263-292 [accessed 23 November 2020].

Koolhaas/Mau, S, M, L, XL, 1995
Koolhaas, Rem/Mau, Bruce, *S, M, L, XL*, New York 1995.

Kosmarski, Grandeur and Decay, 2011
Kosmarski, Artyom, Grandeur and Decay of the "Soviet Byzantium": Spaces, Peoples and Memories of Tashkent, Uzbekistan, in: Darieva, Tsypylma/Kaschuba, Wolfgang/Krebs, Melanie, eds, *Urban Spaces after Socialism. Ethnographies of Public Places in Eurasian Cities*, Frankfurt a.M. 2011, pp. 33–56.

Kreis, Abbruch und Aufbruch, 1995
Kreis, Georg, Abbruch und Aufbruch: die 'Entfestigung' der Stadt Basel, in: Gyr, Ueli, ed., *Soll und Haben. Alltag und Lebensformen bürgerlicher Kultur*, Zurich 1995, pp. 213–228.

Lagae, From Patrimoine partagé, 2008
Lagae, Johan, "From Patrimoine partagé" to "whose heritage"? Critical reflections on colonial built heritage in the city of Lubumbashi, Democratic Republic of the Congo, in: *Afrika Fokus*, 21/1 2008, pp. 11–30.

Lamers, Il viaggio nel Sud, 1995
Lamers, Petra, *Il viaggio nel Sud dell'Abbé de Saint-Non: il „Voyage pittoresque à Naples et en Sicile"; la genesi, i disegni preparatori, le incisioni*, Napoli 1995.

Landphair, The Forgotten People of New Orleans, 2007
Landphair, Juliette, "The Forgotten People of New Orleans": Community, Vulnerability, and the Lower Ninth Ward, in: *Journal of American History*, 94/2007, pp. 837–845, http://archive.oah.org/special-issues/katrina/Landphair57a.html?link_id=dev_9thflood [accessed 25 October 2020].

Langen, Anschauungsformen, 1965
Langen, August, *Anschauungsformen in der deutschen Dichtung des 18. Jahrhunderts. Rahmenschau und Rationalismus*, Darmstadt 1965.

Langford, Our Heritage – Your Playground, 1983
Langford, Rosalind F., Our Heritage – Your Playground, in: *Australian Archaeology*, 16/1 1983, pp. 1–6.

Leanti, Lo stato presente della Sicilia, 1761
Leanti, Arcangiolo, *Lo stato presente della Sicilia, o sia breve, e distinta discrizione di essa, del sig. abate Arcangiolo Leanti da Palermo, e dè patrizi di Noto. Accresciuta colle notizie delle isole aggiacenti, e con vari rami, aggiunte, e correzioni*, 2 vols, Palermo 1761, https://babel.hathitrust.org/cgi/pt?id=gri.ark:/13960/t0qr9nm64;view=1up;seq=7 [accessed 5 August 2020].

Le Blanc, Cost of removing Confederate monuments, 2017
Le Blanc, Paul, Cost of removing Confederate monuments in New Orleans: $2.1 million, in: *CNN*, 12 June 2017, https://edition.cnn.com/2017/06/12/us/new-orleans-confederate-monument-removal-price-trnd/index.html [accessed 13 January 2021].

Le Corbusier, Urbanisme, 1925
Le Corbusier, *Urbanisme* (Collection de L'Esprit Nouveau), 6th ed., Paris 1925.

Le Corbusier, La ville radieuse, 1935
Le Corbusier, *La ville radieuse. Éléments d'une doctrine d'urbanisme pour l'équipement de la civilisation machinist*, Boulogne 1935.

Le Corbusier, Les trois établissements humains, 1946
Le Corbusier, *Les trois établissements humains*, Paris 1946.

Le Corbusier, Concerning Town Planning, 1948 (1946)
Le Corbusier, *Concerning Town Planning* (original title: Propos D'Urbanisme, 1946), translated by C. Entwistle, New Haven 1948.

Le Corbusier, L'Urbanisme des Trois Établissements humains, 1959
Le Corbusier, *L'Urbanisme des Trois Établissements humains*, Paris 1959.

Le Corbusier, Œuvre complète, 1960
Le Corbusier, *Œuvre complète*, vol. 1: 1910–1929, 7th ed., Zurich 1960.

Le Corbusier, The Athens Charter, 1973 (1933)
Le Corbusier, *The Athens Charter* (original title: La Charte d'Athènes, 1933), translated by A. Eadley, New York 1973.

Le Corbusier, The City of To-morrow, 1987 (1925)
Le Corbusier, *The City of To-morrow and its planning* (original title: Urbanisme, 1925), translated by F. Etchells, New York, 1987.

Le Corbusier, Precisions on the present State, 2015 (1930)
Le Corbusier, *Precisions on the present State of Architecture and City planning* (original title: Précision sur un état présent de l'architecture et de l'urbanisme, 1930), translated by E. Schreiber-Aujame, Zurich 2015.

Lettere Del Signor Abate Domenico Sestini, 1779-1784
Lettere Del Signor Abate Domenico Sestini Scritte Dalla Sicilia E Dalla Turchia A Diversi Suoi Amici In Toscana, 7 vols, Livorno 1779–1784.

Lindahl, Legends of Hurricane Katrina, 2012
Lindahl, Carl, Legends of Hurricane Katrina: The Right to Be Wrong, Survivor-to-Survivor Storytelling, and Healing, in: *The Journal of American Folklore*, 125/496 2012, pp. 139–176.

Lipp, Heritage Trends, 2014
Lipp, Wilfried, Heritage Trends – Im Wandel gesellschaftlicher Werte und Befindlichkeiten / Heritage Trends in the Context of Changing Social Values and Sensibilities, in: Franz, Birgit/Vinken, Gerhard, eds, *Denkmale – Werte – Bewertung. Denkmalpflege im Spannungsfeld von Fachinstitution und bürgerschaftlichem Engagement / Monuments – Values – Assessment. Heritage conservation between professional institutions and popular engagement* (Arbeitshefte des AK Theorie und Lehre der Denkmalpflege e.V. 23), Holzminden 2014, pp. 72–83.

Lipp/Petzet, Vom modernen zum postmodernen Denkmalkultus, 1994
Lipp, Wilfried/Petzet, Michael, eds, *Vom modernen zum postmodernen Denkmalkultus? Denkmalpflege am Ende des 20. Jahrhunderts* (Arbeitshefte des Bayerischen Landesamtes für Denkmalpflege 69), Munich 1994.

Long, The Great Southern Babylon, 2004
Long, Alecia P., *The Great Southern Babylon: Sex, Race, and Respectability in New Orleans, 1865–1920*, Baton Rouge 2004.

Long, Rethinking the Notion of Sexually Liberal New Orleans, 2019
Long, Alecia P., "Queers, Fairies, and Ne'er-Do-Wells": Rethinking the Notion of Sexually Liberal New Orleans, in: Adams, Thomas J./Sakakeeny, Matt, eds, *Remaking New Orleans. Beyond Exceptionalism and Authenticity*, Durham/London 2019, pp. 179–198.

Lorenz, Stadtgeschichte Taschkents, 2012
Lorenz, Torsten, Die Stadtgeschichte Taschkents, in: Meuser, Philipp, ed., *Architekturführer Usbekistan*, Berlin 2012, pp. 95–119.

Loth, Essens Wiederaufbau, 2005
Loth, Winfried, 1945 – Essens Wiederaufbau nach dem Krieg, in: Borsdorf, Ulrich/Grütter, Heinrich T./Scheytt, Oliver, eds, *Gründerjahre, 1150 Jahre Stift und Stadt Essen*, Essen 2005, pp. 113–135.

Löw, Schwarzsein als kollektive Praxis, 2010
Löw, Martina, Schwarzsein als kollektive Praxis in Salvador de Bahia. Stadtsoziologie aus kulturtheoretischer Perspektive, in: Frank, Sybille/Schwenk, Jochen, eds, *Turn over. Cultural Turns in der Soziologie*, Frankfurt a.M. 2010, pp. 137–157.

Löw, The City as Experiential Space, 2013
Löw, Martina, The City as Experiential Space: The Production of Shared Meaning, in: *International Journal of Urban and Regional Research*, 37/3 2013, pp. 894–908.

Löw, Space Oddity, 2015
Löw, Martina, Space Oddity. Raumtheorie nach dem Spatial Turn, in: *sozialraum.de*, 1/2015, https://www.sozialraum.de/space-oddity-raumtheorie-nach-dem-spatial-turn.php [accessed 12 December 2020].

Löw, The Sociology of Space, 2016 (2001)
Löw, Martina, *The Sociology of Space. Materiality, Social Structures, and Action* (original title: Raumsoziologie, 2001), translated by D. Goodwin, New York 2016.

Löw, In welchen Räumen, 2020
Löw, Martina, In welchen Räumen leben wir? Eine raumsoziologisch und kommunikativ konstruktivistische Bestimmung der Raumfiguren Territorialraum, Bahnenraum, Netzwerkraum und Ort, in: Eickhoff, Jonas/Reichertz, Jo, eds, *Grenzen der Kommunikation – Kommunikation an den Grenzen*, Weilerswist 2020, pp. 149–164.

Löw, Re/figure(e)/ation, 2020
Löw, Martina, Re/figure(e)/ation. An Essay on Space and Boundaries in Late Modernity, in: Kittelmann, Udo/Knapstein, Gabriele, eds, *Katharina Grosse. It wasn't us* (exhibition catalogue), Berlin 2020, pp. 170–177.

Löw/Vinken, Die Dichte der Entleerung, 2007
Löw, Martina/Vinken, Gerhard, Die Dichte der Entleerung, in: *Zwanzig 10. Neue Bilder. Andere Worte. Journal der Ruhrstadt*, 1/2007, pp. 74–82.

Löw/Vinken, Anpassung und Wirkung, 2012
Löw, Martina/Vinken, Gerhard, Anpassung und Wirkung. Anforderungen an Stadtentwicklung und Baukultur heute, in: *Hoff*, Gregor M., ed., *Verantworten. Salzburger Hochschulwochen 2012*, Innsbruck 2012, pp. 181–211.

Lynch, The Image of the City, 1960
Lynch, Kevin, *The Image of the City*, Cambridge 1960.

Mackenthun/Nicolas/Wodianka, Circulation of Knowledge, 2017
Mackenthun, Gesa/Nicolas, Andrea/Wodianka, Stephanie, *Travel, Agency, and the Circulation of Knowledge*, Münster/New York 2017.

Marek, Rekonstruktion und Kulturgesellschaft, 2009
Marek, Katja, *Rekonstruktion und Kulturgesellschaft: Stadtbildreparatur in Dresden, Frankfurt am Main und Berlin als Ausdruck der zeitgenössischen Suche nach Identität* (diss., Art University of Kassel 2009), http://kobra.bibliothek.uni-kassel.de/bitstream/urn:nbn:de:hebis: 34-2009101330569/7/DissertationKatjaMarek.pdf [accessed 4 June 2020].

Martelli, Oltre la capitale, 2012
Martelli, Sebastiano, Oltre la capitale. Il viaggio di Johann Heinrich Bartels nel Mezzogiorno di fine Settecento, in: Sabbatino, Pasquale, ed., *Il viaggio a Napoli tra letteratura e arti* (Viaggio d'Europa 20), Naples 2012, pp. 307–337.

Materialien zum Sanierungsgesetz, 1945/1956
Materialien zum Sanierungsgesetz (State Archives of the City of Basel/Staatsarchiv Basel. StA BS BD-Reg A 801/1 – 1945–56).

Matyakubova, Tashkent City, 2018
Matyakubova, Dilmira, Who Is "Tashkent City" For? Nation-Branding and Public Dialogue in Uzbekistan, in: *CAP Paper (CAAF Fellows Papers)*, 205/2018, pp. 1–14, https://voicesoncentralasia.org/who-is-tashkent-city-for-nation-branding-and-public-dialogue-in-uzbekistan/ [accessed 21 February 2020].

Maurer, Neue Impulse, 1999
Maurer, Michael, ed., *Neue Impulse der Reiseforschung*, Berlin 1999.

Meier, Ein unsäglich schönes Land, 1987
Meier, Albert, ed., *Ein unsäglich schönes Land. Goethes "Italienische Reise" und der Mythos Siziliens*, Palermo 1987.

Meier, Basler Arbeitsrappen, 1984
Meier, Eugen A., *Der Basler Arbeitsrappen 1936–84: die Geschichte eines genialen Sozialwerks und dessen Auswirkungen auf die städtebauliche Entwicklung Basels*, Basel 1984.

Meier, Basel einst und jetzt, 1993
Meier, Eugen A., *Basel einst und jetzt: der Wandel des Basler Stadtbildes im Lauf der Zeit*, Basel 1993.

Meier, Die normannischen Königspaläste, 1994
Meier, Hans-Rudolf, *Die normannischen Königspaläste in Palermo. Studien zur hochmittelalterlichen Residenzbaukunst* (Manuskripte zur Kunstwissenschaft in der Wernerschen Verlagsgesellschaft 42; diss., University of Basel 1994), Worms 1994.

Meier/Scheurmann, 2010
Meier, Hans-Rudolf/Scheurmann, Ingrid, eds, *DENKmalWERTE. Beiträge zur Theorie und Aktualität der Denkmalpflege. Georg Mörsch zum 70. Geburtstag*, Berlin/Munich 2010.

Meier, Spolien, 2021
Meier, Hans-Rudolf, *Spolien. Phänomene der Wiederverwendung in der Architektur*, Berlin 2021.

Meier/Will, Paradigmenwechsel, 2005
Meier, Hans-Rudolf/Will, Thomas, Dehio 2000! Paradigmenwechsel in der modernen Denkmalpflege? In: Scheurmann, Ingrid, ed., *ZeitSchichten. Erkennen und Erhalten – Denkmalpflege in Deutschland. 100 Jahre Handbuch der Deutschen Kunstdenkmäler von Georg Dehio* (exhibition catalogue), Munich/Berlin 2005, pp. 320–329.

Menne-Thomé, City-Bildung, 1995
Menne-Thomé, Käthe, City-Bildung in der mittelalterlichen Altstadt. Zum langsamen Umbau von Köln, in: Fehl, Gerhard/Rodríguez-Lores, Juan, eds, *Stadt-Umbau. Die planmäßige Erneuerung europäischer Großstädte zwischen Wiener Kongreß und Weimarer Republik* (Stadt, Planung, Geschichte 17), Basel/Berlin/Boston 1995, pp. 149–167.

Mentges, The Role of UNESCO, 2012
Mentges, Gabriele, The Role of UNESCO and the Uzbek Nation Building Process, in: Bendix, Regina F./Eggert, Aditya/Peselmann, Arnika, eds, *Heritage Regimes and the State* (Göttingen Studies in Cultural Property 6), Göttingen 2012, pp. 213–226.

Meuser, Architektur in Zentralasien, 2012
Meuser, Philipp, Architektur in Zentralasien, in: Meuser, Philipp, ed., *Architekturführer Usbekistan*, Berlin 2012, pp. 39–73.

Mitscherlich, Unwirtlichkeit unserer Städte, 1965
Mitscherlich, Alexander, *Die Unwirtlichkeit unserer Städte. Anstiftung zum Unfrieden*, Frankfurt a.M. 1965.

Mock, The Fight to Remove, 2016
Mock, Brentin, The Fight to Remove the Andrew Jackson Monument in New Orleans, in: *Bloomberg CityLab*, 29 September 2016, https://www.bloomberg.com/news/articles/2016-09-29/in-new-orleans-a-renewed-fight-over-andrew-jackson [accessed 25 October 2020].

Möller, Situationen des Fremden, 2016
Möller, Reinhard M., *Situationen des Fremden. Ästhetik und Reiseliteratur im späten 18. Jahrhundert*, Paderborn 2016.

Morgen/Morgen/Barrett, Finding a Place, 2006
Morgan, David W./Morgan, Nancy I. M./Barrett, Brenda, Finding a Place for the Commonplace: Hurricane Katrina, Communities, and Preservation Law, in: *American Anthropologist*, new ser. 4/108 2006, pp. 706–718.

Morrison, Historic Preservation Law, 1974
Morrison, Jacob H., *Historic Preservation Law*, 2nd ed., Washington 1974.

Mörsch/Vereinigung der Landesdenkmalpfleger, Denkmalpflege 1975, 1976
Mörsch, Georg/Vereinigung der Landesdenkmalpfleger, Denkmalpflege 1975. Versuch einer Beschreibung, in: *Deutsche Kunst und Denkmalpflege*, 34/1976, pp. 87–89.

Moskowitz, How to Kill a City, 2017
Moskowitz, Peter, *How to Kill a City: Gentrification, Inequality, and the Fight for the Neighborhood*, New York 2017.

Müller-Raemisch, Frankfurt am Main, 1996
Müller-Raemisch, Hans-Reiner, *Frankfurt am Main: Stadtentwicklung und Planungsgeschichte seit 1945*, Frankfurt a.M./New York 1996.

Müller-Raemisch, Frankfurt am Main, 1998
Müller-Raemisch, Hans-Reiner, *Frankfurt am Main. Stadtentwicklung und Planungsgeschichte seit 1945*, Frankfurt a.M./New York 1998.

Muir Whitehill, The Right of Cities, 1966
Muir Whitehill, Walter, The Right of Cities to be Beautiful, in: *With Heritage so rich* (ed. The National Trust for Historic Preservation), New York 1966 (Reprint 1999), pp. 149–169.

Mullin, American Perceptions, 1977
Mullin, John R., American Perceptions of German City Planning at the Turn of the Century, in: *Urbanism Past and Present*, 3/1977, pp. 5–15.

Murtagh, Keeping Time, 2006
Murtagh, William J., *Keeping Time. The History and Theory of Preservation in America*, 3rd ed., Hoboken 2006.

Nerdinger, Geschichte der Rekonstruktion, 2010
Nerdinger, Winfried, ed., *Geschichte der Rekonstruktion – Konstruktion der Geschichte* (exhibition catalogue), Munich et al. 2010.

Nertz, Umgang des Baslers, 1991
Nertz, René, Der Umgang des Baslers mit seiner Altstadt, in: Baudepartement Basel-Stadt, ed., *Neues Wohnen in der alten Stadt. Die Sanierung staatlicher Liegenschaften in der Basler Altstadt 1978–1990*, Basel 1991, pp. 98–106.

New Orleans baut Bürgerkriegsdenkmale ab, Süddeutsche Zeitung, 18 December 2015
New Orleans baut Bürgerkriegsdenkmale ab, in: *Süddeutsche Zeitung*, 18 December 2015, https://www.sueddeutsche.de/politik/symbole-fuer-sklaverei-new-orleans-baut-umstrittene-suedstaaten-denkmale-ab-1.2788538 [accessed 13 January 2021].

Nietzsche, Untimely Mediations, 1997 (1873–1876)
Nietzsche, Friedrich, *Untimely Mediations* (original title: Unzeitgemäße Betrachtungen, 1873–1876), translated by R. J. Hollingdale, Cambridge et al. 1997.

Nipperdey, Kölner Dom als Nationaldenkmal, 1983
Nipperdey, Thomas, Der Kölner Dom als Nationaldenkmal, in: Dann, Otto, ed., *Religion – Kunst – Vaterland. Der Kölner Dom im 19. Jahrhundert*, Cologne 1983, pp. 109–120.

Nora, Between memory and history, 1996
Nora, Pierre, Between memory and history, in: Nora, Pierre/Kritzman, Lawrence D., eds, *Realms of the memory. Rethinking the French Past – Volume 1: Conflicts and Divisions*, translated by A. Goldhammer, New York 1996, pp. 1–20.

Nora, Les Lieux de Mémoires, 1997 (1984–1992)
Nora, Pierre, *Les Lieux de mémoire* (1984–1992), 3 vols, Paris 1997.

O'Doherty, Inside the White Cube, 1986
O'Doherty, Brian, *Inside the White Cube*, Santa Monica 1986.

Osman, Invention of Brooklyn Brownstone, 2001
Osman, Suleiman, *The Invention of Brooklyn Brownstone. Gentrification and the Search for Authenticity in Postwar New York*, New York 2001.

Ostendorf, The Mysteries of New Orleans, 2016
Ostendorf, Berndt, The Mysteries of New Orleans: Culture Formation and the Layering of History, in: Antenhofer, Christina, et al., eds, *Cities as Multiple Landscapes. Investigating the Sister Cities Innsbruck and New Orleans* (Interdisciplinary urban research 21), Frankfurt a.M./New York 2016, pp. 107–120.

Osterkamp, Sizilien Reisebilder, 1986
Osterkamp, Ernst, ed., *Sizilien. Reisebilder aus drei Jahrhunderten*, Munich 1986.

Osterkamp, Geschichte der deutschen Sizilienwahrnehmung, 1987
Osterkamp, Ernst, Zur Geschichte der deutschen Sizilienwahrnehmung im 18. und 19. Jahrhundert, in: Meier, Albert, ed., *Ein unsäglich schönes Land. Goethes "Italienische Reise" und der Mythos Siziliens*, Palermo 1987, pp. 138–157.

Osterkamp, Riedesels Sizilienreisen, 1992
Osterkamp, Ernst, Johann Hermann von Riedesels Sizilienreise. Die Winckelmannsche Perspektive und ihre Folgen, in: Jäger, Hans-Wolf, ed., *Europäisches Reisen im Zeitalter der Aufklärung*, Heidelberg 1992, pp. 93–106.

Osterloh, Versammelte Menschenkraft, 2016
Osterloh, Malte, *Versammelte Menschenkraft: die Großstadterfahrung in Goethes Italiendichtung*, Würzburg 2016.

Oswald/Demydovets, Bauten und Projekte, 2012
Oswald, Ansgar/Demydovets, Maryna, Bauten und Projekte in Taschkent, in: Meuser, Philipp, ed., *Architekturführer Usbekistan*, Berlin 2012, pp. 167–296.

Pahnke, Spaziergang durchs papierne Jahrhundert, 2018
Pahnke, Gabi, *Spaziergang durchs papierne Jahrhundert. Das Netzwerk von Johann Gottfried Seume*, Berlin 2018.

Pancrazi, Antichità siciliane, 1751/1752
Pancrazi, Giuseppe M., *Antichità siciliane spiegate colle notizie generali di questo regno cui si comprende la storia particolare di quelle città, ... Opera del padre d. Giuseppe Maria Pancrazj ... Tomo primo diviso in due parti. Nella prima si contengono le notizie generali di quest'isola. Nella seconda la pianta, le varie vedute, e la descrizione dell'antico Agrigento*, Napoli 1751/1752.

Pantano, Jean Hoüel, 2003
Pantano, Francesca G., *Jean Hoüel, Voyage a Siracusa; le antichità della città e del suo territorio nel 1777*, Palermo 2003.

Paskaleva, Ideology in Brick and Tile, 2015
Paskaleva, Elena, Ideology in Brick and Tile: Timurid Architecture of the 21st Century, in: *Central Asian Survey*, 34/4 2015, pp. 418–439.

Paterno, Viaggio per tutte le antichità della Sicilia, 1781
Paternò Castello, Ignazio, *Viaggio per tutte le antichità della Sicilia descritto da Ignazio Paternò principe di Biscari e dedicato a sua eccellenza Giuseppe Bologni Beccatelli marchese della Sambuca ... e primo segretario di stato, e degli affari esteri del re Ferdinando III.*, Napoli 1781, https://arachne.dainst.org/entity/2124257 [accessed 8 August 2020].

Pehnt/Strohl, Rudolf Schwarz, 1997
Pehnt, Wolfgang/Strohl, Hilde, *Rudolf Schwarz 1897–1961: Architekt einer anderen Moderne* (exhibition catalogue), Ostfildern 1997.

Petrilli, L'urbanistica, 2006
Petrilli, Amedeo, *L'urbanistica di Le Corbusier*, Venice 2006.

Petrus, From Gritty to Chic, 2003
Petrus, Stephen, From Gritty to Chic: The Transformation of New York City's SoHo, 1962–1976, in: *New York History*, 84/1 2003, pp. 50–87.

Petzet, Zukunft für unsere Vergangenheit, 1975
Petzet, Michael, Eine Zukunft für unsere Vergangenheit? – Denkmalpflege im Denkmalschutzjahr 1975, in: Deutsches Nationalkomitee für das Europäische Denkmalschutzjahr, ed., *Eine Zukunft für unsere Vergangenheit: Denkmalschutz in der Bundesrepublik. Europäisches Denkmalschutzjahr 1975*, Munich 1975, pp. 7–37.

Petzet, Reversibility, 1992
Petzet, Michael, Reversibility – Preservation's Fig Leaf? In: Krieg, Stefan W., ed., *Reversibilität – das Feigenblatt in der Denkmalpflege?* (ICOMOS – Journals of the German National Committee 8), Munich 1992, pp. 81–85.

Petz, Stadtsanierung im Dritten Reich, 1987
Petz, Ursula von, *Stadtsanierung im Dritten Reich. Dargestellt an ausgewählten Beispielen* (Dortmunder Beiträge zur Raumplanung 45; diss., University of Dortmund 1984), Dortmund 1987.

Pinault, Voyage en Sicile, 1990
Pinault Sørensen, Madeleine, *Houël, Voyage en Sicile: 1776–1779* (exhibition catalogue), Paris 1990.

Pinder, Rede am Tag für Denkmalpflege und Heimatschutz, 1934
Pinder, Wilhelm, Rede am Tag für Denkmalpflege und Heimatschutz im Rahmen des ersten Reichstreffens des Reichsbundes Volkstum und Heimat 1933 in Kassel, in: *Denkmalpflege und Heimatschutz im Wiederaufbau der Nation: Tag für Denkmalpflege und Heimatschutz im Rahmen des Ersten Reichstreffens des Reichsbundes Volkstum und Heimat, Kassel 1933*, Berlin 1934, pp. 123–134.

Pinho, African-American Roots, 2008
Pinho, Patricia, African-American Roots. Tourism in Brazil, in: *Latin American Perspectives*, 35/3 2008, pp. 70–86.

Plosky, Fall and Rise of Pennsylvania Station, 1999
Plosky, Eric J., *The Fall and Rise of Pennsylvania Station. Changing Attitudes Toward Historic Preservation in New York City* (master's thesis, Massachusetts Institute of Technology 1999), http://www.subjectverb.com/www/writing/thesis.pdf [accessed 13 May 2020].

Plyer, Facts for Features, 2016
Plyer, Allison, Facts for Features: Katrina Impact, in: *The Data Center. Independent Analysis for Informed Decisions in Southeast Louisiana*, 26 August 2016, https://www.datacenterresearch.org/data-resources/katrina/facts-for-impact/ [accessed 14 January 2021].

Pötschke, Dreißig Häuser sind keine Altstadt, 2007
Pötschke, Günter, Dreißig Häuser sind keine Altstadt – zum Ersatzbau für das Frankfurter Technische Rathaus, in: Deutscher Werkbund Hessen, ed., *Standpunkte. Zur Bebauung des Frankfurter Römerbergs*, Frankfurt a.M. 2007, pp. 13–16.

Powell, Contrarian's Lament, 2010
Powell, Michael, A Contrarian's Lament in a Blitz of Gentrification, in: *The New York Times*, 19 February 2010, http://www.nytimes.com/2010/02/21/nyregion/21gentrify.html [accessed 12 May 2020].

Pred, Place as Historically Contingent Process, 1984
Pred, Allan, Place as Historically Contingent Process: Structuration and the Time-Geography of Becoming Places, in: *Annals of the Association of American Geographers*, 74/2 1984, pp. 279–297.

Prescia, Restauri a Palermo, 2012
Prescia, Renata, *Restauri a Palermo. Architettura e città come stratificazione*, Palermo 2012.

Pugin, Contrasts, 1836
Pugin, Augustus W. N., *Contrasts: Or, A Parallel Between the Noble Edifices of the Fourteenth and Fifteenth Centuries and Similar Buildings of the Present Day. Shewing the Present Decay of Taste. Accompanied by Appropriate Text*, London 1836.

Pugin, Contrasts, 1841
Pugin, Augustus W. N., *Contrasts; Or, A Parallel Between the Noble Edifices of the Middle Ages and Corresponding Buildings of the Present Day*, 2nd ed., Leicester 1841.

Pugin, Gothic Architecture, 1920 (1821-1838)
Pugin, Augustus W. N., *Gothic Architecture selected from various Ancient Edifices in England*, 5 vols, London 1821–1838, quoted after reprint in 2 vols, Cleveland 1920, https://archive.org/details/gothicarchitectu00pugi/mode/2up [accessed 5 February 2021].

Rader, Die Kraft des Porphyrs, 2009
Rader, Olaf B., Die Kraft des Porphyrs: Das Grabmal Kaiser Friedrichs II. in Palermo als Fokus europäischer Erinnerungen, in: Buchinger, Kirstin/Gantet, Claire/Vogel, Jakob, eds, *Europäische Erinnerungsräume*, Frankfurt a.M./New York 2009, pp. 33–46.

Rampley, Identity in Central and Eastern Europe, 2012
Rampley, Matthew, ed., *Heritage, Ideology, and Identity in Central and Eastern Europe. Contested Pasts, Contested Presents*, Woodbridge 2012.

Ratschläge, 315, 1864 / Ratschläge, 2257, 1919 / Ratschläge, 3769, 1939
Ratschläge und Gesetzesentwürfe des Regierungsrates Basel-Stadt an den großen Rat, Basel 1819ff. (State Archives of the City of Basel/Staatsarchiv Basel. StA BS Signatur DSBS9).

Reichelt, Erlebnisraum Lutherstadt Wittenberg, 2013
Reichelt, Silvio, *Der Erlebnisraum Lutherstadt Wittenberg. Genese, Entwicklung und Bestand eines protestantischen Erinnerungsortes* (Refo500 Academic Studies 11; diss., University of Halle-Wittenberg 2011), Göttingen 2013.

Reichow, Organische Stadtbaukunst, 2005 (1948)
Reichow, Hans B., Organische Stadtbaukunst (1948), reprinted in: Lampugnani, Vittorio M./Frey, Katia/Perotti, Eliana, eds, *Anthologie zum Städtebau*, vol. 3: Vom Wiederaufbau nach dem Zweiten Weltkrieg bis zur zeitgenössischen Stadt, Berlin 2005, pp. 56–62.

Reitter, Heine in the Bronx, 1999
Reitter, Paul, Heine in the Bronx, in: *The Germanic Review*, 74/4 1999, pp. 327–336.

Ricca, Shifting Symbolism, 2005
Ricca, Simone, Heritage, Nationalism and the Shifting Symbolism of the Wailing Wall, in: *Jerusalem Quarterly*, 24/2005, pp. 39–56.

Rich, Jungleland, 2012
Rich, Nathaniel, Jungleland, in: *The New York Times Magazine*, 21 March 2012, https://www.nytimes.com/2012/03/25/magazine/the-lower-ninth-ward-new-orleans.html [accessed 25 October 2020].

Riedesel, Voyage en Sicile, 1773
Riedesel, Johann H. von, *Voyage en Sicile et dans la Grande Grèce adressé par l'auteur à son ami Mr. Winckelmann, traduit de l'Allemand, accompagné de notes du traducteur et d'autres additions intéressantes*, Lausanne 1773, https://www.e-rara.ch/zuz/doi/10.3931/e-rara-34386 [accessed 15 August 2020].

Riedesel, Reise durch Sicilien, 1965 (1771)
Riedesel, Johann H. von, *Reise durch Sicilien und Grossgriechenland* (1771), quoted after reprint: Schulz, Arthur, ed., *Johann Hermann von Riedesels Reise durch Sizilien und Großgriechenland*, Berlin 1965.

Riegl, Der moderne Denkmalkultus, 1903
Riegl, Alois, *Der moderne Denkmalkultus. Sein Wesen und seine Entstehung*, Vienna/Leipzig 1903.

Riegl, Neue Strömungen, 1905
Riegl, Alois, Neue Strömungen in der Denkmalpflege, in: *Mittelungen der K.K. Zentralkommission für Erforschung und Erhaltung der Kunst- und historischen Denkmale*, 3rd ser. 4/1905, col. 85–104.

Riegl, The modern Cult of Monuments, 1982 (1903)
Riegl, Alois, The modern Cult of Monuments. Its Character and Its Origin (1903), translated by K. W. Forster and D. Ghirardo, in: *Oppositions. A Journal for Ideas and Critisism in Architecture*, 25/1982, pp. 20–51.

Riegl, Der moderne Denkmalkultus, 1995 (1903)
Riegl, Alois, Der moderne Denkmalkultus. Sein Wesen und seine Entstehung (1903), reprinted in: Kemp, Wolfgang, ed., *Alois Riegl. Gesammelte Aufsätze. Mit einem Nachwort zur Neuausgabe von Wolfgang Kemp*, Berlin 1995, pp. 144–193.

Riegl, Neue Strömungen, 1995 (1905)
Riegl, Alois, Neue Strömungen in der Denkmalpflege (1905), reprinted in: Bacher, Ernst, ed., *Kunstwerk oder Denkmal? Alois Riegls Schriften zur Denkmalpflege* (Studien zu Denkmalschutz und Denkmalpflege 15), Vienna et al. 1995, pp. 217–233.

Riphahn, Grundgedanken zur Neugestaltung, 1945
Riphahn, Wilhelm, *Grundgedanken zur Neugestaltung Kölns*, 14 July 1945 (Historical Archive of the City of Cologne/Historisches Archiv der Stadt Köln, Acc 1225/229).

Roscher, Lexikon der griechischen und römischen Mythologie, 1884
Roscher, Wilhelm H., *Ausführliches Lexikon der griechischen und römischen Mythologie*, vol. 1, Leipzig 1884.

Rossi, The Architecture of the City, 1984 (1966)
Rossi, Aldo, *The Architecture of the City* (original title: L'Architettura della citta, 1966), translated by D. Ghirardo and J. Ockman, Cambridge/London 1984.

Roth, Vorstellung des alten heiligen Köln, 1998
Roth, Erik, "... um die Vorstellung des alten heiligen Köln wach zu halten". Das Kölner Rheinviertel – Sanierung und Wiederaufbau 1900–1956, in: *Köln – 85 Jahre Denkmalschutz*

und Denkmalpflege (Stadtspuren – Denkmäler in Köln 9), vol. 2: Texte von 1980–1997, Cologne 1998, pp. 580–607.

Rotolo, Cinque nuovi murals, 2018
Rotolo, Alessia, Palermo ha cinque nuovi (giganteschi) murals: rinarce il centro tra santi e simboli, in: *Balarm Magazine*, 31 July 2018, https://www.balarm.it/news/palermo-ha-cinque-nuovi-giganteschi-murales-rinasce-il-centro-tra-santi-e-simboli-21299 [accessed 28 June 2019].

Ruskin, The Seven Lamps, 1849
Ruskin, John, The Seven Lamps of Architecture, London 1849.

Saint Non, Voyage pittoresque, 1781-1786
Saint Non, Jean C. R. de, *Voyage pittoresque ou Description des Royaumes de Naples et de Sicile Paris*, 5 vols, Paris 1781–1786.

Sammons, Restoration of the Heine Monument, 1999
Sammons, Jeffrey L., The Restoration of the Heine Monument in the Bronx, in: *The Germanic review*, 74/4 1999, pp. 337–339.

Sandmeier/Selitz, Das Kommunale Denkmalkonzept, 2020
Sandmeier, Judith/Selitz Lisa Marie, Das Kommunale Denkmalkonzept Bayern. Städtebauliche Denkmalpflege als integrierte Praxis, in: Altrock, Uwe, et al., eds, *Stadterneuerung in Klein- und Mittelstädten* (Jahrbuch Stadterneuerung 5), Wiesbaden 2020, pp. 155–180.

Sauerländer, Erweiterung des Denkmalbegriffs, 1975
Sauerländer, Willibald, Erweiterung des Denkmalbegriffs? In: *Deutsche Kunst- und Denkmalpflege*, 33/1975, pp. 117–130.

Scheurmann, Vom Konservieren und Restaurieren, 2005
Scheurmann, Ingrid, Vom Konservieren und Restaurieren. Anmerkungen zur Rezeption Georg Dehios, in: Scheurmann, Ingrid, ed., *ZeitSchichten. Erkennen und Erhalten – Denkmalpflege in Deutschland. 100 Jahre Handbuch der Deutschen Kunstdenkmäler von Georg Dehio* (exhibition catalogue), Munich/Berlin 2005, pp. 48–59.

Scheurmann, Konturen und Konjunkturen, 2018
Scheurmann, Ingrid, *Konturen und Konjunkturen der Denkmalpflege. Zum Umgang mit baulichen Relikten der Vergangenheit*, Cologne/Weimar/Vienna 2018.

Schlungbaum-Stehr, Das Martinsviertel, 1991
Schlungbaum-Stehr, Regine, Das Martinsviertel, in: Architekten- und Ingenieurverein Köln e.V., ed., *Köln – seine Bauten 1928–1988*, Cologne 1991, pp. 85–92.

Schlungbaum-Stehr, Das Martinsviertel, 1999
Schlungbaum-Stehr, Regine, Das Martinsviertel, in: Kier, Hiltrud, et al., eds, *Architektur der 30er und 40er Jahre in Köln. Materialien zur Baugeschichte im Nationalsozialismus*, Cologne 1999, pp. 35–46.

Schmickle, Politics of Historic Districts, 2007
Schmickle, William E., *The Politics of Historic Districts. A Primer for Grassroots Preservation*, Lanham 2007.

Schmidt, Einführung in die Denkmalpflege, 2008
Schmidt, Leo, *Einführung in die Denkmalpflege*, Darmstadt 2008.

Schneider/Schneider, Reversible Destiny, 2003
Schneider, Jane C./Schneider, Peter T., *Reversible Destiny. Mafia, Antimafia and the Struggle for Palermo*, Berkeley/Los Angeles/London 2003.

Schnitzler, Restaurierung des Berliner Doms, 2013
Schnitzler, Katja, Restaurierung des Berliner Doms: Wiederaufbau gegen Widerstände, in: *Süddeutsche Zeitung*, 6 June 2013, https://www.sueddeutsche.de/reise/restaurierung-des-berliner-doms-wiederaufbau-gegen-widerstaende-1.1689582 [accessed 9 April 2020].

Schröder, Baugestalt und Raumprogramm, 2002
Schröder, Jochen, *Die Baugestalt und das Raumprogramm des Berliner Doms als Spiegel der Ansprüche und Funktionen des Bauherrn Kaiser Wilhelms II* (diss., University of Marburg 2002).

Schubert, Kampf um das erste Heine-Denkmal, 1990
Schubert, Dietrich, Der Kampf um das erste Heine-Denkmal. Düsseldorf 1887–1893, Mainz 1893–1894, New York 1899, in: *Wallraf-Richartz-Jahrbuch: Westdeutsches Jahrbuch für Kunstgeschichte*, 51/1990, pp. 241–272.

Schultze-Naumburg, Kulturarbeiten, 1901-1917
Schultze-Naumburg, Paul, *Kulturarbeiten*, 9 vols, Munich 1901–1917.

Schulz, Riedesels Reise, 1965
Schulz, Arthur, ed., *Johann Hermann von Riedesels Reise durch Sizilien und Großgriechenland*, Berlin 1965.

Schulz, Humboldt Forum bekommt Kreuz, 2020
Schulz, Bernhard, Humboldt Forum bekommt Kreuz. Der Streit um die Kuppel des Berliner Stadtschloss – eine Chronik, in: *Der Tagesspiegel*, 29 May 2020, https://www.tagesspiegel.de/kultur/humboldt-forum-bekommt-kreuz-der-streit-um-die-kuppel-des-berliner-stadtschloss-eine-chronik/25858830.html [accessed 30 May 2020].

Schwarz, Stadtlandschaft Diedenhofen, 1943
Schwarz, Rudolf, *Stadtlandschaft Diedenhofen*, 1943, Estate Rudolf Schwarz (Historical Archive of the Cologne Archdiocese/Historisches Archiv des Erzbistums Köln, Estate Maria Schwarz).

Schwarz, Von der Bebauung, 1949
Schwarz, Rudolf, *Von der Bebauung der Erde*, Heidelberg 1949.

Schwarz, Das neue Köln, 1950
Schwarz, Rudolf, Das neue Köln – Ein Vorentwurf, in: Stadt Köln, ed., *Das neue Köln: Ein Vorentwurf*, Cologne 1950, pp. 3–64.

Schwarz, Wegweisung der Technik, 1979 (1928)
Schwarz, Rudolf, Wegweisung der Technik (1928), reprinted in: Schwarz, Maria/Conrads, Ulrich, eds, *Wegweisung der Technik und andere Schriften zum Neuen Bauen: 1926–1961* (Bauwelt Fundamente 51), Braunschweig/Wiesbaden 1979, pp. 12–91.

Schwarz, Gegenstand des Städtebaus, 1997 (1948)
Schwarz, Rudolf, Was eigentlich ist der Gegenstand des Städtebaus? (1948), reprinted in: Pehnt, Wolfgang/Strohl, Hilde, *Rudolf Schwarz 1897–1961: Architekt einer anderen Moderne* (exhibition catalogue), Ostfildern 1997, pp. 216–219.

Schwarz, Der Aufbau zerstörter Städte, 1997 (1955)
Schwarz, Rudolf, Der Aufbau zerstörter Städte (1955), reprinted in: Pehnt, Wolfgang/Strohl, Hilde, *Rudolf Schwarz 1897–1961: Architekt einer anderen Moderne* (exhibition catalogue), Ostfildern 1997, pp. 219–221.

Selitz, Erhalten, Erhalten – Erneuern – Beteiligen, forthcoming 2021
Selitz, Lisa M., *Erhalten – Erneuern – Beteiligen. Partizipation als Verhandlungsgegenstand der städtebaulichen Denkmalpflege* (working title, diss., University of Bamberg), forthcoming 2021.

Selitz/Vinken, Kommunales Denkmalkonzept, 2017
Selitz, Lisa M./Vinken, Gerhard, Kommunales Denkmalkonzept als Chance. Ein Beitrag zu einer historisch informierten Stadtplanung, in: Bayrisches Landesamt für Denkmalpflege, ed., *Das Kommunale Denkmalkonzept. Den historischen Ortskern gemeinsam gestalten und entwickeln* (Denkmalpflege Themen 8), Munich 2017, pp. 24–26.

Seume, Spaziergang, 2003 (1802)
Seume, Johann G., *Spaziergang nach Syrakus im Jahre 1802* (1802), Munich 2003.

Shkuda, Lofts of SoHo, 2016
Shkuda, Aaron, *The Lofts of SoHo. Gentrification, Art and Industry in New York, 1950–1980* (Historical Studies of Urban America), Chicago/London 2016.

Siegfried, Basels Entfestigung, 1923
Siegfried, Paul, Basels Entfestigung, in: *Basler Jahrbuch*, 1923, pp. 81–146.

Sievers, Uzbekistan's Mahalla, 2002
Sievers, Eric W., Uzbekistan's Mahalla: From Soviet to Absolutist Residential Community Associations, in: *The Journal of International and Comparative Law at Chicago-Kent*, 2/2002, pp. 91–158, https://scholarship.kentlaw.iit.edu/cgi/viewcontent.cgi?article=1015&context=ckjicl [accessed 28 June 2020].

Silverman, Contested Cultural Heritage, 2011
Silverman, Helaine, ed., *Contested Cultural Heritage. Religion, Nationalism, Erasure, and Exclusion in a Global World*, New York 2011.

Silver, Lost New York, 1968
Silver, Nathan, *Lost New York*, New York 1968.

Simmel, Sociology, 2009
Simmel, Georg, *Sociology: Inquiries into the Construction of Social Forms*, 2 vols, Leiden 2009.

Smecca, Three travel writers, 2009
Smecca, Paola D., *Three travel writers in Italian translation: Brydone, Strutt and Paton*, Lugano 2009.

Smith, Things You'd Imagine, 2019
Smith, Felipe, "Things You'd Imagine Zulu Tribes to Do": The Zulu Parade in New Orleans Carnival, in: Adams, Thomas J./Sakakeeny, Matt, eds, *Remaking New Orleans. Beyond Exceptionalism and Authenticity*, Durham/London 2019, pp. 93–116.

Smith, Uses of Heritage, 2006
Smith, Laurajane, *Uses of Heritage*, London/New York 2006.

Smith, Cultural Heritage, 2007
Smith, Laurajane, ed., *Cultural Heritage. Critical Concepts in Media and Cultural Studies*, 4 vols, London et al. 2007.

Söderström, Urban Cosmographies, 2009
Söderström, Ola, et al., *Urban Cosmographies. Indagine sul cambiamento urbano a Palermo* (Babele 54), Rome 2009.

Souther, America's Most Interesting City, 2003
Souther, J. Mark, Making "America's Most Interesting City": Tourism and the Construction of Cultural Image in New Orleans, 1940–1984, in: Starnes, Richard D., ed., *Southern Journeys: Tourism, History, and Culture in the Modern South*, Tuscaloosa/London 2003, pp. 114–137.

Souther, The Disneyfication of New Orleans, 2007
Souther, J. Mark, The Disneyfication of New Orleans: The French Quarter as Facade in a Divided City, in: *The Journal of American History. Through the Eye of Katrina: The Past as Prologue?* 94/3 2007, pp. 804–811.

Sovremennoi mahalle radi ne vse, GazetaUz, 20 August 2017
Sovremennoi mahalle radi ne vse: zhiteli Belarik vystupaiut protiv stroitel'stva sovremennoi mahalli, in: *GazetaUz*, 20 August 2017, https://www.gazeta.uz/ru/2017/08/20/mahalla/ [accessed 20 September 2019].

Spelsberg, Il patrimonio culturale, 2011
Spelsberg, Irmela, Il patrimonio culturale italiano visto da Johann Wolfgang Goethe. "Viaggio in Italia 1786–1788", in: *Quaderni del Dipartimento Patrimonio Architettonico e Urbanistico*, 19/20 2009/10, 37/40 2011, pp. 107–114.

Stackmann, Integrität als Konzept, forthcoming 2021
Stackmann, Sophie, *Integrität als Konzept für das Erbe der Vergangenheit – eine kritische Lektüre* (working title, diss., University of Bamberg), forthcoming 2021.

Stahr, Tage in Palermo, 1986 (1845)
Stahr, Adolf, Tage in Palermo (1845), reprinted in: Osterkamp, Ernst, ed., *Sizilien. Reisebilder aus drei Jahrhunderten*, Munich 1986, pp. 149–162.

Stalin, Deviations on the National Question, 1942 (1930)
Stalin, Joseph, Deviations on the National Question (1930), in: Stalin, Joseph, *Marxism and the National Questions. Selected Writings and Speeches*, New York 1942, pp. 203-214.

Sterl, Tausendfüßler in Düsseldorf, 2015
Sterl, Karin A., *Der Tausendfüßler in Düsseldorf. Städtebauliche und denkmalpflegerische Implikationen einer Hochstraße der 1960er Jahre* (unpublished master's thesis, University of Bamberg 2015).

Sternbergh, Embers of Gentrification, 2007
Sternbergh, Adam, The Embers of Gentrification, in: *New York Magazine*, 9 November 2007, https://nymag.com/news/features/40648/index4.html [accessed 13 May 2020].

Stolz/Bühler, Basel im 19. Jahrhundert, 1979
Stolz, Peter/Bühler, Hans, Basel im 19. Jahrhundert, in: *Regio Basiliensis*, 20/1979, pp. 165–201.

Strausbaugh, The Village, 2013
Strausbaugh, John, *The Village. 400 Years of Beats and Bohemians, Radicals and Rogues*, New York 2013.

Stronski, Tashkent, 2010
Stronski, Paul, *Tashkent: Forging a Soviet City, 1930–1966*, Pittsburgh 2010.

Sublette, The World that made New Orleans, 2008
Sublette, Ned, *The World that made New Orleans. From Spanish Silver to Congo Square*, Chicago 2008.

Takahashi, Berlin Heritage Conservation, 2018
Takahashi, Johanna, Berlin: Denkmalpflege zwischen Gentrifizierung und behutsamer Stadterneuerung am Beispiel von Kreuzberg und Prenzlauer Berg / Berlin: Heritage Conservation between Gentrification and Cautious Urban Renewal, in: Selitz, Lisa Marie/Stackmann, Sophie, eds, *Wertzuschreibungen und Planungslogiken in historischen Stadträumen. Neue Beiträge zur städtebaulichen Denkmalpflege / The Ascription of Values and Logics in Planning within Historic City Spaces. New Contributions to the Conservation of Urban Heritage* (Forschungen des Instituts für Archäologische Wissenschaften, Denkmalwissenschaften und Kunstgeschichte 7), Bamberg 2018, pp. 123–152.

Talen, New Urbanism and American Planning, 2005
Talen, Emily, *New Urbanism and American Planning: The Conflict of Cultures*, New York 2005.

Taylor, Hepburn's former brownstone, 2010
Taylor, Candace, Katharine Hepburn's former brownstone available for $27,500 per month, in: *TheRealDeal*, 31 August 2010, http://therealdeal.com/2010/08/31/katharine-hepburn-s-former-brownstone-available-for-27-500-per-month-1/ [accessed 12 May 2020].

The Equal Rights Trust, After the Padishah, 2016
The Equal Rights Trust, ed., *After the Padishah. Addressing Discrimination and Inequality in Uzbekistan* (The Equal Rights Trust Country Report Series 8), London 2016, https://www.equalrightstrust.org/ertdocumentbank/Uzbekistan_EN_0.pdf [accessed 25 June 2020].

The present state of Sicily and Malta, modern travellers, 1788
The present state of Sicily and Malta, extracted from Mr. Brydone, Mr. Swinburne, and other modern travellers, London 1788, https://books.google.it/books?id=9hYIAAAAQAAJ&pg=PA142&dq=intitle:The+present+state+of+Sicily+and+Malta+1788&as_brr=1&hl=de&source=gbs_toc_r&cad=3#v=onepage&q&f=false [accessed 5 August 2020].

Toll, Zoned American, 1969
Toll, Seymour I., *Zoned American*, New York 1969.

Tönnesmann, Paris ist tot, 1993
Tönnesmann, Andreas, Paris ist tot – es lebe Paris! Le Corbusier und seine Stadt, in: Beyer, Andreas/Lampugnani, Vittorio/Schweikhart, Gunter, eds, *Hülle und Fülle. Festschrift für Tilmann Buddensieg*, Alfter 1993, pp. 585–603.

Troisi, Schools adopt monuments, 1998
Troisi, Sergio, Schools adopt monuments in Palermo, in: Council of Europe, ed., *Cultural Heritage and Its Educational Implications: A Factor for Tolerance, Good Citizenship and Social Integration – Seminar Proceedings* (Cultural Heritage 36), Strasbourg 1998, pp. 51–53.

Tuzet, La Sicile au XVIIIe siècle, 1955
Tuzet, Hélène, *La Sicile au XVIIIe siècle vue par les voyageurs étrangers*, Strasbourg 1955.

US-Supreme Court, United States Reports, 1955
US-Supreme Court, *United States Reports: Cases Adjudged in the Supreme Court at October Term, 1954*, vol. 348, Washington 1955, https://tile.loc.gov/storage-services/service/ll/usrep/usrep348/usrep348026/usrep348026.pdf [accessed 18 March 2021].

Venturi/Brown/Izenour, Learning from Las Vegas, 1972
Venturi, Robert/Brown, Denise S./Izenour, Steven, *Learning from Las Vegas*, Cambridge 1972.

Vinken, Die künstlerische Entdeckung, 2001
Vinken, Gerhard, Die künstlerische Entdeckung der Mark. Schinkel – Blechen – Wegener – Fontane, in: Haus der Brandenburgisch-Preußischen Geschichte, ed., *Marksteine. Eine Entdeckungsreise durch Brandenburg-Preußen* (exhibition catalogue), Berlin 2001, pp. 337–350.

Vinken, Die neuen Ränder, 2005
Vinken, Gerhard, Die neuen Ränder der alten Stadt. Modernisierung und 'Altstadt-Konstruktion' im gründerzeitlichen Basel, in: Lampugnani, Vittorio M./Noell, Matthias, eds, *Stadtformen. Die Architektur der Stadt zwischen Imagination und Konstruktion*, Zurich 2005, pp. 130–141.

Vinken, Gegenbild, 2006
Vinken, Gerhard, Gegenbild – Traditionsinsel – Sonderzone. Altstadt im modernen Städtebau, in: Scheurmann, Ingrid/Meier, Hans-Rudolf, eds, *Echt – alt – schön – wahr. Zeitschichten der Denkmalpflege*, Berlin/Munich 2006, pp. 190–201.

Vinken, Sonderzone Heimat, 2006
Vinken, Gerhard, Sonderzone Heimat. Altstadt im modernen Städtebau, in: Schwarte, Ludger, ed., *Auszug aus dem Lager. Zur Überwindung des modernen Raumparadigmas in der politischen Philosophie*, Bielefeld 2007, pp. 285–294.

Vinken, Ort und Bahn, 2008
Vinken, Gerhard, Ort und Bahn. Die Räume der modernen Stadt bei Le Corbusier und Rudolf Schwarz, in: Jöchner, Cornelia, ed., *Räume der Stadt. Von der Antike bis heute*, Berlin 2008, pp.147–164.

Vinken, Patrimônio Cultural e Globalização, 2010
Vinken, Gerhard, Patrimônio Cultural e Globalização. Espaços Urbanos Históricos entre a Mercantilização e a Articulação do Típico [Kulturerbe und Globalisierung. Historische Stadträume zwischen Marktförmigkeit und Artikulation des Eigenen], in: *Salvador-Hamburgo – Passado e Presente da Globalização*, Salvador 2010, pp. 120–130.

Vinken, Zone Heimat, 2010
Vinken, Gerhard, *Zone Heimat. Altstadt im modernen Städtebau*, Munich/Berlin 2010.

Vinken, Freistellen, 2011
Vinken, Gerhard, Freistellen – Rahmen – Zonieren. Räume und Raumtheorie in der Denkmalpflege, in: Alpsancar, Suzana/Gehring, Petra/Rölli, Marc, eds, *Raumprobleme – Philosophische Perspektiven*, Munich 2011, pp. 161–180.

Vinken, Lokale Sinnstiftung, 2011
Vinken, Gerhard, Lokale Sinnstiftung – Die Bedeutung der Denkmale, in: Löw, Martina/Terizakis, Georgios, eds, *Städte und ihre Eigenlogik. Ein Handbuch für Stadtplanung und Stadtentwicklung* (Interdisziplinäre Stadtforschung 11), Frankfurt a.M./New York 2011, pp. 73–82.

Vinken, Kampf um die Mitte, 2011
Vinken, Gerhard, Wiederaufbau als "Kampf um die Mitte". Stadtplanung zwischen technischer Erneuerung und Kontinuitätsversprechen, in: Franz, Birgit/Meier, Hans-Rudolf, eds, *Stadtplanung nach 1945 – Zerstörung und Wiederaufbau* (Arbeitshefte des AK Theorie und Lehre der Denkmalpflege e.V. 20), Holzminden 2011, pp. 14–21.

Vinken, Reproducing the City, 2012
Vinken, Gerhard, Reproducing the City? Heritage and *Eigenlogik*, in: *Urban Research & Practice*, 5/3 2012, pp. 325–334.

Vinken, Unstillbarer Hunger, 2013
Vinken, Gerhard, Unstillbarer Hunger nach Echtem. Frankfurts neue Altstadt zwischen Rekonstruktion und Themenarchitektur, in: *Forum Stadt. Zeitschrift für Stadtgeschichte, Stadtsoziologie, Denkmalpflege und Stadtentwicklung*, 40/2 2013, pp. 119–136.

Vinken, Amt und Gesellschaft, 2014
Vinken, Gerhard, Amt und Gesellschaft. Bewertungsfragen in der Denkmalpflege / The State Office and Society at Large. Questions of Value Assessment in Heritage Conservation, in: Franz, Birgit/Vinken, Gerhard, eds, *Denkmale – Werte – Bewertung. Denkmalpflege im Spannungsfeld von Fachinstitution und bürgerschaftlichem Engagement / Monuments – Values – Assessment. Heritage conservation between professional institutions and popular engagement* (Arbeitshefte des AK Theorie und Lehre der Denkmalpflege e.V. 23), Holzminden 2014, pp. 18–28.

Vinken, Das Erbe der Anderen, 2015
Vinken, Gerhard, ed., *Das Erbe der Anderen. Denkmalpflegerisches Handeln im Zeichen der Globalisierung / The Heritage of the Other. Conservation Considerations in an Age of Globalization* (Forschungen des Instituts für Archäologische Wissenschaften, Denkmalwissenschaften und Kunstgeschichte 2), Bamberg 2015.

Vinken, Pranger von Bahia, 2015
Vinken, Gerhard, Der Pranger von Bahia, das Kreuz von Pommersfelden. Globalisierungsdiskurse und lokale Aushandlungsprozesse als Herausforderungen für die Denkmalwissenschaften, in: Vinken, Gerhard, ed., *Das Erbe der Anderen. Denkmalpflegerisches Handeln im Zeichen der Globalisierung / The Heritage of the Other. Conservation Considerations in an Age of Globalization* (Forschungen des Instituts für Archäologische Wissenschaften, Denkmalwissenschaften und Kunstgeschichte 2), Bamberg 2015, pp. 19–30, https://fis.uni-bamberg.de/handle/uniba/21817 [accessed 30 January 2021].

Vinken, Gefühlssache, 2016
Vinken, Gerhard, Gefühlssache. In der Ferne so nah: Heinrich Heine in der Bronx. Hans-Rudolf Meier zum 60. Geburtstag, in: Franz, Birgit/Scheurmann, Ingrid, eds, *Strukturwandel – Denkmalwandel. Umbau, Umnutzung, Umdeutung. Städtische und ländliche Räume unter Umnutzungsdruck* (Veröffentlichung des Arbeitskreises Theorie und Lehre der Denkmalpflege e.V. 25), Holzminden 2016, pp. 16–18.

Vinken, Im Namen der Altstadt, 2016
Vinken, Gerhard, Im Namen der Altstadt. Stadtplanung zwischen Modernisierung und Identitätspolitik. Einführung in eine wechselhafte Geschichte, in: Enss, Carmen M./Vinken, Gerhard, eds, *Produkt Altstadt. Historische Stadtzentren in Städtebau und Denkmalpflege*, Bielefeld 2016, pp. 9–26.

Vinken, Neue Heimat or Constructing the Old Town, 2016
Vinken, Gerhard, Neue Heimat or Constructing the Old Town. The Example of Cologne, 1930–1960, in: *Studies in Urban Humanities*, 8/1 2016, pp. 67–95.

Vinken, Erbe ist kein Dokument, 2017
Vinken, Gerhard, Erbe ist kein Dokument. Berlin zwischen Ruin und Restauration, in: *Österreichische Zeitschrift für Kunst und Denkmalpflege*, 71 2/3 2017, pp. 156–161.

Vinken, Escaping Modernity, 2017
Vinken, Gerhard, Escaping Modernity? Civic Protest, the Preservation Movement and the Reinvention of the Old Town in Germany since the 1960s, in: Baumeister, Martin/Bonomo, Bruno/Schott, Dieter, eds, *Cities Contested. Urban Politics, Heritage, and Social Movements in Italy and West Germany in the 1970s*, Frankfurt a.M./New York 2017, pp. 169–191.

Vinken, Vorbild Amerika, 2017
Vinken, Gerhard, Vorbild Amerika? 'Historic Districts' und städtebauliche Denkmalpflege in den USA, in: *Forum Stadt. Zeitschrift für Stadtgeschichte, Stadtsoziologie, Denkmalpflege und Stadtentwicklung*, 44/3 2017, pp. 251–270.

Vinken, Geschichte wird gemacht, 2018
Vinken, Gerhard, Geschichte wird gemacht – es geht voran? Die neue Frankfurter Altstadt ist so banal wie fatal, in: Sturm, Philipp/Schmal, Peter C., eds, *Die immer Neue Altstadt. Bauen zwischen Dom und Römer seit 1900* (exhibition catalogue), Berlin 2018, pp. 160–167.

Vinken, From Monument to Heritage, 2018
Vinken, Gerhard, Vom Denkmal zum Erbe. Ein Plädoyer / From Monument to Heritage: An Appeal, in: Bogner, Simone, et al., eds, *Denkmal – Erbe – Heritage. Begriffshorizonte am Beispiel der Industriekultur / Monument – Patrimony – Heritage. Industrial Heritage and the Horizons of Terminology* (Veröffentlichung des Arbeitskreises Theorie und Lehre der Denkmalpflege e.V. 27), Holzminden 2018, pp. 238–241, https://doi.org/10.11588/arthistoricum.374.531 [accessed 28 June 2019].

Vinken, Vom Kampf gegen Riesen, 2018
Vinken, Gerhard, Vom Kampf gegen Riesen – und von deren Zähmung. Denkmalpflege und moderne Großstrukturen, in: Utku, Yasemin, et al., eds, *Im großen Maßstab: Riesen in der Stadt* (Beiträge zur städtebaulichen Denkmalpflege 7), Essen 2018, pp. 14–27.

Vinken, Altstadtkonjunktur und Modernefeindlichkeit, 2020
Vinken, Gerhard, Altstadtkonjunktur und Modernefeindlichkeit. Häuserkampf, Bürgerbewegung und städtische Denkmalpflege seit den 1960er Jahren, in: Brassat, Wolfgang, ed., *Komplexität und Diversität des kulturellen Erbes* (Forschungen des Instituts für Archäologische Wissenschaften, Denkmalwissenschaften und Kunstgeschichte 10), Bamberg 2020, pp. 153–168.

Vinken, Räume des Denkmals, 2020
Vinken, Gerhard, Die Räume des Denkmals. 'Bildmacht' als Ergebnis räumlicher Praktiken, in: Hesberg, Henner von/Kunow, Jürgen/Otten, Thomas, eds, *Die Bildmacht des Denkmals – Ikonisierung und Erleben archäologischer Denkmäler im Stadtbild* (Schriftenreihe des Arbeitskreises Bodendenkmäler der Fritz Thyssen Stiftung 5), Regensburg 2020, pp. 145-157.

Vinken, Palermo oder Überleben, 2020
Vinken, Gerhard, Palermo oder Überleben als Erinnern, in: Kren, Reinhard/Leisch-Kiesl, Monika, eds, *Kultur – Erbe – Ethik. "Heritage" im Wandel gesellschaftlicher Orientierungen. Festschrift für Wilfried Lipp* (Linzer Beiträge zur Kunstwissenschaft und Philosophie 12), Bielefeld 2020, pp. 349–361.

Vinken, Erbe und Emotionen, forthcoming 2021
Vinken, Gerhard, Erbe und Emotionen. Zur überfälligen Re-Politisierung der Denkmalpflege, in: Herold, Stephanie/Vinken, Gerhard, eds, *Denkmal_Emotion. Mobilisierung, Bindung, Verführung* (Veröffentlichung des Arbeitskreises Theorie und Lehre der Denkmalpflege e.V. 30), forthcoming 2021.

Viollet-le-Duc, On Restoration, 1875
Viollet-le-Duc, Eugène-Emmanuel, *On Restoration* (original title : Dictionnaire raisonné de l'architecture française du XIe au XVIe siècle, vol. 8, 1875), London 1875.

Vogts, Die Kölner Altstadtgesundung, 1938
Vogts, Hans, Die Kölner Altstadtgesundung als Aufgabe der Denkmalpflege, in: *Rheinische Heimatpflege. Zeitschrift für Rheinische Heimatpflege*, 10/1938, pp. 432–466.

Vogts, Betrifft Wiederaufbau, 1943
Vogts, Hans, *Betrifft Wiederaufbau Köln*, 10 August 1943 (Historical Archive of the City of Cologne/Historisches Archiv der Stadt Köln, Acc 229/426).

Vogts, Gesundungsmaßnahmen, 1997 (1936)
Vogts, Hans, Gesundungsmaßnahmen im Kölner Rheinviertel (1936), reprinted in: *Köln – 85 Jahre Denkmalschutz und Denkmalpflege* (Stadtspuren – Denkmäler in Köln 9), vol. 1: Texte von 1912–1976, Cologne 1997, pp. 170–180.

Vogts, Gesundungsmaßnahmen, 1998 (1935)
Vogts, Hans, Gesundungsmaßnahmen für das Kölner Rheinviertel (1935), reprinted in: *Köln – 85 Jahre Denkmalschutz und Denkmalpflege* (Stadtspuren – Denkmäler in Köln 9), vol. 2: Texte von 1980–1997, Cologne 1998, pp. 580–607.

Wackenroder/Tieck, Outpourings, 1975 (1797)
Wackenroder, Wilhelm H./Tieck, Ludwig, *Outpourings of an Art-Loving Friar* (original title: Herzensergiessungen eines kunstliebenden Klosterbruders, 1797), translated by E. Morin, New York 1975.

Warnke, Bau und Überbau, 1984
Warnke, Martin, *Bau und Überbau: Soziologie der mittelalterlichen Architektur nach den Schriftquellen*, Frankfurt a.M. 1984.

Warnke, Natur nach dem Fall, 1994
Warnke, Martin, Natur nach dem Fall der Mauern, in: *Dialektik. Enzyklopädische Zeitschrift für Philosophie und Wissenschaft*, 2/1994, pp. 29–34.

Wesenberg, Nationalgalerie Berlin, 2001
Wesenberg, Angelika, ed., *Nationalgalerie Berlin. Das XIX. Jahrhundert. Katalog der ausgestellten Werke* (collection catalogue), Leipzig 2001.

Wetzsteon, Republic of Dreams, 2002
Wetzsteon, Ross, *Republic of Dreams. Greenwich Village: The American Bohemia, 1910–1960*, New York 2002.

Weyeneth, Historic Preservation for a Living City, 2000
Weyeneth, Robert R., *Historic Preservation for a Living City: Historic Charleston Foundation, 1947–1997*, Columbia 2000.

Whalen, A City Destroying Itself, 1965
Whalen, Richard J., *A City destroying itself: an angry view of New York*, New York 1965.

Wiktorin, Der historische Atlas Köln, 2001
Wiktorin, Dorothea, et al., eds, *Der historische Atlas Köln: 2000 Jahre Stadtgeschichte in Karten und Bildern*, Cologne 2001.

Willer, Kulturelles Erbe, 2013
Willer, Stefan, Kulturelles Erbe. Tradieren und Konservieren in der Moderne, in: Willer, Stefan/Weigel, Sigrid/Jussen, Berhard, eds, *Erbe. Übertragungskonzepte zwischen Natur und Kultur*, Berlin 2013, pp. 160–201.

Willer/Weigel/Jussen, Übertragungskonzepte, 2013
Willer, Stefan/Weigel, Sigrid/Jussen, Berhard, eds, *Erbe. Übertragungskonzepte zwischen Natur und Kultur*, Berlin 2013.

Winckelmann, Anmerkungen über die Baukunst, 1968 (1759)
Winckelmann, Johann J., Anmerkungen über die Baukunst der alten Tempel in Girgenti in Sicilien (1759), reprinted in: Rehm, Walther, ed., *Johann Joachim Winckelmann. Kleine Schriften: Vorreden, Entwürfe*, Berlin 1968, pp. 174–185.

Wohlleben, Theoretische Grundlagen, 1999
Wohlleben, Marion, Theoretische Grundlagen zum Substanzbegriff in der Denkmalpflege, in: Hammerschmidt, Valentin, ed., *Dokumente und Monumente. Positionsbestimmungen in der Denkmalpflege* (Veröffentlichung des Arbeitskreises Theorie und Lehre der Denkmalpflege e.V. 10), Dresden 1999, pp. 53–58.

Wohlleben, Gibt es ein neues Verständnis, 2014
Wohlleben, Marion, Gibt es ein neues Verständnis vom Denkmal? Überlegungen zum aktuellen Denkmalbegriff / Has Our Understanding of the Monument Changed? Thoughts on the current concept and definition, in: Franz, Birgit/Vinken, Gerhard, eds, *Denkmale – Werte – Bewertung. Denkmalpflege im Spannungsfeld von Fachinstitution und bürgerschaftlichem Engagement / Monuments – Values – Assessment. Heritage conservation between professional institutions and popular engagement* (Arbeitshefte des AK Theorie und Lehre der Denkmalpflege e.V. 23), Holzminden 2014, pp. 28–36.

Wolf, Monarchen als religiöse Repräsentanten, 2004
Wolf, Christiane, Monarchen als religiöse Repräsentanten der Nation um 1900? Kaiser Wilhelm II., Königin Viktoria und Kaiser Franz-Joseph im Vergleich, in: Haupt, Heinz-Gerhard/Langewiesche, Dieter, eds, *Nation und Religion in Europa. Mehrkonfessionelle Gesellschaften im 19. und 20. Jahrhundert*, Frankfurt a.M./New York 2004, pp. 154–160.

Wood, Preserving New York, 2008
Wood, Anthony C., *Preserving New York: Winning the Right to Protect a City's Landmarks*, New York 2008.

Wuthenow, Die erfahrene Welt, 1980
Wuthenow, Ralph-Rainer, *Die erfahrene Welt: europäische Reiseliteratur im Zeitalter der Aufklärung*, Frankfurt a.M. 1980.

Wyss, Basler Spuren, 1987
Wyss, Alfred, Basler Spuren zum Thema, in: *Bauen in historisch wertvollen Bereichen – Kontinuität und Wagnis. ICOMOS-Kolloquium 86 vom 25. und 26. September 1986 in Basel*, Basel 1987, n.p.

Wyss, Denkmalpflege in Basel, 1988
Wyss, Alfred, Denkmalpflege in Basel 1988. Zum 75jährigen Bestehen der Freiwilligen Basler Denkmalpflege, in: *Freiwillige Basler Denkmalpflege 1984–87*, 1988, pp. 23–37.

Zapperi, Vito Maria Amico, 1960
Zapperi, Roberto, Amico, Vito Maria, in: *Dizionario Biografico degli Italiani*, vol. 2, 1960, http://www.treccani.it/enciclopedia/vito-maria-amico_(Dizionario-Biografico)/ [accessed 17 August 2020].

Zern, Die Entdeckung Siziliens, 2014
Zern, Rubina, *Die Entdeckung Siziliens. Ansichten deutscher Reisender zwischen 18. und 20. Jahrhundert*, Würzburg 2014.

Zilcosky, Learning How to Get Lost, 2017
Zilcosky, John, Learning How to Get Lost. Goethe in Italy, in: *Eighteenth-century studies*, 50/4 2017, pp. 417–435.

Zinn, A People's History, 1980
Zinn, Howard, *A People's History of the United States*, New York 1980.

Zinzendorf, Mémoire, 1773 (1766)
Zinzendorf, Karl von, *Mémoire sur le Royaume de Sicile* (1766), Appendix to: Riedesel, Johann H., *Voyage en Sicile et dans la Grande Grèce adressé par l'auteur à son ami Mr. Winckelmann, traduit de l'Allemand, accompagné de notes du traducteur et d'autres additions intéres-*

santes, Lausanne 1773, pp. 267–349, https://www.e-rara.ch/zuz/doi/10.3931/e-rara-3438 6 [accessed 15 August 2020].

Zukin, Naked City, 2009
Zukin, Sharon, *Naked City. The Death and Life of Authentic Urban Places*, Oxford 2009.

Websites

Website Administrative Code of the City of New York
Website *Administrative Code of the City of New York*, Title 25: Land Use, Chapter 3: Landmarks Preservation and Historic Districts, Sect. 25-301 – 25-322, http://ny.elaws.us/law/adc_t25_ch3 [accessed 18 May 2020].

Website Alte Stadt aus neuen Häusern
Website *Alte Stadt aus neuen Häusern. Ein Projekt von Sarah Bonnert*, http://aufbruch-abbruch.de/ [accessed 3 June 2020].

Website AltstadtForum Frankfurt
Website *AltstadtForum. Für den Wiederaufbau der historischen Mitte Frankfurts*, http://www.altstadtforum-frankfurt.de [accessed 15 January 2013].

Website American Planning Association, Jackson Square
Website *American Planning Association*, Jackson Square: New Orleans, Louisiana, https://www.planning.org/greatplaces/spaces/2012/jacksonsquare.htm [accessed 25 October 2020].

Website Archives and Special Collections Library
Website *Archives and Special Collections Library*, With Heritage so Rich: Report of Special Committee on Historic Preservation (1966), http://abacus.bates.edu/muskie-archives/ajcr/1966/Heritage%20so%20Rich.shtml [accessed 12 October 2016].

Website Backstreet Cultural Museum
Website *Backstreet Cultural Museum*, https://www.backstreetmuseum.org/ [accessed 20 October 2020].

Website Berliner Dom, Drittes Reich
Website *Berliner Dom*, Drittes Reich, https://www.berlinerdom.de/besuchen-wissen/ueber-den-dom/drittes-reich/ [accessed 9 April 2020].

Website City of New Orleans, HDLC: Bywater Historic District
Website *City of New Orleans*, Historic District Landmarks Commission (HDLC): Bywater Historic District, https://nola.gov/nola/media/HDLC/Historic%20Districts/Bywater.pdf [accessed 14 January 2021].

Website Curbed New York, Hepburn's Turtle Bay House
Website *Curbed New York*, Katharine Hepburn's Turtle Bay House for Rent at $27.5K/Month, Sara Polsky, 31 August 2010, https://ny.curbed.com/2010/8/31/10505200/katharine-hepburns-turtle-bay-house-for-rent-at-27-5k-month [accessed 18 May 2020].

Website DomRömer Frankfurt
Website *DomRömer Frankfurt*, https://www.domroemer.de/english-information [accessed 3 June 2020].

Website DomRömer Frankfurt, marketing trailer
Website *DomRömer Frankfurt*, marketing trailer, https://www.domroemer.de/der-film [accessed 3 June 2020].

Website Düsseldorf Blog, Ein Schuss Achterbahn
Website *Düsseldorf Blog*, Ein Schuss Achterbahn, 24 February 2013, http://www.duesseldorf-blog.de/2013/02/24/ein-schuss-achterbahn/ [accessed 25 February 2020].

Website Freunde Frankfurts
Website *Freunde Frankfurts*, http://www.freunde-frankfurts.de/projekte/altstadt.html [accessed 3 June 2020].

Website Governo da Bahia/Secretaria da Cultura e Turismo
Website *Governo da Bahia / Secretaria da Cultura e Turismo*, Resultados recenteese metas do turismo baiano 2001–2020 (2007), http://www.sct.ba.gov.br/estaticticas/tabela33.asp [accessed 30 March 2014].

Website Greenwich Village Society for Preservation
Website *Greenwich Village Society for Preservation*, http://www.gvshp.org/_gvshp/about/index.htm [accessed 2 March 2016].

Website HDLC, Historic District Maps
Website *Historic District Landmarks Commission (HDLC)*, Historic District Maps and Location Information, https://nola.gov/hdlc/map/ [accessed 25 October 2020].

Website House of Dance and Feathers
Website *House of Dance and Feathers*, http://houseofdanceandfeathers.org/ [accessed 20 October 2020].

Website House of Dance and Feathers, Marching Cultures
Website *House of Dance and Feathers*, Marching Cultures, http://houseofdanceandfeathers.org/marchingcultureneworleans/socialaidandpleasureclubs/ [accessed 20 October 2020].

Website La Repubblica Palermo, slideshow
Website La *Repubblica Palermo*, slideshow: La festa in piazza Magione, https://palermo.repubblica.it/cronaca/2013/05/23/foto/23_maggio_la_festa_in_piazza_magione-59448979/1/#1 [accessed 28 June 2019].

Website Le Musée de f.p.c.
Website *Le Musée de f.p.c.*, https://www.lemuseedefpc.com/ [accessed 13 January 2021].

Website LonelyPlanet, New Orleans
Website *LonelyPlanet*, New Orleans, Sights, https://www.lonelyplanet.com/usa/new-orleans/in-location/sights/a/nar/1a1f87e3-fc05-4351-bf6d-772e9e33db14/362207 [accessed 13 January 2021].

Website Louisiana Digital Library, The Ninths Ward's Tribute
Website *Louisiana Digital Library*, The Ninths Ward's Tribute to Men in Service in the World War, https://louisianadigitallibrary.org/islandora/object/hnoc-p15140coll1:935 [accessed 25 October 2020].

Website LouisianaTravel, African American Heritage Trail
Website *LouisianaTravel*, African American Heritage Trail, https://www.louisianatravel.com/african-american-heritage-trail [accessed 13 January 2021].

Website Matador Network, To see the best art and architecture
Website *Matador Network*, To see the best art and architecture in Tashkent, ride the subway, Angelo Zinna, 31 May 2019, https://matadornetwork.com/read/best-architecture-tashkent-subway-uzbekistan/ [accessed 25 June 2020].

Website National Park Service, List of National Historic Landmarks
Website *National Park Service*, List of National Historic Landmarks by State, https://www.nps.gov/subjects/nationalhistoriclandmarks/list-of-nhls-by-state.htm#onthisPage-18 [accessed 13 January 2021].

Website National Park Service, NHL nomination for Jackson Square
Website *National Park Service*, NHL nomination for Jackson Square, https://npgallery.nps.gov/NRHP/GetAsset/NRHP/66000375_text [accessed 25 October 2020].

Website NOAAM, History
Website *New Orleans African American Museum (NOAAM)*, History, https://www.noaam.org/history [accessed 13 January 2021].

Website New York City's Historic Districts Council
Website *New York City's Historic Districts Council (HDC)*, https://hdc.org/ [accessed 17 May 2020].

Website Obits, Sylvester Francis
Website *Obits*, Sylvester Francis, https://obits.nola.com/obituaries/nola/obituary.aspx?n=sylvester-francis&pid=196760804&fhid=4524 [accessed 13 January 2021].

Website RootsWeb, The Victory Arch in Macarty Square
Website *RootsWeb*, The Victory Arch in Macarty Square, New Orleans, Louisiana, http://freepages.rootsweb.com/~neworleans/military/ [accessed 25 October 2020].

Website RootsWeb, To Commemorate Services of Men who served in War
Website *RootsWeb*, To Commemorate Services of Men who served in War, http://freepages.rootsweb.com/~neworleans/military/victory_arch/1919_news_article.html [accessed 25 October 2020].

Website Scouting New York, Sylvan Terrace
Website *Scouting New York*, Sylvan Terrace: A hidden Gem in Washington Heights, 7 September 2011, http://www.scoutingny.com/a-hidden-treasure-in-washington-heights/ [accessed 1 October 2016].

Website ShortsblogBerlinale, An Interview with Michal Pietrzyk
Website *ShortsblogBerlinale*, An Interview with Michal Pietrzyk about "All on a Mardi Gras Day", 27 February 2019, https://shortsblog.berlinale.de/2019/02/27/4049/ [accessed 25 October 2020].

Website Spolien der Frankfurter Altstadt
Website *Spolien der Frankfurter Altstadt*, Stadtplanungsamt Stadt Frankfurt am Main, https://web.archive.org/web/20140407104042/http://www.frankfurter-spolien.de/ [accessed 3 May 2020].

Website Stadtplanungsamt Frankfurt am Main, Dom-Römer-Areal
Website *Stadtplanungsamt Frankfurt am Main*, Dom-Römer-Areal. Urban revitalization of the Dom-Römer complex, https://www.stadtplanungsamt-frankfurt.de/dom_r_mer_areal_5208.html?langfront=en [accessed 10 July 2020].

Website Stadtplanungsamt Frankfurt am Main, Leitlinien für die Gestaltung
Website *Stadtplanungsamt Frankfurt am Main*, Leitlinien für die Gestaltung, http://www.stadtplanungsamt-frankfurt.de/show.php?ID=5638&psid [accessed 15 January 2013].

Website TakeEmDownNOLA, Past Actions
Website *TakeEmDownNOLA*, Past Actions, http://takeemdownnola.org/actions [accessed 20 October 2020].

Website TakeEmDownNOLA, The Symbols
Website *TakeEmDownNOLA*, The Symbols, http://takeemdownnola.org/symbols [accessed 13 January 2021].

Website The Bronx Ink, Lorelei Fountain
Website *The Bronx Ink*, Lorelei Fountain survived wars and valdals, Rani Molla, 24 November 2011, http://bronxink.org/2011/11/24/20101-lorelei-fountain-survived-wars-and-vandals/ [accessed 5 March 2016].

Website The New York Preservation Archive Project, 1961 New York Zoning Resolution
Website *The New York Preservation Archive Project*, 1961 New York Zoning Resolution, http://www.nypap.org/preservation-history/1961-new-york-city-zoning-resolution/ [accessed 15 May 2020].

Website The New York Preservation Archive Project, New York City Landmarks Law
Website *The New York Preservation Archive Project*, New York City Landmarks Law, http://www.nypap.org/preservation-history/new-york-city-landmarks-law/ [accessed 15 May 2020].

Website UNESCO, Arab-Norman Palermo
Website *UNESCO*, Arab-Norman Palermo and the Cathedral Churches of Cefalú and Monreale, https://whc.unesco.org/en/list/1487 [accessed 11 August 2020].

Website UNESCO, Convention Concerning the Protection
Website *UNESCO*, Convention concerning the Protection of the World Cultural and Natural Heritage (1972), http://portal.unesco.org/en/ev.php-URL_ID=13055&URL_DO=DO_TOPIC&URL_SECTION=201.html [accessed 30 May 2020].

Website UNESCO, Historic Centre of Salvador de Bahia
Website *UNESCO*, Historic Centre of Salvador de Bahia, http://whc.unesco.org/en/list/309 [accessed 30 May 2020].

Website Uzbek Travel, About Uzbekistan
Website *Uzbek Travel*, About Uzbekistan: The life in Uzbeka mahalla, 7 December 2017, http://uzbek-travel.com/about-uzbekistan/facts/uzbek_mahalla/ [accessed 25 June 2020].

Website Wikimedia Commons, Virtuelles Altstadtmodell Frankfurt am Main
Website *Wikimedia Commons*, Virtuelles Altstadtmodell Frankfurt am Main, https://commons.wikimedia.org/wiki/Category:Virtuelles_Altstadtmodell_Frankfurt_am_Main?uselang=de [accessed 3 June 2020].

Website Wikipedia, Equestrian statue of Andrew Jackson
Website *Wikipedia*, Equestrian statue of Andrew Jackson (Washinton, D.C.), https://en.wikipedia.org/wiki/Equestrian_statue_of_Andrew_Jackson_(Washington,_D.C.) [accessed 13 January 2021].

Website Wikipedia, Greenwich Village
Website *Wikipedia*, Greenwich Village, https://en.wikipedia.org/wiki/Greenwich_Village [accessed 15 May 2020].

Website Wikipedia, Jumel Terrace Historic District
Website *Wikipedia*, Jumel Terrace Historic District, https://en.wikipedia.org/wiki/Jumel_Terrace_Historic_District [accessed 15 May 2020].

Website Wikipedia, List of World Heritage Sites in Uzbekistan
Website *Wikipedia*, List of World Heritage Sites in Uzbekistan, https://en.wikipedia.org/wiki/List_of_World_Heritage_Sites_in_Uzbekistan [accessed 25 June 2020].

Website Wikipedia, National Register of Historic Places
Website *Wikipedia*, National Register of Historic Places listings in Orleans Parish, Louisiana, https://en.wikipedia.org/wiki/National_Register_of_Historic_Places_listings_in_Orleans_Parish,_Louisiana [accessed 13 January 2021].

Website YouTube, Building for the Future, marketing trailer UKIP
Website *YouTube*, Building for the Future. Learning from the Past, marketing trailer of the UK Independence Party – UKIP 2012, https://www.youtube.com/watch?app=desktop&v=L0EkIahdooM&feature=youtu.be [accessed 24 January 2021].

Illustration Credits

Chapter 2

Figs 1–6: Willy Boesiger and Hans Girsberger, *Le Corbusier 1910–65*, Basel, Boston, and Berlin 1999

Figs 7, 8, 11: Rudolf Schwarz, *Das neue Köln. Ein Vorentwurf*, ed. by the City of Cologne, Cologne 1950, pp. 3-64

Figs 9, 10: Rudolf Schwarz, *Von der Bebauung der Erde*, Heidelberg 1949

Fig. 12: Robert Venturi, Denise Scott Brown, and Steven Izenour, *Learning from Las Vegas*, Cambridge, Mass. 1972

Chapter 4

Fig. 1: G. E. Franklin, *Palestine depicted and described with 350 illustrations*, 1911; https://de.wikipedia.org/wiki/Datei:Western_Wall_circa_1910.jpg [accessed 25 March 2019]

Fig. 2: ©Photo by EvgeniT, 2013; https://de.wikipedia.org/wiki/Datei:Klagemauer_Panorama.jpg [accessed 25 March 2019]

Fig. 3: ©Photo by Jérôme Blum, 2006; https://commons.wikimedia.org/wiki/File:Notre-Dame_de_Paris_2792x2911.jpg [accessed 25 March 2019]

Fig. 4: Le Corbusier, *The City of To morrow and its Planning*, Paris 1925

Fig. 5: ©Kupferstichkabinett. Staatliche Museen zu Berlin, SM 17b.2.

Fig. 6: ©Staatsarchiv Basel-Stadt, AL 45, 1-121-2.

Fig. 7: Le Corbusier, *Urbanisme* (Collection de L'Esprit Nouveau), 6th ed., Paris 1925

Fig. 8: ©Photo by Marius Moldovan, 2019

Chapter 5

Figs 1, 3–9: ©Photos by Johanna Blokker, 2014

Fig. 2: ©Photo by RyansWorld, 2009; https://en.wikipedia.org/wiki/Amir_Timur_Museum#/media/File:Timur_Lane_Museum,_Tashkent,_Uzbekistan.JPG [accessed 25 March 2021]

Fig. 10: ©Photo by Varandej, 2015 https://varandej.livejournal.com/757164.html [accessed 22 October 2015]

Chapter 6

Fig. 1: Augustus Welby Northmore Pugin, *Contrasts, or a Parallel Between the Noble Edifices of the Fourteenth and Fifteenth Centuries and similar buildings of the Present Day*, Salisbury 1836 (2nd Edition Leicester 1841)

Fig. 2: Jean Baptiste Arnout: Vue de Bâle. Pris au dessus de la gare du chemin de fer, Lithograph 1865 (©Staatsarchiv Basel-Stadt, BILD Wack. C 80)

Figs 3–5: ©Staatsarchiv Basel-Stadt, AL 45, 6-30-1; AL 45, 1-116-4; NEG 641

Figs 6–7: Arbeitsbeschaffungsbehörden des Kantons Basel, ed., *Altstadt heute und morgen. Ausstellung der projektierten Massnahmen für die Sanierung der Altstadt von Basel*, Kleines Klingental, 23. September – 31. Oktober 1945 (exhibition catalogue), Basel 1945

Fig. 8: Photo by Eidenbenz, 1962, ©Kantonale Denkmalpflege Basel-Stadt

Fig. 9: Photo by Hoffmann, ©Kantonale Denkmalpflege Basel-Stadt

Fig. 10, 11: ©Kantonale Denkmalpflege Basel-Stadt

Fig. 12: Photo by Peter Heman, 1957, ©Peter Röllin / Kantonale Denkmalpflege Basel-Stadt

Fig. 13: Photo by Eidenbenz, 1984, ©Kantonale Denkmalpflege Basel-Stadt

Chapter 7

Fig. 1: https://glassian.org/Prism/Gallery/NewYork/penn_station.html [accessed 20 March 2019]

Fig. 2: http://behindthescenes.nyhistory.org/shirley-hayes-and-the-battle-of-washington-square-park-1952-1959/ [accessed 20 March 2019]

Fig. 3: https://en.wikipedia.org/wiki/Jane_Jacobs [accessed 20 March 2019]

Fig. 4: ©Photo by imke.sta, 2017; https://www.flickr.com/photos/11264282@N02/38223335294/in/photostream/ [accessed 20 March 2019]

Fig. 5: ©Photo Beyond My Ken, 2011; https://commons.wikimedia.org/wiki/File:Haughwout_Building_from_south.jpg [accessed 20 March 2019]

Fig. 6: http://www.shorpy.com/node/9747?size=_original) [accessed 20 March 2019]

Fig. 7: http://occ123.com/id8.html [accessed 20 October 2016]

Fig. 8: ©Photo by Sailko, 2010; https://commons.wikimedia.org/wiki/File:NYC,_Sylvan_Terrace.JPG [accessed 20 March 2019]

Fig. 9: ©Photo by Sailko, 2017; https://en.wikipedia.org/wiki/Park_Place_Historic_District_(Brooklyn)#/media/File:Park_Place_Historic_District_651-75_Park_Place_Crown_Heights.jpg [accessed 20 March 2019]

Fig. 10: https://streeteasy.com/property/7882793-88-mac-dougal-street-th) [accessed 20 March 2019]

Chapter 8

Fig. 1: ©Photo by Michael Brix, ca. 1974

Fig. 2: ©Photo by Sebastian Suchanek, 2010

Fig. 3: ©Photo by Simsalabimbam, 2018; https://de.wikipedia.org/wiki/Neue_Frankfurter_Altstadt#/media/Datei:Dom-Roemer-Projekt-Huehnermarkt-06-2018-Ffm-Altstadt-10008-9.jpg [accessed 20 March 2019]

Fig. 4: ©Photo by Heinz Gräf, 1961/ ©Stadtarchiv Düsseldorf, No 034_370_001

Fig. 5: ©FSWLA Landschaftsarchitektur GmbH, Düsseldorf und Molestina Architekten Gesellschaft für Architektur GmbH, Köln/Madrid

Fig. 6: Le Corbusier, *Urbanisme* (Collection de L'Esprit Nouveau), 6th ed., Paris 1925

Fig. 7: Le Corbusier, *Précisions sur un état présent de l'architecture et de l'urbanisme. Avec un prologue américain, un corollaire brésilien. Suivi d'une température parisienne et d'une atmosphère muscovite*, Paris 1930

Fig. 8: ©Photo by Johann H. Addicks, 2006; https://de.wikipedia.org/wiki/Datei:Tausendf%C3%BC%C3%9Fler_D%C3%BCsseldorf,_Unterseite_s%C3%BCdliche_Abfahrten,_2006.jpg [accessed 26 March 2021]

Fig. 9: ©Photo by Perlgrau, 2013; https://commons.wikimedia.org/wiki/File:Tausendf%C3%BC%C3%9Fler-Abriss-D%C3%BCsseldorf,_7.April_2013-DSC01107_easyHDR-BASIC-2.jpg [accessed 26 march 2021]

Chapter 9

Fig. 1: Woodcut by Anton von Worms, 1531; https://de.wikipedia.org/wiki/Datei:Koeln-1531-holzschnitt-anton-von-worms_2-1200x680.jpg [accessed 26 March 2021]

Fig. 2: Photograph by August Sander: Rheinfront, Dom bis Sankt Martin, nach Kriegsende, 1946, in: Köln wie es war (Kölnisches Stadtmuseum; Photo://©Rheinisches Bildarchiv, rba_090893; www.kulturelles-erbe-koeln.de)

Fig. 3: *Köln 1945 - Zerstörung und Wiederaufbau*, Beiheft zur Ausstellung des Historischen Archivs der Stadt Köln, Cologne 1993

Fig. 4: Rudolf Schwarz, *Das neue Köln. Ein Vorentwurf*, ed. by the City of Cologne, Cologne 1950, pp. 3-64

Fig. 5: ©Photo Dr. Mann, Stadt Köln, Archiv Konservator. Hans Vogts, Gesundungsmaßnahmen im Kölner Rheinviertel (1936), wiederabgedruckt in *Köln – 85 Jahre Denkmalschutz und Denkmalpflege 1912-1997*, voll. I-II, Cologne 1997/98, I, pp. 170-180 (*Stadtspuren*, voll. 9.1, *Denkmäler in Köln., Texte von 1912-1976*)

Fig. 6: Adenauer, Hanna, Die Pflege der profanen Denkmäler in Köln, in: Rheinischer Verein für Denkmalpflege und Heimatschutz, ed., *Die Heimat lebt – Vermächtnis und Verpflichtung*, Neuß 1955/1956, pp. 159–173

Fig. 7: ©Stadt Köln, Archiv Konservator. Erik Roth, Um die Vorstellung des alten heiligen Köln wach zu halten. Das Kölner Rheinviertel – Sanierung und Wiederaufbau 1900-1956, in: *Köln – 85 Jahre Denkmalschutz und Denkmalpflege 1912-1995*, voll. I-II, Cologne, Köln 1997/98, II, pp. 580-607

Fig. 8: B. Funck, *Wilhelm Riphahn in Köln. Eine Bestandsaufnahme*, Cologne 2004, 278

Fig. 9: Hans Vogts: Die Kölner Altstadtgesundung als Aufgabe der Denkmalpflege, in: *Rheinische Heimatpflege. Zeitschrift für Rheinische Heimatpflege* 10/1938, S. 432 – 466 (zugleich: Denkmalpflege in der Stadt. Jahrbuch der Rheinischen Denkmalpflege 16/1939)

Fig. 10: *Der historische Atlas Köln. 2000 Jahre Stadtgeschichte in Karten und Bildern*, ed. Dorothea Wiktorin a. o., Cologne 2003

Fig. 11: U. v. Petz, *Stadtsanierung im Dritten Reich*, IRPUD, Dortmund 1987, pp. 135-66 (Dortmunder Beiträge zur Raumplanung, voll. 45)

Chapter 10

Figs 1–2: ©Photos by Gerhard Vinken, 2020
Fig. 3: ©Photo by Manfred Brückels, 2010; https://commons.wikimedia.org/wiki/File:Schinkelplatz_Berlin_1.jpg
Fig. 4: ©Photo by picture-alliance/Tagesspiegel | Kitty Kleist-Heinrich TSP, 2015
Fig. 5: ©Franco Stella; http://www.architektur-urbanistik.berlin/index.php?threads/stadtschloss-humboldtforum.30/ [accessed 1 November 2016]
Fig. 6: ©Photo by picture-alliance/ dpa | Reinhard Kaufhold, 1979
Fig. 7: ©Photo by picture-alliance / dpa | Arno Burgi, 2008

Chapter 11

Figs 1–7: ©Photos by Gerhard Vinken, 2019

Chapter 12

Figs 1, 4: ©DomRömerGmbH
Figs 2, 5, 6, 10: ©Gerhard Vinken, 2019
Fig. 3: ©Photo by Sarah Bonnert, 2011
Fig. 7: ©KPS Architekten Engel / Zimmermann)
Figs 8, 9: ©HHVISON, DomRömerGmbH
Fig. 11: ©Photo by Richard Dorrell, 2010; https://commons.wikimedia.org/wiki/User:Richard Dorrell [accessed 26 March 2021]

Chapter 13

Figs 1, 4, 12: ©Photos by Gerhard Vinken, 2019
Fig. 2: "Spaziergang in Palermo", Painting by Franz Ludwig Catel, 1846 https://commons.wikimedia.org/wiki/File:Franz_Ludwig_Catel_Spaziergang_in_Palermo.jpg [accessed 26 March 2021]
Figs 3, 5, 6–9: Engravings by Antonio Bova in: Arcangiolo Leanti, Lo stato presente della Sicilia (…), 2 vols, Palermo 1761 (Vol. 1, Pl. 6, 3, 5, 7, 12; Vol. 2, Pl. 35); Scan ©Hathi Trust Digital Library/University of California (https://catalog.hathitrust.org/Record/101716453) [accessed 26 March 2021]
Fig. 10: Bartels, Johann Heinrich: *Briefe über Kalabrien und Sizilien*, 3 vol., Göttingen 1787-92, vol. 2 (1789): endpaper, in some editions on page 240. Scan ©Bayrische Staatsbibliothek digital; https://reader.digitale-sammlungen.de/de/fs1/object/display/bsb10466283_00273.html [accessed 26 March 2021]
Fig. 11: Houël, Jean-Pierre-Laurent, *Voyage pittoresque des isles de Sicile, de Malte et de Lipari* (…), 4 vols, Paris 1782–1787, Vol. 1, Pl. 36 (Scan ©Hathi Trust Digital Library: https://babel.hathitrust.org/cgi/pt?id=gri.ark:/13960/t3906sb2n&view=1up&seq=7 [accessed 6. March 2021]

Chapter 14

Fig. 1: ©Photo by Jim Henderson, 2010; https://commons.wikimedia.org/wiki/File:Kilmer_Park_Loreley_jeh.jpg [accessed 6 March 2021]

Fig. 2: Caricature by Otto Marcus from "Der wahre Jacob", 1895. Scan ©Universität Heidelberg http://digi.ub.uni-heidelberg.de/diglit/wj1895/0164 [accessed 3 March 2016]

Fig. 3: ©Photo by Phyllis Cohen, 1986; http://bronxink.org/2011/11/24/20101-lorelei-fountain-survived-wars-and-vandals/nggallery/image/image-260/ [accessed 6 March 2021]

Chapter 15

Figs 1, 2, 5: ©Photos by Gerhard Vinken 2014

Fig. 3: ©Photo by Alexandre Magno Teles Zimerer, 2014; https://commons.wikimedia.org/wiki/File:Capoeira_em_Len%C3%A7%C3%B3is,_na_Chapada_Diamantina,_Bahia_Brasil.jpg [accessed 6 March 2021]

Fig. 4: ©Photo by Rodrigues Pozzebom, Agência Brasil, 2008; http://pt.wikipedia.org/wiki/Ficheiro:Baiana-acarajé-Salvador.jpg [accessed 6 March 2021]

Chapter 16

Figs 1, 2, 5–10: ©Photos by Gerhard Vinken 2020

Fig. 3: ©Photo by Irina Vinnitskaya/archdaily, 2013; https://www.archdaily.com/356483/the-debate-over-making-it-right-in-the-lower-ninth-ward/516235b2b3fc4b2ba7000271-the-debate-over-making-it-right-in-the-lower-ninth-ward-photo [accessed 27 March 2021]

Fig. 4: ©Photo by Lombana, 2012; https://commons.wikimedia.org/wiki/File:MardiGrasIndians.jpg/Lombana [accessed 27 March 2021]

Acknowledgments

These essays have been written over a period of almost 15 years. Numerous people have contributed to this work, providing hints and advice, access and information, and support of all kinds. I would like to thank them all most sincerely. Many of the texts were researched and written in the course of sometimes lengthy stays and travels abroad. I would like to express my deep gratitude to the people and institutions that made this possible, namely the German Research Foundation (DFG), the German Academic Exchange Service (DAAD), the Goethe-Institute Salvador-Bahia, the International Center for Cultural Studies (Vienna), the Gerda Henkel Foundation (Düsseldorf), the Volkswagen Foundation, the Hessian State Offensive for the Development of Scientific and Economic Excellence (LOEWE), New York University, and, last but not least, the University of Bamberg, where I have been teaching and researching since 2012.

Without Martina Löw, with whom I was fortunate to explore so many cities, this would have been a very different book.

All texts, unless otherwise indicated, were translated by Graeme Currie, to whom I would like to express my sincere thanks for his skillful and conscientious work. Chapters 2, 3, and 9 were translated by Gerrit Jackson, who sadly passed away at far too young an age. The translations have benefited considerably from the accurate expert revisions of Johanna Blokker, to whom I am deeply indebted. The translations were made possible by funding from the Bamberg Centre for Heritage Conservation Studies and Technologies (KDWT). I would like to thank Farah Maria Berger for standardizing the heterogeneous templates and carefully editing the texts. Finally, I would like to thank transcript Verlag for their professional and extremely accommodating support for the book.

Many of the essays collected here have already been published, mostly in German. I would like to thank the editors of the publications listed below for permission to use material that appeared previously under their auspices.

Chapter 1 is a slightly modified version of: *Vinken, Ort und Bahn 2018* (courtesy of Dietrich Reimer Verlag); Chapter 3 is a revised version of: *Vinken, Reproducing the City, 2012* (courtesy of Routledge); Chapter 4 is an amended and partially expanded version of: *Vinken, Freistellen, 2011* (courtesy of Wilhelm Fink Verlag); Chapter 6 was first published as: *Vinken, Gegenbild, 2006* (courtesy of Deutscher Kunstverlag); Chapter 7 is a revised and considerably expanded version of: *Vinken, Vorbild Amerika, 2017* (courtesy of Forum

Stadt Verlag); Chapter 8 is an edited and expanded version of: *Vinken, Vom Kampf gegen Riesen, 2018* (courtesy of Klartext Verlag); Chapter 9 was first published as: *Vinken, Neue Heimat or Constructing the Old Town, 2016* (courtesy of The University of Seoul); Chapter 10 is an extended version of: *Vinken, Erbe ist kein Dokument, 2017* (courtesy of Verlag Berger); Chapter 11 is a modified version of: *Vinken, Palermo oder Überleben, 2020* (courtesy of transcript Verlag); Chapter 12 was first published as: *Vinken, Unstillbarer Hunger, 2013* (courtesy of Forum Stadt Verlag); Chapter 14 is a slightly modified version of: *Vinken, Gefühlssache, 2016* (courtesy of Verlag Jörg Mitzkat); Chapter 15 is an extended version of the first part of an article published as: *Vinken, Pranger von Bahia, 2015* (courtesy of Universitätsverlag Bamberg).

Soziologie

Michael Volkmer, Karin Werner (Hg.)
Die Corona-Gesellschaft
Analysen zur Lage und Perspektiven für die Zukunft

2020, 432 S., kart., Dispersionsbindung, 2 SW-Abbildungen
24,50 € (DE), 978-3-8376-5432-5
E-Book:
PDF: 21,99 € (DE), ISBN 978-3-8394-5432-9
EPUB: 21,99 € (DE), ISBN 978-3-7328-5432-5

Gabriele Winker
Solidarische Care-Ökonomie
Revolutionäre Realpolitik für Care und Klima

März 2021, 216 S., kart.
15,00 € (DE), 978-3-8376-5463-9
E-Book:
PDF: 12,99 € (DE), ISBN 978-3-8394-5463-3

Wolfgang Bonß, Oliver Dimbath,
Andrea Maurer, Helga Pelizäus, Michael Schmid
Gesellschaftstheorie
Eine Einführung

Januar 2021, 344 S., kart.
25,00 € (DE), 978-3-8376-4028-1
E-Book:
PDF: 21,99 € (DE), ISBN 978-3-8394-4028-5

**Leseproben, weitere Informationen und Bestellmöglichkeiten
finden Sie unter www.transcript-verlag.de**

Soziologie

Bernd Kortmann, Günther G. Schulze (Hg.)
Jenseits von Corona
Unsere Welt nach der Pandemie –
Perspektiven aus der Wissenschaft

2020, 320 S., Klappbroschur, Dispersionsbindung,
1 SW-Abbildung
22,50 € (DE), 978-3-8376-5517-9
E-Book:
PDF: 19,99 € (DE), ISBN 978-3-8394-5517-3
EPUB: 19,99 € (DE), ISBN 978-3-7328-5517-9

Detlef Pollack
Das unzufriedene Volk
Protest und Ressentiment in Ostdeutschland
von der friedlichen Revolution bis heute

2020, 232 S., Klappbroschur, Dispersionsbindung,
6 SW-Abbildungen
20,00 € (DE), 978-3-8376-5238-3
E-Book:
PDF: 17,99 € (DE), ISBN 978-3-8394-5238-7
EPUB: 17,99 € (DE), ISBN 978-3-7328-5238-3

Juliane Karakayali, Bernd Kasparek (Hg.)
movements.
**Journal for Critical Migration
and Border Regime Studies**

Jg. 4, Heft 2/2018

2019, 246 S., kart.
24,99 € (DE), 978-3-8376-4474-6

**Leseproben, weitere Informationen und Bestellmöglichkeiten
finden Sie unter www.transcript-verlag.de**